HISTORY AND

Dame Veronica Wedgwood, one of
ever to be made a member of the Order of Merit, began
writing history when she was a child. Her first book was
published in 1935, and she has been writing ever since.
Among her best-known works are *The Thirty Years' War*,
William the Silent, *The King's Peace*, *The King's War*, *The
Trail of Charles I* and *The Spoils of Time*.

HISTORY AND HOPE

The Collected Essays
of
C. V. WEDGWOOD

FONTANA PRESS

First published in 1987 by William Collins Sons and Co. Ltd
This Fontana Press edition first published in 1989 by
Fontana Books, a division of the Collins Publishing Group,
8 Grafton Street, London W1X 3LA

Copyright © C. V. Wedgwood 1946, 1960, 1987

Printed and bound in Great Britain by
William Collins Sons and Co. Ltd, Glasgow

CONTENTS

INTRODUCTION

Most of these essays were originally published in two collections – *Velvet Studies* in 1946 and *Truth and Opinion* in 1960 – although the present volume contains a few later pieces, some given as lectures.

This is all a long time ago, and perhaps not unnaturally my opinions and sympathies, historical, political and moral, have changed in some respects since some of the pieces were written. But it would be absurd to try to rewrite them and I have not done so. They must stand or fall as the spin-offs or loose ends of a life mainly devoted to the writing and reading of history, but involved also in journalism and in the literary and artistic worlds of my time.

It is over half a century since my first book was published. In those days historical giants seemed to me to be around. (I was proud to learn that G. M. Young in a letter to G. M. Trevelyan referred to me as 'Stunner Wedgwood' – a wonderfully Victorian epithet.) Since then the study of history has undergone many contradictory changes. The amount of source material has increased to an extent which threatens to drown us all, not only in respect of later and near-contemporary periods, but thanks to the boom in archaeology, for early times as well. Computer-based research is now commonplace. In turn economic, social and industrial history have been elevated almost to the exclusion of politics and narrative.

At the same time fewer and fewer historians seem willing to try to summarize all this material for the ordinary reader, who is kept at arm's length or embraced only by the historical novelist or romantic biographer. Scholarship digs deep and mines much gold, but very little is put on display to the public.

Although the mass of people may perhaps know, from television or other superficial sources, more history than their forebears knew, the average well-educated man almost certainly knows less than his father or grandfather did. It is not long since it was fashionable to regard history as an 'irrelevant', useless, or even damaging study – 'a heap of dust' as someone called it. The tide may now be turning but certainly the description by the seventeenth-century writer Thomas Fuller, of history as a Velvet Study, which I quoted in my first collection of essays, would today be regarded by most people as quite inept.

For myself I am unrepentant. I have had immense pleasure in travelling in those 'realms of gold', the past (or grubbing in that 'heap of dust' according to how you look at it), and in trying to convey that pleasure to other people.

The enlargements of horizons, the rediscovery of ancient ways of thought, the unravelling of some intricate sequence of events, the successful guess at motives or intentions, the re-creation of a 'landscape with figures', the feeling of contact with the minds and personalities of hundreds of people who lived before us, these are some of the rewards of studying history which I have tried to share with others.

C. V. Wedgwood
1987

Truth and Opinion[*]

*It is not truth but opinion that can travel
the world without a passport.*

The quotation from Sir Walter Raleigh which provides the title for this collection of essays may seem an unduly defeatist maxim for a historian, as though there were no possibility of establishing, let alone of propagating, the truth. It is not as pessimistic as it sounds, for some opinions are closer to truth than others and the historian lives in the hope that his work may lead to a closer connection between them.

Several of the essays in this book deal directly with ways of approaching the truth and ways of communicating it. Some of them deal with the problem of morality in history, and some with scenes, incidents and arguments from the past. For twenty-five years I have been looking for a philosophy of history without finding one in which I could believe, either in the works of philosopher-historians ancient and modern, or by my own meditations. But in the last years it has seemed to me that the practice of writing history, pursued certainly with passion and I hope with honesty, can produce if not a philosophy, at least a point of view clear enough to give purpose and perspective to what is written.

My writing experience has led me to set a very high value on investigating *what* men did and *how* things happened. Pieces like 'The Last Masque' and 'Captain Hind the Highwayman' were written partly to provide entertainment; they are small literary diversions. But they were also written because limited and relatively simple subjects like these, where passion and prejudices play little part, give the historian an opportunity for the purest kind of enquiry. The apparent objectives may seem light and even

[*] Introduction to the collection of essays of the same title (1960).

frivolous, but the experiment in reconstructing as accurately and fully as possible a detached incident or a character *without attempting to prove any general point or demonstrate any theory whatsoever* is a useful exercise. I have found by experience that in the course of such neutral enquiries unexpected clues are found to far more important matters. 'The Last Masque' gave me numerous indications for lines of enquiry into the Court and administration of Charles I and 'Captain Hind' has left me with a handful of hints, ideas and sources for the social consequences of the Civil War.

The older historians concentrated more on narrative than on analysis, on the *How* rather than the *Why* of history. But now, for several generations, *Why* has been regarded as a more important question than *How*. It is, of course, a more important question. But it cannot be answered until *How* is established. The careful, thorough and accurate answer to the question *How* should take the historian a long way towards answering the question *Why*; but for this purpose narrative history must be written with depth and reflection, thought through stage by stage, and recorded comprehensively and with unremitting attention to chronology. As long as this narrative aspect of history is neglected, as long as the *How* is imperfectly apprehended, the answers given to the question *Why* will be imperfect. There will be (indeed, there is) much learned putting of carts before horses and offering of abstruse explanations for sequences of events which present no problem at all if the historic landscape is looked at as a whole and not divided into unnatural sections. No development in history is self-contained or self-explanatory, and though specialization is essential for learning it is fatal to understanding. General history stands both at the beginning and at the end of all the questions.

I have been told that to write only of how things happened is to abdicate the historian's function, which should be to draw conclusions and explain processes. But are we to presume that no one but ourselves is capable of making deductions from facts? Must the historian, like an old-fashioned writer for the young, be for ever pointing out the lesson as well as telling the story? Is not the intelligent reader of history, like the intelligent reader of poetry or novels, able to take the points for himself, without underlining, repetition, and summing up? 'Work it out for yourself' is the tacit message of most creative writers to their readers. Why then should the historian assume that his readers alone have too little imagination, perception and responsive power to take the challenge? I cannot feel that it is the function of the historian to do all the thinking for his public. If history is educational – and I have a vested interest in believing it to be so – it must be an education in thinking not merely in remembering.

An interest in how things happened and a great desire to find out do not make a philosophy of history. But the quest for facts, past or present, provides some experience for a philosophy of life. These essays mark a few of the stages, the halts and the recreations on a journey towards that always retreating horizon where truth and opinion meet.

1959

The Velvet Study

*If you fear to hurt your tender hands with thornie school-
questions there is no danger in meddling with history which
is a velvet study and recreation work.*

Thomas Fuller

If I was not born a historian I was an aspirant at six and a practitioner at twelve. 'Nothing that is paper can scape me when I
have time to write and tis to you', wrote Dorothy Osborne to
William Temple. I needed no object and I made my own time.
Nothing that was paper could scape me even though the physical
labour of writing opposed a frustrating barrier between me and
my goal, and the mind had five acts complete before the pencil
(blunt at one end and chewed at the other) had got further than
Dramatis Personae copied from the front of a Temple Shakespeare.

Dramatis Personae, or as I learnt to put later, *Characters in order
of appearance* – the first inspiration was evidently dramatic though
the taste for history had come earlier. It began presumably with the
shiny picture on rollers like a map which, in the echoing play-
room at my grandmother's house, presented to my unrecognizing
eye Caradoc before Caesar, captive but unbowed. Not until my
first history lesson was the remembered picture suddenly clothed
with meaning. I was six; a world of inexhaustible possibilities
opened before me – real people, real things that had really happened to them. Britons, Romans, an invasion, people with the
most complicated names. I remembered them all; as soon have
forgotten the names of my neighbours in class. The walk home
that afternoon, up the tree-lined Kensington streets, was too
short. With difficulty I compressed into it for my companion's
benefit the substance of Caradoc's interesting fate, 'So he said to
Caesar: Why did you want to invade us? and Caesar said . . .' But
the Yale key was already in the lock and upstairs in the nursery
tea was on the table and it was 'Run along and wash your hands'.
Only some weeks later when I instituted a brief oral examination

of the term's work did I find to my dismay that I had been talking all the while to unlistening ears. It was an early lesson in the difficulty of imparting even the most interesting information.

Writing did not come until a year or two later, and then for a time the spell of imaginary characters was greater than that of real ones. There was my first theatre: the tiered immense semi-circle of darkness, the sudden, noiseless lifting of the curtain, and there against a mist-blue distance, lovelier than anything eye had seen or heart imagined, was a beautiful and evidently shipwrecked lady asking a group of pirates but perhaps they weren't pirates – 'What should I do in Illyria?' From that charmed frame of light wherein they moved, the starry language flowed over me, meaningless as stars and as beautiful. It seemed reasonable on getting home to start in at once, between cocoa and bedtime, to write like Shakespeare.

In the end only the stage directions were like Shakespeare. I copied them faithfully. The failure did not greatly disconcert me. Shakespeare was acknowledged to be without an equal and I was young. Double figures lay all ahead. Meanwhile there were other impressions cramming and tumbling into my mind: Shelley and Herrick and Coleridge, *The Little Duke*, *The Pilgrim's Progress* and *Pinocchio*, and with these, unsorted and unclassified, from sources of every kind, a heroic multitude from epic and saga and ballad, fairy-tale and folk-lore: Roland and Achilles, Guy of Warwick and Lohengrin, Galahad and the Red Cross Knight, Beowulf, Theseus, and the Thrice-wise Helena, the Percy and the Douglas (and like Sir Philip Sidney, I too found my heart moved more than with a trumpet). There were handsome books with gilded tops and coloured plates, there were squat little books 'told to the children', forbidding books of unrelieved print and wonderful French picture-books, Job's Napoleon on the bridge at Lodi and Boutet de Monvel's pale Joan of Arc.

Not books only, but the cool splendours of the National Gallery, Raphael's shapely virgins, the flame glow of Rubens and the mysterious darkness of Zurbaran's Franciscan. There were the culminating glories of the Diaghilev Ballet, with Tamar waving her rose-red scarf and the Fire-bird darting, brilliant, beneath the tree with the golden fruit, and the Swan Princess parting by moonlight from her handsome lover. One afternoon a man in a black frock-coat came sidling on between the dancers and said: 'Ladies and Gentlemen, the peace treaty has been signed.' After that there was a procession with generals on horses and a great number of royal tournaments.

Looking back now it is possible to analyse the peculiar dualism of childhood. One part of the mind stored these over-violent impressions to release them suddenly in fiery inspiration or panic fear, for the Baba Yaga came crackling through the Chiltern beechwoods, the dreadful northern Stalo creaked and whispered among the London planes. Clerk Saunders's ghost followed me on the stairs and Prince Lucifer himself sometimes lurked under the bed. But at other times an unwritten masterpiece flashed all-glorious through my brain and the blunt stumblings of the pencil no longer mattered.

Yet alongside these moments of dazzling and fearful imagination, there were the agitated sortings and classifyings of a painfully industrious mind. And since the fears and the imaginings were less evident than the albums of old masters and the charts of dates it was as an unimaginative child with a memory for facts that my elders saw me. Certainly there were long periods, as I grew older, during which the strain of classifying, dating and placing the artist, the school, the style of poem or picture prevented all spontaneous enjoyment. Yet though the arts came thus, for some years, to be drained of pleasure, the past never lost its enchantment. A cross, difficult, lumpish child, I felt more at home in it than in the present. Among the friendly dead, being bad at games did not seem to matter.

New shapes and patterns gradually emerged. The disjointed procession of kings and statesmen spaced along the years assumed in perspective interesting formations. They were linked in chains of progress or movement, fascinating to follow as the pencil line which on the puzzle page of *The Rainbow* (my secret vice) could be drawn from dot No. 1 to dot No. 56 until there, complete, was a duck or a rabbit. Behind these emerging arabesques of development the jumbled backgrounds fell into place, poetry, pictures and cathedrals, and more remotely conceived, but quite clear even to me, an enormous population of nameless human beings.

The perception of form in history gave me I suppose the first discoverer's excitement. I caught it once again with all its old enchantment, when I found in Maitland the whole architecture of a period built up from the analysis of its detail. It is the excitement which comes again, sudden and spasmodic, at those rewarding moments when – after long study – the logic of an incomprehensible situation suddenly becomes clear. With this discovery of form in history came the parallel recognition that truth has more than one face.

Three things after that: all together, or at least so close as to make their chronology too hard to disentangle: my father's sobering advice on writing, my discovery of documentary evidence and the *Decline and Fall of the Roman Empire*.

By the time I was twelve my writing had grown dangerously swift. There was a special kind of writing pad called 'The Mammoth', two hundred pages, quarto, ruled feint; under my now practised pencil Mammoths disappeared in a twinkling. 'You should write history,' my father said, hoping to put on a brake. 'Even a bad writer may be a useful historian.' It was damping, but it was sense. It was, after all, unlikely that I would ever be Shakespeare.

Soon after came the electrifying discovery of the document. My temperament being neither scientific nor inquiring I had not given much thought to the sources of the historical information which I acquired. One day at school our teacher read us letters to illustrate a lesson, and a fragment of a diary. The immense revelation dazzled me. Here was direct knowledge for the asking. Immediate contact could be made with these dead, so distant yet so tantalizingly near. After that, certain of my goal but uninstructed how to reach it, I breathed for hours on the showcases of the British Museum copying out all the documents on view. I ransacked the historical tomes of my father's library for anything between inverted commas. I found Pepys of course and was puzzled and rather shocked, Clarendon and was swept out of my depth, the Verney papers and regained my footing.

Whether it is that I have never quite outgrown the first excitement of that discovery, I find in myself to this day an unwillingness to read the secondary authorities which I have difficulty in overcoming. Indeed it is rather the fear of some learned reviewer's 'the author appears to be ignorant of the important conclusions drawn by Dr Stumpfnadel' than a desire to know these conclusions for their own sake which, at the latter end of my own researches, drives me to consult the later authorities.

Yet there was at this time a more subtle influence at work of which the documents were but one outward sign. Certainly I could name the hour and the place of my starting-point on the long road I have followed since: it was a small class-room on the topmost floor of a majestic stuccoed house in Kensington. Out of the windows, far below, the traffic passed up and down the tree-lined street like clockwork. It must have been summer, for the trees were in leaf and the sun was shining. The class-room was painted dark green and white; at one end there was a picture of William III landing at Torbay and at the other of Wolfe scaling the Heights of Abraham. It was here that I found, in the witty, determined grey-haired lady, who dominated the scene from behind a very large desk on a very small rectangular platform, the teacher who knew how to unlock the sluice gates between the arid flats of my intellect and the flood-waters of my imagination. The desert burgeoned; the Mammoth pads flowered into an enormous History of England.

Almost immediately afterwards came Gibbon, an imposing birthday present, half a challenge. I got down to it at once, ostentatiously out of bravado, but went on out of insistent passion, evening after evening, in the yellow nursery light. 'Understandest thou what thou readest?' my grandfather mocked. I understood this much: that here was a master, here was material shaped and subdued, men and centuries brought into order, a whole world frozen in the sharp, dispassionate light of a single mind. Before this immense achievement I stood amazed; almost, for the first time, humbled. But certain: this was the star for my wagon.

At twelve I had no theory of history. Since then I have had many, even for some years the theory that in the interests of scholarship it is wrong to write history comprehensible to the ordinary reader, since all history so written must necessarily be modified and therefore incorrect. This was I think always too much against my nature to have held me long.

Acquaintance with the work of foreign historians sharpened my consciousness of the different angles from which the same events may be viewed. The associations of places, the evidence of ballad and tradition, the 'accepted' errors revealed to me little by little the delicate embroidery which can be wrought by legend on fact, embroidery which may have value as well as beauty, since it may reveal a significance in the fact not apparent from the fact itself. My own varying estimates of the facts themselves, as the years passed, showed me too clearly how much of history must always rest in the eye of the beholder; our deductions are so often different it is impossible they should always be right.

Reading Bacon's *Novum Organum* I recognize in middle life how much I am a Platonist, how given up to the doctrine of acatalepsy. For the whole value of the study of history is for me its delightful undermining of certainty, its cumulative insistence on the differences of point of view. But a writer greater than I can ever hope to be and a better historian than many historians will allow* has said that to write history three things are necessary: 'a capacity for absorbing facts, a capacity for stating them, and a point of view'. But what point of view can emerge from the deliberate multiplication of points of view? It is therefore in search of an ultimate point of view that I am now pursuing my velvet study back to its source.

If poetry and colour and shape have all been important to me, it is evidently in that initial *Dramatis Personae* that the ultimate reason lies. For human life is essentially dramatic; it is born and exists in conflict, conflict between men, conflict between men and circumstances, or conflict within the confines of a single human skull. This conflict is the core of every development in time. It is this conflict with which all life is bound up and on which is poised the whole powerful and awful potentiality of human endeavour. In the individual conflict lies the first reason for those mysterious abstracts, economic trends and social movements, which in our text-books are apt to become disembodied concepts. The individual – stupendous and beautiful paradox – is at once infinitesimal dust and the cause of all things.

The danger of this point of view for the practising historian is evident. The selective winnowing of time leaves only a few recognizable individuals behind for the historian to light on. Thus the

* Lytton Strachey, who has suffered from imitators who have neither his learning nor his style and who mistake a kind of vulgar derisiveness for the delicately percipient malice of the master.

historian who finds the human being more interesting than what the human being has done must inevitably endow the comparatively few individuals he can identify with too great an importance in relation to their time. Even so, I prefer this overestimate to the opposite method which treats developments as though they were the massive anonymous waves of an inhuman sea or pulverizes the fallible surviving records of human life into the grey dust of statistics.

The human mind is too vast in all its activities for one mind to master. The attempt, foredoomed to failure, must yet be made. Not to understand is to admit defeat. Nothing is outside the province of the historian, however much may be outside his personal scope. Prejudice is a failure of the understanding, and lack of prejudice may safely be aimed at, for it will not be achieved. In any case, it is not lack of prejudice which makes for dull history, but lack of passion.

The human mind, in all its baffling strangeness and variety, is yet to be charted. One common humanity can produce a Napoleon and a Buddha, the guards at Buchenwald and the nuns of Leper Island. This immense contradiction is the historian's province; he has all the past to practise on and all the time that is left to us to solve the problem.

Or has he? For in the end he is only another ant industriously working away at his own particular conflict in the gigantic, indifferent ant-heap. When the megalomania which Mr E. M. Forster believes, not without justification, to be the occupational disease of historians begins to affect me, I hear the voice of the royal layman apostrophizing England's greatest historian: 'Another damned thick book! Always scribble, scribble, scribble! Eh, Mr Gibbon?' That at least is a salutary reminder of the deafness of the world. To check other vanities and other ambitions there is the measured dictum of England's second greatest historian that to be great in this profession is perhaps 'the rarest of intellectual distinctions'.

1946

The Origins of Germany

Germany has no frontiers; not only no natural frontiers but no self-explanatory political frontiers. The sea is the most effective of natural frontiers, with mountains – provided they are high and barren enough – a good second; rivers are a perennial source of dispute. It is, however, only necessary to look at the physical map of Europe to see that Germany has no evident framework. Geographically, there is no reason whatever for her existence. This is of course true of other countries: a nation is a political, not necessarily a geographical, entity, and although an indisputable boundary – like Great Britain's – is an advantage to the state as valuable as it is unusual, it is not indispensable to healthy growth.

The German problem was, however, intensified by the fact that this shapeless state of ill-defined and changing frontiers occupied a position of great economic importance. For centuries Germany dominated the overland trade routes and inland waterways of Western Europe. Her geographical position thus made of her a highway and a clearing station. While the commercial advantages were great the attendant political disadvantages proved to be even greater, for the interests of the people were drawn continually away from their own country, while the state lacked the necessary centripetal force to counteract the outward magnetism. The political development of Germany was, and is, out of step with her cultural and economic progress, a discrepancy which accounts for some of the contradictions in her conduct.

No other nation-state has changed its outline or shifted the balance of its governing authority so often as Germany. From the beginning her growth was haphazard. The upheaval of population in central Asia, which in the fourth and fifth centuries sent wave after wave of barbarian tribes to submerge the Roman Empire was slow to subside. Latecomers found the civilized lands beyond the Rhine and the Danube already saturated. Germany, never, except in the south and west, more than an outpost of the Empire, now became the overflow. It was not a fortunate position, since pressure from the still nomadic tribes to the eastward continued long after further movement to the west had become impossible. Though it would be rash to determine the political characteristics of the numerous tribes from whom the future German race was to spring, it is worth noting that they were from the beginning a people of 'have-nots', a people forced to make do with the un-cultivated wilds because the Goths, the Lombards and the Vandals had already occupied Roman Gaul and Roman Spain, Roman Italy and Roman Africa.

Whether the German character was indeed affected by this halting of their westward march, it is impossible to say. It was certainly affected in a negative manner by exclusion from the sphere of Roman influence. Some German historians have sought to trace throughout their country's history a sharp fissure between the western and south-western districts, along the Rhine and the upper Danube, which had belonged to the Roman Empire, and the regions in the outer darkness beyond. The distinction is not as clear as theory can make it appear, but it is certainly true that mellowing and beneficent influences in German history come more often from these regions, only to be dispersed in the bleak atmosphere of the northern plain.

No historical division is ever clear cut. There was no moment during the migrations when the last tribe squeezed itself into the pale of the Roman Empire and slammed the gates in the face of the next. Just as a fringe of Roman provinces in the west and south were ultimately to be part of Germany, so in the north we find one tribe half in and half out of the old Empire. The Franks gave their name to France; they also gave it to the province of Franconia (Franken) in Germany. Had the Franks maintained their supremacy in the north-western section of Europe some kind of amalgamation between the romanized and the barbarian world might have been possible. They were a people who com-bined the enormous vitality of the barbarian with considerable adaptability and political instinct. Moreover, they produced several leaders of unusual ability and one of genius.

It is typical of the modern German attitude to history that they have rejected Charlemagne as a Frenchman. Charlemagne, the greatest of the Frankish kings, subdued the pagan Saxons along the Weser and thus laid the first outpost of Germany's eastward expansion, brought under control most of the disordered peninsula of Italy and revived in his own person the Roman Empire of the West. The lands which he ruled covered virtually the whole of modern France, about a third of modern Germany and something over half of Italy. It was not by any means an ideal state, geographically speaking. Italy at any rate was superfluous. Yet had this Franco-German Empire survived it must have been a consolidating force in Europe, controlling, as it would have done, the problematical German tribes. Its capital was situated significantly in the borderland between civilization and barbarism at Aix la Chapelle on the Rhine.

French and German historians alike trace the troubles of the Rhenish frontier to the disintegration of this Empire. It could not indeed have happened in a more unfortunate manner. Charles, the youngest of Charlemagne's grandsons, took most of modern France; Lewis, the second, known as Lewis the German, took the regions east of the Rhine; Lothar, the eldest and the stupidest, was given as narrow a strip of land as could possibly be carved out to include the two capitals of the Empire, Aix la Chapelle the administrative centre, and Rome the spiritual head. A ribbon of country, including most of the Rhine and the Alpine passes, was thus stretched out under the control of a weak ruler, at the mercy of two strong neighbours. Charles and Lewis made short work of Lothar. Over the spoils they came near to making short work of each other. No one can now exactly trace the battlefield of Fontanetum where they and their followers clashed, but it lies somewhere on the Flemish border ringed round with a hundred later battle-fields. Later they signed a treaty at a pivotal point on the new frontier: at Strasbourg. The debatable land had been created. As for Lothar, the only mark he left on Europe was the echo of his name in the province of Lorraine.

To the east of the debatable land Germany now began to develop as a separate entity. Here, far more strongly than within the ancient Roman Empire, tribal organizations persisted as an undercurrent long after the tribes themselves had ceased to wander, and the country had been parcelled out under the feudal system. Traces of tribal law can be felt in the more brutal persistence of the blood-feud in Germany, and in the obstinate refusal of local privilege to be assimilated in any general system of justice. The occasional protests of criminals that they had a right to be tried by the law of their own people wheresoever in Germany their crime had been committed occur as late as the seventeenth century.

The most serious consequence of this failure of the nation to dissolve the tribe was its effect on German feudalism. In no other country of western Europe did the barons attain to, or hold for so long, such far-reaching rights. In their struggle against the centralizing authority of a King or Emperor, they could rely on a support from their own people which had something in it of tribal devotion to a chieftain.

This powerful force increased the danger of disintegration which was always inherent in Germany's geographical situation. That part of Germany which had been part of the Frankish Empire covered roughly the western third of what is Germany today. Threatened and battered along its eastern edge by still unsubdued tribes, the German state grew at the expense of these neighbours. Building out into the uncivilized land first a bulwark, then a colony, then a further bulwark beyond, Germany stepped gradually eastward from river to river, from the Weser to the Elbe, from the Elbe to the Oder.

The migrations of peoples do not halt of themselves: when the Germanic tribes were brought up short in their westward march, the tribes in the rear were still pressing on. They continued to do so for centuries. The Germans, determined to hold at least what they already had, turned and fought. They are hardly to be blamed for that; where they made their error was in not knowing where or when to stop. They acquired simultaneously a panic-terror of encirclement and a highly aggressive frame of mind towards their neighbours. Insensibly the establishment of defensive lines towards the east, the gradual assimilation of heathen and barbarous peoples, the legitimate colonization of waste land developed into a policy of attack. The *Drang nach Osten*, which is so marked a characteristic of early German history, could only be checked by two things: a geographical barrier or a cultural barrier. But there is no geographical barrier on this eastern frontier; the monotonous sandy plain was an irresistible temptation.

It was a cultural barrier which stopped them. Quite suddenly the *Herrenvolk* came into collision with a civilization different from, but fully as advanced as, their own. This was the civilization of the Slav peoples. At this point colonization frankly gave way to aggression. Held back, defeated, they retired only to come again. The spontaneous need for expansion exhausted itself; it was kept alive by the policy of German rulers. In the seventeenth century the Czechs were ruthlessly subjected to Austria; in the eighteenth the King of Prussia and the Empress Maria Teresa divided Western Poland.

None of this, however, really gave to Germany frontiers which her rulers or her people regarded as satisfactory. Held up on the west because the Roman Empire had reached saturation point before they came, they were held up on the east because the Slav nations had stabilized and solidified in their rear. It is a fundamental maxim in German policy that existing frontiers are merely provisional.

While the frontiers remained thus wilfully undecided, the heart of Germany also failed to materialize. Anatomically speaking, the state was a monster. Conditions on the frontiers were partly to blame; German energies were dispersed round the perimeter instead of being concentrated at the centre of the kingdom. The power of the Emperors (German Kings had resumed the ridiculous title of Roman Emperor in the tenth century) was perpetually drawn off to the extremities of their kingdom, or more serious still, into Italy, where for centuries they sought to establish a true imperial authority.

In the centre, meanwhile, with its roads and its waterways, a commercial Germany of a different kind was developing independently of the imperial state. The same thing happened among the cities of the northern coasts whose commercial interests united them with England, France and the Scandinavian countries more closely than with the rest of Germany. Against a central government which was rarely more than a name, the active merchants of Germany soon established rights of their own. The free cities which were to be for centuries the true centre of German wealth and civilization contributed little or nothing to the idea of the German state. They had made their own laws, existed independently of each other, levied their own taxes, even entered into their own agreements with foreign powers. Nor were the free cities the only independent powers in Germany. Some clever dynasts had succeeded in accumulating large provinces in their hands, shaping virtually independent states like Saxony and Brandenburg; but the pettiest barons and knights had often managed to establish an independence no less absolute. Goethe's Götz von Berlichingen boasted that he was dependent on no one but 'God, the Emperor and myself'. Dependence on the Emperor, it should be added, was theoretical.

The imperial dignity, faintly following the Roman model, was elective. Naturally enough the magnates responsible for choosing an Emperor were careful to avoid setting up a man or a dynasty stronger than themselves. As a result of the sudden switching from dynasty to dynasty in the Middle Ages, the German state had no chance to solidify (as the French did) about the personal lands of one family. The centre of gravity was constantly moving. We find it at Aix la Chapelle and generally along the Rhine during the ninth and tenth centuries, with a swerve eastwards to the Harz Mountains and Goslar in the eleventh, then farther south to Swabia with great assemblies at Bamberg under the Hohenstaufen. The Rhineland, with Speyer for the city of the Imperial Diet, was favoured by the earlier Habsburg; their later descendants converted Regensburg on the Danube into the official meeting-place, but used their own lands in Austria as the basis of their power, their capital at Vienna. Under the Emperor Charles IV in the fourteenth century Prague was to all intents the capital of the Empire; he himself, King of Bohemia by inheritance, partly Czech, and of the dynastic ruling family of Luxembourg, was perhaps the only Emperor whose private lands might have solved the German problem. He held as it were both frontiers – the Latin at Luxembourg, the Slav in Bohemia. A statesman of vision and patience, he might have achieved much had he had successors worthy of him. He, like Charlemagne, has a 'bad press' in Germany. Certainly his Empire would have solved the German problem by submerging the German centre between the French and Czech outer provinces.

In the sixteenth century the marriages of royal families began to make astonishing patterns in European geography, more particularly the marriages of the Austrian Habsburg. Charles V, on whom all the chief possessions of his family devolved, was elected Emperor in 1520. He controlled, besides Austria, Spain and the Netherlands. The Netherlands at this time were at least technically a part of the Empire, and their relations with the Rhineland and North Germany were exceptionally close. Charles V left them by will to his son, the King of Spain. This of course did not in theory prevent them from being still a part of the Empire; but imagine a situation in which an outlying province of great importance, controlling the delta of the Rhine and the Narrow Seas, is deliberately placed under the control of a foreign power. Yet so ill-developed was Germany as a nation that anomalies of this kind became in the ensuing century the rule rather than the exception. We find the Kings of France, Sweden and Denmark holding lands inside Germany, and German princes holding lands outside it.

The Reformation, meanwhile, had divided the country against itself. Both Protestants and Roman Catholics sought foreign allies; in the first half of the seventeenth century the Empire degenerated into little more than the fighting ground for all Europe, as one foreign power after another was called in to settle a problem which the German nation had failed to solve for itself. Spanish, Swedish, Danish, Flemish, French and Hungarian armies wasted the land for thirty years while German patriots vainly longed for a saviour who would bring union to their distracted country, and once or twice imagined that they saw him upon the horizon.

There were in fact two possibilities during the war. The first and that which came nearest to realization, was the amalgamation of the entire country under Roman Catholic Habsburg sway, ruled from Austria. The weakness and division of the northern provinces and the genius of the imperial commander-in-chief Wallenstein made the realization of this plan all but possible. The state created would have pivoted on the River Elbe – the reason for this being that Wallenstein was a Czech and moreover a man of great personal ambition. He sought to build up a new political entity based on an extension of his own country Bohemia, and in particular of his own lands. When he had dispossessed the Duke of Mecklenburg and carried the Austrian eagles to the Baltic to lay siege to Straslund, it looked as if the new state had been born.

At this moment the King of Sweden, Gustavus Adolphus, intervened. For the preservation of his own control of the Baltic it was evident that he must throw back the encroaching Habsburg state. But he was a man of profound religious convictions and of no less Napoleonic vision than Wallenstein. His plan for Germany was a northern confederation linked up with the Scandinavian powers, from which the Habsburg south could secede if it liked, a broken and emasculated fringe. His death in battle and Wallenstein's murder a year later put an end to both plans.

What actually happened during the Thirty Years War was the final destruction of imperial prestige – henceforward the Habsburg dynasty was to concentrate only on ruling its private dominions – and the collapse of the cities. The discovery of the ocean routes and the diversion of trade to all quarters of the globe had in any case robbed the free cities of their glory before the war. The war completed the process. There grew up instead the eighteenth-century Germany of small despotic principalities, principalities where the arts – on the French model – flourished, and which left monuments more beautiful, more civilized, more perhaps to our taste than the ornate Gothic of the cities. Such was the Zwinger at Dresden, or the noble episcopal palace at Würzburg with its lovely Tiepolo ceilings. Yet politically it was a vicious civilization, based on a class of subservient officials, and neither recognizing nor fulfilling any function in the political education of the people.

It was moreover a more feeble civilization nationally than any which had preceded it. The egoism and weakness of German rulers yielded the western frontier step by step to France, and the nineteenth-century neurosis about the Rhine was thus added to the others which had accumulated through the centuries. Yet this was something for which Germany had herself to blame.

The withdrawal of Austria from all pretensions to control the north made way for the unexpected growth of another power. Prussia-Brandenburg, in the seventeenth century the most contemptible of Germany's larger states, bankrupt, mortgaged and infertile, with a miserable capital city built of wood, soared into the ascendant under the rule of successive able and unscrupulous rulers. With an eye to essentials they cleared the Swedes off the Pomeranian coast and acquired the means to sea-power, solved the frontier question almost to their satisfaction by dividing up Poland with Austria and Russia, and gained both a strategic outpost to the south-east and invaluable mineral resources by annexing Silesia from a protesting Austria. The unification of Germany under Prussia in the nineteenth century was the logical conclusion. Taking advantage of the resurgent nationalism of the time and the evident incapacity of the other German states, Bismarck re-created the Empire with Prussia at its head. It was left, however, for Hitler, who combined in his person all the neuroses diffused among the German people, to realize the wildest of all Germanic imperial dreams, to re-incorporate Austria in the Reich and extend German dominion over half Europe.

The interaction of geographical position and political development has made of the German people a problem which all but defies solution. Their achievement in all spheres except the political has been creditable, in some cases outstanding. But it is the achievement of individuals, or at most, of small groups. They have not in the course of their history shown the least political insight. They are not merely bad neighbours, they are in the last resort bad citizens, lacking self-assurance and self-respect. For fifteen hundred years they have found themselves unable to accept their position in the European continent. What that position will be in future no longer rests with them.

1944

Martin Luther

——————⋘◇⋙——————

There is no escape from Martin Luther. Whether we accept or reject him, admire or hate him, know him or are ignorant of him, we cannot evade the consequences of what he did to Europe, and through Europe to that great part of the world which has been affected by European thought. It would seem reasonable therefore to try to know him; yet of all the great controversial figures of history he is perhaps the most controversial, the most difficult to see with objectivity or precision. Since that week in April 1521 when at the Diet of Worms the obstinate monk faced the obstinate Emperor and the apparent unity of western Christendom cracked, it has been impossible to see Luther except from one side or the other of that great divide.

On the one hand there is the monumental pastor with the stubborn kindly face of German picture-book and German statuary, a foursquare giant caught for posterity in a perpetual utterance of his 'Here I stand, I can do no other'. There is the opposing legend of the gross, lying monk gnawed with the egoist's unspeakable despair. There have been other fashionable versions – the German nationalist or the *petit bourgeois* ranged in his correct posture in the class war. Although none of these versions is wholly without foundation in the immense and inconsistent material which Luther's works provide, all are partial and therefore misleading, and there is not one among them all which is, or will ever be, universally acceptable. What Martin Luther was has long been submerged in what he did, and what he did varies, more than the achievement of any other European, according to time, place and point of view.

Yet a periodic reassessment of Martin Luther is a necessity, not only in the pursuit of objective truth, here so elusive, but in order to analyse and so to guide those powerful forces inherited from the past which live and work in the world to-day. The influence of Luther alike for good and for ill is not yet exhausted, and this moment, four centuries exactly since his death at Eisleben on 18 February 1546, provides an occasion for examining afresh where we stand with him and he with us.

In the last fifty years two developments have deeply modified the conception of Luther. The first is the decline of religion as a controlling force in the western world and the second is the political career of Germany. It is the measure of the hold which Martin Luther still exercises over our imaginations that the blame for both these phenomena has been from time to time ascribed to him: for the first because he divided and – it is argued – therefore weakened the hold of organized faith, for the second because of his part in creating the German nation.

A distressful tract of history divides us from the time when Robert Browning's 'grand rough old Martin Luther' was the widely accepted view of the great Reformer in this country. The same tract divides us from the days when Carlyle rejoiced that the defeat of vapouring, vainglorious France had assured the happy ascendancy of sober, God-fearing Germany over our continent. The events which have shown Carlyle a mistaken prophet have not spared Luther's reputation, for the part which he played in creating the German nation was fundamental. 'There has never been a German', wrote Döllinger, 'who so completely understood, nay whose spirit I should say has been so completely imbibed by his nation . . . The mind and spirit of the Germans were under his control, like the lyre in the hands of a musician.' Luther indeed, less than any other great figure which that nation has produced, can escape the consequences of having been a German; and the consequences to-day are no longer what they once were. Writing in 1900 Dr T. M. Lindsay concluded his *Luther and the German Reformation* with the comfortable reflection that 'Luther is the type of the best German manhood, in his patient industry, his enjoyment of quiet home life among wife and bairns, his love of music and his power to kindle when occasion arises into the slow-burning fire which consumes opposition'. The modern school which sees in Luther Hitler's spiritual ancestor sees in him another type of German manhood. The difference between the points of view is not so much the result of intervening discovery and research as of the two world wars for which Germany is responsible.

The position of Luther has been more subtly compromised by the failure of the liberal experiment of the nineteenth century. In so far as Luther was accepted, however oddly, in the liberal tradition as one of the great liberators of the human spirit, the esteem in which he was held has wilted with the growing cynicism and desire for authority which characterize this century.

With this shifting emphasis on the one hand, has gone on the other hand, an attack on Luther's obsequious political doctrines and on his personal subservience to authority. While one group of critics, yearning after the beautiful, disciplined and united Christendom which (on inadequate evidence) they imagine once to have existed, condemned him for its destruction, a second group, no less critical, condemned him for having given his large sanction to the authoritarian state. The man who had once been seen as the liberator of the human spirit was now more often represented as the man who had subjected spiritual to material values and the Church to the State. Matthew Arnold's penetrating phrase 'the greatest of the Philistines' was cheaply echoed by those who detected the Philistine but failed to see the greatness.

Luther thus faces the judgment of the twentieth century through a distorting perspective. The distortion must be corrected if we are to come to any clearer understanding of the man and his thought, and it is important that we should, for Luther has a part still to play in the regeneration of his own people, and in the struggle between material and spiritual values which has reached so acute a phase in our own time. It is indeed because our time differs fundamentally from his in the very premises on which human life and actions are based that so much misunderstanding of his teachings has arisen. Only by the effort to eliminate that misunderstanding and to see what Luther's theory meant in his own time, what was the balance and what the limitations of his outlook, can we once again grasp the heart of his message.

The elements which made up his volcanic power are not difficult to distinguish both from his own writings and from the comments of his contemporaries. He was a remarkable speaker, with a 'fine, distinct, pure voice', fluent, emphatic yet 'no great shrieker', possessed above all of the sympathetic power to fit his words to his audiences. The outspoken enemy of the pretentious, scholastic sermon, he believed in preaching to the humble in language familiar to them. It came to him easily, perhaps too easily, bursting forth in plentiful homely images, gross, earthy, graphic. He was one of the first great stylists of popular speech and he used the half-formed language of the people, with its immense potentialities of rhythm and colour and vehemence, with an artist's mastery. In his unashamed and unaffected handling of the ordinary words of ordinary men and women, no less than in the affectionate care which he took to appeal to lowly hearers he showed a democracy of the heart, in startling contradiction to his political teaching. It is for this reason above all that he has become so deeply a part of his country's tradition. He dominates a language in which there is no single influence comparable to that of his Bible, perhaps the most astonishing, impressive and highly personal translation ever compassed.

Martin Luther had further that colossal assurance without which no great Reformer can exist. True, he was subject to doubt, introspection and the dark torment of an egocentric bred in a strongly mystical tradition; but despair in him yielded always to the great overwhelming certainties. It would be vain to deny the ingenuousness of some of those certainties. The Scriptures were his measuring rod of the truth, but the interpretation, and in the end the translation too, was his. What he said of them, what he *made* of them thus became the truth. He rejected as inauthentic what did not suit him, the Epistle of St James for instance, which carries his marginal note 'This is false'. Furthermore in that key passage of the Epistle to the Romans through which he himself had found his own great certainty – that salvation is by faith alone – he inserted in the German version that necessary missing word 'alone' to clinch the argument. 'It is true these four letters *sola* do not stand in the Latin and Greek texts,' he defended himself, adding with some fierceness, 'and the blockheads stare at them like cows in front of a new gate.' Some might think the scholars thus dismissed as blockheads had the right of it, but Luther, deeply convinced that he knew what St Paul had meant, would not budge.

With this great certainty went also, undeniably, a great courage. Because the dangers he ran were less considerable than those braved by many other reformers we forget too easily that they were very great, and seemed so to Luther. His posting of his Thesis at Wittenberg and still more his burning of the Papal Bull were acts of defiance performed against a background of popular support. But the journey to face the Emperor at the Diet of Worms, notwithstanding Luther's popularity in Germany and the protection of the Elector Frederick of Saxony, needed real courage. John Huss, in circumstances not wholly dissimilar, had been seized and burnt at Constance, and Luther, only a few months earlier, had in the course of a disputation with Eck admitted that he did not believe certain of the opinions held by Huss to be heretical. Thus when he spoke of going to Worms to stand 'in the mouth of Behemoth between his great teeth and to acknowledge Christ' he was neither boasting nor jesting. The courage which he brought to that occasion must not be underestimated because the great teeth of Behemoth did not in fact gnash until he was well beyond their reach, and the imperial ban of the Empire was flung in vain against the defiant heretic monk already safe in hiding in the Wartburg.

Luther added to his assurance and courage an energy both of mind and body which gushed forth in a torrent of words, written, spoken, preached. He was well aware that his energy betrayed his scholarship; loose-knit and rough-hewn argument was the price he paid for readiness and vigour. In this he contrasted himself with the cautious Melanchthon. 'I hew the trees,' he said, 'Philip planes them.' Erasmus he described contemptuously as *Verba sine re*, but he described himself as *Res sine verbis*, seeing clearly how with him the impulse to action outran the slower processes of thought. He would have his ideas out and fighting before they were fully formulated as ideas. It has been well said of him that 'his words were half battles'. In that lay their strength while he lived and uttered them, and their weakness when exposed, in the static silence of the printed page, to unfriendly analysis.

In the early sixteenth century the spoken word was still as

potent as the written. The sermon and the disputation carried a weight equal to and in some cases greater than that of the printed page. A whole orchestration of gesture and tone added to or modified a meaning and men were convinced by the ear in a fashion which is incomprehensible to us to-day. (The wireless will presumably in time redress the balance once more against the printed word: it is beginning to do so.) This change in emphasis has provided yet another subsidiary cause for the misunderstanding of Luther, whose subtler meanings were often and evidently associated with a rich expressiveness of voice and gesture and timing, which is wholly lost to us.

For this, among other reasons, too much has been made of that violence of expression which went with his stupendous verbal felicity and facility. Not that violence and coarseness are surprising in a sixteenth-century Saxon of peasant and mining stock, handling a vernacular which has at no period been remarkable for refinement. Words poured from him in torrents in the pulpit, at table, in religious controversy or domestic chatter; the crumbs alone, the Table Talk, fill six quarto volumes in the authoritative Weimar edition of Luther's works. This unexpurgated flood, bottled in season and out of season by scribes whose accuracy is not always beyond reproach, provides material enough for many portraits of Luther, including – with a little judicious selection – that of the brutal, mawkish, servile German of some modern critics. It is easy to generalize from selected instances where the material is so vast; it is easy to compare Luther's moods of blustering defiance to his expressions of grovelling obsequiousness to princes, or to set against the savagery of his attack on the revolted peasants – that notorious passage in which he exhorted the princes to slaughter them like mad dogs – the tears he shed over a frozen violet. As there was inconsistency, and room for inconsistency, in Luther's powerful, productive mind, so in his character there was baseness. It was indeed an essential part of his greatness, the key to '*das Allgemein Menschlich*' in him, which gave, and still gives, him his irresistible force. But to make by smart analogies and cheap juxtapositions a case against the whole character of Luther is merely misleading.

Few would now deny that Luther's political influence, on

Europe and on Germany, was unfortunate. His innate conservatism, his deliberate subjection of the Church to the State and the doctrine of submission to the temporal power which was implicit in this laid an effective foundation for the bureaucratic–autocratic state. It should, however, be remembered by those who blame him most vigorously for Germany's political failings that the first examples of the secular state to which he had given so great an impetus were outside Germany, in the France of Richelieu for instance. Moreover, the prevalence of his religious teaching in the Scandinavian countries does not appear to have had political effects in any way comparable to those it had in Germany.

The plain truth about Luther's political teaching is that time has played tricks on it for which he himself can hardly be held responsible. He could not be expected, living in an age which was profoundly religious, to foresee what would be the consequences of his political views in an age when the religious premisses on which they were based had ceased to be effective. He accepted the temporal power with submissive acquiescence because the temporal power, being of this world, was of very little account. The spiritual, inner life of man, his only true life, was to be lived separately from his material life. Luther belonged heart and soul to an age of belief. He could hardly have imagined a world in which the spiritual life of man was very largely, and the next world totally, at a discount. His attitude to the State rested on his estimate of the relative importance of the temporal and the spiritual – an estimate so unflattering to the former that it was hardly worth more than intermittent and casual attention. There is in Luther's writing no clearly worked out theory, rather a series of impatient assumptions tending to the acceptance of the established order. This in the late Renaissance meant the acceptance of strong authority and, since religious sanction was necessary, the quasi-sanctity of the temporal power. God had set up the princes for this imperfect and transitory world. Luther's political beliefs must therefore be seen in strict relevance to his contempt for the world. It was, to him, the 'devil's inn' and he thought it to be approaching its last apocalyptic moments. It is fundamental to Luther's teaching that the temporal is not important. This attitude, pushed to a doctrine, has justified man's acquiescence in monstrous systems;

but it has also produced a standard of Christian values outside and above all systems and provided the individual with a spiritual strength that no system of material politics can break. One point has in any case been insufficiently considered: did Luther's views of the State produce the notorious political weaknesses of the German people, or did the German people merely adapt certain aspects of Luther's teaching to suit circumstances which were by no means of his making?

What is needed today is to redress the balance of Luther's teaching more especially in Germany by a renewed emphasis on his religious experience. For here he taught a doctrine which is pure democracy. Here he escaped the restraining bonds of politics – necessarily perverting to religion since the Kingdom is not of this world. Here in this central core of his belief he is no longer the obsequious dependant of a temporal prince or the defender of property and law against revolt and anarchy. He is a man with a revelation.

His revelation, that the just shall live by faith *alone* (he must have his '*alone*' for it was part of his revelation, whether or not it was a part of St Paul's), postulates the active responsibility of the individual. The act of belief has to be made; the change of heart is everything. Like all great revelations, his was a very simple one and not new, though to *him* it was new, and at once so personal and so overwhelming that, in the corrupt atmosphere of his time, he could feel only the necessity of making it general throughout the Church. He demanded for the whole Church as he knew it the change of heart, and certainly with Tetzel hawking Indulgences to a patter worthy of Autolycus a change of heart seemed overdue.

The Church met the challenge by manoeuvring him into heresy and demanding his retraction. He would not retract. So that instead of Reform there was a schism, and because there was a schism there was a weak young schismatic Church which had to grow (Luther had no choice) in the shelter of the temporal power. Hence the paradox: the subservience of the Lutheran Church arose from the bold assertion of the independence of man's soul which Luther had made. It is not the only paradox. It may be claimed that Luther completed the work of Hildebrand by shattering the Holy Roman Empire; and equally that he destroyed the work of the great medieval Popes by shattering the supremacy of Rome. It may be claimed that he was the architect of German unity and equally that he retarded German unity for centuries by creating the religious schism. But the greatest paradox of all was that his theory of man's inner responsibility towards himself and God led to the practice of his temporal subjection to the State which could alone guarantee the survival of the Reform.

A man with a revelation cannot be held down to the practical effects of his teaching in the narrow sphere of politics; and it is unjust to Luther to forget that his true province was not the State, but the soul of man.

1946

The Divisions Harden

W as the question of the Reformation in England settled
by 1603 when Queen Elizabeth died? Was it settled
for the other nations of western Europe? Luther had
been dead for more than half a century. There had been three
generations of knotted argument, wars, martyrdoms, massacres –
justification enough for Francis Bacon's comment:

> Surely this is to bring down the Holy Ghost, instead of the likeness
> of a dove, in the shape of a vulture or raven; and to set out of the
> bark of a Christian church a flag of a bark of pirates and assassins.[1]

Another Englishman, that great Anglican Richard Hooker,
writing at the close of the troubled sixteenth century, breathed a
spirit of reconciliation and compromise over England. On the
mainland of Europe it appeared that rulers and churchmen of
different faiths were content, or at least resigned, to accept co-
existence with one another. The princes of the numerous German
states were, since the Peace of Augsburg, free to impose their own
religion on their subjects, so that Roman Catholic and Lutheran
states existed together (and within a few years Calvinist states also)
within the loose framework of the Holy Roman Empire and under
the suzerainty of a Roman Catholic Emperor. In France the
Huguenots had, by the Edict of Nantes, gained the right to practise
their religion, a right further secured by military and territorial
concessions. Though the dominions of the King of Spain remained
closed to Protestant influences, the hereditary lands of their Habsburg cousins in Austria, Hungary and Bohemia were infiltrated
with Protestantism, and in 1609 the Protestants of Bohemia
secured a guarantee of toleration. Such arrangements made it

look as though, after a long period of struggle, diversity of religion and coexistence would be henceforward accepted.

But what in fact happened in the seventeenth century – that century which we see, in the perspective of time, as the beginning of the modern world: the scientific age, the century of Galileo and Newton? Contrary to what might have been expected, religious passions blazed up afresh. One after another settlements which had seemed to promise peace were violently overthrown. Thus in England the armed forces of Puritanism for a time destroyed the Anglican settlement and sent both the Archbishop of Canterbury and the King to the scaffold. In France the Huguenots were attacked and gradually deprived of their special privileges, until in 1685 the Edict of Nantes was withdrawn and thousands were compelled either to change their religion or to go into exile. In central Europe, in 1618, more than a century after Luther had nailed up his theses at Wittenberg, the Thirty Years War began. It started as a Protestant rising in Bohemia, and developed into the bloodiest and the most bitter of the wars stemming from the Reformation. It was also the last. When it came to an end, at the exhausted Peace of Westphalia in 1648, Protestantism had suffered heavy losses. It had been suppressed in Bohemia, in all the Austrian domains and in large areas of south Germany.

But how important was the religious element in the conflicts which mark the second century after the Reformation? It is true, as indeed it had been in the earlier stages of the story, that princes and governments of the same religion were by no means always on the same side. The dynastic rivalry between the ruling families of France and Spain in this century, as in the previous one, prevented united action on the part of the Roman Catholic powers.

Statesmen living at the time would often assert that the religious aspirations of their opponents were nothing but a cover for political ambition or economic greed. Their own religious motives, on the other hand, were wholly sincere. Thus, for instance, Father Joseph, the pious adviser of Cardinal Richelieu in France, was convinced that the King of Spain and the Habsburg dynasty in general only upheld the Roman Catholic cause so that, under the pretext of religion, they could increase their own power. To take an example from the other side: the revolt of the Presbyterian Covenanters in

Scotland against King Charles I was described by his authoritarian minister Strafford in these terms:

> This is not a war of piety for Christ's sake, but a war of liberty for their own unbridled inordinate lust and ambition, such as threw Lucifer forth of heaven.[2]

Nothing in history is harder to establish than motive, and religious fervour had never been the only motive in the disputes arising from the Reformation. It is none the less apparent that beliefs, sincerely held, played a part which was never negligible and was sometimes significant. With some individual protagonists religious zeal was undoubtedly the dominant force, although it was rarely free from an admixture of other elements. The renewed violent wave of religious conflict which swept over Europe in the seventeenth century arose, in great part, from the natural rivalry of growing nation states, but national and dynastic antagonism were heightened and inspired among Catholics by the crusading spirit of the Counter-Reformation, and among Protestants by the influence of Calvin and his followers.

The idea of a powerful centralized nation state, usually, though not always, a monarchy, had developed fast in the sixteenth century. It continued to do so in the seventeenth, and reached its most formidable expression in the France of Richelieu and later of Louis XIV. A religion therefore which challenged the authority of the ruler or was potentially hostile to the interests of the State was bound to become an object of persecution. Calvinism, the most dynamic of the Protestant creeds, presented an obvious challenge to the secular State and particularly to monarchy because it aimed at a theocracy and the rule of God's elect.

The persecution of the Huguenots in France, of the Puritans in England, and of the Presbyterians in Scotland was the logical expression of the centralizing policy of the Crown. But the religious motive cannot be discounted. Richelieu thought it a principal duty of a sovereign to re-convert his heretical subjects to the true faith, and the genuine piety of Louis XIV under the austere influence of Madame de Maintenon was undoubtedly a factor in the ultimate repeal of the Edict of Nantes. The devotion of Charles I to the Church of England is, of course, unquestionable.

On the other hand, the resistance aroused in the Puritans by persecution in Scotland and England undoubtedly gained much of its force from the religious fervour which transfigured and accompanied the more worldly motives of these rebels. The Covenanting movement in Scotland began as a protest against episcopal government and the Anglican liturgy, but in its earliest form it was by no means a purely religious protest. National pride, resentment against the English, the fear of the nobles that the spoils of the Reformation might be taken from them, and personal ambition for power: all these things played a part. But the history of the movement is remarkable for the emergence of a dominant, rigidly religious group; these men, rather than compromise with their consciences, excluded potential allies, purged the military command and so narrowed the range of their supporters as to bring inevitable disaster to their cause. There was more faith than self-interest here.

In England the motives behind what used to be called the Puritan revolution were more complex. We know it as a constitutional struggle between Parliament and the Crown. The desire of the gentry in Parliament to extend their political power, to maintain and improve their economic position and to establish their freedom of action against the authority of the Crown – these things have become evident in the light of modern research. But we must not leave out of account the organic links between the English struggle and the religious war which was raging in Europe. Calvinist doctrine captured a high proportion of the English gentry in the earlier part of the seventeenth century, so that Puritanism became the religion of the opposition to the Crown. The situation was made more acute after the outbreak of the Thirty Years War by the foreign policy of James I and Charles I, who – apart from a short interlude – aligned themselves with the Spanish–Austrian Habsburg, that is with the militant Roman Catholic party in Europe: this meant, of course, with the traditional enemy, the Spaniard, whose sea power was still a block to English maritime and colonial expansion. Religious and economic objections to the King's policy thus reinforced each other.

The position was further complicated by the favour shown by the King to the Arminian clergy in the Anglican church. Arminius was a Dutch reformer whose lenient views on predestination, election and Grace had been declared heretical by the Synod of Dort in 1619. The Synod of Dort was for orthodox Calvinists what the Council of Trent was for Roman Catholics: hence educated Puritans in England were dismayed at the encouragement of Arminian influence in the Anglican church. But what perturbed educated and uneducated alike was not so much the doctrine of Arminius as the ritual which his Anglican followers reintroduced into worship. Candles, vestments, genuflections – they took these for popery.

A king who encouraged these unwelcome elements in the Church and also maintained an alliance with Roman Catholic Spain could hardly fail to provoke opposition, some of it sincerely religious. After all, fellow Protestants in Europe were suffering heavy reverses in the 1620s and 1630s. Bohemia was lost, the Rhineland occupied by Spanish troops; destitute Protestant refugees were familiar figures in England. Such things provoked righteous indignation against the King's policy.

Turning from England to Europe we find an equal confusion of motives. The Bohemian revolt of 1618, which began the Thirty Years War, was partly religious, partly nationalist, and partly the work of an ambitious faction among the nobility. In putting down the revolt and suppressing all forms of Protestantism in his hereditary dominions the Habsburg emperor Ferdinand II consolidated his power. He also found it convenient to pay his supporters and the commanders of his army by grants of Bohemian land. An enlightening comparison can be made between the expropriation of the Protestant Bohemians by Ferdinand and of the Catholic Irish by Oliver Cromwell for similar reasons. But, although Ferdinand had strong secular motives for his attack on Protestantism, he was also acting in accordance with a solemn vow which he had made in his youth at the shrine of Our Lady of Loretto, to extirpate heresy in his lands.

Much of the literature and many private letters and diaries of this period bear witness to a deep and far-reaching renewal of religious faith. Among extremists, both Catholic and Protestant, there are even signs of a renascent hope that, through a Holy War, Christendom may be united in one faith once again. A French ambassador in Scotland in 1643 reported the opinions of the Covenanters in these words:

> They say openly they will push their fortune as far as France . . . they are convinced that they would beat all the princes in Christendom. . . . General Leslie lately in a large meeting of nobles said: Consider what a glorious thing it would be before God and man, if we managed to drive the papists out of England and follow them to France . . . and plant *nolens volens* our religion in Paris and thence go to Rome, drive out anti-Christ and burn the town that disseminates superstition.[3]

Of course, this was ridiculous boasting, but it was not isolated. The same idea occurs, for instance, in Andrew Marvell's 'Horatian Ode on Cromwell's Return from Ireland':

> *What may not then our Isle presume*
> *While Victory his Crest does plume!*
> *What may not others fear*
> *If thus he crown each Year!*
> *A Caesar he ere long to Gaul,*
> *To Italy an Hannibal,*
> *And to all States not free*
> *Shall clymacterick be![4]*

On the Roman Catholic side it certainly looked at one time as though the reconquest of Europe for the Church might be achieved. In 1629 the imperial armies of Ferdinand II reached the Baltic and the extinction of Protestantism in northern Europe seemed almost a possibility.

What prevented the work of the Counter-Reformation from going farther was, once again, the rivalry between the two leading Roman Catholic powers, France and Spain. Dr Elton has described the way in which the Habsburg–Valois conflict favoured the spread of the Reformation up to 1555. Nearly a century later the basic pattern is unchanged. The Habsburg still ruled over the Spanish–Austrian combine, and the dynastic jealousy of the Valois in France had been inherited by their successors, the Bourbon. When Austrian Habsburg armies, sweeping up from south Germany and Bohemia, reached the Baltic, when Spanish Habsburg armies were on the Rhine, it was high time for France to act. And so Cardinal Richelieu subsidized Gustavus Adolphus, the Protestant King of Sweden, to invade Germany and turn the tide of war. After his death at the Battle of Lützen in 1632 the Protestant cause came to rely more and more on French money and French troops. Just as the Valois–Habsburg rivalry had favoured the spread of the Reformation, now Bourbon–Habsburg rivalry checked the further advance of the Counter-Reformation.

In the face of the renewed Roman Catholic attack there had been some movements towards unity among Protestants. But these came mostly from preachers and thinkers and were not reflected in the views of Lutheran or Calvinistic rulers. For more than forty years, from 1630 onwards, the sad figure of John Dury flits through Protestant courts and assemblies. Himself a Calvinist, he longed for a union of the Protestant churches and worked for it vainly all his life. Time and again, in private letters and public statements, he urged on rulers and theologians the need for mutual trust:

> Let our aim be . . . to purge our heart from a design to serve the interests of one side, mainly to cross another. For he that looks upon his brother with the eye of a party, has put out the eye of a Christian . . . He that doth not confide in his neighbours, doth hinder them to confide in him, and he that doth fear others, doth beget in them causes of fear against himself . . . For if I cannot bring my spirit to trust my neighbour, how can I expect that his spirit should be brought to trust me?[5]

Dury aimed at *union*: he did not aim at toleration, and he did not believe in it. In a closely wrought argument, published in 1644, he rejected the plea of the English Independents to a separate existence and form of organization:

> The liberty whereunto we are called in Christ, doth not give occasion to singularity, or permission to break the bonds of spiritual unity; which by the allowance of a public toleration of different Church Government may be occasioned.[6]

Toleration was still in the middle years of the seventeenth century regarded with dismay even by moderate men. The ideal of union, by which different but not dissimilar beliefs could find room in a single church – this had been Hooker's ideal. It was also John Dury's. Union and conciliation were good, but toleration was bad because it led to licentious excesses. There had been the frenzied outburst of the Anabaptists at Münster in the previous century which had frightened Protestants as much as, or even more than, Catholics. It was generally felt that if religion was not in some way controlled there would be no end to ignorant self-appointed prophets teaching blasphemous and immoral doctrines. Amsterdam, where a large measure of freedom was permitted, was notorious for the number of sects which had sprung up, and jocose references were often made to their 'Amsterdamnable opinions'.

During the Civil War in England, when government censorship was relaxed, preachers of all kinds multiplied, and some valuable ideas took root, and have survived to this day. The Baptists were the most widespread of the numerous Independent groups. Scores of prophets and preachers appeared during this period of religious anarchy; George Fox, the founder of the Quakers, was to prove in the end the most remarkable and the most influential. Many were, however, merely ignorant and hysterical ranters, condemned, not without justification, by the more sober Anglicans and Puritans alike:

> These kind of vermin swarm like caterpillars,
> And hold conventicles in barns and cellars,
> Some preach or prate in woods, in fields, in stables,
> In hollow trees, in tubs, on tops of tables,
> To the expense of many a tallow taper
> They toss the holy scripture into vapour . . .
> I write of separatists and schismatics
> Of shallow-pated, hair-brained heretics . . .
> Whom neither law nor sense can curb or bridle,
> Who ne'er are well employed, nor never idle.[7]

Toleration it was widely believed would only encourage such people. The desire for it came therefore in the first place only from the 'separatists and schismatics' themselves. Roger Williams, for instance, left England for greater liberty in New England, but withdrew from the more rigid Calvinism of Massachusetts to found his own colony in Rhode Island. In his famous attack on what he called the 'Bloody Tenet of Persecution' published in 1644 he asserted that it was consonant with the spirit of Christianity to tolerate pagans, Jews and Turks as well as all kinds of Christians. His ideas combined a wide vision with practical sense:

> An enforced uniformity of religion throughout a nation or civil state confounds the civil and religious, and denies the principles of Christianity and civility . . . The permission of other consciences and worships than a state professeth, only can, according to God, procure a firm and lasting peace; good assurance being taken, according to the wisdom of the civil state, for uniformity of civil obedience from all sorts.[8]

Roger Williams put his finger on a critical point. If civil obedience could be assured, there ought to be no difficulty in tolerating purely religious opinions. The unsolved problem was that so many religious opinions still at this date involved political action that could endanger the State. As long as religion was a pretext for war between nations, so long differences of religion within the State might cut across national loyalties.

Meanwhile it was still strongly felt that certain opinions were so blasphemous as to constitute a moral danger to society. Four years after Roger Williams published his appeal for toleration the English Parliament, with a Presbyterian majority, promulgated an 'ordinance for the punishing of blasphemous heresies' which made the teaching of atheism or of disbelief in the Trinity a capital offence. It is perhaps fair to point out that only the *teaching* of such doctrine, not just the belief in itself, was a crime; and no one, in fact, suffered death under this retrograde measure.

The idea of toleration grew slowly, and usually under the pressure of personal disaster. Thus after the annihilating defeat of the Scottish Covenanters, at the Restoration of Charles II, Samuel Rutherford, one of the most rigid of their leaders, could bring himself to say that perhaps their cause had failed through a lack of the spirit of love.

Our work in public was too much in sequestration of estates, fining and imprisoning, more than in a compassionate mournfulness of spirit towards those whom we saw to oppose the work. In our assemblies we were more upon citations and suspensions from benefices, than spiritually to persuade and work upon the conscience with the meekness and gentleness of Christ . . . It had been better had there been more days of humiliation and fasting . . . and if the meekness and gentleness of our Master had got so much place in our hearts that we might have waited on gainsayers and parties contrary minded; and we might have driven gently as our master Christ, who loves not to overdrive but carries the lambs in his bosom.[9]

Something of the same kind had been said by Jeremy Taylor in 1650 from the Anglican side of the barrier in the days of their persecution.

I have lived to see religion painted upon banners and thrust out of churches, and God to be worshipped not as he is, the Father of our Lord Jesus . . . but rather as the Lord of Hosts, which title he was pleased to lay aside when the kingdom of the Gospel was preached by the Prince of Peace.[10]

Yet in England with the Restoration of Charles II the triumph of the Anglican Church was marked by a fresh outburst of persecution of the Nonconformist sects. The motives behind this were now frankly political, and after the deposition of James II the Toleration Act of 1689 gave to the English Nonconformists the right to practise their religion unmolested. It should, however, be remembered that this was not an absolute toleration, because the State church defended itself against any political danger from the Nonconformists by excluding them from the universities and from all public offices. Such a solution, which, in effect, turned all non-Anglicans into second-class citizens, would have been unthinkable and quite unacceptable to the Puritans of an earlier age. But generations of persecution made relief in any form welcome, and the enormous expansion of English commerce and industry which was just beginning gave the Nonconformists the outlet that they needed for their energies and talents.

But toleration, often of a tacit, illegal kind, came most often through a lowering of the religious temperature. Thus Huguenots who had not gone into exile continued in eighteenth-century France to exercise their religion privately and discreetly; and were only at intervals the object of persecution. The same thing can be said of Roman Catholics in England. New speculations, other than those of religion, were beginning to occupy the minds of men. The tide of intellectual fashion had ebbed away from theology. Descartes, in regions of thought the most influential mind of the century, had said that questions concerning God and the soul 'ought to be demonstrated by philosophical rather than theological argument'. This was to remove the problem into a calmer sphere. The more ardent spirits and the best minds were turning above all towards natural philosophy and the exploration of the universe. The dispute about religion ceased to be of vital importance. The ordinary man by the end of the seventeenth century no longer had much interest in theological argument and denunciation. His point of view could perhaps be summed up in the words of the poet Dryden:

> *Faith is not built on disquisitions vain;*
> *The things we* must *believe, are* few, *and* plain . . .
> *'Tis some Relief, that points not clearly known,*
> *Without much hazard may be let alone:*
> *And, after hearing what our Church can say,*
> *If still our Reason runs another way,*
> *That private Reason 'tis more just to curb,*
> *Than by Disputes the publick Peace disturb.*
> *For points obscure are of small use to learn:*
> *But* Common quiet *is* Mankind's concern.[11]

1965

NOTES

[1] Francis Bacon, 'Of Unity in Religion', in *Essays*, ed. A. W. Pollard, 1900, p. 8.

[2] Cited in C. V. Wedgwood, *Thomas Wentworth. A Revaluation*, 1961, p. 251.

[3] *Diplomatic Correspondence of Jean de Montereul*, ed. J. G. Fotheringham for the Scottish History Society (Edinburgh, 1899), II, pp. 550, 556.

[4] *Poems and Letters of Andrew Marvell*, ed. H. M. Margoliouth (Oxford, 1952), I, pp. 89–90.

[5] John Dury, *A Peacemaker without Partiality*, 1648, pp. 1–3.

[6] John Dury, *An Epistolary Discourse*, 1644, p. 22.

[7] John Taylor, *A Swarme of Sectaries*, 1641, pp. 7, 17.

[8] Roger Williams, *The Bloody Tenet of Persecution*, 1644, p. 3.

[9] Samuel Rutherford, *A Testimony* (Lanark, 1739), p. 6.

[10] Jeremy Taylor, 'Epistle Dedicatory', in *The Rule and Exercise of Holy Living*, 1650.

[11] 'Religio Laici', in *The Poems of John Dryden*, ed. James Kinsley (Oxford, 1958), I, p. 322.

Shakespeare – The Close of an Epoch

On 24 March 1603 Queen Elizabeth died. The 'fair vestal throned by the West' who had reigned in England for forty-four years was succeeded on the throne by her cousin the King of Scots –

> *Our* omne bonum *from the wholesome North*
> *Our fruitful Sovereign James.*

The quotation is from one of the many laudatory verses offered to the king by his English subjects. The author, Thomas Dekker, was admittedly a purveyor of popular poetry, and therefore one who moved with the times. For him, the new king's journey from his native Scotland into his new realm was a progress accompanied by all the hosts of Heaven:

> *Silver crowds*
> *Of blissful angels and tried martyrs tread*
> *On the star-ceiling over England's head. . . .*[1]

But James VI, King of Scots, who was now James I, King of Great Britain (a name that he hoped would henceforward replace altogether the separate names of England and Scotland), was not accompanied by crowds of blissful angels as he journeyed southwards. He was accompanied by hordes of greedy suitors. In the first unrestrained, and indeed rather endearing, pleasure which he showed at his accession to the long-coveted Crown of England, he lavished honours and prizes with open hands. He was so free with the knighthoods that soon the wits would be referring to the 'cob knights' because like cob nuts they came in clusters. He was also surrounded, as the English courtiers had feared, with a host of Scots who got their share – the English said more than their share – of the royal bounty. Later in his reign, with that good humour which was always his most disarming characteristic, King James would say that he had looked upon his first years as a kind of Christmas with presents for all.

As the new king entered into his inheritance the mood in England was one of expectancy, relief and rejoicing. His peaceful accession was in itself a matter for general congratulation, and there was, by and large, less regret for the passing of the great queen and the end of her remarkable reign than hope for the future.

This was natural enough, especially among those who were dependent on the Court and ever ready to 'crook the pregnant hinges of the knee' to the current dispensers of favour. They looked for benefits to come from a living king and had no further concern for benefits received from the dead queen; King James had already shown that he responded much more quickly to suitors than the more wary Elizabeth had done. Shakespeare had lived in no other reign than that of Elizabeth, but he knew the common human tendency and had put brief bitter comment on it into the mouth of Hamlet, Prince of Denmark:

> It is not very strange; for my uncle is King of Denmark, and those that would make mows at him while my father lived, give twenty, forty, fifty, an hundred ducats a-piece for his picture in little.
>
> (II. ii. 358ff.)

At the change of sovereigns, he was one of those who remained silent, offering no elegy to the departed Elizabeth, and no poetic welcome to King James. Later on he would include the usual complimentary references to the monarch in his plays. In the closing scene of *King Henry VIII*, James would be compared to a mountain cedar with wide protective branches, and the three weird sisters would mount a pageant for Macbeth indicating the glories of the house of Stuart – 'a show of eight Kings, the last with a glass in his hand'. At the third apparition Macbeth had already seen enough –

> *Filthy hags!*
> *Why do you show me this? A fourth! Start, eyes!*
> *What, will the line stretch out to the crack of doom?*
> *Another yet! A seventh! I'll see no more:*
> *And yet the eighth appears, who bears a glass*
> *Which shows me many more; and some I see*
> *That two-fold balls and treble sceptres carry . . .*
>
> (IV. i. 115ff.)

The glass of the future showed no other successors to the Stuart kings, descended from Banquo, crowned in England as well as Scotland, and ruling also in Ireland; with their double orbs and triple sceptres they marched steadily on. More subtle flattery was contained in Shakespeare's treatment of Banquo, the mythical forefather of King James. The disreputable ruffian of legend, who had been Macbeth's accessory to the murder of Duncan, was metamorphosed into a brave and honourable warrior. Court flattery? Perhaps; but this is also a stroke of genius, for what better foil to the introspective, hag-ridden Macbeth than this open-hearted straightforward gentleman?

The change of sovereigns was to be no loss to Shakespeare. Whatever can be said against the extravagant, often disorderly, sometimes ridiculous Court of King James, it was lavish of entertainment and generously appreciative of the theatre. The queen consort, Anne of Denmark, came of an exuberant and gifted family, and shared with her brother, Christian IV, a taste for the more spectacular arts. The reign was to see a series of original and elegant court masques, and the establishment of Inigo Jones as a principal designer of scenery and dresses.

In May 1603 the Lord Chamberlain's Men, with Shakespeare's name mentioned third, became the King's Men, and Shakespeare and his fellow actors marched behind King James on his formal entry into the City of London. In the course of the next decade the court witnessed performances of *Othello*, *Measure for Measure*, *King Lear* and *Macbeth*, the last being given during the uproarious celebrations which marked the state visit of the Queen's brother, Christian IV, in 1603. At the wedding festivities of the king's daughter Elizabeth, in 1604, no less than seven plays by

Shakespeare seem to have been performed at different times – including *Much Ado about Nothing*, *The Winter's Tale*, *The Merry Wives of Windsor*, *Othello* and *Julius Caesar*, as well as the famous and apposite performance of *The Tempest* with its tale of a royal betrothal brought about by the all-wise father of the bride.

We have, for convenience sake, to make divisions in the continuous flow of history. The end of a reign, the end of a dynasty and the end of a century came very close together with the death of Queen Elizabeth I in 1603, which has therefore been selected as a suitable historic milestone. But in the life of Shakespeare, as in the lives of most, if not quite all, Englishmen, the elements of continuity were greater than the elements of change between the two reigns.

Elizabeth's first minister, Robert Cecil, continued to be the first minister of King James, whom he had done his best to prepare for the exacting task of ruling England by some preparatory advice during the last years of Elizabeth's reign. Sir Edward Coke, attorney-general under Elizabeth, continued to serve the Crown as attorney-general under James, and by the zeal of his services, especially in his ferocious manner at the trials of Ralegh and the Gunpowder plotters, gave no inkling of his future activities as the great champion of the Common Law. This later and much more significant part of his career was not to begin until King James had the unfortunate idea of making him Chief Justice of the Common Pleas, where he esteemed it his duty and made it his business to prevent the encroachments of the prerogative courts and the extension of the royal power.

Both Puritans and Roman Catholics were to be disappointed of any radical change in the sovereign's religious policy. The dragging Spanish war was to be concluded in 1604, but the pacific policy of King James was welcome in these early years. Peace had been Queen Elizabeth's desire, when it could be had with safety, and the blessing of peace is a constant theme in Shakespeare's plays which does not alter, and had no need to alter, with the change of sovereign.

The deep and searing changes in English life had come in the generation before Shakespeare was born. Their ultimate consequences might not yet be fully worked out, but at the end of

Elizabeth's reign, when Shakespeare was in his fortieth year, there was a relative stability.

King James had frankly looked forward to an easy time in England after his troubled years in Scotland, combating a violent and still powerful nobility and an angrily Calvinist clergy. 'St George', he had written, 'surely rides upon a towardly riding horse, while I am daily daunting a wild unruly colt.'[2] His English subjects, too, were at first disposed to welcome the evident advantages of his rule. In the last years of Elizabeth they had never been free from anxiety about the succession or from the fear that her death might be the signal for rebellion at home and possibly invasion from abroad. Once James was securely on the throne these anxieties faded. In place of a childless old woman, the sovereign was now a man in the prime of his life with a growing family of children. The succession ceased to be a problem and the spectre of invasion vanished when the peace with Spain was concluded.

It is true that the union with Scotland was felt to be something of a mixed blessing. Centuries of hostility could not be wiped out in a moment, and relations between the English and the Scots who came into their country seemed at times so bitter that one foreign envoy at least believed that a war between the two nations was ultimately inevitable. While the English resented the presence of Scotsmen seeking their fortunes in England, the Scots had more serious cause for complaint. Their king was now an absentee for years at a time, and where the interests of Scotland and England were at variance, especially in matters of foreign trade and foreign alliances, those of England were inevitably preferred. There were lesser irritations; in the newly designed flag the cross of St George had been superimposed on the cross of St Andrew. But England derived one substantial advantage from the union; there was no longer in international affairs any danger of an alliance between Scotland and France.

At the beginning of King James's reign it was not yet apparent that the monarchy as Queen Elizabeth had maintained it was doomed. Parliament had been growing more insistent and more troublesome in its demands, but at no point had the Queen lost control of the situation. The elements of future trouble were indeed present, but the problems did not yet appear insoluble. If it was becoming clear that the distribution of power between Crown and Parliament would have to be substantially altered, no one would have foretold that the alteration would plunge the country into civil war.

By the time of Shakespeare's death almost every disastrous element in the situation had fully declared itself: the chronic insolvency of the Crown, the growing aggressiveness of the Commons, the declining prestige of the Dynasty and its servants, and the steady growth of Puritan influence. If we are to talk of the end of an epoch and the beginning of another, this date, 1616, would serve the purpose better than the change of dynasty in 1603.

To solve the perennial problem of finance, Robert Cecil had tried to guide through Parliament a statesmanlike plan known as the Great Contract. The King was to receive a fixed income in return for the surrender of his more irksome feudal rights, especially wardship and purveyance. But the Commons tried to drive too hard a bargain, the King lost patience, and the plan foundered. With the collapse of this plan there was no hope left of any effective solution of the money quarrel between King and Parliament. Both would assert their rights until the crisis of 1640 exploded into civil war.

Robert Cecil died eighteen months later, and with him ended the succession of loyal, well-informed and judicious ministers who had supported the greatness of the Tudor monarchy. The Stuarts were never to be so fortunate in their servants; they were bad choosers.

In 1613 the King's eldest son, Prince Henry, died. Whether this attractive, headstrong, aggressive young man could have been a successful king in the difficult conditions which lay ahead it is impossible to guess. But he had the popular touch which his father and his younger brother lacked, so that the affection and respect in which the monarchy was traditionally held suffered by his death. King James had retained from his stormy years in Scotland an understandable timorousness of crowds which made him dislike public appearances. His younger son grew up with a fastidious distaste for the common people. Thus, at a time when the personal popularity of the sovereign might have done much to buttress the threatened power of the throne, the royal family tended to withdraw into the private and extravagant world of the Court.

For rhe Court, however admirable in its patronage of the arts, now rapidly acquired a reputation for loose spending and loose living. In the week that Shakespeare died, April 1616, the King was at Royston with his new favourite, George Villiers, later to become Duke of Buckingham. His previous favourite, Robert Carr, had just been sent to the Tower with his wife, jointly charged with the murder of Thomas Overbury, who had been removed some years earlier to stop him from giving evidence which would have made it impossible for Carr's wife to divorce her previous husband, the Earl of Essex. The King, who at that time had been foremost in securing the Essex divorce, was now only interested in getting rid of Carr to make way for Villiers. The whole business was squalid and public. It did the Crown no good.

Meanwhile, the King's second Parliament, rightly named the Addled Parliament, had met and had been dissolved after three weeks of arid squabbling. It was clear from this how complete the deadlock between the Commons and the Crown had become. The King, in the unceasing quest for money, had started, cautiously at first but with increasing recklessness, the deplorable practice of selling honours. This he did sometimes directly, sometimes by granting the right to create and sell titles to his favourites. Villiers was to clear nearly twenty-five thousand pounds in Ireland from nine peerages and eleven baronetcies. Irish titles were relatively cheap. The average English peerage began at about twenty thousand, but the price had sunk to about a quarter of this by the end of the reign.

There was nothing new in the steady rise of the wealthy into the ranks of the nobility, but the passage was now easier, and the frankness of the buying and selling brought the Crown rather than the nobility into disrepute. Money and power will always command a certain awe, but the Crown, which was held to be the fountain of honour, became tainted in reputation by this huckstering. James was aware of this; so was his son Charles, but they could not afford to give up the lucrative trade.[3]

The lower ranges of Jacobean society were also fluid; position was acquired by wealth as it had been for the past century. The formalities of social distinctions remained as rigid as ever, and the pleasures of crossing them were not the least reward awaiting the tradesman who made his way up in the world, or married his well-dowered daughters into the aristocracy. The new gentry were probably not so many as the frequency of contemporary comment on them would lead us to suppose, but they were noticeable. So at the conclusion of *The Winter's Tale* Shakespeare depicts the sudden rise in fortune of two humble folk. The shepherd and his clownish son who had found and brought up the infant Perdita are loaded with honours and fine clothes at the court of her father. The old shepherd says proudly to his son:

> Thy sons and daughters will be all gentlemen born.

The son, gorgeous in his new attire, revels in the humiliation of Autolycus, who had previously twitted him on his low birth:

> You are well met, sir. You denied to fight with me this other day, because I was no gentleman born. See you these clothes? Say you see them not and think me still no gentleman born; you were best say these robes are not gentleman born: give me the lie, do, and try whether I am not now a gentleman born.
> *Autolycus.* I know you are now, sir, a gentleman born.
> *Clown.* Ay, and have been so any time these four hours.
>
> (V. ii. 124ff.)

While the prestige of the Crown dropped steadily, the danger from the Puritan minority steadily increased. They were estimated by foreign observers to be about a third of the king's subjects. The popular appeal of some of their preachers was by this time a double threat to the theatre. Not only did they preach against players, but the dramatic eloquence of their sermons made the pulpit a competitor of the playhouse. About the time of Shakespeare's death one of London's most popular actors, Nathan Field, protested against the denunciations of the stage currently issuing from the pulpit of St Mary Overy in Southwark. There was nothing, he argued, positively against acting in the Scriptures, and as His Majesty patronized the stage it was disloyal to denounce it.[4]

But the Privy Council thought it advisable to listen to the protests of the godly from time to time. They forbade one Rossiter to build a new theatre at Puddle Dock because it was so near to Blackfriars Church that the performances would interrupt 'divine service upon weekdays'. Not long after this the city fathers of Norwich would be appealing to the Council against 'players, tumblers, and such as carry about pageants and shows and the like', on the grounds that entertainments of this kind drew the poor citizens of Norwich away from 'their works and labours' so that the manufactures, on which they and the town subsisted, were 'in such sort neglected as causeth daily no small loss and damage'.[5]

There had always been a strong undercurrent of opposition to the theatre, with local mayors and justices ready to forbid performances. But by the second decade of the century a measure of popular support was building up behind it. In 1617 a crowd, to the number of many thousands, assembled in Lincoln's Inn Fields and attempted to pull down a playhouse. Such attempts were to be repeated; the crowds involved were usually said to consist of 'loose and lewd persons', but there was an admixture of London apprentices as well as the 'exceeding great multitude of vagrant rogues as there always are about the city'. The influx into London of masterless men from all over the country was an increasingly serious problem. Slums were forming in the suburbs, and it became even more difficult to keep control over the casual labour which accumulated and proliferated round the great seaport.

The London mob was, within a short time of Shakespeare's death, to become a factor in politics. During the clash between King Charles I and his second Parliament over the impeachment of Buckingham in 1626, the Council got wind of a plan to start a riot at the Globe Theatre, and forestalled it in time by closing the theatre on the critical day. Two years later a mob gathered outside the Fortune Theatre and lynched the unfortunate Dr Lamb, alleged to be Buckingham's tame necromancer, as he came out.[6] These dangerous mixed crowds of apprentices, vagrants and seamen would, a few years later, on the eve of the Civil War, surge round the Parliament house preventing the members they disliked from taking their seats, and would threaten the ill-guarded and vulnerable palace of Whitehall itself.

Less immediately terrible but much more serious in the long

run was the growing weight of Puritan opinion among the educated gentry. The late Elizabethan foundation of two markedly Puritan colleges at Cambridge, Emmanuel and Sidney Sussex, was having its effect both in the ministry and among laymen. It is an odd chance that on the day of Shakespeare's death a tough young gentleman from East Anglia matriculated at Sidney Sussex – *Oliverius Cromwell Huntingdoniensis*.[7]

Puritanism was the influence which was to make the most immediate modification in the character of English life and politics. But deeper and far more significant changes were beginning over the whole of western Europe. Galileo, born in the same year as Shakespeare, was at the time of his death completing the astronomical observations which were to change the picture of the universe for Western man. Francis Bacon was urging the foundation of a college devoted entirely to the experimental study of the natural sciences. William Harvey was already lecturing in London on the circulation of the blood. The scientific revolution had begun. The close of one epoch marked the beginning of another.

In this last period of Shakespeare's life, what were his compatriots like? Seen through the eyes of visitors to this country our Jacobean ancestors present some unexpected features. Almost all observers agreed that the English were a lively and volatile race. Their self-satisfaction was a byword.

> No nation in Europe is more haughty and insolent nor more conceited of its superior excellence. Were they to be believed, understanding and common sense were to be found only among them. . . .[8]

So wrote the Duc de Sully, ambassador to King James I from Henry IV of France. No doubt he was prejudiced, for as the Venetian envoy noted, 'The English and French hate one another, as is usual between neighbours'.[9]

The frequent corruption of justice and in the management of public affairs shocked this same Venetian deeply. 'Bribery', he wrote, 'is the one method for solving all problems in this country.' But he was impressed by the energy of the people, their business acumen, the great fortunes now frequently amassed by English merchants in overseas trade, and the busy and varied shipping which filled the Thames. London Bridge was too narrow for the traffic it had to carry and was always a danger to the boats passing up and down the river and negotiating the rapids under its arches. But it was amusing for foreign visitors to hear the English boasting about their relatives among the heads of traitors at either end of the bridge.

Thames transport was well organized and on the whole comfortable, with cushioned seats and coverings against wet weather, and the Thames watermen were extremely skilful – and needed to be. English women were fair and generally pretty, English beer was excellent, and was indeed in demand abroad. The English were reputed good soldiers, but liked their comforts and were therefore not so good as the Scots; they were good sailors, but better pirates.[10]

Apart from the proud conviction that there was no place or people better than England and the English in the world, the national character is not instantly recognizable from these accounts of the earlier seventeenth century. The impression is of a noisier, gayer, more fickle, more demonstrative people than we have since become. They like noise, one foreigner reported, and will go into a church and ring the bells simply for fun.

Their skill as actors was famous and English strolling players were popular abroad. The fact that they delighted foreign audiences indicates their liveliness, energy and skill in mime, for their language was not widely understood. Though English acting was admired, the English language was not. This awkward mixture of Saxon and French – as it seemed to visitors – could sometimes sound attractive when spoken by the natives. But it was not a language that an educated man needed to acquire. Foreigners engaged in trade mastered it when necessary, but diplomatic representatives, however long resident in the country, rarely took the trouble. Though they often reported with pleasure dramatic representations at Court and elsewhere, the treasures of the language were poured out for them in vain. They remained unaware that they were listening to one of the richest languages of the world at its greatest moment. Had they been told so, they would no doubt have thought it another absurd manifestation of English conceit.

But the English themselves – their writers at least – were very well pleased with their language. They praised its rhythmic qualities, its mingling of strong consonants and open vowels, its wealth of forceful monosyllables, and the huge variety of its idioms. Its flexibility and beauty, its fitness for all and every subject, were continually demonstrated by poets, dramatists and translators. It was the era of the great dictionaries – Florio's Italian dictionary, Cotgrave's French dictionary, Minsheu's Spanish and polyglot dictionaries; all these bore witness to the inexhaustible variety of English and its capacity to express every shade of meaning.

Such a language had a great future, as Samuel Daniel predicted in lines which have become famous:

> *And who in time knows whither we may vent*
> *The treasure of our tongue? To what strange shores*
> *This gain of our best glory shall be sent*
> *T'enrich unknowing nations with our stores?*
> *What worlds in th' yet unformed occident*
> *May come refin'd with th'accents that are ours?*[11]

Certainly there was poetry now being written in English that would in time to come circle the globe –

> *How sweet the moonlight sleeps upon this bank!*
> *Here will we sit, and let the sounds of music*
> *Creep in our ears: soft stillness and the night*
> *Become the touches of sweet harmony.*
> *Sit, Jessica. Look how the floor of Heaven*
> *Is thick inlaid with patines of bright gold:*
> *There's not the smallest orb which thou behold'st*
> *But in his motion like an angel sings,*
> *Still quiring to the young-eyed cherubins;*
> *Such harmony is in immortal souls;*
> *But whilst this muddy vesture of decay*
> *Doth grossly close it in, we cannot hear it.*
>
> (*M. of V.*, V. i. 54ff.)

Such lines are for all time, and it is strange to think that they were written in a language of small circulation and less prestige, for a public, enthusiastic and appreciative indeed, but limited to the town-dwelling, theatre-going minority of a country at that time only on the perimeter of the intellectual world.

The expansion had already begun. The treasure of the tongue that Shakespeare spoke was already reaching strange shores, especially in the yet unformed Occident, which English enterprise was doing its best to form to its own heart's desire. The Virginian colony was struggling to establish itself. It was in the year of Shakespeare's death that the Indian princess Pocahontas was received at Court and became the talk of the town. Soon the poet and colonial venturer George Sandys would spend his leisure time, among the dangers and hardships of life in Virginia, translating the *Metamorphoses* of Ovid into English verse – the first work of English literature to be produced in America.

Shakespeare himself had been inspired by the misadventures of the Virginian colonists in the setting of *The Tempest*. In 1609 a fleet bound for Virginia was scattered by a storm of unexampled fury. It was thus described by a survivor:

> An hell of darkness turned black upon us . . . we could not apprehend in our imaginations any possibility of greater violence, yet did we still find it, not only more terrible but more constant, fury added to fury, and one storm urging a second more outragious than the former . . . our clamours drowned in the winds and the winds in thunder. Prayers might well be in the hearts and lips but drowned in the outcry of the officers. . . . The sea swelled above the clouds and gave battle unto Heaven. It could not be said to rain, the water like whole rivers did flood in the air. . . . Upon Thursday night Sir George Summers being upon the watch, had an apparition of a little round light, like a faint star, trembling and streaming along with a sparkling blaze, half the height upon the main mast, and shooting sometimes from shroud to shroud, tempting to settle as it were upon any of the four shrouds; and for three or four hours together, or rather more, running sometimes along the main yard to the very end and then returning . . .[12]

This scene of darkness, storm and dismay, lit by St Elmo's fire, is very close to the storm so wonderfully conjured up in the opening scene of *The Tempest* and later described as a spectator by the frightened Miranda, and as the agent of the storm by Ariel. Thus Miranda:

> If by your art, my dearest father, you have
> Put the wild waters in this roar, allay them.
> The sky, it seems, would pour down stinking pitch,
> But that the sea, mounting to the welkin's cheek,
> Dashes the fire out. . . .

(I. ii. 1ff.)

and later Ariel:

> I boarded the King's ship; now on the beak,
> Now in the waist, the deck, in every cabin,
> I flamed amazement; sometimes I'ld divide,
> And burn in many places; on the topmast,
> The yards and bowsprit would I flame distinctly,
> Then meet and join. Jove's lightnings, the precursors
> O' the dreadful thunderclaps, more momentary
> And sight-outrunning were not; the fire and cracks
> Of sulphurous roaring the most mighty Neptune
> Seem to besiege, and make his bold waves tremble,
> Yea, his dread trident shake.

(I. ii. 196ff.)

The storm-tossed adventurers had already given themselves over for lost, when Sir George Summers saw land, and they ran ashore off an island. This turned out to be one of 'the dangerous and dreaded islands of the Bermuda', believed to be inhabited by devils and therefore 'feared and avoided of all sea travellers alive above any other place in the world'. But on further investigation they found this 'most prodigious and enchanted place' to be little short of an earthly paradise, abounding in food of all kinds, fish, fruit, hogs and turtles. Here they were able to refresh themselves plentifully, to build new ships, and proceed in the spring to Virginia.

Thus Shakespeare's last play, with its visionary dreamlike quality and theme of reconciliation, is linked to the true story of the misfortunes and deliverance of the Virginian colonists. Shakespeare had a vicarious interest in the venture through several of his friends, and it is as certain as such things can be that the accounts he read of the adventure, in print and in manuscript, inspired him to the setting and the dramatic opening of this play. But in his use of the material, the old and the new world, the past and the future have been marvellously combined. He uses the details of the shipwreck off the 'still vexed Bermoothes', but he sets his own enchanted island back in the old world, in the Mediterranean between Naples and the African coast.

There is something impertinent in attempting to attach the life and world of so transcendent a genius to the commonplaces of economic or social history. None the less, the outline of Shakespeare's life and career is in harmony with this period of expansion and social change. He can be seen as a man of the sixteenth century whose mind responded to the times, who built up his position in the world and acquired possessions and social status as he acquired wealth. He accumulated a competent fortune; in his later life he lived well, bought the best house in Stratford and ended his days as its most distinguished citizen. Very soon after his death, passing visitors would be proudly shown in his parish church 'a neat monument of the most famous English poet Mr William Shakespeare'.

But changes were happening in the Stratford that Shakespeare knew. Within a few years the River Avon, in Shakespeare's time not navigable by 'a boat of any burden', would be made passable from Tewkesbury to Stratford for barges of thirty tons.[13] The iron manufacture of Birmingham was growing steadily. In the Civil War it would be supplying swords – not very good ones, these 'Brummagem blades' – to whichever side happened to have gained control of it.

Changes in fashion and taste were meanwhile altering the theatre. With the lessening respect for the Crown, dramatists and players became bolder in handling contemporary themes. There was the extraordinary daring of Middleton's *A Game at Chess*, a savage attack on the King's policy of Spanish marriage for his son, against which the Spanish ambassador protested. But the Court was out of London, and the play ran to packed houses for eleven nights before it was ordered to be taken off.[14]

This ferocious political play was a sign of the times; if few playwrights ventured quite so far as this, the fashion was now all for plays about matters of immediate and most ephemeral interest. The generation after Shakespeare's death produced a stream of social comedies on currently popular topics, of value to historians, but rarely of any permanent quality. Aubrey was in the right of it when he contrasted these playwrights to their disparagement with Shakespeare: 'His comedies will remain wit as long as the English tongue is understood, for that he handles *mores hominum*. Now our present writers reflect so much upon particular persons and cox-combeities that twenty years hence they will not be understood.'[15]

Shakespeare was as acutely conscious as any good dramatist must be of the tastes and fashions of his day. He spoke of actors as 'the abstracts and brief chronicles of the time'. But the topical and personal allusions in his plays are incidental, never structural. Yet it can perhaps be argued that the creeping political uncertainty of King James's reign is reflected in the atmosphere of the later plays wherever these touch on political themes or on the exercise of human power which is the stuff of politics.

Shakespeare was as deeply concerned as any respectable citizen must be for the good government of his country. Growing up under the shadow of disturbing changes, reaching his maturity at a time when the threat of foreign invasion was real and the national danger a constant preoccupation, his recurrent themes are the necessity of strong and *legal* government. The House of Lancaster falls because of this basic flaw in its right, in spite of the triumphant interlude of King Henry V. Above all, Shakespeare prizes the blessings of peace. The great dramatic epic that he devoted to the Wars of the Roses, their causes and their cure, was essentially an indictment of civil war as the worst of disasters.

The political themes of his later plays are less consistent and more disillusioned. Octavius, who should be the Henry VII of the Roman civil wars, is treated in such a way as to alienate sympathy and discourage admiration. One feels that Shakespeare's political judgement is divided, or rather, that his understanding of individuals is now so mature and so perceptive that the simple handling of a political theme is too coarse for him. These plays have politics in them, but they are not about politics; they are about people.

Is it too fanciful to suggest that a mounting political disillusion, a disillusion about the nature of human power, can be traced not only in the Roman plays, but also in *Macbeth*, in *Othello*, most strongly of all in *King Lear*? The intractability of the problem of regal power was becoming evident in the England of Shakespeare's maturity; the dangers were growing. The indications are necessarily vague, but the political uneasiness of the later plays is in sharp contrast to the clear political line of his earlier work.

Twenty-five years divided the death of Shakespeare from the foundering of his country into a second Civil War, a war which – both for the principles involved and the character of the protagonists – would have provided better material for Shakespeare's genius than the baronial struggles of the fifteenth century. During that interval his plays continued to hold the stage and, with their publication, to delight readers. We find a young English courtier travelling in Italy with 'Shaxper's book' for a companion. At Venice he crossed one afternoon to San Giorgio – 'St George's' he calls it – and spent the afternoon with a friend reading in the book. They must have been reading aloud to each other, since only one book is mentioned – there in the sunny cloister in the lagoon, declaiming the uncouth language which the Italians despised, and in which some of the loveliest poetry in the world had been created.[16]

A few years later, a harassed civil servant, struggling to shore up the fast-collapsing Government of Charles I, with too many calls on his time and too little help, protests to a friend that he cannot 'play Pyramus and Thisbe and the Lion, too'.[17] Soon after, Queen Henrietta Maria, marching down from the North with arms and supplies for her husband – a gayer and less vindictive Margaret of Anjou – will pass the night at Stratford, at New Place, as the guest of Shakespeare's daughter. Later, the King, a prisoner at Holmby House, will read the plays for recreation and annotate his folio here and there in his delicate neat handwriting. At a still grimmer moment in the struggle John Cook, the attorney-general, preparing to arraign the King in the name of 'my clients the people of England', will brood over the rumoured poisoning of King James by Buckingham and the unwillingness of Charles to investigate the matter. Had the king read the Scriptures more, and Shakespeare less, wrote Cook with vindictive glee, he would have known that it was his duty to avenge his father's death.[18] Had John Cook known his Shakespeare as he knew his Bible he might have remembered Hamlet.

With the changed taste of the Restoration, Shakespeare came back to the stage, played in a different manner and sometimes in an altered text. The women's parts were now played by women. Prince Rupert, stern veteran of wars by land and sea, feel in love with the first recorded Desdemona, ash-blonde Margaret Hughes with her soft Welsh voice, wooed her and made her his own –

> *She loved me for the dangers I had passed,*
> *And I loved her that she did pity them. . . .*

A little later Dryden offered his amended version of *The Tempest* to the sophisticated Restoration audience, with some apology for refurbishing this old-fashioned stuff –

> *As when a tree's cut down the secret root*
> *Lives under ground, and thence new branches shoot;*
> *So from old Shakespeare's honoured dust, this day*
> *Springs up and buds a new reviving play. . . .*

Dryden was too good a poet and too good a critic not to reverence Shakespeare, but he felt that the magical element in the plot needed some excuse in the age of the newly founded Royal Society, of Christopher Wren and Robert Boyle and Isaac Newton.

> *I must confess 'twas bold, nor would you now*
> *That liberty to vulgar wits allow,*
> *Which works by magic supernatural things . . .*
> *Those legends from old priesthood were received,*
> *And he then writ as people then believed.*

What Shakespeare believed or did not believe is matter for speculation still. He does not work by supernatural, but by natural magic. Today, when the Scientific Revolution, just beginning when he died, has wrought unimaginable changes in every sphere of thought, in every corner of our lives, his magic still works. He speaks to us differently, but no less truly than he did to our ancestors in the England of King James and Queen Elizabeth I.

Before beauty and truth of such depth and harmony, historical

reflections on the nature of an epoch and the poet's relation to it
seem irrelevant –

> *The cloud-capp'd towers, the gorgeous palaces,*
> *The solemn temples, the great globe itself,*
> *Yea, all which it inherit, shall dissolve,*
> *And, like this insubstantial pageant faded,*
> *Leave not a rack behind. We are such stuff*
> *As dreams are made on; and our little life*
> *Is rounded with a sleep.*

1964

NOTES

[1] *The Non-Dramatic Works of Thomas Dekker*, ed. A. B. Grosart, London, 1884, vol. I, p. 99.

[2] *Correspondence of James VI with Robert Cecil and Others*, ed. J. Bruce, Camden Society, London, 1861, vol. lxxxviii, pp. 31–2.

[3] Lawrence Stone, 'The Inflation of Honours', *Past and Present*, November 1958.

[4] William Haller, *The Rise of Puritanism*, Columbia, 1938, pp. 19ff.; *Calendar of State Papers, Domestic Series, 1611–18*, p. 419.

[5] *Acts of the Privy Council, 1615–16*, p. 292; *1621–3*, pp. 517–18.

[6] S. R. Gardiner, *History of England*, vol. vi, p. 319.

[7] Abbott, *Writings and Speeches of Oliver Cromwell*, vol. I, p. 27.

[8] *Memoirs of the Duke of Sully*, translated from the French, London, 1778, vol. iii, p. 229.

[9] *Relazioni degli Stati Europei. Lettere al Senato degli Ambasciatori Veneziani nel secolo decimo settimo.* ed. N. Barozzi and G. Berchet, Fourth Series, Venice, 1863, p. 64.

[10] ibid., pp. 27–30, 92–3.

[11] *The Complete Works of Samuel Daniel*, ed. A. B. Grosart, 1885, vol. I, p. 255.

[12] *The Tempest*, Arden edition, London, 1954, Appendix A.

[13] W. H. B. Court, *Rise of the Midland Industries, 1600–1838*, Oxford, 1938, p. 10.

[14] *Acts of the Privy Council, 1623–24*, p. 305; Leslie Hotson, *Shakespeare's Wooden O*, London, 1959, pp. 16ff.

[15] *Aubrey's Brief Lives*, ed. Oliver Lawson Dick, London, 1949, p. 276.

[16] Helen Kaufman, *Conscientious Cavalier*, London, 1962, p. 137.

[17] *Calendar of State Papers, Domestic Series, 1639*, p. 272.

[18] John Cook, *King Charles His Case*, London, 1649.

Cavalier Poetry and Cavalier Politics

The restlessness of the seventeenth century is a massive restlessness, reflected in gigantic convolutions of stone and tempestuous statuary. In western Europe this was perhaps the most unhappy century until our own time, and it is closer to our own than any other in the causes of that unhappiness. Between the joyous experimentalism of the sixteenth century and the intellectual serenity of the eighteenth, it interposes a period of bewilderment: a time (like ours) in which man's activities had outrun his powers of control.

The change from a land to a money basis for society, and the conflict between State and individual were important elements in the unrest of the time, but they were not its fundamental cause, while the struggle between Catholic and Protestant was a mere pendant of political issue. A mental conflict stronger than the material quarrels which set Europe's entangled dynasties and growing nations against each other divided the mind of the individual against itself: the struggle between reason and revelation.

Mysteriously, slowly, the planets, in the sixteenth century, were seen to move. The solar system became apparent through the eyes of Copernicus. When Galileo, in the early seventeenth century, set the world itself spinning, the Holy Office stepped in; too late. Only a few years afterwards William Harvey discovered a yet more intimate circulation, that of the blood in the human body. The static world dissolved in motion.

But at the beginning of the seventeenth century, the ordinary educated man lived, as he had lived for the past thousand years, by revelation. The daytime of the faith was over, but the sun had not set: far and fading, it was still the light men knew. Saint Teresa was newly dead and very newly canonized. Men had seen miracles and were to see them for some years more. The curtains had not yet been drawn and the artificial lamps of reason lit. There was the deceptive conflict of the inward and the outward light. Not until the latter half of the century was a renewed and circumscribed security to be found whose foundation was the *cogito ergo sum* of Descartes.

The political storms which blew up over Europe at this time were not physically more horrible than those which had gone before, but they were more demoralizing. In the sixteenth century men had known very well what they were doing, whether they were poisoning rival princes in Italy, or harrying silver fleets in mid-Atlantic. It was a cocksure century. The seventeenth century was not. An anxious or resigned uncertainty, a doubt embracing both motives and aims obscured men's minds. Witchcraft and witch-hunting rose in horrible crescendo; astrology gained fantastic hold; extraordinary religions sprang up like mushrooms.

It is significant that only in the victorious, comfortable Dutch republic did a highly realist school of painting develop. Elsewhere the artist – with few exceptions – transmutes or subordinates reality. Even as sharp an observer as Callot handles his 'Misères de la Guerre' with a light and airy line. *Simplicissimus*, the nightmare novel of the Thirty Years War, was not written until a generation after the war itself, could not have been written until then. Compare the neat, topographical drawings done by Hollar when he accompanied Lord Arundel on an embassy to Germany at the height of the conflict with the horrified jottings of Lord Arundel's secretary. The artist has deliberately closed his eyes. Compare also the symbolic grandeur of Rubens' painting of the Habsburg leaders meeting on the eve of the Battle of Nördlingen: below, well-fed symbolic figures of the Danube and its tributaries; above, the graceful young princely generals, Spanish and Austrian, their cloaks and love-locks streaming in the wind, their left hands doffing, one the plumed sombrero, the other the Hungarian bonnet, their right hands clasped in brotherly greeting; behind each in artfully dissimilar groups the idealized officers of their staff; and beneath their clasped hands the distant spire of Nördlingen church. Tomorrow will be fought the battle in which ten thousand men will die and the scattered remnants of a routed army carry disease and vermin from the Lech to the Rhine.

In civilizations, as in human beings, recognizable phenomena signalize certain epochs. In periods of transition an inward uneasiness is often expressed by affectations designed to conceal it; baroque performed this function in the civilization of western Europe, bridging the gap between the crude assurance of the Renaissance and the polished assurance of the eighteenth century. All would ultimately yield again to man's control: science would be organized, the passions embanked, the arts regulated, religion reduced to formula; but in the meantime thoughts were directionless and men unhappy.

To this general oppression, a further weight was added in England. The young northern country of between three and four million inhabitants had recently come thrusting forward among the powers of western Europe, had gained one or two spectacular successes against the gigantic power of Spain and suffered some ignominious checks. Her people, or rather her educated classes, accepted the former as the most natural thing in the world and blamed convenient scapegoats for the latter.

The phenomenal vigour and precosity of the Elizabethans had created a false expectation among their successors. The English knew already that they were the chosen people, their habitation a demi-paradise, their prowess by sea and land unmatched, their swords ever drawn and ever victorious in just causes. The deceits, the shifts, the betrayals, the total eclipse of the seventeenth century shook their faith in almost everything except their country. The King, the Commons, the idle rich, the idle poor, the gentry, the City – you could take your choice which to blame, much as you can today. But nobody seems to have recognized the simple fact that England, with a quarter the population of France and a third that of Spain, with few discovered resources, with all her wealth in private hands, could not maintain the position she had intermittently reached under Elizabeth.

The total insignificance of their country in the European scene was all the harder for the average Englishman to understand, since it went with a period of comparative economic prosperity at home. One should not pay too much attention to the perennial English complaint that everything was going to the dogs, nor to evidence of local depressions. Local depressions there are always. Still less should one be misled by the poverty of the Crown; wealth was in private hands, and the Crown's powers of taxation were so limited that it had no means of tapping the wealth of the community either in its own or the public interest. But great wealth there certainly was, and the things which should – but do not always – go with wealth: a growing interest in the arts and education, leisure for thought and the cultivation of the graces.

Nor were wealth and civilization confined to the capital. England, a small country, was beginning to be fairly well roaded; communications improved, posts were instituted. If London continued to be the only town of first-class importance, and the two universities the sources from which the intellectual life of London was fed, innumerable country houses were the centres of local constellations of talent. Everything points to a period of comfort and ease such as the Elizabethans had hardly known.

All the more inexplicable, therefore, to contemporaries was the insignificance of their country in European politics. The independent gentry who stalwartly refused to give loans to the Crown were the first to throw up outraged hands when bankrupt preparations for war ended in disaster. 'Since England was England she got not so dishonourable a blow . . .' The causes for which they cared were being betrayed and defeated on the continent of Europe, while their Government did nothing, or, fatally, too little. Puzzled, indignant, conscience-stricken, some of them volunteered in foreign armies. Others stayed at home and blackguarded their rulers. Still others justified the inglorious epoch, though for the wrong reasons:

> White Peace (the beautifull'st of things)
> Seems here her everlasting rest
> To fix, and spreads her downy Wings
> Over the Nest:
>
> As when great Jove, usurping Reign,
> From the plagu'd World did her exile,
> And ty'd her with a golden Chain
> To one blest Isle:

> *Which in a Sea of plenty swam*
> *And turtles sang on every Bough*
> *A safe retreat to all that came*
> *As ours is now.*

Thus Sir Richard Fanshawe, in 1630, a moment when religious liberty and the Protestant cause had been wiped out almost to the shores of the Baltic. Two years later, when the King of Sweden had smashed the Catholic armies back to the Danube and the younger generation in England strained at the leash to join in, another courtier, Thomas Carew, took up the refrain:

> *. . . What though the German drum*
> *Bellow for freedom and revenge, the noise*
> *Concerns not us, nor should divert our joys;*
> *Nor ought the thunder of their carabins*
> *Drown the sweet airs of our tun'd violins.*

But it was not 'white Peace the beautifull'st of things' any more in the 1630s than in the 1930s; it was a wretched, uneasy peace with a bad conscience, and the tuned violins quivered with foreboding.

Foreboding as much of inward as of outward disaster. The signs of political unrest in this country where the turtles were singing on every bough were apparent to anyone not blinded by its material prosperity. Church, State and society suffered from a succession of insignificant or unsuitable leaders. Intelligence was not lacking, but something – confidence, style, character even – was. The prestige of the Crown would hardly have survived any successor to Elizabeth; James I, who might have been a distinguised eccentric don, was clearly impossible. His son Charles acquired a tragic pathos at his latter end, but was not, reigning, an impressive king. The archbishops were little better: Bancroft portentous, not impressive, Abbot cantankerous and bigoted (having shot a beater while hunting, he was ultimately suspended for manslaughter: an unreassuring thing to happen to the archbishop), and last of all fussy little Laud, trotting briskly round snuffing out abuses. Society shook with the kind of scandals that had either been concealed, or been carried off with more style, in the days of Elizabeth: the Essex divorce, the Overbury murder trial, the case of Lord Audley, the prosecution of Lady Purbeck for adultery.

Small things, but educated England was a small, inbred society. This smallness gave importance to single personalities, and a negative importance to the lack of them.

A political crisis was evidently approaching at terrific speed. The government could not continue bankrupt in the 'sea of plenty'. Either the Crown must find means to tap the wealth of the country, or it must cede its authority to those who could. The same crisis had already broken in most European countries. Kings who could not be masters were liable to become victims. King James might survive; King Charles was obviously doomed. From Elizabeth's death in 1603 until 1630 the situation built up towards the crisis. Then came ten years of postponement when Charles threw the opposition out of gear by refusing to call Parliament. It was never anything but an unexpected interlude, and never – except to those who were wilfully blind – appeared as anything else. The inevitable clash was postponed for a decade, the unrestful, mock-happy thirties.

> *Ten years the world upon him falsely smiled*
> *Sheathing in fawning looks the deadly knife –*

Fanshawe again, writing of the King his master; but he might be speaking for many of his contemporary poets, for the whole of his precocious generation.

The combination of spiritual unrest with material comfort – a combination never again so strikingly apparent until our own time – seems to be in England at least a fruitful one for poetry. The astonishing harvest of the second quarter of the seventeenth century has, reckoned in numbers alone, rarely been equalled. But of this great population of poets very few made an attempt to grapple with the problems of their times. The recurring note is, if worldly, insouciance; if unworldly, retreat.

The two obvious exceptions, Milton and Marvell, were both to be found among the opponents of the King. Milton is too complicated and individual a genius to conform to any general rules, but in Marvell, born in 1621 and maturing as a poet during the most restless and disastrous years of the century, many of the characteristics of the Cavalier poets are apparent. He was unlucky by so narrow a margin in missing the interlude of the thirties:

> *The forward youth that would appear*
> *Must now forsake his Muses dear*
> *Nor in the shadows sing*
> *His numbers languishing.*
>
> *Tis time to leave the books in dust*
> *And oil the unuséd armour's rust . . .*

Unhappy 'forward youth', Marvell was only twenty-one when war broke out. The sense of threatened happiness was never more graphically expressed than in his

> *But at my back I always hear*
> *Time's wingéd chariot hurrying near:*
> *And yonder all before us lie*
> *Deserts of vast eternity.*

He, too, could retreat at times from the pressure of the world to embroider prettily on country themes. There are his glow-worms:

> *Ye Country Comets, that portend*
> *No war, nor prince's funeral*
> *Shining unto no higher end*
> *Than to presage the grasses fall.*
> *Ye glow-worms, whose officious flame*
> *To wandering mowers shows the way . . .*

Evidently close kin to Herrick's glow-worms whose services were called in to light Julia to bed. Yet the bedrock of his poetry is not retreat, but acceptance and understanding. It is only necessary to compare the fearless political grasp displayed in his celebrated 'Horatian Ode on Cromwell's Return from Ireland' with Abraham

Cowley's 'Ode to Charles I' after the first abortive Scots War. Marvell manages to compress a whole political theory as well as an extremely striking *aperçu* of the situation into his lines: Cowley makes no attempt to write anything but good verse. Neat and accomplished the empty phrases ring:

> *Others by war their conquest gain*
> *You like a god your ends obtain*
> *Who when rude chaos for his help did call*
> *Spoke but the word and sweetly order'd all . . .*

The King had in fact been forced to yield to the Scots rebels without fighting because he realized in time that he had no army with which to fight them. Two years later, when he risked a war, the results were so disastrous that even Cowley had no words for them.

But the poets were mostly on the King's side. The reason can hardly have lain in the patronage afforded by the Court to literature. It was notoriously poor. The truth was that the poets of this period, however young and fashionable, belonged to the *arrière*, not to the *avant garde*. Their whole trend of thought reached back into a receding past, away from the cold and probing realism, both in thought and politics, which was gradually submerging the older world. They were in fact anti-political, just as the King's view was anti-political – an attempt to do without politics, not an attempt to reform them. This, in the political field the fatal weakness of the King's side, was its attraction for them, and its charm for posterity.

Revealed religion had dominated the dying world, and revealed religion is the refuge of one large group of these poets, the impregnable fortress into which they retreated from the anxious pressure of the time. Donne, from whom the poetic inspiration of his successors was partly derived, stands outside the group. He was thirty by the time Elizabeth died, and like all who reached manhood in that more robust epoch, his torments came mostly from within. There is no retreat in his religious verse, rather a fierce grappling with the mysteries of dogma and the hideous reality of death. He does not, like the later metaphysical poets, soar into the Empyrean, or abandon himself in feminine surrender to the arms of God. The earth is solid under him.

His successors, without exception, are in flight before the world; escape is their only message, whether they speak with the pellucid ingenuousness of Herbert, the lofty sweetness of Vaughan, the ecstasy of Crashaw, the liquid fluency of King, the vibrating rapture of Quarles. Occasionally and far off, one catches the echo of the world without:

> *But hark! My pulse like a soft drum*
> *Beats my approach, tells thee I come,*
> *And slow howe'er my marches be,*
> *I shall at last sit down by thee.*

The military simile has a hint of menace in King's peaceful elegy on his wife.

Each individual case is, of course, different. George Herbert, of noble birth, forsook the prospect of a worldly career for quiet at Bemerton; Henry Vaughan, a simple doctor in remote Brecknock, had little opportunity to know the world; Francis Quarles, who had been a courtier and travelled abroad, knew from what he was retreating; Henry King and Richard Crashaw felt the wind of politics at its keenest, the former losing his bishopric and, worse still, his library, the latter his Cambridge fellowship. King's quiet conscience and sweet disposition made his troubles the easier, and Crashaw, who died in poverty at Loretto, had found in the Catholic faith shelter from the blast.

Quarles, describing only his individual case, gives reason for them all:

> *Like to the arctic needle, that doth guide*
> *The wand'ring shade by his magnetick pow'r,*
> *And leaves his silken Gnomon to decide*
> *The question of the controverted hour;*
> *First Franticks up and down, from side to side,*
> *And restless beats his crystall'd Iv'ry case*
> *With vain impatience: jets from place to place,*
> *And seeks the bosom of his frozen bride;*

At length he slacks his motion, and doth rest
His trembling point at his bright Poles' beloved brest.

Ev'n so my soul, being hurried here and there,
By ev'ry object that presents delight
Fain would be settled, but she knows not where;
She likes at morning what she loathes at night;
She bows to honour; then she lends an eare
To that sweet swan-like voice of dying pleasure,
Then tumbles in the scatter'd heaps of treasure;
Now flatter'd with false hope; now foyl'd with fear
Thus finding all the world's delights to be
But empty toyes, good God, she points alone to thee.

Less secure than this total retreat from the world was the mere country retreat of Herrick, who lacked the quality of mind necessary for more arduous contemplation than that of violets. Not that he contemplated violets with much assiduity (he had at first bitterly resented being cut off from the gaieties of the capital). A close observation of nature is markedly absent from his, as from most, contemporary verse. He evokes the colour and the climate of the English summer with what proves to be on examination an astonishing vagueness of accurate detail. Therein lies his genius. Comfortably settled at Dean Prior in Devonshire, well connected, by nature and breeding contentedly obsequious ('Great Caesar,' he apostrophizes the minuscule Charles I and wreathes verses like garlands round the baby Duke of York), he was in a position to bury his head, not in the sand, but in a bank of wild flowers. He sang as he himself said

of Maypoles, hock-carts, wassails, wakes,
Of bridegrooms, brides and of their bridall cakes,
I write of Youth and Love and have Accesse
By them to sing of cleanly wantonnesse.

'Cleanly wantonnesse' – but for a few coarser outbursts at the expense of personal enemies – does indeed hit off Herrick very neatly. But his gifts, nourished on a diet of material, if simple, pleasures could not apparently contend with adversity. Driven out of his rectory, he was pleased at first with the prospect of returning to London, but things were not what they had been, his Great Caesar beheaded, his pretty Duke of York in exile and well on the way to becoming the far from pretty James II. The honeysuckle talent withered.

The fact was that in the seventeenth century – as in our own – escape was impossible. There is matter for reflection in the fact that its major poet, Milton, went out to meet the political problem of his time and to some extent subdued it to his verse. With few exceptions the others, when caught, were caught unwillingly. For there was no escape: not in contemplation at Little Gidding, not in the common rooms of Oxford and Cambridge, not in the rectories of Devonshire or the country mansions of the Cotswolds, least of all in the gardens of Whitehall. It was the politician's century, and the poet was already being pushed away, driven back, as it were, into his own society. Hence the flourishing of cliques, the Oxford clique with Will Cartwright, the Cambridge clique with Cowley and Crashaw, the 'sons' of Ben Jonson, the Whitehall clique of gentry. Hence the private jokes, the adulation of friends, the lampooning of enemies, the sly topical scandals and oblique references which make great tracts of their verse incomprehensible.

The false forward spring of the thirties brought on the flowering of innumerable talents; verses flowed gracefully from a hundred fluent quills, Carew, Davenant, Waller, Godolphin, Lovelace, Townshend, Habington. They were all quiet-needing talents, born in rich soil and germinated by showers of applause. Flowering in the sunshine of the thirties their delicate blossoms were later to fall unquickened or hang withered on the bough. But they were most of them, however short their bloom or few their verses, something more than mere fashionable practitioners of *vers d'occasion*. The anthological immortality of so many of the lyrics – an immortality which makes them too hackneyed for quotation – is itself a tribute to the astonishing felicity of their touch. 'Go lovely Rose', 'The lark now leaves his wat'ry nest', 'Tell me not, sweet, I am unkind' – each is unique, each perfect. Artificial in design, their poetry is yet unforced. Its effortlessness makes it at first glance seem almost too easy. There is nothing, not even observation, to give body to their works. Their natural phenomena are almost always wrong. Even gardens, a form of tamed and sophisticated nature in which they delighted, they never closely observed or accurately described. Yet at times their poetry seems all compact of sunlight and green lawns, of bright flowering borders and the white-thorn hedgerows of an English spring. Marvell's bees go to bed in the tulips, a freak of nature equalled by Lovelace's grasshopper snugly tucked up in a carved acorn. Their convention was not the laboured convention of accuracy. They relied on the rightness of sound and rhythm, and the associations which one happy phrase can call to mind. Their appeal is through the senses to the imagination, never laboriously to the inward eye which was Wordsworth's bliss of solitude but emphatically not theirs.

Imagination was their refuge, as faith was that of the metaphysical poets: imagination so strong that in most of them the poet and the man led separate lives. Some intrigued at Court, some planned a *coup d'état*, some when war came raised troops of horse, many distinguished themselves in the field and more in the dangerous parts of spies and messengers. Their experience of life was vivid, harsh and dangerous, anxious and despairing, the experience of the defeated. Hardly a breath of it reaches their verse, unless it be a soft melancholy like that of a summer evening: life is short, beauty is shorter, and the cool shadow of not unwelcome death lengthens across the garden.

The *carpe diem* theme recurs in innumerable variations. Lighthearted in Cowley's

> *To-day is ours, what do we fear?*
> *To-day is ours, we have it here.*
> *Let's treat it kindly that it may*
> *Wish at least with us to stay.*

Didactic in Herrick's 'Gather ye Rosebuds', *moqueur* in Jordan's irrefutable statement that his mistress 'will be damnable mouldy a hundred years hence', faintly menacing in Jasper Mayne's

> *Time is the feather'd thing*
> *And, whilst I praise*

79

> *The sparklings of thy looks and call them rays*
> *Takes wing.*
> *Leaving behind him as he flies*
> *An unperceivéd dimness in thine eyes*

But apart from this general preoccupation with the shortness of time, they search after beauty rather than truth, manner and not matter. Occasionally, but very occasionally, genuine personal feeling forces a way through. Cowley's lament for his friend William Harvey opens on a note almost harsh with pain:

> *It was a dismal and a fearful night,*
> *Scarce could the Morn drive on th' unwilling light,*
> *When sleep death's image left my troubled breast*
> *By something liker death possessed*
> *My eyes with tears did uncommanded flow*
> *And on my soul hung the dull weight*
> *Of some intolerable fate.*
> *What bell was that? Ah me! Too much I know.*

But this is the exception. For death, however keenly felt, as for love, however genuine, there were the accepted patterns, the tender, plaintive strain, the Grecian vegetation, the mourning shepherds. Life could be met only on these terms, feeling expressed only under the customary disguises. From the country peace of Bemerton George Herbert mildly protested:

> *Is it no verse, except enchanted groves*
> *And sudden arbours shadow coarse-spunne lines?*
> *Must purling streams refresh a lover's loves?*
> *Must all be vail'd, while he that reads, divines,*
> *Catching the sense at two removes?*

George Herbert could dispense with such veils. The 'sweet and vertuous soul' had made peace with heaven and had no more to fear on earth. He was lucky, too, in dying before the crisis of the time.

But for those who must go on living in the world the pretence was essential. Unlike Milton, they were not on terms with it. So while the King's government went finally bankrupt, while the Scots overran the northern counties, while Strafford was beheaded in front of a gigantic crowd of jubilant spectators, and the little Archbishop escaped by a back way from the mob and the King fled the capital and the Queen fled the country, and after a hundred and fifty years of peace England was at war with herself, these poets were imploring Amarantha to unravel her hair, giving the nightingale winter quarters in their lady's throat, asserting that birds and flowers mistook her coming for the dawn, with a hundred other irrelevancies.

When the assumed mood breaks down, it gives place to a venomous or ribald parody on itself. Equivocal words and a whole alphabet of symbols invest the pretty gallantries with other meanings. Most of these poets are adept at disguising obscenity; Suckling's sleight of hand is positively insolent. From his brilliantly accomplished verse, indeed, a savage, go-getting, tomorrow-we-die materialism emerges almost naked. Gambler and society playboy, he never had any doubt of the fate in store for the lilies of the field, planned to have his good time and had it. Whether or not he killed himself, preferring poison to an uglier end, is a matter of indifference; but he died in Paris and in poverty during the opening months of the Civil War. The first whiff of gunpowder had been enough for him.

His fellows, more sympathetic for that reason, cultivated their wilful blindness to the end, their 'careless heads with roses bound' within the doomed walls of Basing House or besieged Oxford, in the shadow of the firing party and the block. Montrose, like Raleigh, was rhyming on the eve of execution. Nor did they mean, as one literal-minded editor has thought, that roses were commonly twined in their hair. The roses were their still lovely imaginings, though the draught whistled under the door in the fireless prison, and a querulous wife with a sheaf of unpayable bills was the material out of which they conjured Althea 'whispering at the gates'.

Theirs was a mental, not a physical, shrinking. Few of them actually failed in courage. Suckling, not unexpectedly, Waller, too; sensitive and vain, with most of his relations on the Parliament side, he fancied himself as an orator in the House of Commons. Later, becoming involved in a plot to betray London to the King, he lost his nerve and betrayed his associates instead, an act which forty subsequent years of blameless life could not altogether wipe out.

> *The soul's dark cottage batter'd and decay'd*
> *Lets in new light through chinks that time hath made,*

he was to write long after, in a poem whose twelve lines sum up perhaps more perfectly than anything else in the English language the mistakes of youth and the regrets of age. None can have known them better.

But Davenant was knighted for valour by the King and employed on dangerous missions. Falling into Parliamentary hands, he was only saved from execution, as some thought, by the intervention of Milton. Cowley, expelled like Crashaw from Cambridge, entered the Queen's service as a secretary and was employed as a confidential agent during the Commonwealth. It did his talent no good. He was never to fulfil the promise of his radiant teens. Sidney Godolphin was killed in a skirmish at Chagford; Cartwright died of camp fever in overcrowded Oxford; Denham, Cleveland, Lovelace, Fanshawe, all were active for the King, and all were dispossessed, imprisoned or exiled.

In debts, defeat and hunger their voices fade out. A few naturally carried over the tradition, with the remains of their lives, into the ensuing period. The individual always exists to blur the lines which historians for convenience must draw precisely. Traherne, born late in the 1630s, closes the exquisite cycle which began with Quarles. The Restoration brought with it the triumph of the scientific approach, the foundation of the Royal Society, and the cynical shelving of moral values which accompanied the new outlook. Smooth, ingenious and satirical was the new and more ordered expression of the poetic impulse. Fantasy and faith were alike dead: they had been the last expression of the nation's wondering and ingenuous adolescence, of a time when men still saw themselves midway between the beasts and the angels. Henceforward man was lord of creation: there was nothing he would not know. The limitless world, inexplicable and impressive, dwindled to the compass of his mind. Descartes, Boyle, Newton – the physical and mental map regained its contours. Men knew once more where they were and whither they were going, but their fancy would never again range so freely, and no one again would say

> *I saw Eternity the other night*
> *Like a great ring of pure and endless light.*

1944

The Causes of the Civil War

Two separate but related questions have to be answered about the conflict that divided England in the middle years of the seventeenth century. What was the nature of the crisis in English government at this time? Could that crisis have been resolved without war, and if not why not?

The conflict had two aspects – it was concerned with problems of government peculiar to England, but it was also a part of the religious wars that affected the whole of western Europe for a century after the Reformation. In so far as the crisis concerned the internal affairs of England, it might have been resolved peacefully. But the dynastic and religious conflict, at that time dividing Europe, introduced elements into the English situation that transformed a political and administrative struggle into a military one.

The political and religious causes of the war are those that have been traditionally emphasized. The King, in common with most European sovereigns of the time, wished to strengthen the central government and was impatient of the hindrances put in his way by Parliament and by the gentry who exercised local power. The gentry, in and out of Parliament, resented interference with what they believed to be their liberties and privileges. This constitutional struggle was intensified by religious feeling. It was a logical part of the King's centralizing policy to insist on uniform religious practices and submission to the state Church. But many of his subjects inclined, with varying degrees of fervour, towards forms of Protestantism which could not, or would not, be included within the Anglican Church. The religious and political opposition to the Crown thus came into very close association.

This is the broad outline of the political picture presented by England in the first half of the seventeenth century. Many details can be added to it, to strengthen and modify the general impression, but it is important to remember that such details are *additions*: they do not basically alter the general situation.

It is usual to emphasize the poverty of the Crown and Parliament's control of subsidies as a cause of tension between King and Commons in this epoch, and as a principal reason for the failure of King Charles's experiment in non-parliamentary government. Certainly the King lacked funds for the effective exercise of power; but it was the lack of government officials, quite as much as the lack of funds, that wrecked the monarchy. King Charles during his personal rule found numerous subterfuges for raising money. Had he developed his industrial monopoly programme more consistently and more thriftily, had he allowed his courtiers less latitude and his financial advisers more, it is conceivable that he might have solved the money problem at least as effectively as any of his contemporaries abroad.

It was not lack of money that prevented him from quelling the revolt of the Scots in 1639 and 1640. Twice over, with or without money, he got an army together and marched it to the North. But the spirit was lacking. The men were deplorably bad material: 'all the rogues in the kingdom,' said Sir Jacob Astley; and they were very unwilling to fight. What undermined the King's policy much more than lack of funds was lack of co-operation. Strafford, the King's chief minister, spoke of 'a general disaffection to the King's service'. Among those responsible for recruiting, equipping and sending the troops, from Lord Lieutenants to Justices of the Peace, the majority shared in this 'general disaffection'. They were at worst hostile to the King's policy, at best bored with it, and their behaviour varied from the indifferent to the actively obstructive. They had neither faith in nor respect for the King's government. The King's government, for its part, had very limited powers of coercion against them, for the simple reason that no other body of men existed to replace them. The King could not get rid of obstructive Justices of the Peace and put in loyal ones, because there were at that time simply not enough loyal gentlemen to be found. When the Short Parliament met, in April 1640, great efforts were made in Yorkshire, under the influence of Strafford, to send devoted King's men as MPs to Westminster. As a result the county was for over a month almost entirely denuded of loyal King's men, the obstructionists had it all their own way at home, while the loyalists, who could not be in two places at once, were serving the King at Westminster. This desperate shortage of support was fatal to the royal administration.

That was the cardinal weakness of King Charles's government. He had no civil service, no country-wide bureaucratic class dependent on him. The royal policy, divulged by proclamation, depended for its implementation on local men, principally on the Justices. These were not officials exclusively dependent on the Crown but gentlemen of standing in their own right who had, over the years, developed their own traditions of behaviour and their own views on what was good for the country – and for themselves. If a majority of them felt no enthusiasm for the policies of the Crown, as far as these affected the internal life of the country, then the policies of the Crown would not be carried out.

In theory, King Charles understood the necessity of controlling the Justices, who were required to report regularly to the central government. But he failed to realize what Queen Elizabeth had always known, that in practice his powers depended on making his policies acceptable to those who were to enforce them. Thus, when it came to the Scots war, the troops were well aware that the gentry, who had unwillingly scraped them together, were no more interested in the war than they were themselves. Desertion, indiscipline and mutiny followed naturally from this knowledge.

A situation had arisen in which government became impossible as soon as the King found himself at loggerheads with the gentry. He had the authority to initiate and plan a policy, but he had not the power to enforce it. The gentry had the power to enforce (or not to enforce) a policy, but had not the power to initiate it. Such a situation could not last. One of two things was bound to happen: either the King had to find means to enlarge an official class dependent on himself – the solution found by Richelieu and most of the European absolutists; or the gentry had to find means of controlling the initiation of policy, so that they would only be required to do what they were willing to do.

A centralizing government policy, whether in Church or State, is quite naturally and inevitably unpopular with those who are accustomed to exercising local power and local discretion, and who do not wish to see their power (or their rights, as they would say) invaded. But this explanation for the opposition to King Charles I has of recent years been felt to be inadequate. It has been suggested that the real cause for the opposition was economic – that the dominant gentry were rich and growing richer, and were consequently irritated at the Crown's medieval interventions in favour of common good and the common people against private profiteering and the unrestricted operation of the capitalist system. Conversely, it is argued that the trouble was caused not by the rich gentry at all, but by the poor gentry: that the epoch was one of economic recession, and that the instability of the gentry's position, and that of landed society in general, caused the unrest that led to war.

Evidence can be found for both these arguments, and this is not in the least surprising since many different reasons for economic unrest did undoubtedly exist in the England of King Charles. The very plentiful surviving evidence by no means lends itself to straightforward interpretation and has hardly yet been fully assembled from all possible sources. The economic policy of King Charles was, in any case, so inconsistent that it was likely to arouse protest – as it did – from almost all types of men. At one moment, he was fining depopulators and profiteers in the interests of the poor; at another, he was encouraging them. At one moment, he was protecting the interests of the cottager against the engrossing landowner, at another, shovelling cottagers and squatters out of the way for the benefit of shareholders in agricultural or industrial schemes, or to improve his deer parks, or simply to raise money by fines. He did whatever suited him at the moment. Thus economic motives for opposition to his policies are all-pervasive, but they are – like the policies themselves – of many different kinds.

The crisis, however, was not in essence an economic crisis. It was a political and administrative crisis. The critical position of the gentry did not arise from their economic power – or lack of it – but from their administrative power. That, and that above all, made a constitutional upheaval of some kind inevitable. The Long Parliament, which met in November 1640, solved the problem by putting through legislation against the prerogative courts, thus curtailing the coercive powers of the Crown, and arrogated to themselves the right to coerce opponents, and to discuss and, by implication, to initiate policy. At this point, the constitutional revolution was complete *without a war*. What turned a peaceful revolution into a shooting war was the European situation, the strategic position of the British Isles and the King's foreign policy.

In Europe, wars of religion had been almost continuous since the Reformation. Under Queen Elizabeth I, England had come to play the part that the majority of her educated people thought the right one – against Roman Catholic Spain, in favour of the Protestant powers and their allies. This policy was natural to a people who were predominantly Protestant, and whose overseas expansion had already brought them into collision with Spain. The fact that John Pym, leader of the Commons in 1640, a strong Puritan, was also secretary of the Providence Company, with its trading interests in the Caribbean, has been often and rightly emphasized. On the European mainland the Habsburg dynasty (Spain–Austria) had made themselves the defenders of the Roman Catholic Church and had, by force of arms, undone the work of the Reformation in Bohemia and much of South Germany. By 1629, when King Charles was on the eve of his experiment in non-parliamentary government, the imperial Roman Catholic armies reached the Baltic. This menacing background to the English situation is too often overlooked. The Protestant Cause – which, in a vague way, meant a great deal to many Englishmen – was in a very depressed state when King Charles's personal rule began.

In the triumphant advance of the imperial Catholic forces, King Charles's brother-in-law, the Protestant Elector Palatine who had rashly accepted the Crown of Bohemia from Protestant rebels of that country, had become a landless and homeless exile. It was a source of frequent, if often uninformed and unreasonable, criticism of King Charles that he had done far too little for his brother-in-law and, after his death, for his widow and children. But the King's sins of omission were less glaring than his sins of commission. Spain was the other half of the Spanish–Austrian Habsburg combine; and Spain was the traditional enemy and rival of England. It is true that, by the 1630s, Spain was a much weakened power and, in some sort, rather the traditional than the actual villain of the piece.

English merchants were beginning to look with equal resentment on the rising power of the Dutch. But the re-orientation of opinion was far from complete. The Spaniards still barred English expansion in the new world, especially in the Caribbean, while Dunkirk, in Spanish control, was a constant menace to English shipping. The Spaniards, for their part, needed the friendship of the English government, if they were to pursue their eighty years' war with the Dutch. A hostile England would threaten the sea route of their money and troops for the Netherlands; a friendly England could give them help and protection against the growing menace of Dutch sea power in the Channel and the Narrow Seas.

In return, therefore, for considerable financial benefits King Charles had given help and protection to the Spaniards. All through the thirties Spanish bullion, for the payment of their troops in the Netherlands, was shipped in English ships by way of London to Antwerp. English ships, being technically neutral, were immune from attacks by the Dutch. In this way, King Charles's government gave valuable aid to Spanish arms against the Protestant Cause. In 1639, when with the loss of Breisach the Spaniards became unable to send their troops overland by the Rhine route into Flanders, King Charles allowed them to send them by sea in English ships. The Dutch, at last exasperated too far, stopped some of these ships; whereupon, to make it easier for the Spaniards, the King allowed them to land their men at Plymouth, march them overland and ship them again from Dover. Not more than a few thousand Spanish troops came in this way, but the operation was sufficiently noticeable to provoke rumours that the King – then at the height of his effort to force Anglican ritual upon the Calvinist Scots – was in league with Catholic Spain, and intended to subdue his Protestant subjects with the help of Spanish troops. Indeed, the whole Scots war was seen by many, in the British Isles and abroad, as the signal for Great Britain to become involved in the European conflict. The Scots would be supported by the Dutch and French, the King by the Spaniards; thus the dynastic-religious wars of Europe would be extended to our shores.

In the autumn of the same year, 1639, after the armistice with the Scots at Berwick, a Spanish Armada was chased into English territorial waters, where it was effectively destroyed by the Dutch Admiral, Marten Tromp. In this conflict, the English fleet did nothing; but the King, before the battle, had allowed the Spaniards to replenish their stores of gunpowder at a price, and he had given orders for the billeting of their troops on the ships in English coast towns, if they should be forced to land. All this looked very bad to his anti-Spanish Protestant subjects. A rumour that he was about to lease the southern Irish ports to the Spaniards as naval bases was, in the circumstances, very widely believed. It was only forty years since the Spaniards had actually occupied Kinsale; and, as events were soon to show, they had still considerable interest in gaining a foothold in southern Ireland for the defence of their sea routes. Whatever the King intended about the southern Irish ports, it is beyond question that, in the summer of 1640, Strafford tried, in his master's name, to arrange a loan of four million ducats from Spain, in return for a regular guard of thirty-five ships of the English navy to convoy Spanish transports through the Channel. Nothing came of this, because the Dutch made it clear that they would consider the arrangement a breach of neutrality; and, much as Charles needed Spanish gold, he could not at that moment risk a Dutch war.

This was the background of recent foreign policy against which the English constitutional revolution took place. Charles had time and again shown himself to be not merely pro-Spanish but willing to accept Spanish subsidies and to give indirect help to Spanish arms in the European war, in defiance of the economic interests and the religious principles of a large majority of his subjects. In the autumn of 1641, revolt broke out in Ireland – a revolt of the Roman Catholic population against Protestant Scottish and English settlers. This revolt was greatly stimulated by fear of what the powerful English Parliament, Protestant and anti-Spanish, might perpetrate in Ireland.

Irish exiles, both soldiers and priests, from the Spanish Netherlands and Spain played a considerable part in the rising, so that the Irish rebellion was from the start associated with the European religious wars. Where did King Charles stand in this revolt? As

King of England, he should have given the utmost of his protection to the Protestant settlers in Ireland. But the insurgents claimed that he had authorized them to act. He denied it, probably with a fair measure of truth; but his previous conduct gave strong colour to the insurgents' claim, and re-doubled the suspicions of Parliament. In the circumstances, Parliament insisted that the ultimate control of the forces to be raised for the suppression of the Irish revolt must lie with them. Suddenly, a dangerous constitutional question, which might otherwise have lain dormant, came into the forefront of debate: the question of the control of the armed forces. Since neither King nor Parliament would give way on this, civil war was the logical outcome.

Thus the immediate cause of the Civil War was a clash over the control of the armed forces. This clash was the logical outcome of the suspicion engendered by the King's foreign policy. Without that suspicion there would have been nothing to make war inevitable or even likely. A constitutional struggle with legal weapons – that there must have been. But what converted a tussle in the law courts and Parliament to a violent clash of fighting men in the field was the state of religious and dynastic war on the Continent, and the King's fatal espousal of what seemed to the majority of his subjects the wrong side. Without that, Parliament would hardly have dared to arrogate to itself the sovereign's right to defend his people. But Charles had shown that he was more interested in Spanish gold than in the immunity of British shores. This caused the Civil War.

1955

Miss Mangnall of the Questions

$\blacktriangleright$ rincess Angelica, only daughter of King Valoroso XXIV of
Paflagonia, it will be remembered by addicts of *The Rose and
the Ring*, was held up as an example to idle pupils by their
governesses. 'She could play the most difficult pieces of music at
sight. She could answer any one of Mangnall's Questions!' Soon
the Paflagonian schoolroom will be the last niche in the temple
of fame left to poor Miss Mangnall, later editions of whose
valuable work, limp from the thumbing of long-dead governesses,
are sometimes to be found in the fourpenny boxes in the Charing
Cross Road. Her book, privately printed in 1800, was later
acquired by the enterprising firm of Longmans, ran into revised
edition after revised edition, and became the mainstay of the pre-
Victorian and early Victorian schoolroom. And what an admirable
mainstay it was. A copy came into my possession from the unworthy source mentioned above – fourpennyworth, as I lightly
assumed, of innocent amusement for a short train journey. I
underestimated Miss Mangnall. Not only was I put to shame by
my own ignorance – did I know that Fuller's Earth was an
'unctuous kind of marl', or even that gratitude was the distinguish-
ing virtue of the Egyptians? – but I was filled with nostalgic
admiration for the balance, the logic, the firm and reasoned outlook of this astonishing lady. With far more confidence would I
place Miss Mangnall's *Questions* in the hands of 'the young person'
than many a modern work sterilized by child-psychology and em-
bellished with the self-consciously ingenuous pictures that children are now supposed to like – as if every right-minded child did
not immediately prefer 'The Boyhood of Raleigh' by Sir John
Everett Millais.

The fact is that Richmal Mangnall, born according to tradition in Manchester in 1769, and for many years head-mistress of Crofton Hall in Yorkshire, belonged to the Age of Reason. Her face, under the neatly fastened turban, is that of a pre-eminently sensible woman: shrewd eyes, kindly mouth, open features. Her *Questions*, which is chiefly devoted to History and Antiquity with a brief section on Astronomy and General Subjects, implies an exalted philosophy of life. Black is black to Miss Mangnall and white is white, the colour being irrevocably determined on the highest moral principles. Her prejudices, which are many and unconcealed, arise from high-mindedness, if a little also from ignorance. Believing what she did of the Hierarchy, the Inquisition and the Mendicant Orders – which 'prevented the dawning light of the thirteenth century from penetrating the regions of darkness' – how could she think well of the Church of Rome? She had none of that unnerving impartiality which in more recent handbooks clouds the youthful mind with doubt. Her later editors and revisers maintained, together with her dignified prose, her upright prejudices and her exemplary freedom from subservience or hypocrisy. To the last Mangnall's *Questions* spoke with Johnsonian authority and fearlessness, the voice of the eighteenth century ringing out over the nineteenth.

As a guide in politics and morality she was, if conventional, yet extremely sound, though here and there infected a little with a plutocratic bias. When asked whether prosperity or adversity most tried the human soul, her pupils were to reply: 'Prosperity, as that condition affords the opportunity of proving either its true greatness or the vices which may be concealed in it.' Lucky hand-loom weavers, fortunate labourers of Speenhamland! Their souls were spared the supreme test. But no fault can be found with her answer to the question, 'What is true glory?' Her definition is precise: 'Active benevolence, fortitude to support the frowns of fortune, evenness of temper in prosperity, patience in afflictions, contempt of unmerited injuries; this is virtue, and the fame of virtuous actions can alone be called true glory.' Politically she was a firm believer in the 'superior excellence' of the English constitution, stalwart in her defence of freedom of conscience, and, as the years went by and new editions appeared, proud of her country's claim to have 'struck off the chains that galled the African slave'.

Nothing was omitted from her scrutiny. Each English reign is credited with its 'principal inventions and discoveries'. The use of the globes was introduced under King Edward I, a period at which 'it is remarkable that wine was sold as only a cordial, in apothecarys' shops'. Starch and the horse-guards come under King Henry VIII, speaking trumpets under Cromwell; the Northern Lights were first observed in the time of King George I.

She was wonderfully absolute too in her classifications. 'Name the four most ambitious men in Rome?' she asked: 'Name the four most temperate Romans? Name the three most luxurious?' There is no arguing about the answers, no protesting that Catiline may have been more ambitious than Marius, or Caesar more luxurious than either. The abominable 'Sylla' figured in both the first and third category. Honour, however, where honour is due. 'The Duke of Wellington was equally eminent in the senate and in the field, sternly upholding the line of duty without fear or favour. It has been said of him that he made the service of public life more masculine: he rebuked by his conduct restless vanity, and reprimanded the morbid susceptibility of irregular egotism.' In sentences like these Miss Mangnall's English achieves lapidary perfection. Nelson, for instance . . . 'after hoisting the English flag over the united fleets of France and Spain, closed his glorious career in death; his grateful country rewarded him with substantial favours while living, and has since raised monuments of brass and marble to a memory more lasting than either'.

Miss Mangnall's scrupulous use of words gives distinction to even the commonest questions. 'Whence are cocoa-nuts procured?' she asks, and not, as you or I would, 'Where do coconuts come from?' thus committing an assault on grammar and condemning one of the pleasantest words in the language, the charming 'whence', to undeserved neglect. But although sensitive to the beauties of literature, Miss Mangnall and her editors were sound on decency. The works of Rabelais, 'a Frenchman', 'were greatly deficient in that delicacy without which genius may sparkle for a moment, but can never shine with pure undiminished lustre'.

The spacious dignity of many of the answers must have enriched the common vocabulary of generations of young English ladies, while doubtless making Miss Mangnall's name hateful for ever in their ears. Like many of the best educationists she was more concerned with the teacher than with the pupil: her manual was designed to preserve the energies and the temper of the harassed governess while supplying her deficiencies of education and character. The first edition of the *Questions* is a pocket volume which could be slipped into reticule or work bag, and unobtrusively propped on the knee beneath the edge of the schoolroom table. Instruction and crochet might thus proceed simultaneously. How many oppressed gentlewomen, from 'poor Miss Taylor' in the elegant parlour at Hartfield to the tameless Brontës in the stuffy schoolrooms of the Yorkshire gentry, as they sat down to face lethargic or hostile pupils, must have breathed a silent thanksgiving for the gift of a strength not their own.

1942

The City of God

My soul, there is a country . . .

Saint Augustine died in his bishopric, the fortress town of Hippo Regius on the north coast of Africa, in the late summer of the year 430. Fifteen months earlier the Vandals, the most brutish of the barbarian tribes who had penetrated the crumbling frontiers of the Roman Empire, had leapt the pillars of Hercules into Africa. Masters of Rome's richest province and lords of the western Mediterranean they were soon, under their King, the ugly and crooked Gaisaric, to hold the Empire up to ransom. With the tide of this last calamity beating round the walls of his earthly city the Saint had died, leaving to his doomed contemporaries and to an unimaginable posterity his *City of God*.

The days of his life were the last of the Roman Empire. Born not long after the death of Constantine he had seen in his youth the deceptive stability established under Valentinian I and Theodosius. The elements of imperial order were still present and the furnishings of civilization were all about him: the baths and the hypocausts, the material wealth and physical comfort, the free food and the free entertainments. The world of learning flourished in disputatious vigour, its roots deep in the culture of centuries. But the Goths were crossing the Rhine and the Vandals the Pyrenees. There was pressure without, and within the paralytic rot – a parasite population and a rigid bureaucracy.

Christianity was the official religion of the Empire, but it was challenged by heresy and troubled by schism. Pagan learning and above all the fine teaching of the Neo-platonists dominated the schools. These were the influences which formed the mind of the young Augustine pursuing his studies at Carthage while the Goths shattered the imperial army and killed the Emperor Valens at the calamitous battle of Hadrianople. This was in the year 378; nine years later Augustine was baptized. By the time he was consecrated to the see of Hippo in 395 the barbarian disintegration of the West was far advanced and the Empire divided between the feeble sons of Theodosius. In 410 Rome fell, to Alaric, King of the Visigoths. Such was the first century of official Christianity: a clouded opening.

In these dismal circumstances Saint Augustine began to compile his *City of God*. He had two motives for his writings. The first was to defend the Christian faith against pagan accusers who saw in the decay of the Empire the vengeance of the forsaken gods. The second was to raise above the wreck of a temporal Rome and beyond the dark horizon of his times the vision of the Heavenly City which has no end.

The first of these tasks, the refutation of paganism, seems remote from us; to Saint Augustine it was urgent. The struggle was a bitter one fought out inside the brain of every educated Roman Christian: the delights of poetry and the intellectual pleasures of a great culture came to these men almost with the odour of damnation about them. The beauty of classical literature, in which they had been bred, was a temptress beauty, and safety – for some of them at least – lay only in renunciation. This inner struggle, which Saint Augustine had himself experienced, reflects the vehemence and reality of the physical struggle which from time to time still came to the surface in the political world and which was always a latent danger. The apostasy of the Emperor Julian had occurred within Augustine's lifetime, and when Alaric was besieging Rome the Senate had decreed the death of Serena, niece of the Emperor Theodosius, who, in a too outrageous display of her contempt, had helped herself to a necklace from the statue of the Mother of the Gods. Paganism was still powerful and seemed more powerful even than it was.

Saint Augustine thus appointed himself the defender of the True God against the dethroned population of false gods, and in chapter after argumentative chapter historically disproved the efficacy of Jupiter and his crew.

The contest in these terms seems unreal to us, and yet the struggle with false gods is perennial and may be in a more desperate state to-day than when Saint Augustine took up the challenge. For it was in the last resort the material values which Augustine challenged, the false faith which measures its gods by the worldly success they choose to bestow and offers material propitiation for material benefit. If we read for the pagan gods of the fifth century the gadget gods of the twentieth, the slogan gods, the scientific gods and the thousand superstitions of rationalism, the struggle is not foreign to us: only the terms in which it is couched. But the materialism of our time has not paganism's redeeming beauties and there is no Saint Augustine.

The second task which Saint Augustine undertook in *The City of God* has, however, the more immediate reality for us – the task of revealing the eternal kingdom beyond the earthly kingdom. Like Augustine we inhabit a threatened world; the threat, being largely of our own making, is different in quality from the threat to the Roman order. Barbarian invasions and atom bombs have necessarily a different impact on human lives and the human mind. But both are unsettling.

Not that civilized society in the twentieth century is so near the abyss as it was in the fifth. Our world has not yet reached that visionary unreality, that hysteric oscillation between terrified excess and terrifying austerity, nor acquired the frantic appetite for public entertainment in the midst of public disaster.

Saint Augustine, citizen of the Roman Empire, belonged to its complex, huge, decayed fabric. It was the earthly city as he understood it. The medieval world with its feudal subdivisions, its territorial loyalties under the circumscribed authority of a Church whose boundaries were never so wide as those of the fallen Empire, would have been beyond his darkest imagining. Yet it was precisely this unimaginable medieval world which took Saint Augustine for its own, and which, through him, caught the great light of Plato, the only pagan who 'came near to the knowledge of Christ'. Otherwise his immense influence on the Middle Ages was one which might well have astonished him. From his well-furnished arsenal of learning and argument, ammunition was to be found for conflicts of which he had not dreamt. From the surge and movement of his style were to come, in echo and paraphrase, some of the loveliest passages in medieval Latin. The sea-beat of his

Quanta erit felicitas, ubi nullum erit malum, nullum latebit bonum, vocabitur Dei Laudibus, qui erit omnia in omnibus?

melts into the bell-chimes of Abelard:

> *O quanta qualia*
> *sunt illa sabbata,*
> *quae semper celebrant*
> *superna curia,*
> *quae fessis requies,*
> *quae merces fortibus,*
> *cum erit omnia*
> *deus in omnibus.*

His ideas illumined Dante; his theories of the State sustained the established Church in Gregory VII and his theories of God undermined it in Wyclif and Luther. For if he believed that the earthly State was the outcome of sin, he also believed that God needed no mysterious intermediaries between himself and his creation. Strange that the Saint whose writings so dominated the Middle Ages should be in spirit so much closer to the Renaissance with its immense rediscovery of the human personality.

There is a satisfying basis of fact to the outlook of Saint Augustine: he understood the earthly city and indeed devoted much of his book to explaining it. After all it is a fact; it has to be lived in, whether it is the Roman Empire or some shield-clashing monarchy of the Franks or, for that matter, a parliamentary democracy. Although it is the result of sin (Adam's sin) it is not necessarily bad. '*Set justice aside* and what are kingdoms but fair thievish purchases?' said Saint Augustine, thereby making it clear that justice is the essential. Nowhere does he suggest that it is the impossible. The earthly city can and should embody it. *The City of God* gives no countenance to the doctrine that the Christian is at liberty wholly to disregard the earthly city. On the contrary, in all those passages which explain the relations of the temporal with the heavenly kingdom – that is of the Christian with the State – there is a classic moderation.

The heavenly city observes and respects this temporal peace here on earth, and the coherence of men's wills in honest morality.

The true Christian,

being a citizen, must not be all for himself, but sociable in his life and actions.

And again:

One may not be so given to contemplation that he neglect the good of his neighbour, nor so far in love with action that he forget divine speculation.

Only when there is evident conflict between the laws of the heavenly and the earthly city must the citizen of the latter take his stand against the temporary and temporal. This was the strength and comfort of Saint Augustine's message to a troubled world, for whatever befalls the earthly city the heavenly city stands firm.

Its citizens know no difference of language or nation; they come from the ends of the earth and are scattered over all the world; their common citizenship is in Christ. Their city was untouched by the Roman disaster; it has been seen in faith since then in every quarter of the globe, on the hills of China and in the jungles of Africa, and once with the brightness of revelation by a tinker in Bedford gaol. Disquieting doubt or dazzling vision, the faith is rooted deep in the hearts of men. It is this faith which to-day still nourishes the lurking doubt that antiseptics and full employment – good though these be – are neither man's ultimate goal nor his salvation and that, beyond the earthly city with its strivings and its power for good or for evil,

> *If thou canst get but thither*
> *There grows the flower of Peace,*
> *The Rose that cannot wither,*
> *Thy fortress and thy ease.*

1946

The Last Masque

The dress designed for King Charles I to wear in the masque which concluded the Christmas festivities of the year 1639–40 was of pale blue embroidered with silver thread. Inigo Jones, who had designed the sets for every masque for the last thirty years, had once again revived the fashions of his youth with their tight-fitting doublets and padded breeches. For the sleeves he had adapted one of his favourite flower motifs: calyx-shaped over-sleeves enveloped the King's shoulders and upper arms, like the inverted cups of gigantic bluebells. The doublet, closely moulded to his slight figure, was so thickly stitched over in silver whorls and posies that the blue background hardly showed. His padded breeches were of slashed blue and silver, the blue edged with filigree thread. Long white silk stockings encased his small but well-made legs, exposed up to the thigh. His dancing pumps were all but concealed under huge silver shoe-roses. A quilled ruff of fine muslin framed his face, and his greying hair, carefully curled, was surmounted by a three-cornered hat of cloth of silver above which nodded two tiers of well-matched ostrich plumes.

King Charles was mature for masquerading. He was in his fortieth year and, but for his Master of the Ordnance, Lord Newport, the oldest performer in that year's festivities. Although the King had been rehearsing with his usual assiduity since the previous October, his more serious and distinguished courtiers had been too deeply engaged in the affairs of the nation to have much time to spare. Apart from the eight lords he had chosen to attend him, the performers were mostly drawn from the pages and musicians, the small fry of Whitehall.

The King's part was suited to his age and dignity. He had only to appear on a throne of honour raised high above the stage and later to partner the Queen in a stately dance. It was the responsibility of Inigo Jones to see that no embarrassing accidents occurred. 'The peece of tymber of ye engyne of ye Kings seate to be strongly nayled and fastened,' he scribbled on his sketch of the backstage mechanics.

The King's seat on the English throne in January 1640 was less comfortable than the stout wooden contraption designed for him by Inigo Jones. The atmosphere of gaiety which normally surrounded the Christmas celebrations of the Court was notably absent, and although both the King and Queen appeared as enthusiastic about their masque as usual, there was in their conduct a hint of pretence. The iron-handed minister, Wentworth, recently recalled from Ireland and created Earl of Strafford, had been in frequent audience with the King. He was not among the masquers. Both his austere presence and that of the buff-coated officers who now haunted the palace disturbed the jocund mood proper to the season.

The words of the masque had been written by William Davenant, the music composed by the Queen's master musician, Louis Richard, a Frenchman long resident at the English Court. In the opinion of everyone, not least of Inigo Jones himself, words and music were secondary to the scenic inventions for which they provided the vehicle. But a plot and a subject of some kind there had to be. King Charles, therefore, would impersonate the character of Philogenes, the lover of his people, a beneficent ruler conferring the blessings of peace upon a chorus representing the grateful nation. The King rehearsed the part in the intervals of the harassing Council meetings at which he decided to equip an army of thirty thousand foot and three thousand horse to keep his rebellious subjects in order.

The trouble had begun a year before in Scotland, but showed signs of spreading southward. In the previous summer, confronted by a superior force of rebel Scots at Berwick, the King had had to make temporary concessions to the rebels and withdraw without striking a blow. It had been a harsh forewarning of difficulties to come. His English troops, raised with difficulty, had been meagre and mutinous. An odd kind of volunteers, a wit had said, for not a man of them had come willingly. Murmurs against the King's church policy, against prelacy and popery, were growing loud in every English county. On the march north against the Scots, Lord Say and Lord Brook had refused to take the special oath of allegiance tendered by the King to all his followers, promising 'most constantly and cheerfully even to the uttermost hazard of life and fortune to assist him against any rebels whatsoever'. He had had to place them under arrest: only for a few days, of course, but it had been an unseemly and perplexing incident. When Lord Say was released he went home and took his contingent of troops with him, announcing that they had come solely as his attendants.

Yet with an obscure tenacity the King rejected the evidence of his subjects' discontent. This must be something superficial, temporary. It could not be that he, King Charles, the good, the just, who referred his every action to God and his conscience, should be wantonly defied merely because he wanted to impose a beautiful uniformity of worship throughout his dominions.

After he had made his temporary concessions to the rebel Scots at Berwick, agreeing to suspend his religious reforms in their country for the time being, he had reviewed the army which had marched against him. The troops, in innocent enthusiasm, threw up their blue bonnets and cried 'God save King Charles and down with the Bishops'. He was not pleased: he would compel them to respect his bishops yet. To the Scots lords who waited on him he had been cold. When they made to kiss his hand, he withheld it and only slightly raised his hat in a general salutation before taking his seat. His puzzled eyes travelled over their faces, seeking the private reasons for their public opposition. To his certain knowledge there were only five or six of them to whom, in his own phrase, 'he had not done courtesies'. In his opinion past courtesies should have secured present loyalty; he could conceive of none but personal motives for rebellion. That these men should seriously, for reasons of conscience or patriotism, object to the liturgy that he had specially composed for Scotland was beyond his imagination.

When he left Berwick after the pacification he had learned his lesson after his own fashion. In future, he announced, 'I shall not command but where I am sure to be obeyed'. He would be patient and wily; opponents could be removed, bribed, persuaded. He would call into being again the old animosity between English and Scots; he would raise a larger army. He would compel obedience. He would do everything except abandon the policy which he knew to be pleasing to God.

As he moved southwards to London the warm reception of his English subjects, profoundly relieved that there was to be no war, applied a deceptive balm to his injured spirit.

> *Others by war their conquests gain,*
> *You, like a God, your ends obtain,*
> *Who, when rude chaos for his help did call,*
> *Spoke but the word and sweetly ordered all . . .*

The Cambridge poet Cowley told him what he wanted to hear. The pacification at Berwick had been of his choosing; he had not been defeated; he, the merciful King, had decided not to fight.

The theme was taken up and elaborated in the masque for which on the afternoon of Tuesday, 21 January 1640, the whole Court, with a number of ambassadors and distinguished guests, had assembled in the building behind the banqueting house of Whitehall. For the occasion the cares of state had to be excluded, like the bleak January weather, beyond the world of expensive make-believe which was to be conjured up on the stage of the Queen's Dancing Barn. The name had been rudely given to the new building by the Puritans, but in reality it was the King's Dancing Barn, for it had been his idea. Once they had used the banqueting hall itself for masques, but since the painted canvases of Rubens had been hoisted into place on the ceiling, the King feared the damaging effect of candles and torches on their colours. He had given order for the temporary wooden building alongside and it had been constructed to the designs of Inigo Jones, with a permanent stage measuring fifty-two feet in height and forty-two feet from side to side of the proscenium arch. The stage itself was raised from seven to eight feet above the floor of the room, allowing for the construction and working of substantial mechanism underneath.

The seats and boxes in the auditorium were designed to accommodate spectators according to their rank. The central place this afternoon was filled by the royal children and their grandmother. The children, of whom the eldest was not yet ten, were a handsome, high-spirited group, taking strongly after their mother's family – large features, high colouring, bouncing vitality. Their maternal grandmother, Marie de Medici, the only adult royalty among the audience, since the King and Queen had disappeared into their robing-rooms, commanded the scene. She was a substantial woman in her later sixties, her fat-enveloped face eloquent of character rather than intelligence.

After quarrelling for the last time with her son, the King of France, she had thrown herself embarrassingly on the hospitality of her daughter, the Queen of England. In the delicate state of English public opinion the presence of the extravagant Italian visitor with a large train of priests and servants made an unfortunate impression. Her manner of living at St James's Palace, which her son-in-law had assigned to her, emphasized inopportunely his Queen's foreign and Roman Catholic connections.

The masque had been devised with the Queen's mother and the royal children in mind. In deference to Marie de Medici's ignorance of English there was little speaking, and the usual interludes of spoken comedy had been replaced by a series of farcical dances. For the delight of the children the scene changes were to be many and all the incidents short.

While the usual preliminary hitches occurred and were dealt with behind the scenes, the audience had plenty to occupy it in deciphering the meaning of the allegorical figures and symbols painted on the cornice, the proscenium arch and the drop-curtain which concealed the stage. In the centre of this curtain appeared the classical name of the performance they were about to see – *Salmacida Spolia* – and those who understood the allusion could explain to those who did not how certain savage tribes had been subdued by the Greeks of Halicarnassus, not by force of arms, but by visiting the fountain of Salmacis, where they saw and learnt to appreciate the superior civilization of the Greeks. So, it was to be understood, the rebellious Scots would learn to appreciate the superior qualities of episcopal government. On one side of the stage two female figures, representing Reason and Intellectual Appetite, were clasping hands. Opposite them 'a grave old man representing Counsel' kept company with an armed woman for Resolution. On the deep cornice which surmounted the stage, figures of women and children with symbolic attributes jostled one another. Here were Fame and Safety, Riches, Forgetfulness of Injuries, Commerce, Felicity, 'Affection to the country, holding a grasshopper', Prosperity and Innocence.

Presently an anticipatory hush foretold the rising of the curtain. Fans of matched and curled ostrich feathers ceased their movement and lay still in velvet laps; white explanatory hands dropped into repose; all faces turned the same way and, rustling over its roller at tremendous speed, up went the curtain.

Before them, in the cavern of the stage, was a scene of gloom and tempest. Trees with tormented branches bowed before the gale. In the distance angry waves broke over a rock and a storm-driven ship shuddered under a lightning-riven sky. The rattling of metal sheets in the wings added to the awful effect. In the middle of the stage stood a huge round object, recognizable from the outlines painted upon it as the great globe itself.

The audience had possessed themselves of the horror of the scene when with a clap of thunder the globe split in half and a hideous Fury 'looking askance with hollow envious eyes' came snarling to the front of the stage, torch in hand. In a harsh male voice, belying her female draperies, the creature began to speak:

> How am I grieved the world should everywhere
> Be vexed into a storm, save only here?
> Thou over happy, too much lucky isle . . .

In rhymed couplets the monster declared her intention of destroying the peace of England. Lest the meaning should be still in doubt, the speaking Fury was joined by three others who emphasized the point in a menacing dance.

This was the opening anti-masque. The first of the scene-changes followed. The shutters forming the wings slid back along grooves out of sight, revealing another series of shutters behind them. The dark clouds which hung down from the top of the scene were wound up creakingly while others of a different hue began to appear. The stormy sea at the back of the stage divided down the middle and slid apart to reveal another painted scene. Since it was not the fashion for the curtain to drop during these operations, there had long been arguments among the producers of masques as to the best way of diverting the attention of spectators. An Italian producer – and the Italians were the acknowledged masters of the masque – advised the placing of stooges far back among the audience to cause a disturbance at the critical moment. The simulated cracking of wood as though a tier of the gallery were collapsing, or a cry of 'Fire! Murder! Help!' could be guaranteed to draw all attention away from the stage. But the stooges sometimes acted too well; there had been panics and whole theatres had been emptied in a stampede for safety. Inigo Jones preferred his own invention – a gyrating coronal of three concentric circles of candles set off by reflectors which, being set in motion when a scene change was to take place, delighted and dazzled the audience so that they had eyes for nothing else.

But there is no sign of the use of this invention, or of anything else, among the numerous sketches which were made for the masque of 1640. The scene-changes in this, the most mechanically ambitious of all his masques, were apparently effected with so much rapidity that they needed no concealment. The scenery was wound off at each side and up and down from below and above. Behind the numerous canvas clouds which were suspended from braces in the roof and lowered or raised at will, all manner of rapid modifications could be made in the scenery and furnishings of the top part of the stage. They were wonderful clouds, carefully painted and cut after the numerous loving and lyrical sketches which have survived in his papers, small and large, round and elongated, billowing cumulus clouds carefully copied from nature to serve the higher ingenuities of his art.

Before the eyes of the spectators, therefore, the stormy sea and lowering sky gave place to a landscape of smiling summer. Across the painted sky jerked a painted Zephyr on a cloud breathing a flowery breeze from his fat cheeks. Below stretched a saffron-yellow cornfield, improbably framed in arching elm trees round whose knotted trunks grape-bearing vines were garlanded.

Meanwhile, below the stage strong hands turned the windlass which governed the silver chariot now slowly descending from the clouds. Two persons were unsteadily seated within it – a woman in blue ornamented with bulrushes, and a young man 'in a carnation garment embroidered all with flowers'. In mid-air the two broke into a duet. The lady, who represented Concord, expressed her reluctance to remain longer among the ungrateful people of Great Britain. Her companion, who was the Good Genius of Great Britain, remonstrated with her. The people might be unappreciative, he admitted, but they had a King whom she must surely find it a pleasure to serve:

> *Yet stay, oh stay, if but to please*
> *The great and wise Philogenes.*

It was true, the couple pursued their argument, that the people were sullen and ungrateful and would not accept their monarch's benevolent control; but to reward so good a King, Concord might yet give his people another chance. The harmonious lecture on politics at an end, the chariot reached stage-level and the two heavenly beings climbed out of it and departed in different directions to see whether their persuasions would soften the hearts of the ungrateful subjects of Philogenes.

Their endeavours would take time, as some of the better-informed members of the audience may well, a little grimly, have been thinking. The passage of time had, however, been allowed for by Davenant in composing his libretto: after their departure the remaining anti-masques, a series of twenty separate comic dances, were to be presented, mostly by the younger members of the Court, pages and young gentlemen, with their fortunes to make, who had grasped the opportunity of displaying their amiable talents before the great. Of this half-hour's frolic nothing has remained but Davenant's brief descriptive note on each entry and a few unidentifiable sketches of grotesques by Inigo Jones. Most of the dances were funny and most of the jokes were topical: ballets about doctors and prescriptions, about Rosicrucians and Roaring Boys, Jealous Dutchmen and Mad Lovers. Occasionally the mind's eye can supply a guess from the stage direction: 'Four

Grotesques or drollities in the most fantastical shapes imaginable';
or, the sentimental interlude, a shepherd dancing a pastoral *pas
seul*; or pure farce, 'a nurse and three children in long coats, with
bibs, biggins, and muck-enders'. Then there was the dance
specially put in for the Queen's dwarf, Jeffrey Hudson: 'three
Swiss, one a little Swiss, who played the wag with them as they
slept'. Three feet high and twenty-one years old, Jeffrey Hudson
concealed an alert intelligence in his mouse-coloured head and a
valiant spirit in his breast. His portraits reveal the full-size personality in the midget figure. A year or two later he would be a
captain of horse and would be knighted, not undeservedly, for
courage in the field.

When he had first been brought to the King, Charles had
already been in possession of two other notable curiosities – his
giant porter, and 'Old Parr', the English Methuselah, said to be
a hundred and fifty years of age, and brought to Court by the Earl
of Arundel. 'You have lived much longer than other men,' said
the King, when the venerable father was presented to him; 'what
have you done that was more remarkable?' The rustic replied
with what had long been his best crack: 'Please your Majesty, I
did penance for a bastard when I was above a hundred years old.'
King Charles uttered a freezing reproof; but if he regretted old
Parr's morals he valued his years and used to boast that his kingdom contained the tallest man, the smallest man, and the oldest
man in the world.

But Old Parr's vitality had not survived the pace of life at Court;
both he and the giant porter were long since dead, and Jeffrey
Hudson, capering waggishly upon the prostrate bodies of his
fellow-dancers, was now the sole survivor of the astounding trio.

The interludes had now lasted for long enough. Concord and
the Genius of Great Britain had assembled the full chorus of the
'Beloved People' of England in the wings. The last ballet, a rollick-
ing affair of a Spanish riding-master and his pupils, galloped off the
stage. The side shutters rattled once more along their grooves,
the clouds were lowered and raised, and the cornfields at the back
changed to a mountain landscape, in the midst of which, on a
high, hollow mountain, above defiles of rock and pine, the clouds
hung mysteriously low. While the scene was changing the chorus

had crowded on to the stage and facing the very centre of the audience began to sing a compliment to the Queen Mother. There she sat, the stupid, stout, unloved widow of Henry of Navarre. 'Your beauty kept his valour's flame alive,' they shamelessly chanted, 'Your Tuscan wisdom taught him how to thrive.'

Now, at last, the great moment had come. The chorus of the Beloved People ranged themselves politely on each side of the stage so as not to impede the view. The low clouds above the mountain rose, the last of the obstructing shutters slid out of the way, 'and the King's Majesty and the rest of the masquers were discovered sitting in the throne of Honour, his Majesty highest in a seat of gold, and the rest of the Lords about him'.

There they stood, in their bluebell doublets, like the King's, their white stockings, their silver hats and ostrich feathers: in the midst Charles himself, looking for once a great deal larger than life, for the sharply narrowing perspective of Inigo Jones's sets made no allowance for the actual size of the performers who were to appear backstage. Larger than life, therefore, and very regal, he sat, with his cousin Lennox on his right, and the Earl of Carlisle on the left, tall young men with fair, horsy, well-bred faces; six other lords were ranged at suitable distances round about. Instantly the Beloved People broke into laudatory song.

> *Since strength of virtues gained you Honour's throne*
> *Accept our wonder and enjoy our praise!*
> *He's fit to govern there, and rule alone,*
> *Whom inward helps, not outward force, doth raise.*

Certainly King Charles's throne rested on no effective outward force in spite of his present efforts to remedy the deficiency. But at the moment the spectators were not paying much attention to the words even if they could distinguish them. The King's throne, lords and all, had been slowly lowered to ground-level; he rose and at the same time there appeared, high up under the cornice, the largest and most solid of the many clouds which had yet descended from the pulleys in the heavens. 'A huge cloud of various colours,' Inigo Jones described it. It was indeed vast, since it concealed – or, to maintain the illusion, it carried – no less than eleven people. As it reached mid-air and mid-stage, it was seen slowly to open, revealing 'a transparent brightness of thin exhalations.' 'Tinsel' is the word scribbled on Inigo Jones's sketch, but it is possible that the rays which broke from the cloud were not all tinsel. There may have been light effects managed by reflectors, for Inigo Jones fancied himself at tricks of the kind. Whatever the nature of the 'transparent brightness', in the heart of it among her 'martial ladies' sat the Queen herself.

When the ladies were rehearsing for the masque, the Earl of Northumberland wrote to his sister that they were the worst set of faces he had ever seen on such an occasion. But he was prejudiced; neither of his own sisters – one the celebrated beauty Lady Carlisle – had been chosen. If their portraits are to be trusted against his word, they were a pretty enough collection. There was the sweet-faced Duchess of Lennox, exchanging eye-signals with her husband on the King's right: they were deeply in love. There was the lymphatic blonde, Lady Carnarvon, a convinced Puritan who had stipulated that she would only appear in the Queen's masque if it was not performed on a Sunday. There was the handsome, headstrong Lady Newport, carrying her sorrows with a high head; no eye-signals here although Lord Newport stood opposite her close by the King. He was the Puritan of this marriage and her adoption of the Roman Catholic religion a year or two back had done more than the bearing of three imbecile children to alienate him from her for ever. There was the glowing bride, Lady Kinalmeaky, whom the King himself had given away three weeks before.

But the Queen herself drew all eyes. In looks she hardly competed with the younger women who surrounded her. She was thirty years old and pregnant for the ninth time. She had lost her looks in her first childbed and was in the habit of saying – judging all other cases from her own – that no woman was beautiful after eighteen. She was a scrawny little woman with an ivory skin, a figure slightly twisted, features too large for the meagre face, and teeth which, as a niece once unkindly said, protruded from her mouth like guns from a fortress. But the King worshipped her and he was not the only one. Plain, old before her time, in wretched health, she dominated her younger and handsomer ladies by the electric animation of her personality. Her prominent eyes sparkled; when her thin, long mouth parted into a smile it was a chord of music. So she sat, mistress of stage and Court, from her throne in the multi-coloured cloud, a diminutive figure in carnation silk with plumed helmet and scarlet baldric and an antique sword at her side, the undoubted Queen of the Amazons.

As her cloudy car touched the ground the King advanced, took her by the hand and led her in procession from the stage to the place where her mother sat among the audience. The lords and ladies sought their wives or the partners allotted to them and followed in stately dance.

The King and Queen were now seated in the midst of the Court, but it remained for the Beloved People to sing a final salutation. For the last time all the handles were being turned off-stage; for the last time the clouds laboured up and down. For the last time the pictured cloths opened to reveal the last backdrop. It was the noblest and most elaborate of all Inigo Jones's effects and his sketch-books show that he had drawn it time and time again before he was satisfied. The scene was one of 'magnificent buildings composed of several pieces of architecture. In the farthest part was a bridge over a river, where many people, coaches, horses and such like were seen to pass to and fro: beyond this, on the shore were buildings in perspective, which shooting far from the eye showed as suburbs of a great city.' The whole represented, by implication, the King's extensive building programme in London to which Inigo Jones himself had so largely contributed. He did not, of course, go so far as to include actual drawings of the Piazza at Covent Garden or the new west front of St Paul's Cathedral – the bridge was frankly modelled on a recent new bridge in Rome – but only the slowest courtier could fail to take his meaning. Here, almost as large as life, was the final representation of the blessings which King Philogenes had poured upon his Beloved, and strangely ungrateful, People.

For the moment the menacing discontent of England and Scotland, the cabals and intrigues of the King's enemies, the rude things that his people wrote on walls and sometimes even in pamphlets, were forgotten. On the final chords of Louis Richard's long-lost music three more cloudy chariots jerked across the sky above the city and opened to reveal all the musicians playing on their instruments to present the music of the spheres. Last of all, in the centre of the stage 'the heavens opened full of deities which celestial prospect, with the Chorus below, filled the whole scene with apparitions and harmony'. In the general exclamation of the audience, the merry accompaniment of the fiddlers, the creaking of the mechanism, Davenant's words may not have been altogether distinguishable. The Beloved People vociferously saluted the wisdom of their reigning King.

> All that are harsh, all that are rude,
> Are by your harmony subdued,
> Yet so into obedience wrought
> As if not forced to it, but taught.
> Live still, the pleasure of our sight
> Both our example and delight . . .

Inigo Jones was delighted with his effects. By his own account they were 'generally approved of, especially by all strangers that were present, to be the noblest and the most ingenious that hath been done here in that kind'. The one other opinion that has come down to us is markedly different. Young Robert Read, nephew of one of His Majesty's principal Secretaries of State, wrote some days later to his cousin Tom Windebanke in Ireland. 'The mask was performed last Tuesday night, myself being so wise as not to see it. They say it was very good, but I believe the disorder was never so great at any.'

There was room for disorder among all those pulleys and cog-wheels, those ascending and descending chariots and clouds, those quadruple scene changes. Which windlass jammed while the stage-hands strained at the handle, what backdrop stuck as it went up, leaving the scene half cornfield and half stormy sea? Did the Beloved People like sheep go astray all over the stage? For a moment the imagination pictures the frantic, furtive signals, the forgotten cue whispered in agitation, the audience sometimes restive, sometimes laughing, and the vacant eyes of Marie de Medici, vaguely aware of compliment, but blind to meaning.

The allegory of tempest giving place to joyous calm, of Philogenes bestowing peace on his applauding people, was defiantly inept. Among the eight blue-and-silver lords about the King there were three at least who vehemently opposed his policy in public, and among the rest not one who did not conceal a dark anxiety under the radiant *mine de circonstance* demanded by the part. Young Lennox, who nine years later was to offer vainly to die in his master's place, knew well and feared the temper of his countrymen in the north. The bewildered Earl of Lanark, a lip-biting, over-burdened, conscientious young man, had in the last few days been presented with the impossible appointment of Secretary of State for rebellious Scotland. Among the English lords there were Russell and Fielding who were well aware from their Puritan kinsmen and friends that the King's reputation in England had never stood so low – an indignant city, a restive gentry, a depressed and uneasy people. The accidental disorders on the stage added their unintentional, tacit note of satire to the last masque ever to be danced by King Charles.

The last chorus ended, the clustered wax candles were lighted in all the sconces, the musicians from their cloudy gallery began to play again, the masquers mingled with the audience and the King and Queen danced among their courtiers. The rhythmic patter and swish of the dancing feet, the hum of voices, the susurration of silks, filled for the last time the Queen's great Dancing Barn.

Beyond the precincts of Whitehall, skewering rashers of bacon from the glowing coals of their winter fires, or warming knotted hands at the blaze of wood and the glow of turf, the people of England in town and country talked of their own affairs, made love or made baskets, darned the day's tears in worn clothes, smoked a pipe of tobacco or took a pot of ale after the day's work, before huddling by families on to their flock mattresses to sleep. A few were talking politics, more than a few were praying. The revolving world carried the island and all on it through the darkness to the late winter dawn and brought nearer by one day that January morning nine years in the future, when King Charles, haggard and dignified, would enact outside Whitehall the last scene in the story of Philogenes.

1950

Strafford

On 12 May 1641, Thomas Wentworth, Earl of Strafford, was beheaded on Tower Hill. Although he inspired one of Macaulay's more terrific indictments and a play by Browning, he is not one of the best known of English statesmen. In the Whig tradition of history he stood out as the evil genius of Charles I, the proud, fearless, wicked man who was the energy and the brains of the King's unparliamentary rule. There was a time when even serious writers accepted unquestioning every private and public scandal connected with his name – how he violently ill-used his opponents, embezzled public funds and seduced the wife of one of his colleagues. Recent research has disproved the more outrageous slanders, and the change in the political climate which has caused a revaluation of Stuart policy has brought some belated recognition for his merits. It is now generally admitted that Strafford was an exceptionally gifted administrator and a statesman of high integrity of purpose.

A wealthy Yorkshire squire, he first attracted notice by refusing to pay the Forced Loan levied by the King in 1626, and in 1628 he led the House of Commons during the session which formulated the Petition of Right. At this point, however, his career took a sharp turn away from the Parliamentary party; he joined the Court side, became Lord President of the Council of the North and was given a seat on the Privy Council. In both these offices he at once made himself felt as a determined reformer, with the welfare of the common man and the intelligent ordering of public affairs at heart. From 1633 until 1639 he was Lord-Deputy of Ireland, where he pursued a sternly benevolent policy, controlled a subservient Parliament, checked the rapacity of the Anglo-Irish nobles and introduced some interesting social and economic legislation. Recalled to England in 1639 when the King's government was on the verge of collapse, he failed in the hopeless task of averting disaster . The royal army was defeated by the rebellious Scots and the King had no choice but to recall Parliament.

The Commons had never forgiven Strafford for his desertion of the Parliamentary side in 1628: he was the arch-traitor. Now, on the collapse of the King's personal rule, he made deliberate use of this fact, sacrificing himself to the animosity of the Commons in the hope of diverting popular ill-feeling from the King to himself. His political judgment may have been at fault in this, but at no time in his career does the individual man appear more noble than in this last attempt to save his master. The letter which he wrote to the King, urging him to appease the Commons by approving the Bill for his execution is at the same time one of the most extraordinary and one of the most moving documents in this language. 'To say that there has not been a strife in me,' he wrote, 'were to make me less man than, God Knoweth, my infirmities make me, and to call a destruction upon myself will find no easy consent from flesh and blood. To set Your Majesty's conscience at liberty, I do most humbly beseech Your Majesty . . . to pass this Bill, and by this means to remove I cannot say this accursed, but I confess this unfortunate, thing forth of the way towards that blessed agreement which God, I trust, shall ever establish between you and your subjects.' That letter alone must confer on Strafford heroic stature.

So much for Strafford the man. But his fall stood for something more than the condemnation of a single man. Because of this larger issue, rather than because of intrinsic qualities, his fate deserves remembrance. His fall, and with it the end of King Charles's personal rule, marked the failure of a political experiment and the defeat of a principle. Although the personal rule of King Charles is now no longer believed to have been an uncompromising tyranny, and although the fair-minded admit that it was in many ways more beneficent to the common man than parliamentary government was to become for many generations, yet it was nevertheless a false start down a dangerous political path. It is therefore for the theory behind the King's actions and behind Strafford's that they must ultimately be judged, rather than for the

intrinsic merits of those actions themselves. It is one of the para-
doxes of history that the just men may sometimes be found
defending the unjust cause while the self-interested may occasionally stumble into a right and noble course.

Writing of Strafford's fall, Archbishop Laud tried to explain it
in personal terms: 'He served a mild and gracious Prince,' he
wrote, 'who knew not how to be, or be made great.' Laud was
wrong, for the fault was not in Charles, but in Charles's theory of
government and in Strafford's too practical contribution towards
it. Strafford's administrative gift was his undoing, for like many
good administrators he believed too much in authority. Much
may be and must be sacrificed to efficiency, but one can sacrifice
too much. That is the first maxim of democracy. To get rid of
sloth and mismanagement Strafford was prepared to set the
authority of the State beyond the reach of criticism. In the Ship
Money case he described Hampden angrily as one of those whose
nature 'leads them always to oppose all that authority ordains for
them'. In the context one may sympathize, for with the seas
infested with pirates and the navy in decay, Hampden's refusal
to pay his contribution to the tax was, to say the least of it, in-
opportune. But in theory Strafford was wrong, for, whatever the
circumstances, Hampden had a right to his opinion and Parliament should have been called. Once remove the citizen's right of
criticism and no guarantee is left against the abuse of authority.

Was Strafford blind to this weakness in his case? Not altogether,
for, like other authoritarians, he sought to surround his beliefs
with a *mystique* – sure sign that he felt the need of a more profound justification than could be found in mere political practice.
Speaking in York, when he assumed his office of Lord President
of the Council, he summed up his theory of the State. 'To the
joint individual well-being of sovereignty and subjection', he
said, 'do I here vow all my cares and diligences through the whole
course of this my ministry . . . The authority of a King is the key-
stone which closeth up the arch of order and government, which
contains each part in due relation to the whole . . . *Whatever he
be that ravels forth into question the right of a King and of a people
shall never be able to wrap them up again into the comeliness and
order wherein he found them.*'

It was the fatal combination, administrative efficiency and the deification of the State. Did Strafford see to what excesses it might lead? Hardly, for he was all his life too busy a man to have time for remote speculation. He died in the conviction that the King's Government and his own must stand or fall by their practical results. A sincere, brave and able man, he lacked the vision to see that the State, like the human soul, cannot be saved by works alone.

1941

Cardinal Richelieu

The portrait of Richelieu by Philippe de Champaigne, which hangs in the National Gallery, is a striking comment on the greatness of his personality. The narrow, determined chin, the pursed mouth, discriminating and sensual, the observant eyes, and intellectual forehead – here, even to the small pointed beard, was the typical Frenchman of European tradition. There are few clearer proofs of the way in which a dominating personality may set a fashion and establish a mould. How many Mussolinis were not to be met with on a short stroll through any Italian town? English character would not be the same without, say, Queen Elizabeth, Oliver Cromwell or Dr Johnson. French character and the French nation would have been different without Richelieu.

The great man is known by his legend, and Richelieu has a gigantic legend. It began even before he died, when he travelled France, a sick man, in a litter huge enough to contain himself, his doctors and his secretaries, a litter which was study, office and bedroom in one, and for whose passage the walls of inns had to be knocked down at night-fall. From this lair the 'secret great Cardinal' directed the destinies of the nation which he had made the greatest in Europe. But historic memory is longer and sharper in France than it is here; no French King, who, like Henry VIII, beheaded his wives and bullied his subjects, would have passed into popular tradition as a fiercer Humpty Dumpty and household joke. Nor has Richelieu been mellowed by the passing of three centuries. As the architect of the French monarchy his memory suffered with the spectacular collapse of his work, and thence fell into the hands of the Romantics who made him theatrical, fiendish and sinister. Rescue work by modern historians has not wholly dispelled the cloud.

The man himself has been obscured by his work, for if his motives are in doubt, his achievements are clear. He made the French monarchy the greatest power in Europe. Heresy and liberty, he used to say, were the two chief enemies, and he dealt with them firmly, almost finally. He broke the Huguenots, disregarded the Estates, started and then controlled the French press, founded the Academy to keep literature in order, and patronized the Sorbonne to do the same for learning; he froze the nobility out of local administration and created a new bureaucracy entirely dependent on the Crown; he dammed up the political aspirations of a vital and intelligent people so formidably that it took them a century and a half to burst the dam. And in Europe he ruthlessly and finally undermined the Habsburg hegemony. Whether these things were to his credit or his discredit depends on how and when you look at them. To-day they are chiefly to his discredit. The man was an early and efficient totalitarian.

But Richelieu differed from the modern dictator in the proportion and sanity of his political perspective. When he said that he hated heresy and liberty, he meant no more than what he said. He did not mean that he hated individuality, enterprise or initiative. He did not regard the State as an end in itself and every man or woman as cogs in the machine. He thought of it as an instrument towards an end, as the mechanism for efficient administration, and no more. It was a harsh view but it was a practical one. Grit clogging the movements of the machine had to be removed; so much the worse if the grit was human. This is a bad principle, but it is a limited one. It leaves, on the whole, great tracts of human activity comparatively free. Moreover, in seventeenth-century France the alternative was political anarchy. It is unfair to condemn Richelieu's solution of the problem of national government because it was not the English one. It could not have been the English one.

The French were not at that time a people with a gift for politics. What they had was a gift for civilization, and what Richelieu did was to make possible the flowering of that unparalleled genius. Like many great innovators, he did, living, more immediate harm than good. Serving the national interests of France, '*le principe sacré de l'égoïsme national*', he laid Germany waste, provoked civil war in Spain, overran Savoy, unleashed murder in the Engadine, sacked Mantua. In order to consolidate an ill-founded Government he tricked and inveigled his opponents to the scaffold, destroyed the innocent with the guilty, jettisoned his assistants and betrayed his friends. Yet on his deathbed, when he was asked to forgive his enemies, he said with perfect sincerity that he had none save the enemies of France. It was true. He was undoubtedly that very questionable thing, a patriot. His ruthless and single-minded work for the French monarchy, his disregard alike of private consciences and private interests, his sweeping away of all, good, bad and indifferent, which stood in the way of the monarchy, made possible the stupendous efflorescence of the French genius, gave to his country that dominating position in the arts of living which she has held through all political vicissitudes for close on three centuries, and which she will surely hold again.

Much of Richelieu's political work is by our standards vicious; much of it is vicious by any standards. Unsound in one particular – he never solved the financial problem – it was bound ultimately to collapse. Nevertheless, he understood, released and guided the essential creative talent of a great people. Man was not made for the State, as he saw it; the State was made for man, and more especially for the French.

He had a curious vanity, a belief that he was a poet. He was never happier, he once astonishingly declared, than when he was writing verses. His career hardly bears out the truth of the assertion, yet the self-deception was typical and significant. Whatever his actions might be, in his heart he knew that the individual creative genius of man was more valuable than the achievements of the statesman.

1942

The Strategy of the Great Civil War

The Civil Wars of England lasted, with one long inter-
mission, for about nine years. It was in September 1642
that first blood was drawn in a skirmish at the village of
Powick Bridge opposite Worcester on the Teme, and in September
again, nine years later, that the battle of Worcester ended the war,
almost in the same fields. The spatter of scars from musket balls
on the south wall of Powick church tower is from the latter, not
the earlier, battle.

The political significance of the Civil Wars is so great that their
military history has been, if not positively neglected, at least submerged. Not entirely, of course, for Cromwell's organization of
the New Model Army and Rupert's famous cavalry have been
obvious subjects of study. But Clarendon, the leading historian
of the war, was a civilian, and few of those who fought, certainly
neither of its two outstanding soldiers, were great hands with the
pen. Cromwell's dispatches are brief, tough, impressive, but
throw all too little light on the purely military side of the war.
Rupert, a proud and silent man, neither boasted of his victories
nor explained his defeats. 'It is a life of honour,' he said of a
soldier's career, 'but a dog would not lead it.'

The Civil War is part of our political heritage; the principles
for which our ancestors fought are still alive to us. It is part of the
literary and romantic tradition of this country, bringing back
nostalgic visions of fluttering banners and Van Dyck faces, of vain
heroism and thundering cavalry charges, of stern-faced men with
Bible and sword going into battle to the chanting of a psalm. For
most of us it is a part of our childhood, for who has not played
Cavaliers and Roundheads? But we do not easily fit these imaginative pictures to what we know of the English countryside, and
the battlefields of the Great Civil War remain for the most part

neglected sites. Occasionally there will be a monument to some distinguished casualty – Hampden has an obelisk at Chalgrove Field; Falkland, Sunderland and Carnarvon share another at Newbury; but at Naseby the monument is in the wrong place and at Edgehill it is the wrong monument, for the grey monolith on the side of the steep slope where the trees end was erected to a soldier who fought at Waterloo.

The strategy of the Civil War in its larger aspects has not been much studied, and this is understandable for the English Civil War is a curiosity of military history with rules of its own outside the ordinary line of development. Its strategy was bound up, one might almost say swaddled up, with the social structure of the country and limited by the peculiarities of the political situation; it could not be planned according to the military rules and practice of Continental fighting, but was amenable to the brilliant manipulation of talented amateurs. It was indeed a war in which the professional soldier was at a disadvantage. Of the numerous Englishmen who had been trailing their pikes in Flanders for want of employment at home and who hurried back to fight either for King or Parliament, few achieved any real distinction, though many were efficient and experienced in the minutiae of their profession. Thomas Fairfax, a man whose sheer thoroughness and determination (he was a Yorkshireman) amounted nearly to genius, and the brilliant, unstable George Goring were perhaps the only two professional soldiers who made any significant mark. More often professional ideas interfered with the freedom of invention and action which English conditions offered.

It is significant that the two men who best understood and exploited the situation were both, if not exactly amateurs, at least beginners in their profession. Cromwell knew nothing whatever of warfare before he acquired his captain's commission in the summer of 1642, and Rupert, although he had served in the Netherlands and Germany, as a ranker in the Prince of Orange's life-guard and later as an officer, had spent his last four years as a prisoner of war when, at the age of twenty-two, he was appointed Lieutenant-General of the King's Cavalry. Cromwell was therefore too ignorant and Rupert too young to be bound by the accepted rules.

The civilian population, too, was ignorant of the rules. No war had been fought in England for a century and a half and the attitude of a fat and prosperous people, used to orderly government, was very different from the embittered, helpless resignation of the German and Flemish peasantry. Foreign towns knew only too well the blackmail of *Brandschatzung* – the indemnity which the general of an occupying army demanded in return for preventing the sack of the town. English towns had never heard of such a thing, and when Rupert, assuming the existence of the custom, exacted a sum from Leicester, great was the indignation of the city fathers and great the speed with which King Charles ordered his nephew to pay it back. It was the first rule of Continental warfare which had to be unlearnt in England, for here each side strove not to terrorize, but to pacify and win over the civil population.

Whence, among this peaceful people, arose the armies which appeared with such terrifying speed in the summer of 1642? England had an antiquated system of defence, the local levies. These hastily mustered yokels were almost entirely untrained, and although provision was supposed to be made for their equipment, very little was ever to be had; a few old pikes with a helmet or two of an Elizabethan model were often as much as could be found for them.

London had its trained bands who had been exercised occasionally in the handling of pikes on fine summer evenings. The King, fearing trouble with the people, had created a small life-guard shortly before the outbreak of the war. For the rest both sides relied on troops of volunteers raised by wealthy or patriotic gentlemen who defrayed the expenses themselves, recruiting the men on their own estates and arming them according to their own caprice. If they chose to equip them with battle-axes or bows and arrows – and on occasion we find both of these antiquated weapons in use – to tie coloured ribbons on their shoulders or encase them from top to toe in armour – as did Sir Arthur Hazelrig with a regiment immediately nicknamed the 'Lobsters' – no one was going to stop them.

The armies of both sides, therefore, presented a variegated appearance. Some were too much armed, some were not armed at all; there was uniformity neither of equipment nor of dress. Some wore red, some wore blue, some undyed cloth – they would dye it in the blood of their enemies. No definite mark distinguished the King's men from Parliament's. Officers of the Royalist forces wore red sashes, Parliamentary officers orange, but it is not to be supposed that the supply of sashes was at first equal to the sudden demand, nor that the reds and oranges hastily bought up or fished out of the oak chest by a thrifty wife did not vary through every shade and approximate inconveniently to each other. Mistakes between friend and foe were frequent and often bloody. A further confusion was added during the opening phase of the war by the Parliamentarian habit of referring to the Royalists as the 'rebels' and themselves as the party of King and Parliament. (One remembers Hampden's device: 'Not against the King I fight, but for the King and the Commons' right.') Some enthusiastic French gentlemen who had hurried over to England to defend their countrywoman, Queen Henrietta Maria, enlisted in error under the wrong flag.

As well as the victims of such strange misunderstandings there was a fluctuating fringe of professional soldiers who changed sides to suit themselves; some were Scots or Irish mercenaries, some Englishmen, one or two came from farther afield, like that Croatian captain of whom John Aubrey tells, who openly declared: 'I care not for your cause but for your half-crowns and your handsome women.'

To the professional trained abroad there was no dishonour in changing sides. The arrangement was a business contract, and an officer who resigned his commission in one Continental army was wholly at liberty to take up a commission in another when he wished. Whole regiments shifted from side to side during the Thirty Years War with no one thinking the worse of them. But in this matter the English war proved to be different. We hear significantly much of prisoners. There was a concentration camp for Royalist soldiers at Coventry, and atrocity stories were told of the sufferings of Parliamentarians in Oxford Castle and of the King's men lodged in the hulks of moored vessels in the Thames. As for the Royalist officers, the Tower of London had rarely been more fully or more gaily populated.

When flowing cups run swiftly round
With no allaying Thames,
Our careless heads with roses bound
Our hearts with loyal flames . . .

The question of prisoners was one on which the rulings of the foreign-trained professionals were an inadequate guide: in the German wars large numbers of prisoners were not taken; the defeated were simply absorbed into the army of the victor. But the English quaintly regarded changing sides as dishonourable; it might be done but never with credit. 'Walter Baskervile', we read in the contemptuous jottings of a Royalist soldier, 'first for the Parliament, then for the King, then theirs, then taken prisoner by us, and with much adoe gott his pardon and now *pro rege*, God wott.'

In other ways, too, the spirit of the English forces was peculiar to these islands. The rank and file, recruited from the peasantry from Wales, Cornwall, West Yorkshire, Lancashire and Cheshire on the King's side, from the eastern and the home counties on Parliament's, shared a strong spirit of individualism and independence. We speak loosely of the survival of 'feudalism' in England, thinking of our ancient landed gentry and the sentiments of loyalty and obligation between squire and tenantry; but in fact feudalism in its final form never developed in England, and the last vestiges of anything which a man from the Continent would have called feudal had vanished a century before the Civil War. No English landowner had rights of life and death over his people; few, if any, English peasants were rigidly bound to the soil. The troops which followed the standards of their local gentry were, taken by and large, more humane, more civilized, more reasonable than their counterparts abroad. But they were also more stubborn, more argumentative and, until they had commanders who understood them, less trainable. Added to this, some of them took a stand on their rights and could not be gainsaid.

The men of the local levies refused to fight outside their own counties, which was indeed one of the presumed conditions of their service, and it was only with extraordinary persuasion that Sir Ralph Hopton managed to bring the Cornish infantry – the finest in the Royalist army – out of its native duchy, nor in spite of a plan of campaign which was intended to end only in the recapture of London, did this particular section of the King's army ever appear farther east than Devizes, where at Roundway Down they had the pleasure of tumbling Sir Arthur Hazelrig's ridiculously encased 'Lobsters' down one of the steepest chalk slopes in the Wiltshire downs.

A further problem in discipline and organization was set by the gentlemen volunteers, who, although only a sprinkling of the whole army and usually grouped together into a troop, were a perennial obstruction to discipline. The gentry of England knew nothing of war – again how un-feudal! – and carried both their pleasant manners, their social distinctions and their strong individuality into battle. At that time nobody was brought up on the military doctrine of 'theirs not to make reply, theirs not to reason why'. They answered back and reasoned why in and out of season, with the utmost nonchalance. What a world of obstructive young subalterns is conjured up by the ingenuous tribute paid by Waller to Cromwell, who, as a junior officer, 'did not argue upon his orders'.

After more than a century of peace England was naturally behind Europe in her armaments, a fact which for once did not matter, since no foreign nation was involved. The demand for arms in the opening months of the war far outran the supply, and officers coming back from abroad must have laughed to see the antiquated pikes and Elizabethan helmets in the ranks of both armies. Everything was in short supply. Birmingham manufacturers, cashing in on the King's necessity, put out a line in cheap swords, for a consignment of which Charles contracted, until Prince Rupert, raging over hundreds of snapped weapons, threatened to resign if his cavalry were issued with any more 'Brummagem Blades'. English pistols too seem at first to have been oddly unreliable: they would go off suddenly, backwards, or misfire altogether. Or perhaps they were only mishandled by amateur soldiers. Prince Rupert, a singularly striking target and frequently the object of deliberate attentions, got through the whole war with nothing but a graze on the shoulder, which suggests a low standard of aiming. It was poor Sir George Lisle, facing the firing squad after the surrender of Colchester, who called to his executioners to come closer, and when they would not, pleaded: 'Friends, I have been nearer when you have missed me.'

Heavy artillery played a larger part than has generally been allowed. It was of inestimable value in sieges, and the Civil War was a great war of sieges. Transport was a perennial problem, for the cannon were enormously heavy for their power, would stick in the muddy roads holding up the progress of an entire army, and as often as not leave a wheel behind them when forcibly hauled out. Yet, in spite of the difficulty of transport, guns were used conventionally in the Continental manner in pitched battle, where they pounded away to very little effect before the opening of the action. When Cromwell in 1648 left his entire artillery behind while he raced in advance to cut off the Scots Royalists at Preston, he was sacrificing superiority in armaments to speed and surprise in a way which a conventional soldier of the time would have thought absurdly dangerous. His decision was fully justified by the event.

But in siege warfare the cannon was really important, and indeed the King's weakness in this arm was certainly one of the factors in his defeat. The battering power of the big culverins and demi-culverins, twenty-pounders and twelve-pounders respectively at close range – about 300 yards – was terrific. A sustained bombardment would smash down the average city wall effectively enough for the besiegers to fight their way in, and comparatively few cities failed to surrender after a serious bombardment.

Banbury was an outstanding exception, for here the Royalist colonel, Sir William Compton, a boy of nineteen, kept the garrison working in shifts day and night throwing up an earthwork behind the outer wall until, after fourteen weeks' resistance, he was at length relieved. Colchester, in 1647, surrendered not so much to hunger as to superior artillery. The batteries of the defenders gave out for lack of ammunition and Fairfax was able to move his heavy guns into a position from which they could have raked the town. Gloucester, besieged by the King in 1643, held out until the trained bands of London, in a fervour of devotion, marched across the Cotswolds to its rescue, simply because the King had not enough ammunition for his guns, and so could not smash his way in. The capture of Waller's guns at the otherwise small skirmish of Cropredy Bridge turned it into an event of importance to the King, and it is notable that at the second battle of Newbury Prince Maurice carried out an elaborate and dangerous manoeuvre in order to secure the King's artillery, first collecting the guns into Donnington Castle and posting a guard over them, then retiring to Oxford, collecting reinforcements and making a lightning advance across the Berkshire downs by night to Donnington, to convoy the guns safely back into Oxford. Not for nothing did the Parliamentarians call Maurice, Rupert's less spectacular brother, the 'good come-off'.

The musket was the most important fire-arm in general use in the seventeenth century, and the musketeers were a class apart, the aristocrats of the infantry. In England, a country even in those days of ditches and copses, and deep lanes fringed with hedges, a skilful captain could do wonders with a handful of musketeers. We find them lining the long hedge on the Royalist right flank at Naseby field, preventing Fairfax from manoeuvring his army or outflanking the King. We find them contesting the transverse hedges and orchard walls in the first battle of Newbury, an engagement which was not so much a pitched battle as a crossword puzzle of single skirmishes in the enclosed market gardens and orchards on the outskirts of the little town. When during the battle Falkland, the King's Secretary of State, tired of a conflict to which he saw no profitable end, rode his horse at a gap in one of the hedges, he knew that there would be musketeers on either side to pick him off; and accordingly found the death he sought. At Langport, where George Goring made the last serious stand for the King against the triumphant Parliamentarian advance into the west in 1645, he held the ridge above the town by investing the narrow lane, which was its only access, with the main strength of his musketeers. A narrow English lane, covered by musketry fire, was a death trap to incautious cavalry. But Fairfax threw in the whole strength of his infantry to fight the Royalists back, foot by foot, at push of pike, from the knotted thorn trees and the high banks.

In hand-to-hand contest it was push of pike which ultimately decided the issue. And the pike, for all its simplicity, was an effective weapon when skilfully handled, both in attack and defence. The Continental pikemen could withstand or at least break the impetus of cavalry attack; the attitude of defence was a lunge, the butt end of the pike resting against the instep of the hinder foot, the shaft steadied against the bent forward leg. In this attitude the skilful pikeman could fend off attack with the point of the pike controlled by the left hand, and keep his right hand free for swordplay.

Could the London trained bands have done anything so complicated? Doubt seems permissible. As for the country levies, they found other uses for their pikes – when they had them. They were convenient for flicking the fruit off orchard trees, for hooking a new shirt from the housewife's line: they could be turned to account for hanging up a cooking-pot, punting a ferry across a stream, or even for chopping wood. 'I cannot conceive what these fellows are doing with their weapons,' grumbled Sir Ralph Hopton when yet another batch of infantrymen reported irrecoverable damage or loss.

The general strategy of the Civil War is obscured by innumerable local quarrels. Parliament strove from the outset to co-ordinate its supporters into associations and groups, of which the most important was the Eastern Association from which sprang Cromwell's army and the ultimate reorganization of the New Model. The King, paradoxically, diffused his energies and played up to local magnates in order to gain widespread support and undermine his opponents throughout the country. In pursuit of this system he fatally dispersed his forces. By garrisoning isolated country houses he reduced the effective strength of the army which he was to put in the field, and in the end the Royalist war came to a close in a series of heroic and useless resistances before, one after another, the fortified manors and fair country seats hauled down the royal standard. Some, like Basing House, fell only to assault and paid the penalty in the blood of the defenders.

One peculiarity of the English landscape assisted time and again in the reduction of these improvised fortresses. This was the position of the village church, so often within a stone's throw of the manor. With its strong square tower the typical village church made a convenient station for a gun, by the threat of which the neighbouring house could be driven to surrender.

Before the King's main army was broken at Naseby and the isolated garrisons successively reduced, many had been the local fights and skirmishes between the small forces in these outposts and Parliamentary troops passing through the country. In the same way, though not so frequently, nests of Parliamentarians recruited and held together by local magnates molested passing Royalists, and in some stretches of country which saw none of the serious fighting, local jealousies and local quarrels kept up spasmodic disturbance.

The main strategic outline of the war is, nevertheless, plain enough. The chief strength of Parliament lay in the south and east; of the King in the north and west. He unfurled his standard in Nottingham, the most southerly point at which he could cross the Trent, in August 1642, struck south across the Midlands collecting his forces, intending to march at once to London. The Parliamentary army under Essex barred his way below the sharp ridge of Edgehill in Warwickshire, but was sufficiently damaged in the action which followed on 23 October to make the capitulation of the city something more than a possibility. But Charles hesitated fatally and by the time his advance guard reached Turnham Green – the main strength of his army carrying Brentford by assault – the trained bands had come to stop him and London was in a state of defence, with chains and barricades across the city streets and the Bowling Green at Hyde Park Corner the pivotal point of a system of outer defences of earthworks and batteries.

The King, however, decided to fall back no farther than Oxford, thus making his headquarters at the apex of a triangle, of which the bases were in Lancashire, Wales and the South-West, extending forward into enemy territory. The Chilterns, with their steep north-westward face against the King, were to prove an insuperable barrier to any bold frontal attack on London; the town of Reading, in the only practicable gap, was bitterly contested, changing hands four times in the course of the war. The strategy planned by Prince Rupert for the reduction of London during the following year, 1643, was the separate advance of the King's forces from the north and west in a pincer movement which was to converge on the estuary of the Thames just below the capital. He did not believe that this port and merchant city would hold out in the face of a threat to its very life-blood, the seaward approaches. He was probably right, but the plan came to nothing owing to the difficulty of moving the armies so far from their recruiting grounds. The men of the western Midlands would not advance on London while the Parliamentary stronghold of Gloucester remained un-reduced in their rear. The West Country men feared with equal reason the raiding of their homes and fields by the Parliamentary garrison which still held Plymouth, and the town of Kingston-upon-Hull was a menace to Yorkshire. The King's two fatal weaknesses prevented him from reducing these three cities. He failed at Gloucester for lack of artillery, and at Plymouth and Hull because such navy as there was had declared for Parliament and kept the garrisons revictualled from the sea.

In the following year, Rupert attempted to save the situation by a double preliminary campaign for the reduction of all subsidiary Parliamentary forces in the west and north before the march on London. The western campaign succeeded with the surrounding and surrender of the Earl of Essex, but the northern campaign ended in disaster at Marston Moor on 3 July 1644. It was a pitched battle which Rupert had not intended to fight, and which was forced on him because Charles's military advisers in Oxford feared that the city might be attacked if the absence of the army were prolonged. In the circumstances one cannot but feel that the choice of so exposed and indefensible a site as Oxford for his headquarters was a disastrous handicap to the King.

The loss of the north was fatal to Charles's hopes. Moreover, the Parliamentary army had now been reorganized under Fairfax and Cromwell. The strength of the Royalist army was annihilated at Naseby in June 1645 and the final mopping-up of the King's scattered garrisons was merely a matter of time and patience. Attempts on the part of the King to stabilize a front farther to the west along the line of the Severn and behind the Cotswolds, with his headquarters at Worcester, failed completely. His last army, from the Midlands and Wales, was surrounded and capitulated at Stow-on-the-Wold in March 1646, his last western army at Truro a week earlier.

Parliamentary strategy, for the first part of the war, being purely defensive, was less interesting. It was also uninspired. In fact the Parliamentary side produced no strategist of the stature of Rupert.

What it had was a superb tactician in Cromwell. Cromwell realized that until Parliament had cavalry which could out-manoeuvre Rupert's they would never be able to pass from defence to attack, and he set himself to develop that cavalry methodically, with infinite patience, making of his heavy-armed, perfectly disciplined, but swift and mobile Ironsides the model for the cavalry of the New Model Army.

Indeed, when we think of that war, of the English countryside alive with the troops of the seventeenth century, it is always of the cavalry that we think. For the whole conformation of the land cried out for the exploitation of this arm. The wide stretches of unfenced common land, the huge sweep of the Wiltshire and Berkshire downs, the innumerable dents and hollows, rises and depressions of the Midlands, made it the perfect country for cavalry fighting – not for pitched battles between charging squadrons of horse, although that might come in, but for skirmishing and raiding. It was the sort of country in which a small number of cavalry, cleverly used, might baffle, divide and defeat far larger forces. Which was precisely what Rupert, left to himself, was perpetually trying to do; as when dodging with lightning speed across the Yorkshire dales he drew the besiegers off from York and slipped in to the relief of the city from the north, while Fairfax was still looking about for him on the western side.

Moreover, cavalry had another advantage for these ill-provided armies, since horse and man could themselves be used as a weapon. Continental cavalry was armed largely with pistols and until the time of Gustavus Adolphus the 'caracole' had been the favourite tactic; each line of cavalry halted, fired, and having fired wheeled off to the rear to wait for their next turn. There was no actual contact with the opposing force. Gustavus preferred the terrifying method of charging without a halt straight into the ranks opposite, firing only at the last minute. Rupert, whose troops, as we have seen, were poorly armed, taught his men to rely almost entirely on shock and impact. He turned horse and man into projectiles, and both at Edgehill and Naseby simply rode down the opposing ranks until they panicked and fled. Cromwell copied and developed the method, improving the armour and equipment of his troops, until the impact of the Ironsides became like the impact of so many miniature tanks. Sheer weight drove them through the enemy.

Just as the English open country was specially suited to the swift and free movement of small bodies of cavalry, so the hedged lanes, the ditches and the banks gave special opportunities to the musketeers. In contrast to the wide scope of cavalry action were the many congested engagements fought out between infantry in the built-up and enclosed outskirts of many a quiet English town, or even in the outbuildings of some large manor-house. When the owners of Compton Wynyates attempted to recapture their house, fortified against them by the Parliamentarians, the outer wall of the park, the inner garden wall, the stable yards became successive points of a frantic and embittered defence. In few wars can there have been quite so many actions in narrowly enclosed spaces or improvised strong-points. The country had few fortresses in a condition of readiness, so fortresses must be made as occasion demanded and offered. In one church at least, Alton in Hampshire, a band of trapped Royalists defended the length of the nave pier by pier, barricading themselves behind pews and tables, surrendering at last on the chancel steps. The conversion of Lichfield Cathedral into a fortress was a more deliberate act, for the Cathedral dominates the town; twice defended it was twice taken, and a great part of its fine red-sandstone Gothic destroyed in the process.

The English climate has not altered very much in three hundred years. Naseby was fought 'about the noon of a glorious day in June', but Naseby was exceptional. The summers of the Civil War were typical summers; 'a blustring cold day, and the evening very wett', or some equally depressing entry, is found time and again in the notes of the contemporaries. That particular blustering cold day was in August. One can sympathize too with the musketeers who were to 'go resolutely forth by Sallies, in a dark, cold, blustring, rainy, tempestuous night'. We all know such nights. But the climate was not subject to great extremes and therefore we hear less than we do in Continental fighting of the formal business of going into winter quarters and abandoning further manoeuvres until the spring. If the larger movements of the war were, as one would expect, seasonal, there was intermittent fighting all the year round. Ice was on the ground in some parts of

England in the August of 1642, but the winters themselves were for the most part mild and muggy.

The Civil War was the last prolonged or serious war to be fought in England itself, and centuries of peace have wiped away the scars. Here and there an ancient helmet or a pair of rusty spurs hangs in a local museum; here and there a church wall is scarred with small shot, an ancient font carries the scratched initials of the soldiers who camped there, or a country house will preserve by oral tradition the story of some private act of heroism, like the story of Arthur Jones's wife and her cool deluding of the Parliamentary soldiers to save her husband's life, which is handed down at Chastleton.

It is hard to see Turnham Green or even Newbury as once they were, and Wigan is no longer the 'pretty village' through which Prince Rupert rode after his relief of Latham House; yet you may trace Cromwell's position with tolerable certainty on the rolling fields of Naseby and follow his brilliant manoeuvres on the bald expanse of Marston Moor, or, walking the by-roads of England, see suddenly that trivial hillock, this unimportant brook re-endowed with the terrible significance of some brief and bloody afternoon three hundred years ago.

1945

Niccolo Machiavelli

When Niccolo Machiavelli, suitably attired in his councillor's robes, withdrew from the living room of his poverty-stricken home to the refuge of his study to compose his two great political works, it was not his intention to start an argument that would last from the sixteenth century to the twentieth. On the contrary, he intended to formulate rules of statecraft which would put an end to argument. It occurred to him, as it has done to some greater and to many lesser men, that the lamentable confusion of contemporary society could be reduced to order if practical rules for political conduct could be established. He sought for those rules where men of learning in his age were accustomed to seek: in the superior wisdom of classical times. His *Discourses* are a penetrating analysis of the events recorded in the first ten books of Livy, and *The Prince*, although in a less explicit manner, derives equally from classical reading.

Machiavelli's material was typical Renaissance material; his way of looking at it was his own. He claimed to have entered upon a path 'as yet untrodden by anyone else', and certainly his analysis of past history and of contemporary events and the conclusions he reached on correct political conduct in a great variety of circumstances impressed and astonished many of his contemporaries. Such a connoisseur of statecraft as Thomas Cromwell warmly recommended his works. Machiavelli's cardinal weakness, as Professor Butterfield has pointed out, is that his conviction of Roman superiority prevents him from approaching his material objectively. In spite of the preconception which partly governs his conclusions, Machiavelli remains a pioneer of the inductive method of reasoning, and by more than half a century the forerunner of Francis Bacon. Whether he is altogether to be praised for this innovation is more doubtful. A method which was to prove valuable in other spheres has particular dangers when applied to history. The material is too doubtful and imprecise to be suited to this treatment, a truth which escaped Machiavelli's penetrating intellect because of the relative simplicity of the historical evidence available to him. He was not particularly worried by conflicting or alternative versions of the facts which he analysed, still less by the existence of indefinable or imponderable elements in any given political situation, elements whose existence would, and indeed often does, make nonsense of his maxims. Nemesis overtook him, or rather his writings; for these very imponderables, these elements on which he had not reckoned, made his practical political handbooks objects of bitter opprobrium within a few years of his death.

He gained the notoriety which has more or less clung to his name ever since, because the nature of politics underwent a violent change in the middle years of the sixteenth century. It has sometimes been said that the divorce of politics from ethics begins with Machiavelli. This was not true in practice; politics and ethics have been through a series of marriages and divorces since the beginning of recorded history. Machiavelli happened to live at a time and in a country where this divorce appeared to be absolute; his observations rested on this assumption. Very shortly after his death European politics entered upon one of the most intensely religious phases through which they have ever passed. A violent reaction from Machiavelli's works was the direct consequence. He had calculated, with resignation, on the natural depravity of man, but he had also calculated that man would act on the whole as a reasonable being. *The Prince* places before rulers patterns of the coolest reason and common sense. The *Discourses* call for the exercise of these qualities by republican governments. The Reformation and the Counter-Reformation produced among a great number of people, and even among ruling princes, a frame of mind which was wholly unreasonable. Religious beliefs and moral convictions became dominating forces throughout western Europe. Individual princes or whole societies were found ready to run impossible risks and to make preposterous sacrifices in order to preserve or restore certain religious observances. Whatever ulterior motives the present fashion may attribute to the men of the Religious Wars there can be no serious doubt that many of them were moved by the most passionate sincerity. This supercharge of inspired irrationality gives to the events of the period an explosive and incalculable quality which cannot be explained merely in terms of social unrest and economic change.

The men of the Counter-Reformation repudiated Machiavelli with the frenetic zeal that they applied to most of their beliefs and prejudices, for he had denied by implication that element in politics which was to them of paramount importance, the salvation of the human soul. The unredeemed materialism of his outlook, though it might still appeal to a rare thinker like Francis Bacon or, with significant reservations, to a practical politician like Cardinal Richelieu, was repellent to the majority of men during the whole of that tumultuous religious century. The men of the new dispensation, particularly in the Roman Catholic Church, led the attack; Cardinal Pole declared that the author of *The Prince* was an 'enemy of the human race'. Pope Paul IV put his works on the Index and the Council of Trent confirmed the condemnation. By one of those paradoxical twists very frequent in that age of fanaticism and propaganda, the Protestants attributed the practice of Machiavelli's doctrines – or what they believed to be his doctrines – to the Catholics in general and the Jesuits in particular. The identical compliment was returned with equal heat. Yet in the case of the Jesuits the slander struck so deep a root that even today Father Walker, Machiavelli's latest translator and editor in English, thinks it advisable in the introduction to his scholarly work specifically to repudiate Machiavelli's more obnoxious views.

Those who accepted the name of Machiavelli as a symbol for close designs and crooked counsels had not always read him. His ideas were so widely and slanderously disseminated at second and third hand that those who most religiously repudiated him often did so in ignorance of what he had actually taught. Only when the vehement rage of the Religious Wars had died down was it possible to look at his work again with a dispassionate eye and to discover with surprise that some of his doctrines were respectable and that all were presented with a precision and judgment which make his works an education to study. The unrelenting materialism is certainly there, but so are reflections on the preservation of liberty in the State and the maintenance of stable popular government which commanded the admiration of Macaulay, and to which the political theory of the Whigs was very considerably indebted. As secretary to the Florentine Republic, Machiavelli had learnt to believe in maintaining a safe political equilibrium by a series of checks and balances. In the words of Jacob Burckhardt, to examine a plan of his drafting is like looking into the works of a clock. In political theory, therefore, he was one of the first to emphasize the value of conflicting interests in the State, so that one may hold the other in check. 'In every republic,' he wrote, 'there are two different dispositions, that of the populace and that of the upper class . . . all legislation favourable to liberty is brought about by the clash between them.' From this and other reflections of the kind it might be argued that Machiavelli, not the devil, was the first Whig.

He can certainly claim to have been the first exponent of utilitarian political theory. The doctrine of the greatest good of the greatest number appears by implication in his political writings and is formulated in almost those words in, of all his works, that ribald little comedy *Mandragola*. It is curious to reflect that the sage formula of Bentham and James Mill was first used to justify a seduction.

In the latter half of the nineteenth century resurgent Italy, looking about for heroes, selected Machiavelli as an early prophet of national unity. His disgust with the ineptitude of Italian petty politics certainly led him to say things which can be so interpreted. He believed in a strong, efficient State and regretted the corruption and enslavement of his country which had been brought about by the quarrelsome inefficiency of its princes and republics. Moreover, like the good public servant he had been, he believed that men should make sacrifices for the common weal. In the passages where he commends the nobility for public spirit, of which the Roman republic could offer such heroic examples, his writing glows with an unusual fervour. Partly on account of these, and still more because of his love for Italy, the greatest of his biographers, Villari, hailed him as the 'least understood and most calumniated personality that history has known'. He even went so far as to add that Machiavelli's burning hope for a free Italy crowned his brows 'with a divine splendour that glorifies the age'.

The heyday of nationalism and *Realpolitik* was evidently the moment for Machiavelli's triumphant return from the Inferno to which the Counter-Reformation had banished him and the limbo of reputation in which he had remained ever since. His sincere belief in a strong united State appealed to the nationalist, and his acute observation of facts to the realist. The moment has passed. His nationalism no longer pleases a generation which has suffered too much from aggressive nations. His glorification of the single-minded civic virtue which sacrifices private interest and private moral standards to the superior needs of the State has an ugly sound to those who have seen the oppression of Leviathan at its worst, whether in his own Italy or elsewhere. His realism appears academic in an age when politics no longer seem to depend on those more or less direct problems of personal decision which figure so largely in Machiavelli's statecraft, but rather on social and economic forces obscurely apprehended and hard to control. There is, moreover, too much in his writing to sicken and dismay. His most ardent admirers cannot deny that he advocates both craft and cruelty as legitimate weapons in statecraft. It is true that he insists that neither should be used for itself alone. It is true that he regards their use as inevitable, given the depravity of man, and fences all his doctrines with the specious plea that statesmen must live as the world lives. The service he hoped to do humanity – and he sincerely believed that he was serving humanity – was that of teaching the wicked to be wicked reasonably, or at least to achieve reasonable and reputable ends by reasonable if disreputable means.

No honest historian can deny that the epochs during which high moral purpose has played a large part in politics have been as disordered and unhappy as those in which it has not. The righteous ruler has not, in practice, necessarily been the best for his people. On the other hand, he has not necessarily been worse or less successful than the unrighteous, nor have epochs of realist and amoral politics been markedly superior in their results to the others. The facts prove nothing, or anything. In the circumstances righteousness might perhaps be given the benefit of the doubt. Examples can be cited in which firmness of moral judgment has triumphed over political wisdom, although Machiavelli cites none. This is the weakness of the Machiavellian method. His claim to objectivity is false. It is false because his admiration for the vanished Roman past controlled and limited his vision, and it is false because his natural taste for subtlety, and his admiration for cleverness and force directed his choice of historical examples.

The real flaw lies in the application of his method to a type of material – historical evidence – which ought not to be treated in this way. Its very nature prevents objective observation. The selection of examples and the kind of conclusions drawn from them is essentially personal. The interpretation of historical facts differs radically from the interpretation of natural phenomena because the same fact does not appear in the same light to any two observers and the relative importance, or even the notice, accorded to individual facts differs with the judgment and character of every historian. Thus Machiavelli's discovery of a method which was later to be valuable when applied to the natural sciences was made in a branch of knowledge where it was liable to be misleading and dangerous. Since his time the practice of assuming general laws from selected historical facts has been practised by hundreds without the tenth part of his dexterity or percipience. It is possible that his most harmful legacy to the modern world is this fallacious practice of arguing to supposed general principles from the insecure and imperfectly apprehended premises which are all that history has to offer.

1955

Scots and English, 1603–40

Clarendon, in his *History of the Rebellion and Civil Wars in England*, states that the disturbances in Scotland which preceded the Bishops' Wars came as a shock to the English councillors of King Charles I. It seems probable that they came as a shock to King Charles himself. The unexampled authority that his father James VI had succeeded in establishing for the Crown in Scotland – an authority which he continued to exercise at long range when he became King of England – was something which Charles I had learnt to take for granted.

His father, addressing his English Parliament in 1607, had announced with pardonable satisfaction:

> Thus I must say for Scotland and may truly vaunt it: here I sit and govern it with my pen: I write and it is done: and by a Clerk of the Council I govern Scotland now, which others could not do by the sword.

There were signs of a weakening in this authority before King James died, if only in the steady increase of lawlessness on the Borders and in parts of the Highlands. But the dominion of the Crown over the major part of the kingdom still appeared intact.

It was therefore all the more startling to his son when the challenge to the royal authority first began to assume a violent form in Scotland, where he had least expected it to do so. Still less had he expected his English subjects to make common cause with his Scottish subjects against him. These two miscalculations, first as to his power in Scotland and secondly as to the state of popular feeling between Scots and English, were fatal to him not only in Scotland but, as it turned out, in England as well.

The consideration of these errors and their possible causes was the starting-point of this enquiry into Anglo-Scottish relations between the union of the kingdoms and the breakdown of the personal rule of King Charles I.

Three phases may be distinguished in the span of thirty-five years which divides the Union of the Crowns from the signing of the National Covenant and the outbreak of revolt in Scotland. First there was the initial short phase during which the King and his two councils, Scottish and English, worked earnestly towards the closer union of the two countries. This phase came to an end when the projected scheme for the Union met with the vehement opposition of the English House of Commons. Since it had become apparent, during the negotiations, that the scheme was almost equally distasteful to both countries, King James abandoned the idea for the remainder of his reign, the only significant move during this second quiescent phase being the reorganization of the Scottish Privy Council, which began with the accession of King Charles I in 1625 and entered on the acute stage which led to the revolt with the King's visit to Scotland in 1633. During this period it was commonly believed that the reorganization of the Scottish Church was to be a step towards its amalgamation with the English Church and that this was in turn to lead on towards a closer union of the two nations. Whether this was true or not, the curious paradox remains that the King's policy, by bringing into being the same kind of opposition in both countries, did in fact bring his subjects of both nations much closer together than ever before, although not at all in the way he had intended.

To return to the first phase: the phase of open effort towards a closer Union of the Kingdoms. King James VI entered on his English inheritance with high and statesmanlike hopes, and also with that optimistic zeal which was one of his most endearing characteristics. He was aware of the technical and emotional problems which the new situation presented but was, it would appear, fully confident of his power to deal with them.

Speaking to the congregation assembled in St Giles's on his last Sunday in Edinburgh before he left for England in April 1603, the King announced:

143

My course must be . . . to establishe peace and religioun and wealth
betwixt both the countries. And, as God has joynned the right of
both the Kingdoms in my persoun, so yee may be joynned in wealth,
in religioun, in hearts and effectiouns. And, as the one countrie has
wealth, and the other has multitude of men, so we may part the gifts
and everie one as they may doe to helpe other . . . And . . . as I have
a bodie als able as anie King in Europ, whereby I am able to travell,
so I sall vissie you everie three yeere at the least.

A year later, in July 1604, he set up a joint commission of both
countries to draft a plan for the Union and in October he sent for
the Scots Chancellor, the Earl of Dunfermline, to London to assist
in working it out. The King followed this by a proclamation 'dis-
chairging and discontinewing the severall names of Scotland and
England' so that the 'hole island with the dependences and perti-
nentis of the same . . . sall keep in all ensewing ages the united
denominatioun of the invincible monarchie of Greit Britane'. This
alteration of two time-honoured names by no other authority than
the royal prerogative was ill-received in both countries, where
from that day to this the general term Great Britain and its colour-
less sub-division into North Britain and South Britain have never
really penetrated into the vernacular. As for the Borders, they
were, as the King had declared at Berwick on his journey to the
south, 'borders' no longer but 'the verie hart of the cuntrey', and
he was anxious to win a general acceptance for a term of his own
invention, the 'Middle Shires', as their new name. The inhabitants
of the re-christened Middle Shires were requested in future to
behave themselves 'as becometh modest, quiet and peacable subjects, forbearing all violent, unlawful and extraordinar behaviour'.
More than proclamations were, however, needed to control the
borderers. Those on the Scottish side had celebrated the death of
Queen Elizabeth and their King's accession to the English throne
with a burst of renewed raiding over which Archbishop Spottiswoode in his *History* reproachfully shakes his head. 'The word no
sooner came of the queen's death,' he states, 'than the loose and
broken men in the borders assembling in companies made incur-
sions upon England, doing what in them lay to divide the two
Kingdoms.' The borders, placed under the control of the Scottish
Privy Council, and provided with an efficient border police, did

however now begin to make progress towards more peaceful conditions.

The joint flag which King James next designed to distinguish the ships of both nations at sea was badly received in Scotland because the cross of St George was superimposed on the cross of St Andrew, an arrangement which the King's Council ventured to suggest might 'breid some heat and miscontentment betwix your Majesteis subjects'.

It was found, when the proposed terms of a closer political and economic union were laid before the English Parliament in the winter of 1606-7, that there were more important things than flags to breed heat and miscontentment. The proposals for freedom of trade between the two countries and for the admission of Scots on equal terms into English trading companies struck against the vociferous and ill-mannered opposition of the English merchants.

The Scots, although more amenable, were on the whole relieved that the onus of opposing the King and preventing any closer union with the neighbour nation had been conveniently shouldered by the English. Although the Scottish Privy Council thought it necessary to object to the offensive tone of some of the speeches made in the House of Commons, there was a broad hint of relief in the letter which they sent to the King:

> It is no littill greif to us to heir quhat just causes of discontentment are ministrat unto your Majestie at all these meetingis for enforceing that Union, *so greatlie hated by thame and so little affected by us*, except in that religious obedyence we aucht to your Majestie not to dislike onything that lykis you.

Their religious obedience, thanks to English opposition, was strained no further; the Scots Parliament passed the Union subject to its passage through the English Parliament as well, and in the English Parliament it suffered shipwreck.

A letter from the three Estates of the Scottish Parliament, when the danger was over in August 1607, has some significant phrases:

> We nevir meant, to except aganis onie confounding as it wer of these two before separated Kingdomes in one glorious monarchie and impyre of the whole Yle, bot onlie that this your Majesteis

auncient and native Kingdome sould not be so disordourit and maid
confusit by turneing of it, in place of a trew and friendlie Unioun,
into a conquered and slavishe province to be governed by a Viceroy
or Deputye, lyke suche of the King of Spaynes provinceis as your
Majestie . . . made mentioun of.

The reference to Spain which James had made when expounding the Union to his English subjects had been singularly tactless
to the Scots. The Spanish dependencies to which he had vaguely
compared Scotland were Naples and Sicily; there was however a
closer parallel in the situation which had arisen between Spain
and the Netherlands, a parallel which would be rather too obvious
to any reasonably well-informed Scottish statesman at the time.
The Netherlands had first given a ruler to Spain, and in the early
stages of this union of sovereignty the Spaniards had resented the
influx of Netherlanders into their country and the overweight of
Netherlandish councillors and favourites round their King, just
as the English in the early years of James's reign were resenting
Scottish influence at the Court. In the following generation the
tables were turned, and an entirely Spaniolated King had provoked the Netherlands to revolt by treating them as a province of
Spain. This familiar sequence of events from comparatively recent
history made Spain an unfortunate example for James to place
before his subjects. There was therefore general relief when the
Union was shelved and the technical readjustments between the
two kingdoms with the one King were reduced to a minimum:
namely, the repeal of all hostile laws, the mutual agreement not
to harbour each other's criminals, and the ruling that the *post-nati*
(those born *after* the King's accession) should be regarded as
automatically naturalized citizens of both countries.

For the rest of his reign James left the Union question alone,
and considerable care was exercised to prevent any infringement
of the separate rights of either nation. The Scots Privy Council
effectively silenced an English borderer who had tried to cite a
Scot in the Star Chamber, and as late as 1632 we find a Scot
referring a subpoena to appear before the English Exchequer to
the Scots Privy Council lest by going to London in obedience to
it he should create a precedent. The naturalization of Scots, born
before the Union, who were elevated to English peerages was

carried out by separate Acts of Parliament for each case in the usual cumbrous way. In the opposite and rarer event of Englishmen being raised to Scottish peerages, it is not quite clear what, if anything, was regularly done. Viscount Falkland certainly became a naturalized Scot; but there seems to be no evidence either way as to whether Lord Fairfax of Cameron did so.

In so far as the King's policy of Union survived, it survived in his continued and drastic reorganization of the Scottish Church to bring it into line with the English one. But he handled the relationship between the two with considerable tact. There was, for instance, the important question of apostolic succession, which according to the Episcopalians had been broken in Scotland by the ascendancy of the non-episcopal Kirk. In England, apostolic succession, thanks to Cranmer, had been preserved intact. It was therefore evident that if the newly appointed Scots bishops were to receive the laying on of hands in the correct manner, they must come to England for it. But the ceremony was not to be performed by the archbishops of Canterbury or York lest this should be held to imply that the Scottish Church was under the authority of either of these metropolitan sees. The bishops chosen to perform the ceremony were the bishops of Ely, Bath and London, whom one contemporary historian alleges to have been selected simply as 'the most ancient bishops' in England.

The precaution was essential, for even so obedient a servant of the King as John Spottiswoode, the archbishop of St Andrews, felt very strongly on this point. A few years later he refused at the funeral of King James to take any other place in the procession except at the side of the archbishop of Canterbury. Having gained this point, he then found that he was expected to conform to English clerical customs and wear lawn sleeves. He refused and he was certainly within his rights, for the late King had regulated the apparel of Scottish bishops in considerable detail – coats of black damask, satin or velvet, and long gowns of velvet or other rich silk, and always 'their tippett of Spanishe taffetty about thair necks'. But when Spottiswoode failed to gain this second point, he refused to appear at the King's funeral, an act of a most unusual spirit from him which gained him the temporary favour of his compatriots, among whom he was not normally popular.

This second phase of King James's policy towards Scotland is marked by the slow decline of the power of his Council in that country. Before he died, his boast that he could govern Scotland with the pen was no longer absolutely true, and his son succeeded to a power, the foundations of which were already crumbling. The theoretical authority and the actual loyalty of the Scottish Privy Council were as strong as ever, but its prestige was dwindling.

The first signs of this diminished effectiveness are to be seen in the serious recrudescence of disorders in the Highlands and on the Borders, which marked the closing years of James's reign, and to which danger signals the King would undoubtedly have paid more heed had not the affairs of England come by this time to occupy the foreground of his attention.

The story of the Borders is particularly significant. The initial effort to turn the stormy debatable land into the peaceful Middle Shires had been extraordinarily successful. The iron gates of some of the border strongholds had been symbolically torn down and beaten into ploughshares and Sir William Cranstoun by a ruthless policy of hanging and deporting temporarily checked the activities of the reivers. One entire border clan, the Grahams, selected as an example no one quite knows why, was systematically exterminated by the destruction of their houses and the deportation of the men. In the year 1606 'above a hundred and forty of the nimblest and most powerful thieves in all the border' ended their lives on the gallows. Their names and nicknames in the reports of the Border Commissioners recall the days of heroic lawlessness commemorated in the ballads -- Hob Armstrong of the Banks, Will Elliott called the Guide, Johnnie Noble called the Grip, Archie Milburne called Cold Archie, John Baty called Bide Him Jock, and Andrew Armstrong, bastard son to Kinmont Willie, hero of the boldest rescue ever made from Carlisle castle, so much celebrated in local verse. Three years later the chancellor, Dunfermline, reported to the King with the utmost assurance that the Commissioners for the Borders had cleared them

of all the chiefest malefactors, robbers and brigands as were wont to reign and triumph there, as clean . . . as Hercules sometime is written to have purged Augeas his ecuries . . . and has rendered all those ways and passages betwixt your Majesty's Kingdoms of Scotland

and England as free and peacable as Phoebus in old times made free and open the ways to his own oracle at Delphos . . . These parts are now, I can assure your Majesty, as lawful, as peacable and as quiet as any part in any civil Kingdom in Christianity.

The peace of the Middle Shires lasted about ten years. In 1621 King James ill-advisedly dissolved the small armed guard which had been created to keep order in the district. The troops had not been gone a year before the reivers were as active as ever. 'Thrift increases michtilie in Annanderdaile, Eskdaill, Ewisdaill, and in the nether pairtis of Nithisdaill,' it was reported, 'the lymmaris ar so insolent and unreullie, because thair is not ane gaird . . . that thai cair not quhat thai do, and sa in this waise the cuntrie is wraikit in all pairtis'. A new joint Commission for the Borders was hastily set up, but it lacked the necessary backing of force and the country appears to have dropped steadily back into its endemic disorders. By 1635 an organized band of brigands was terrorizing almost the whole of the Borders. They are described as leading about

> as well by day as by night ane armed power to attempt and committ diverse wicked and lewde attempts . . . by ill using, assaulting, wounding, mayming and wickedlie killing diverse of our subjects and others, robbing and spoyling of their goods and some taking and imprissoning and in prison keeping in extreme hunger and cold even unto death, untill they sall make great and greevous fynes for the redemptioun of their persons, and also committing murthers, manslaughters, burglereis, ravishementis, robreis, felloneis, waists, besides burning of houses and barnes full of corne . . . and minassing and threatning with panes of life and death all such as sall in our courts of justice prosecute anie of the offenders for the offences foresaid.

Thus all that seemed to have happened on the Borders, until their local disturbances are submerged in the general agitation of the Civil Wars, was that the old border raiding with certain tacit rules and chivalries had given place to the ganging together of a ruthless dispossessed banditti.

The same disintegration of authority is visible in the Highlands and Islands. King James had initiated an extensive onslaught on

Highland disorders and on the Highland way of life in general
before he left Scotland. The famous outlawry of the entire Mac-
Gregor clan, who were thus handed over to the mercy of the
Campbells and the Colquhouns, was dated the same week that he
departed for England. The MacLeods of Lewis were coolly dispossessed to make way for a company of gentlemen adventurers
from Fife who saw possibilities of developing the island. That
extraordinary chieftain, Patrick, Earl of Orkney, himself an illegitimate kinsman of the royal family, who with a brood of illegitimate
brothers and sons had established virtually a separate power in
Orkney, deriving its revenues from piracy, was executed, with one
of his sons, in Edinburgh. Meanwhile, a small naval expedition
had been sent against the Western Isles and the major chiefs,
having been kidnapped during a dinner-party on board one of
the King's ships, the able and wily bishop of the Isles, Andrew
Knox, persuaded those that were left to subscribe the Statutes of
Icolmkill, a programme for the pacification of the Isles in which
the chiefs agreed, among other things, to send their eldest sons to
be educated in the Lowlands. The King had, at the same time,
continued his policy of settling the blood feuds of the northern
nobility by a system of compulsory marriages between the leading
families.

But in the second and third decades of the century the disorders
began to multiply again. The MacLeods proved altogether too
much for the gentlemen adventurers from Fife, whose survivors
twice beat a retreat before what the contemporary poet Lithgow
has called 'the desperate courage of these awful Hebrideans',
twice came back, and finally sold their rights to the Mackenzies,
thus leaving the 'awful Hebrideans' to fight it out between themselves. Beyond the immediate sphere of Campbell control, in the
Western Highlands, the Camerons and the Mackintoshes were
again carrying on furious warfare. In 1624 the murder of two of
the Gordons by the Crichtons of Frendraught undid years of
pacifying work in the Eastern Highlands. When King Charles
visited Scotland in 1633, the Privy Council commanded the 'prin-
cipalls and chiftans of the clans in the Yles' to repair to Edinburgh
to greet the King and to prove to the English visitors 'that the most
remote part of this Kingdome and Yles thairof ar settled under ane

perfyte obedience and peace'. The demonstration was a necessary piece of window dressing, for the power of the Privy Council to establish even the most imperfect obedience and peace was by this time more than doubtful. An outrageous case of wrecking on the coast of Lewis in the ensuing year seems to have gone quite unpunished.

The decline in the prestige and therefore in the power of the Scots Privy Council which had begun under James VI was unintentionally accelerated by Charles I. It was not the least of this King's misfortunes that he was always too much of a Scotsman for England and too much of an Englishman for Scotland. In many ways he was the type of the absentee Scot, rootless in England and uprooted from Scotland, a type which the circumstances of the Union of the Crowns had made very frequent about the English Court. He surrounded himself from choice with men of the same kind: the Duke of Lennox, the Marquis of Hamilton, Will Murray. In this way he created for himself the illusion of being in touch with Scottish feeling when in fact he had lost contact with it.

The Council which James VI had left to carry out his will in Scotland had been well chosen, in the King's own eloquent phrase, of such men as he could correct or were hangable. But they did also sufficiently represent the prestige and power of the Scots lords. Having created such a Council, he let it alone, merely filling the vacancies as they occurred. Charles I, a young man with ideas but no experience and very little acquired knowledge of Scottish politics, tampered incessantly both with the organization and the composition of the Council. He reconstituted it shortly after his accession, insisting on the exclusion of any members who were also Lords of Session. This not only removed men with the kind of legal experience and standing necessary on the Council, but also incapacitated its most assiduous attenders, because the judges only had to cross the road to reach the Council Chamber. Charles then, contrary to all advice, fixed too large a quorum. No king with an elementary knowledge of the transport problems of Scotland could have made so simple a mistake, particularly after excluding all those who found attendance easy. His subsequent steady appointment of the bishops to seats on the Council was chiefly intended to forward his Church policy, against which, especially the revocation of all grants of Church land to laymen since the Reformation, the Council had at first warmly protested. He may also have believed that clerics, with no family lands demanding their attention, could be relied on to devote themselves more exclusively to the work of the Council. But the very frequent changes that he made in its personnel produced an atmosphere of fidgets and intrigue very unsuitable to the conduct of affairs.

Thus, in creating what he thought would be a wholly obedient Council, Charles lost sight of the one essential, that it should also be an efficient Council, a united, respected and powerful body. He was to find when he came to impose his Church policy that the Council was willing but was impotent. He had fatally lessened its prestige and its effectiveness by omitting too many of the Scots lords who felt they had a right to sit on it. The most extraordinary omission was probably that of the young Earl of Montrose whose father had been on the Council for over twenty years, whose grandfather had been chancellor and whose family tradition had been one of service to the Crown for the past century. The appointment of a coming young man of this background ought to have been automatic. There were other less startling instances of the same kind. The effect of such omissions was to create exactly what James VI had been most careful to avoid, namely a focus of discontent, combined with power and prestige, *outside* the Council. Thus at the same time Charles weakened his own Council and set up rival factions. In the course of his royal visit in 1633 Charles moreover added nine Englishmen to the Council in Scotland. These appointments were scarcely more than nominal, as the English were unlikely to be present again in Scotland after the royal visit, and moreover Charles might fairly have argued that the number of Scots with official appointments in England far outweighed the number of Englishmen with appointments in Scotland. Nevertheless this dilution of the Council by nominal members who were ignorant of Scots affairs was not calculated to strengthen its prestige.

This treatment of the Council is worth emphasizing, for nationalist resentment in Scotland – not so much against the English partner-nation, as against an absentee monarch – was steadily growing. The promise made by King James of revisiting his native land every three years had not been kept. He came back only once, in 1617; King Charles postponed his first visit until 1633 – eight years after his accession. The loss to the smaller towns which had counted on the almost annual visits of their King to bring a bustle of visitors and trade was considerable. Perth was described by John Taylor the Water-Poet as early as 1618 as being 'much decayed, by reason of the want of his Majesty's yeerely comming to lodge there'. William Lithgow in his flowery welcome to King Charles in 1633 puts into the mouth of Scotland lines suitable to a deserted wife:

> True, and most true it is, the Proverbe proves,
> That age is still injur'd, by younger loves:
> And so am I, thine eldest Region made,
> A prey to dark oblivion's winter shade.

It was thus with a weakened Council and with a nation acutely sensitive to the fact that their King preferred his other kingdom that Charles set out to complete his father's work and bring Scotland into religious conformity with England. Strong as was the purely religious element in the opposition which gathered against him, the nationalist element must not be underestimated.

Charles made a certain allowance for national feeling; but as it turned out, not nearly enough. The popularly miscalled Laudian liturgy, the new Service Book which he attempted to introduce in 1637, was in fact largely a Scottish compilation, and the bishops on whom Charles relied to introduce it in Scotland – Spottiswoode, Sydserf and the spirited Whitford, who read it with a pair of pistols on the pulpit in front of him – were pure Scots by birth, breeding and education. A certain amount of care had thus been taken by the King not to offend Scottish susceptibilities; but he lacked the imagination to see that his precautions needed to go far deeper. He could not wipe out the cumulative effect of his own and his father's absences, of the English appointments to the Privy Council, of the bustling up and down to London of the Scots bishops charged with the preparation of the Prayer Book. A sense of neglect and long-pent-up national resentment were strongly mingled with the religious feeling which caused the riots in Edinburgh at the introduction of this 'Popish-English-Scottish-Mass-Service-Book'. The document of protest drawn up by the opposition and largely managed by the noblemen whom Charles had deliberately and mistakenly kept off the Council, was significantly named the *National* Covenant.

This was, however, nationalism with a difference. The Scots were perfectly well aware that there was considerable opposition to the King's religious policy in England. They were careful to prepare an 'Information for All Good Christians within the Kingdom of England' setting forth their case to possible sympathizers south of the border. King Charles for his part found when it came to a war with the Scots that, for perhaps the first time in history, the English were not prepared to fight even to prevent an invasion, so deeply were they infected with sympathy for the Scots revolt.

The royal miscalculation was not wholly inexplicable. King Charles seems to have made the mistake of judging the relations between the two peoples exclusively from the official knowledge he had of them, a knowledge based on the narrow limits of his own court and the various official disputes which came to his notice. Officially Anglo-Scottish relations had often been strained, and had never been really cordial since the Union of the Crowns.

The joining together of two nations of which one was incomparably the wealthier had been bound to produce some unhappy consequences. The English resented the influx of Scottish adventurers of all classes, and the Scots resented the English assumption that their commercial interests should always have the first consideration. The Union plan had broken down because English merchants would not admit Scots merchants to equal privileges with themselves, and although the Scots were glad enough that the plan had broken down, they resented the reason. Later there had been ugly disputes about the allotment of land in Nova Scotia, incontrovertibly started as a Scottish colony; English adventurers had quite shamelessly attempted to get the charter to the Scots cancelled in their favour. Again the Greenland Company of London not only trespassed in waters to which the Scots had been granted a prior right, but in 1629, the Scots complained, 'seazed upon thair chellps, medled with all the provisioun being thairin, and have takin thair men prisonners and used thame with all rigour, sua that the shippes quhilks wer reiked furth for that voyage at ane verie great charge ar now returned emptie, to the heavie loss and discouragement of the undertakers'.

In commerce the English undoubtedly had the whip hand and used it. Thus when the Scots, perturbed at the alarming increase in the consumption of English beer – a brew which had become astonishingly more fashionable than any native one – tried to keep it out by putting up the duty against it, the English instantly retaliated with a threat to raise the duty on wool and coal, the two chief Scottish exports, a counterblow which, if it had been put into effect, would have been disastrous to Scottish trade. However, an attempt by the English some years later, in 1623, to compel the Scots to sell all their raw wool exclusively to England was successfully resisted on the ground that a monopoly of this kind would enable the English to fix the price as they liked. Rumours and echoes of this foiled plan, so advantageous to the English, rumble on for some years; the Commission appointed to enquire into the depression in the English cloth trade in the early years of Charles I, for instance, reproachfully cites the sale of Scots wool to foreign manufacturers as one contributory cause of the English depression.

The English, for their part, saw very much the worst of the Scots during the early years of the century. It was evident that the more populous and more prosperous southern country offered better opportunities for the work-shy to pick up a livelihood. Gangs of sturdy beggars from Scotland soon found it worth their while to save enough to persuade friendly sea captains to set them down at convenient places on the English coast, whence they swarmed over the country in such quantities that it was necessary to issue five – evidently inadequate – prohibitions between 1606 and 1620 against the unlicensed carrying of 'beggarlie passengeris' to England. The prohibitions were felt to be essential for the preservation of good social relations between the countries, lest, as one order of the Privy Council phrased it, the crowding of 'idill suitaris and uncomelie people' into England should give an impression that there were 'no persones of good rank, comlynes nor credite' in Scotland. Certainly the tone of some English lampoons on the Scots at this date does suggest that this was the impression made. A further order commanded all recruited soldiers going from Scotland to Europe to go direct by sea and not to cross over England, where the unruly behaviour of groups of Scots asserting themselves to be soldiers travelling to foreign wars 'procures the privat grudge and miscontentment of the people of that land against his Majesteis subjectis of this kingdome'.

King James himself was aware of the psychological difficulties presented by the arrival of a Scottish king with Scots courtiers in England. To do him justice – and he is a king to whom less than justice is persistently done – he sent back the greater part of his Scottish household servants as soon as he arrived in London and found Queen Elizabeth's palaces already fully staffed with English men and women. His extreme liberality to his Scots favourites he excused to the Parliament in 1607 with the endearing phrase that both he and they had regarded the first three years of his reign as a sort of Christmas. On the whole he made a consistent effort to avoid or soften the jealousies which might arise between the two nations at and around the court. Thus when his eldest son was installed as Prince of Wales he created only five Scottish Knights of the Bath to twenty Englishmen, a very reasonable proportion.

The insults that the members of either nation lightly hurled at the other were punished with considerable severity from time to time. Balfour records with evident pleasure the execution in Edinburgh of Thomas Ross, who had nailed up a number of anti-Scottish theses on the door of the University Church in Oxford and offered to defend them in disputation. An English traveller who, in course of a heated dispute with a Scot in a ship, lying off Civita Vecchia, was reported to have said that 'any merchant in London was able to buy all Edinburgh' was called up in front of the Council in London, where he protested that he had only said 'some four merchants of London dealt for as much merchandise as all Edinburgh did'.

King James would have liked men to believe that the English had the monopoly of bad manners, and went so far as to assert in an address to his English Parliament that no Scot had used opprobrious terms of the English. The contrary seems, however, to be proved by the existence of a Scottish Act of Parliament of 1609 prohibiting the publication or uttering of 'pasquillis, libellis, rymis, cokalanis, comedies and siclyk' against the English.

It was in England, however, that the ill-feeling between the two peoples most often came to a violent expression, for the fairly obvious reason that while there was a nucleus of Scots to provoke national resentments in England and chiefly round London, there was no equivalent group of English in Scotland, where the visitors were few, were on the whole well-behaved, and were usually made very welcome.

The King was on the whole fairly faithfully supported by his courtiers and by his Scots and English Councils in preventing unnecessary trouble. There was the notorious incident in 1612 at Croydon races when a Scot named Ramsay hit the Earl of Montgomery in the face and the Earl of Montgomery failed to respond in kind, so that, as a contemporary sourly observed, there was 'nothing lost but the reputation of a gentleman'. Montgomery's friends asserted that he stomached the insult in order to prevent a free fight between Scots and English, and to be fair, it seems very probable that this was indeed his reason, though he never quite lived down having lost his reputation. Altogether the year 1612 was an uneasy time for Anglo-Scottish relations in London, and things very nearly came to an outburst again over the case of Lord Sanquhar who had hired a couple of assassins to murder an English fencing master who had accidentally put out his eye. None of his compatriots in high place, however, took Lord Sanquhar's part in the matter, and he was hanged, to the gratification of the English and to no regret of the Scots.

There is, however, one other aspect of the situation in and round the court which it is not out of place to consider here, because it has not been much noticed and it undoubtedly had a considerable effect on the position of the Crown in Scotland. The departure of the King had broken up the cadre of the Scottish court. What was created in England was essentially an English court with a Scottish, or as time went on, an Anglo-Scottish enclave within it. Although such men as Hamilton and Lennox, the most outstanding examples of the anglicized Scots nobleman, were evidently men of high authority, the reputation in general of the anglicized Scots did not stand very high north of the Border. There certainly seems to have grown up a substantial group of Scots lords who preferred to disassociate themselves from their compatriots at the English court, which meant of course to disassociate themselves from the court altogether. Lord Gordon, for instance, who became Huntly in 1636, we find making long visits to the French court and comparatively short ones to the English, to which he almost deliberately did not belong. The same thing was significantly true of the young Montrose. This was a dangerous situation for the King to allow to grow up, because it was a bare generation since the Scots nobility had at last been gathered into some kind of order and allegiance under the Crown. To allow distinguished Scots peers to revert to an uninterrupted independence, and to feel not even the social magnetism of the court – let alone any other – was to increase the risk of ultimate rebellion.

Meanwhile more than thirty years of a common sovereignty had insensibly strengthened links between the Scottish and the English peoples of which the King, dealing only with the political surface, remained unaware. English travellers, with few exceptions messengers of goodwill, had been well received in Scotland and had acquired a respect for some at least of what they saw there. Both the prolific poet and journalist John Taylor in 1618 and Sir William Brereton in 1636 were awed by the physique of the Highlanders. Taylor, an irrepressible tourist, boldly penetrated as far as Braemar to join in the hunting, borrowed a kilt for the occasion from the kindly Earl of Mar and can thus probably claim to have been the first but emphatically not the last Englishman to masquerade unconvincingly in borrowed romance. He was impressed too by the bounty of Scottish hospitality and the patriarchal households of the lairds who generously gave him lodging in the course of his tour.

Sir William Brereton's record of 1636, on the eve of the outbreak of the religious troubles, is more significant. Like Taylor, he was impressed by the patriarchal manners of the Scottish gentry to their families and servants. He also writes approvingly of the demonstrations which some congregations in Scotland had made against ministers who in accordance with the royal instructions had tried to introduce kneeling and other Popish ceremonies. It is evident, from the way in which he writes of these things and the introductions which he had, that the close connections which had once existed between the Reformed kirk in Scotland and the Elizabethan Puritans – Cartwright, it will be remembered, had been offered a chair at St Andrews – had outlasted the Union of the Crowns and been strengthened by the fact that both were now equally exposed to attack from above.

But the forcing house of understanding between the two nations was neither in England nor in Scotland, but on the mainland of Europe. There had been very extensive recruiting in Scotland for the Protestant powers involved in the Thirty Years War. There was much volunteering from England. The muster rolls of Swedish, Dutch and Danish armies show interesting mixtures of names from both countries. In parenthesis, on the Catholic side, the murder of Wallenstein in 1634 must have been planned and carried out entirely in the English language between an Irish colonel, a Scottish colonel and an English major. But it was in the Protestant armies, especially the Dutch and Swedish, that bonds of personal friendship and above all of common religious convictions were being increasingly formed between the representatives of the two nations.

An influence of equal importance came from the English-speaking churches in the Netherlands. These seem to have been truly Anglo-Scottish, and were all of them closer to the Dutch Calvinist model than to the Anglican establishment to which they were only very vaguely attached. Their powers of ordination had long caused anxiety to the Anglican Church at home and they were the source of a steady trickle of ministers to both England and Scotland whose doctrines and practice were wholly at variance with the forms that Archbishop Laud was trying to impose. The dictates of the English Privy Council commanding them to conform to Anglican measures were disregarded by them and were politely deprecated by the Dutch government under whose protection they existed. The Low Countries thus became the convenient resort of those who opposed the government on religious grounds, and it was here that the dissident godly of both nations made significant friendships.

To all of this King Charles was insufficiently alive, although his opponents seem to have been perfectly aware of it. The English sympathy for the Scots revolt early caused the moving spirit of the National Covenant, Lord Rothes, to note piously that 'some growth of Christian affection amongst neighbours may prove this cord to be twisted by a hand from above', meaning presumably that God had taken a hand in bringing English and Scots together against the church policy of their common King.

Thus in the first thirty-five years of the Union of the two countries under one sovereign, the King's attempts to achieve either an economic or a religious union, by policy directed from the centre, had both broken down: the first on English resentment, the second on Scottish intransigence. The first real movement of mutual help and affection between the two peoples was created not by the policy of the Crown but by resistance to it. It is an interesting and possibly an instructive paradox.

1958

Principles and Perspectives

E very scholar and every writer who seriously embarks on the study of history must sooner or later become aware of the moral problems which that study involves and must take measures to solve them. Whether the historian embarks upon some all-embracing account of world events and seeks to find a pattern and meaning for the whole story of man, or whether he confines himself to a brief period and a small region, say the administrative history of Galloway during the minority of King David II, he will be dealing with the actions of men, though seen in a different perspective and on a different scale. He may lean by temperament towards the romantic and biographical approach so that history is for him dominated by the deeds and ideas of great men and women and foot-noted with anecdotes of their lives; or he may pursue his studies in impersonal terms, seeing men and women as merely incidental to the evolution of institutions, to the rise and fall of societies, the interplay of economic forces; he may devote himself to the personal career of Napoleon, or the decay of the feudal system, or spend a lifetime compiling from the available sources figures showing the number of vessels trading to Hamburg during the Thirty Years War and the character of their cargoes. But he must always at some point become aware of the desire to say that such a thing was good or bad, such an action right or wrong. He may believe this to be an important part of the historian's function and have no doubts in his mind as to how it should be done. He may hold that moral judgments are no part of his task and dismiss from his mind all conscious thought of them. But however strongly he may believe in the dispassionate approach, if he is honest with himself he will know that his opinions and his judgments are the outcome of the personal beliefs, fears and prejudices implanted in his mind by the people with whom he grew up and the events in the world about him, and that these things will show in his work, if not openly, then between the lines.

It is impossible for the historian to avoid making value judgments and it is difficult for him to define precisely on what grounds he makes them. Quite apart from the numerous moral and political prejudices to which he is subject, the dimension of time adds a further complication. Great distances of time reduce the intensity with which we feel about moral issues. What Cromwell did to the people of Wexford is much closer in time, and therefore much more imaginable, and therefore much more distressing, than what the Emperor Theodosius did to the people of Thessalonica. Questions of right and wrong, of humanity and inhumanity ought to be equally significant to the historian whatever the period in which they happen. But it is evident that they are not; few accounts of the September massacres are written without some sign of passion or sympathy on one side or the other, but the story of the Sicilian Vespers can be told with apparent detachment.

The history of a nation as told by a foreigner, and as told by a native are totally different things; the same history may look different again if told by a member of a dominant group or of a minority. It is not only that the appearance of facts changes, that the Union of 1707 does not look the same to an Englishman and to a Scot, or that the American Civil War reveals wholly different aspects to a native of New England and to a native of South Carolina. The perspective and the emphasis, the relationship between different facts and their relative importance also changes. In the changing perspectives of time and place the intelligence and the morality of almost all actions, the virtues and the vices, the advantages and disadvantages of almost all events, can be, and are, differently assessed. The right of one generation is the wrong of another, the right of one nation or class is the wrong of another.

Liberal historians of the nineteenth century believed in progress and believed that the creation of nation states and the liberation of oppressed peoples were a right and proper part of progress. Most of them also believed that toleration, variously equated with Rationalism or Protestantism, was also right, though this clear and simple alignment occasionally caused embarrassment. What for instance was Samuel Rawson Gardiner to do with the Irish Rebellion of 1641? He could not deny that this rising was a fervent expression of national spirit and he accorded a cautious approval to this noble feeling. But no one had explained to the Irish that, to satisfy liberal historians of a later date that they were properly equipped for setting up a nation state, they should have been Protestants – like for instance the Dutch whose revolt against Philip II was much and rightly applauded by liberal-minded historians.

The Irish were emphatically not Protestants, and more in sorrow than in anger, Gardiner had to point out that their rising was thus doomed from the outset not because they were, after ten years, outnumbered and out-gunned by the Puritan English, but because they were 'throwing themselves athwart the line of historical progress'. This would be more convincing as an explanation of failure if all Catholic-national revolts at this epoch could be shown to have collapsed. But Gardiner had overlooked, strangely, the exactly contemporaneous revolt of Portugal against Spain. The Portuguese, of whose national fervour there is no question, also made the same mistake as the Irish; they were nationalist without being Protestant. But they threw themselves athwart the line of historical progress with complete success.

Generalizations, even from the most learned and judicious writers, often come to look foolish when the beliefs which made them acceptable have lost their force. That might be a warning against making generalizations at all, but the historian cannot do entirely without a moral and political framework within which to arrange his facts and make his deductions. The past has to be measured as the present is measured against the standards and beliefs on which, consciously or unconsciously, the historian conducts his own life.

This is the first paradox. The things which we believe to be right, the things which we believe to be true, vary widely from age to age and the same holds good for the past times which are the historian's province. If we make no allowance for these variations we become rigid and stultified, lacking in human imagination, unable to bring full understanding either to the present or to the past, accepting received ideas and traditional prejudices instead of judging for ourselves. If we make too much allowance for the changing standards and the shifting of opinions we begin to lose all sense of moral stability. Historical thinking has always fluctuated between these two dangers, the danger of having no perspective at all, and the danger of having one only; the danger of having no principles at all and the danger of having principles that are too rigid.

It has recently been most persuasively argued by the scientist-philosopher Professor Michael Polanyi in *The Study of Man* that historians by emphasizing the relativity of moral standards and their inconstant shiftings from age to age have exercised an important influence in undermining, or at least unsteadying, our capacities to make moral judgments. The accusation deserves serious consideration. The original intention of historians, when they argued that men should be judged strictly within the framework of their own time, was a generous one. It arose from the desire to do justice to men and motives in the past. This was also a sound idea, in relation to inquiry, because it is evident that the historian who has a full understanding of the principles and standards of the people and societies he is studying will be able to interpret the evidence they have left behind them with a far better prospect of discovering the truth than the historian who is without this understanding or has it only in a very imperfect degree.

The wars of religion have left their mark on the institutions, the society and the prejudices of most of the peoples of western Europe. These bitter and distracting conflicts are not only dismal and deplorable but largely incomprehensible until we can bring to them some understanding of the beliefs which guided the protagonists. We must understand and accept the idea that, however self-interested their conduct may appear, the rulers of that epoch (all of them in theory and many of them in practice) believed that it was their duty and their function to legislate for their people not only in time but in eternity: that they were responsible in the first place for their subjects' souls and only in the second place (if at all) for their physical welfare on earth.

The examination of the economic revolution caused by these religious troubles and of the economic motives which were undeniably important throws much light on certain aspects of the subject, but it does not illumine the whole. It must be added to, and not substituted for, an understanding of the spiritual issues involved. It is, incidentally, a curious symptom of our own time that the purely materialist interpretation of history, and the present popularity of economic determinism are at least in part a moral and spiritual revolt against the uncertainty and fluidity of historicism. The aggressively materialist view of the historical process was seized upon by many, from my own generation onwards, to satisfy a spiritual thirst, the thirst for certainty, which the historicists left unsatisfied.

Historicism, this way of thinking about the past, or attempting to think about it in its own terms, was the outcome of an idea both humane and scholarly. But it had and still has very grave dangers, as Lord Acton clearly saw and as clearly taught. He never ceased to exhort postulant historians to apply, in the last resort, the highest ethical standards to their historical judgments. 'In judging men and things,' he wrote to Creighton, 'ethics go before dogma, politics and nationality.' Belief in the moral law must lie at the root of all sound historical judgment. Failing this, the historian, in trying to apply different standards to different epochs, will confuse himself, and ultimately his readers, by taking the explanation of conduct for the justification of it. We cannot understand why King Philip II imposed the Council of Blood on his subjects in the Netherlands, or why Cromwell massacred the Irish unless we understand the beliefs which made them hold these things to be right and just. But explanation is not justification: these things were not in themselves right and just. Given the framework of belief within which King Philip II or Oliver Cromwell reasoned, we can say that their own responsibility for actions in themselves evil was relatively less than was, for instance, the responsibility of Hitler for actions in themselves evil. The religious beliefs and the moral standards of the sixteenth and seventeenth centuries on the whole supported these atrocious actions. That does not make evil actions in themselves less evil, but it makes the motives of those who perform them less depraved. It was possible in the sixteenth and seventeenth centuries for very evil things to be done by men who were not necessarily evil, who were even, on balance, good men. The same argument could hardly be sustained, at least as far as racial and religious persecution is concerned, in the twentieth century. But to say that those who perform evil actions are less culpable at some times and in some contexts than they are in others is not to minimize the evil of the actions themselves. The confusion is all too easily made; from explaining an action we move insensibly towards justifying it, and from thence towards a general blurring of the moral issues and a comfortable belief that circumstances are always to blame, and men and women are not.

This is the confusion into which historians fall when they make allowances for 'the standards of the age'. Their intention is to understand and be just to the past, but the result in the long run may be unfair to the present, because this outlook steadily and stealthily fosters the conviction that nothing is good or bad in itself but only in relation to its surroundings.

Historians who subscribe to this view fall into two classes according to temperament. If by temperament they are mainly interested in people, that is in individual human problems, they will act in the belief that to understand all is to forgive all. *Tout comprendre c'est tout pardonner*: discover all the relevant facts, make the imaginative effort to understand why a particular man took a particular decision or performed a particular act, and it will be possible to view his conduct, however deplorable or however vicious, with a dispassionate benevolence.

This is neither wise, sensible nor responsible conduct. The aspiration to understand and to forgive is noble and valid in personal relationships between the living. It is also, in actual and everyday personal relationships, by no means easy to achieve. It is harder to understand and to forgive the personal irritations and annoyances, let alone the wrongs, that we suffer or think we suffer at the hands of our contemporaries than it is to forgive all the crimes of the Emperor Domitian. The first requires an effort in self-control and self-forgetfulness, and some sacrifice of personal pride; the second is merely an intellectual exercise. The application of the principle of understanding and forgiveness to historical personages is a sentimental fallacy. The historian has suffered nothing at their hands; it is not for him to pronounce an absolution. But it is for him to make sure that the crime or crimes really were as they have been handed down, and that their authors were the people to whom they have been attributed. That is the proper function of the historian, but that is quite a different story.

If the historian deals rather with impersonal matters, with the development of institutions, with mass-movements, with the growth and decline of societies or ideas, this 'historicist' attitude may cause him simply to suspend conscious judgment: to discover, to record, but to make no open comment. A concealed and perhaps unintentional comment he will be hardly able to avoid. He may trace the origins of the Inquisition, explain its function and its practices, consider what made it appear necessary and be endurable to the society which created and sustained it; but he will desist from openly saying whether it was good or bad. It simply *was* and is to be considered dispassionately in relation to its historical background. He may study the institution of slavery through the ages, noting its various forms from the ancient world to the present time. He may examine the effects of the system on the societies which practised it, and the different conditions under which slaves have lived at different times and in different parts of the world, but if he holds to the view that no judgment should be made except in relation to the standards of the epoch, he will offer no explicit opinion on the institution itself. The people who accepted the system evidently approved of it, and once the idea is accepted that an epoch or a society should only be judged on its own terms, there is nothing further for the historian to say.

This sentimentality in judging people, and this refusal to judge things, both arise from the highest of motives, the desire to be just. Historicism has undoubtedly deepened and widened the outlook of historians and of their readers. The historians who wrote before the idea of historicism had been developed have greater assurance in their own wisdom; their words have an air of confident moral and political authority; but they can be strangely narrow. It did not occur to Voltaire or to Gibbon to look at the actions of their forefathers from any angle but their own. In our own era of confused issues and tottering principles, the great eighteenth-century historians are a tonic to read because of their unhesitating certainty and their conviction of their own well-grounded reasonableness. But their vision as historians, though detailed and clear, was limited. They could make no sense of points of view widely different from their own or institutions that they did not understand. What they did not understand they scorned. Few of them could penetrate, for instance, the Gothic gloom which, for them, obscured the lively society of Europe's Middle Ages.

This was left to the romantics, when the Age of Reason had been shocked into its grave by the French Revolution. The romantics, above all, influenced historians towards the adoption of a more sympathetic attitude towards individuals, and a more tentative, more eager and inquiring, less contemptuous approach to extraordinary ideas and unfamiliar institutions. Of all the romantics Sir Walter Scott had the widest influence on the approach to history not only in Great Britain but over the whole of Western Europe, for he wanted, like all writers of imagination, to be on terms with his characters, whether they were intended for contemporary figures, or drawn from the past. This was equally true whether he was writing novels or history, whether he was drawing an imaginary figure or one like Rob Roy or Montrose for whom he had genuine material to use. This desire to be on good terms with his characters made him take pains to find out how they would have thought and felt. He was not always successful in this, but the effort and the intention were always there. He wanted to talk the language of the past with the men of the past. The preromantic historians had no such desires. If by some midsummer magic in the Eildon Hills, where True Thomas met the Faery Queen, Walter Scott had found a means of conversing with men and women of bygone centuries, he would have embraced it with joy. But would Edward Gibbon have done so? In the first place he would not have believed the thing possible. But even if it had been possible, he hardly wished for any closer acquaintance with Belisarius or the Emperor Julian than he had already acquired; let the centuries keep their distance.

The study of modern history as we know it, in all its depth and richness, owes much to the romantics and to historicism. But as understanding increased and sympathies became more fluid moral certainties declined. Scott himself was a child of the eighteenth century, and the assured standards of the Age of Reason prevented his generation from carrying the principles, or rather the lack of principle, of historicism to its logical conclusion. In ensuing generations, as historical scholarship became ever more extensive and more detailed, the danger increased. The youthful Ranke greatly intensified it by setting up the ideal of dispassionate truth. All preconceived views, all religious and political prejudices must be set aside: the historian's task was to find out and state 'what actually happened'. This was a noble ideal but it was also impossible of achievement, and rigidly applied it certainly implied the abdication of any function of moral judgment.

Ranke did not – indeed he could not – live up to his ideal. His pupil Burckhardt, the least deceived of nineteenth-century historians, viewed the great illusion of the master with a kind of exasperated admiration. While he stood amazed and in awe before the gigantic learning and the colossal achievement of Ranke – the volume upon volume of European history, much of it based on pioneer research – he was amused and irritated by the way in which the great man slid his personal prejudices into his writing under his superficially dispassionate manner, and constantly implied value judgments often of an extremely simple kind. He admired the clarity and vitality of his mind and his indefatigable energy, but he was irritated and sometimes shocked by his naïveté, his self-deception and at times his small-mindedness. It is not irrelevant to record that in 1870 Ranke, the apostle of the dispassionate approach to history, could justify the Franco-Prussian war on the grounds that 'we are fighting against Louis XIV'; a classic example of misapplied history and deep national prejudice.

The sincerity and the genuine idealism of Ranke's conception of dispassionate history won for it a wide acceptance. But though nothing could sound more noble than the dispassionate pursuit of truth, the ultimate effect of this teaching was to be sadly ignoble. History dispassionately recorded nearly always sounds harsh and cynical. History is not a moral tale, and the effect of telling it without comment is, inevitably, to underline its worst features: the defeat of the weak by the strong, the degeneration of ideals, the corruption of institutions, the triumph of intelligent self-interest. It was no accident that the age of Ranke was also the age of *Realpolitik*.

A subsequent and yet more disturbing development was to

follow from this elevation of the idea of dispassionate truth. On almost every historical point, except the simplest, it is very hard to establish truth. Napoleon once rudely described history as 'une fable convenue'; but an agreed fable, a generally accepted legend, can provide a stable and comfortable background. When the new disciplines and techniques of historical research were turned upon the various agreed fables which had served men well enough for several generations, these fables naturally disintegrated. They were replaced not by new, better and more truthful fables, but by furious arguments. Over almost the whole field of history – especially modern history – the increase in knowledge has brought a decrease of certainty: too many perspectives and too few principles. The accepted designs were shattered, the recognizable forms and figures would no longer do, and history, like other forms of art, entered on a period of abstraction.

The violent times through which we have lived were not foreseen by Ranke, who believed confidently in progress. They were foreseen with uncanny accuracy by the more gloomy and more perceptive Burckhardt. Their effect on historical thinking has been, inevitably, to bring about a return to a more rigid and less fluid way of thought. On the one hand there is the revival of the almost religious attitude to history, the desire to find in it the handwriting of God and to deduce from our now enormously increased factual knowledge some idea of the pattern of world events past, present and to come. Hence the inspiration and the wide popularity of Toynbee's *Study of History*: hence also the strong academic resistance to it. Hence the growth of the influence of determinist views of history. History, told within the Marxist pattern, gives answers to all the important questions; they may not be the right answers, but to many people a definite answer is a right answer. For what they want from history is not the truth about the past – which only interests a very small minority – but ideas and directives for conduct in the present.

If such a demand exists, it is evidently more dangerous to leave it unsatisfied than to satisfy it. The great historians have rarely lost sight of their ultimate responsibility to their readers. Historicism enlarged and enriched the scholar's understanding of the past, but it left the present out of account. Dispassionate scholars to-day are vainly trying to hold a position, which they have themselves disintegrated and undermined, against the advance of the new and revived philosophies of history, which offer not a flickering and uncertain truth about the past, but plausible answers to insistent modern questions. The position can only be restored and held, as Acton saw, by the insistence on a moral standard.

1956

Social Comedy
in the Reign of Charles I

O n 2 September 1642 the London theatres were closed by an ordinance of the Lords and Commons, phrased in terms which would not have disgraced a tragedy:

> Whereas the distressed Estate of Ireland steeped in her own Blood and the distressed Estate of England threatened with a Cloud of Blood by a Civil Warre, call for all possible meanes to appease and avert the wrath of God appearing in these Judgments . . . and whereas publike Sports doe not well agree with publike Calamities, nor publike Stage playes with the Seasons of Humiliation, this being an Exercise of sad and pious solemnity, and the other being Spectacles of pleasure, too commonly expressing lascivious Mirth and Levitie: it is therefore thought fit and ordeined by the Lords and Commons in this Parliament Assembled, that while these sad Causes and set times of Humiliation doe continue publike Stage playes shall cease and bee forborne.

There was as much policy as moral reprobation in the decision of Parliament to close the theatres. Political and social comment, by no means always favourable to the government, had become increasingly common on the stage during the first half of the seventeenth century. During the Ship Money disputes Massinger had put these words into the mouth of a tyrannous King:

> *Moneys? We'll raise supplies what ways we please,*
> *And force you to subscribe to blanks in which*
> *We'll mulct you as we shall think fit.*

Before the play was licensed the King marked this in the margin: 'This is too insolent and to be changed' so that the offending words never reached the public, but it is an interesting comment on the amount of liberty allowed to dramatists that Massinger introduced them at all. On other occasions the King's policy had come under open criticism from the theatre. During the religious troubles with Scotland the players at the Fortune Theatre introduced into one of their plays a mockery of the Laudian ritual which was received with great enthusiasm by the audience until the government prohibited the performance and confiscated the properties. Undeterred, the company retaliated by putting on a play called *The Valiant Scot* which dealt with the heroic resistance of Sir William Wallace to Edward I. The modern analogy was perfectly understood by the Londoners who sympathized with the Scots in their current rebellion against King Charles and the Laudian liturgy.

Since the accession of King Charles I the taste for topical comedy, immensely stimulated by Ben Jonson earlier in the century, had become fully established. Dramatists like the veteran Philip Massinger and Richard Brome, the one-time servant and assiduous imitator of Ben Jonson, as well as the fashionable James Shirley and a number of lesser men, both amateurs and professionals, made use of contemporary incidents and contemporary controversies in their comedies. Davenant, in his *Platonic Lovers* (1636), Brome in his *Court Beggar* (1632), Chapman and Shirley in *The Ball* (1632) exploited subjects of current interest and Thomas Heywood in *The Late Lancashire Witches* (1634) took his material almost unaltered from the accounts of the famous witch trial in Lancashire in the previous year. The realistic representation on the stage of familiar places of public resort – as in Brome's *Covent Garden Weeded* (1632) and Shirley's *Hyde Park* (1632) – underlined the contemporary character of stage comment on manners, morals and even politics. The closing of the theatres was thus an obvious counsel of prudence on the part of Parliament when serious trouble began. Puritan prejudice against these 'sinful heathenish lewd ungodly spectacles and most pernicious corruptions' provided a moral justification for an act of policy. The players, as the abstract and brief chronicles of the time, were far too dangerous to be left at liberty to utter what they would to excitable London audiences during the Civil War.

The fifteen years before the Civil War is not one of the great epochs of English drama. The veteran Ben Jonson complained that amateurs were spoiling the stage:

> *Now each Court Hobby horse will wince in rhyme;*
> *Both learned and unlearned, all write plays.*

Shackerley Marmion, a professional playwright of a younger generation, complained of 'this licentious generation of poets' who troubled the peace of the whole town by turning everything that happened into a play. So that a scrivener could not lose his ears,

> *Nor a Justice of the Peace share with his clerk,*
> *A lord can't walk drunk with a torch before him,*
> *A gallant can't be suffer'd to pawn's breeches*
> *Or leave his cloak behind him at a tavern,*

but the poets would be writing about it. The chief sinners, in James Shirley's estimation, were the young university men who would come up to London 'like market women with dorsers full of lamentable tragedies and ridiculous comedies'.

Certainly, but for the three great plays of John Ford, the thirties were not remarkable for poetry on the stage. Both tragedy and pastoral were blown out with wordy pretentiousness and had come to depend too much on over-ingenious intrigues, on magnificent costumes and on scenic effects imitated from the masques.

> *In scene magnificent and language high*
> *And clothes worth all the rest . . .*

complained Richard Brome, thinking perhaps of the insipid works of writers like Ludovic Carlell or the courtier Sir John Suckling's absurd *Aglaura*. But Brome was hardly fair in suggesting that the clique which admired such plays had taught the public to

> *. . . despise all sportive merry wit*
> *Because some such great play has none of it.*

To judge by the number of comedies written, the demand for comedy was as strong as ever. If the public sometimes had a mind to sugared kickshaws and wished to see imaginary Kings, Queens, knights and ladies performing improbable actions, at other times it robustly clamoured for the beef and bag-pudding of topical comedy.

The comedies of this time are not of course purely topical. They share a number of stock situations and stock characters – often frank plagiarisms of Ben Jonson – with the comedies of the two previous generations and some with the comedy of all time. The pert page, the sly waiting woman, the talkative old nurse belong to comedy through the ages. The comic Justice of the Peace, and the stupid constable are peculiar to England, though not to one decade rather than another. Justice Bumpsey, Justice Testy, Justice Cockbrayne are followers in the tradition of Jonson's Overdo and Shakespeare's Shallow. If these gentlemen had fairly represented the average ability of the Justices of the time it would be hard to understand how the administration functioned, more especially if they were seconded by Constables of the line of Dogberry. Constable Busy in *A Match at Midnight* (1633) locks up 'twelve gentlewomen, our own neighbours', for being in the street after dark on their way to help a friend in labour. He will have none of their excuse for going out at night; their friend should have 'cried out at some other time'.

The comic Frenchman – usually a dancing master – the comic Dutchman, drunk and valiant, the comic Welshman, fiery and boastful but good-humoured and brave, were all popular figures. So were the low-life characters – the bawds, the cut-purses, the confidence tricksters, and the unemployed soldiers living by their wits. The last have a long pedigree in English comedy but they became more common in the comedies of the thirties just as their prototypes were becoming more common about the streets of London. England stood neutral in the wars of Germany and the Netherlands; and both, or rather all, sides recruited indifferently in the British Isles. The officer from the foreign wars, known by his 'taff'ta scarf and long estridge wing' was a familiar figure in the London taverns. The indifference of the professional to the cause which employed him was now and again the subject of comment. Young Palatine in Davenant's *The Wits* (1634) mocks a more scrupulous warrior with

> *What is't to thee, whether one Don Diego*
> *A Prince, or Hans van Holme, fritter seller*
> *Of Bombell, do conquer that parapet*
> *Redoubt or town, which thou ne'er saw'st before?*

But Justice Cockbrayne, in Brome's *Covent Garden Weeded*, probably overdid the part when he disguised himself as a soldier and boasted: 'I have seen the face of war, and serv'd in the Low Countries, though I say't, on both sides.'

While the stock types still continued popular in the reign of Charles I, the introduction of some new figures and the development, or the more frequent appearance, of certain older ones, point to the pre-occupations of the time. The decayed gentleman or dispossessed landowner (Dryground, Monylack), the city usurer (Bloodhound, Hornet, Vermin, Quicksands), the feckless courtier living by his wits, the tradesman – and occasionally the yeoman – turned gentleman, the citizen's wife with ambitions beyond her station: all these turn up with almost monotonous regularity.

The comedies do not present an exact picture of what was going on, but by the exaggeration of some elements in the social situation and emphasis on others they clearly reflect the prejudices and anxieties of the audiences who watched them. Wealth was changing hands; the structure of society was being modified by the upward thrust of yeomen and tradesmen into the gentry, while the intelligent gentry consolidated their position by engaging in trade. Examples of this shifting and coalescence of classes are repeatedly given in the comedies of this period, sometimes with a direct, sometimes with only an implied comment. 'I am a gentleman,' claims one Startup in Shirley's *Constant Maid* (1640), 'my father was a yeoman, my grandfather was a nobleman's footman.' Sir Paul Squelch, the Justice of the Peace in Brome's *Northern Lass* (1632), is the son of a rich grazier and the grandson of a ploughman. Massinger in *The City Madam* (1632) comments on the invasion of trade by the gentry:

> *masters never prospered*
> *Since gentlemen's sons grew prentices: when we look*
> *To have our business done at home, they are*
> *Abroad in the tennis court.*

But there is one surprising characteristic of the social commentary of this period. The Puritans are let off very lightly. In King James's reign Ben Jonson had dealt ruthlessly with them in *Bartholomew Fair* and in *The Alchemist*. But Zeal-of-the-land Busy, Tribulation Wholesome, and Ananias had few imitators, perhaps because it was felt that no better could be done. During King Charles's personal rule, when the anti-Puritan stage might have been expected to pursue the godly with relentless ridicule, few comic Puritans are to be found. There are references to them of course, allusions to silenced ministers, and to preaching sectaries of both sexes, mockery of their attitude to love-locks, Sunday pastimes and maypoles. But the criticism is on the whole good-natured, and lacks entirely the bitterness and bite of Jonson's attack. In Davenant's *News from Plymouth* (1635), Cable, the sea-captain wooing a widow of Puritan sympathies, tells her:

> *I know*
> *You love to frequent the silenc'd parties;*
> *Let but their lungs hold out, and I'll listen*
> *Till my ears ache.*

In case this should not prove his sincerity he gaily adds a promise to cut down his mainmast because it resembles a maypole. In Davenant's *Wits* occurs that description, much quoted by modern economic historians, of the 'weaver of Banbury that hopes to entice Heaven by singing to make him lord of twenty looms'.

Cartwright, himself an Anglican divine, makes the strongest attack on the Puritans in *The Ordinary*, but even this hardly goes beyond the bounds of good nature. In the last scene the gang of rogues who frequent 'The Ordinary' from which the play has its name decide to seek their fortunes in New England. The inhabitants, who have

> *one eye*
> *Put out with Zeal, th'other with ignorance,*

ought to be easy game. The tricksters will need only to cut their hair to the right length and

> *Nosing a little treason gainst the King,*
> *Bark something at the Bishops,*

and garnish their talk with 'now and then a root or two of Hebrew'.

It is fairly evident from this mild treatment that the public, while ready to laugh at the excesses of fanatics, was no longer in the mood to think Puritan-baiting as funny as it had been twenty years before. The King was doing too much of it and the sympathies of the Londoners were not with him.

The treatment of the Anglican clergy had scarcely altered since Shakespeare's time. The curate appears only as a comic figure or as a necessary convenience to the plot, like Sir Boniface the down-at-heel pedant who marries runaway couples in Heywood's *Wise Woman of Hogsden* (1638). Frequently he has not even a name and appears at the foot of the Dramatis Personae among servants and supers as *Curate*. When he is given a name it will be something unflattering like Quailpipe, my lord's chaplain in Brome's *The Antipodes*. His wife, when he has one, fares no better. Davenant paints her unkindly:

> *Mother Spectacles, the curate's wife*
> *Who does inveigh 'gainst curling and dyed cheeks,*
> *Heaves her devout, impatient nose at oil*
> *Of jesamine, and thinks powder of Paris more*
> *Profane than th'ashes of a Romish martyr.*

Two of the least reputable clergy appear in Cartwright as 'clubbers at the Ordinary'. Sir Christopher, a rather low-church divine whose wordy sermons Cartwright parodies in the play, declares bitterly that 'poor labourers in divinity can't earn their groat a day'. His companion, Vicar Catchmey, a 'singing man' out of a job, is equally poor and both are represented as hovering in want and bewilderment very near the brink of the criminal underworld.

This attitude to the unfortunate Anglican clergy reflects the popular opinion of the time. Lack of respect for the ministers of the established Church was quite as great a block in the path of Laudian policy as the active opposition of the Puritans.

The religious controversy was a theme too dangerous and too inflammable to be openly touched on by the dramatists. But the social problem, the changes in society, the pretensions of the new rich and the troubles of the new poor were freely discussed. Even the King's financial shifts were treated as the subject of comedy and the sale of titles provided good material for jokes.

In Shirley's *Love in a Maze* (1631) the foolish new-made knight Sir Gervase Simple is contemptuously described:

> one that has
> But newly cast his country skin, come up
> To see the fashions of the town, has crept
> Into a knighthood, which he paid for heartily,
> And, in his best clothes, is suspected
> For a gentleman.

In John Carvell's play, *The Soddered Citizen*, the title-buyer is a lord, but

> He's of our city breed . . . he bought
> His raw green honour with the overplus
> Of what his father left, of purchasing,
> Got in his shop, by 's 'What dee lack?' and fawning.

The great number of the new knights who came into being when the King, to increase his revenues, revived the old knighthood fees, could hardly pass without comment. In Brome's *The Damoiselle* these ordinary knights are compared to cob nuts –

> He was one of the cob knights in the throng
> When they were dubbed in clusters.

An unpleasant young snob in Shirley's *The Ball* (1632), who can go nowhere without boasting that he is cousin to a lord, shows his mettle by announcing:

> *I care no more for killing half a dozen knights of the*
> *Lower House, I mean that are not descended from nobility,*
> *Than I do to kick my footman.*

Davenant makes use of the royal sale of honours to mock the pretensions of ladies who elevate their chambermaids into 'waiting gentlewomen'. Widow Carrack in *News from Plymouth* tells her maid Smoothall:

> *I may make thee a gentlewoman, though thy mother*
> *Was Goody Smoothall, and do it by my lord's patent*
> *When I am a baroness: 'tis now in fashion*
> *To metamorphose chambermaids. The King*
> *Dubs knights, and new stamp't honour creates gentry.*

Neither the dramatists nor the audience held the view that rising in the world, acquiring an estate or buying a title, was in itself wrong. Worth deserved a material reward and wealth that had been honestly earned was wholly respectable. In Brome's *The Damoiselle* a citizen who has acquired gentility by acquiring land is thus defended against the criticisms of a born, but impoverished, gentleman:

> *Land lordship's real honour*
> *Though in a tradesman's son: when your fair titles*
> *Are but the shadow of your ancestry:*
> *And you walk in 'em, when your land is gone*
> *Like the pale ghosts of dead nobility.*

But the honest acquisition of wealth as a theme, the success story of the old Dick Whittington variety, was out of fashion. On the contrary plays were now more often written on the theme of successful dishonesty, as in Mayne's *City Wit* or Davenant's *The Wits*.

Bewildered as they usually were by the operations of capitalism

which surrounded them, the dramatists and the great majority of
the audience were disposed to think that any transaction by which
money was made to multiply, without the labour of the owner,
must be dishonest. Usurers, goldsmiths, lawyers, scriveners and
all such as dealt in loans and mortgages, were natural villains on
the stage.

> *That man who has the readiest way to cheat*
> *Wins all the glory, wealth, esteem, grows great,*

reflects the villainous goldsmith in Carvell's *Soddered Citizen*. He
next enters into an ingenious plot with a friend. They will buy an
estate jointly. One of them will then dispose of it to some unsus-
pecting innocent. After the sale, the other will make his appearance
with title deeds showing that the estate was jointly owned and has
been sold without his permission. The victim will be forced either
to relinquish the estate or to buy him out. In either case there will
be proceeds to share.

The most famous of all the blood-suckers is the veteran
Massinger's tremendous creation, Sir Giles Overreach, the dark,
overshadowing villain of *A New Way to Pay Old Debts* (*c.*1623).
Beside him, financiers like Brome's Vermin and Shirley's Hornet
are mere pygmies. Massinger, whose boldness, force and colour
belonged to an earlier generation of dramatists, was a much
more violent satirist than the younger men who rose to fame
in the 1630s. Overreach shared his Christian name and some of
his characteristics with Sir Giles Mompesson, a financier once
greatly favoured at Court, who had been attacked by Parliament
and had crashed to ruin in 1621. One of the relatively few references
to enclosure occurs in this play, where Overreach is described as
'the grand incloser of what was common'. The younger generation
of dramatists tended to write almost exclusively about London,
where enclosure was not a topic of the first interest. Massinger
and his generation still drew on the whole countryside for their
themes, and Overreach is not a city figure, but one of the new
financier-landowners who, by fair or foul practices, were building
up large estates in the country.

Overreach, like all the successful rich men of the epoch, has to establish his social position and plans to do so by marrying his daughter to a lord. To make certain of this alliance he suggests to the girl that she should lure the lord into a compromising position so that he can be compelled to marry her. The girl's innocence and the lord's shining virtue prevent any such thing happening and Overreach is effectively over-reached in the last act.

The theme of intermarriage between the children of the self-made and the decaying nobility and gentry could be, and was, variously handled. James Shirley, in *The Witty Fair One* (1628) expressed pity for the young women and contempt for those who sought this way of bolstering up their fortunes:

> *not a virgin*
> *Left by her friends heir to a noble fortune*
> *But she's in danger of a marriage*
> *To some puffed title.*

A character in Shackerley Marmion's *A Fine Companion* takes a more severely practical view: 'Why, sir, your citizens' widows are the only rubbish [i.e. rubble] of the kingdom, to fill up the breaches of the decayed houses.' Celestina in Shirley's *Lady of Pleasure* (1635), a young rich widow herself, although anxious not to be carried off too soon, has no great aversion to the probable fate which will overtake her, when the court gentleman

> *Claps in with his gilt coach and Flandrian trotters*
> *And hurries her away to be a countess.*

William Davenant, a courtier, regrets the necessity which compels the 'female issue of our decay'd nobility' to

> *quarter arms with the City*
> *And match with saucy haberdashers' sons.*

The opportunities for comedy afforded by the more innocent and more absurd pretensions of the new rich, and especially their wives, were freely exploited. In Massinger's *City Madam* (1632), the rich citizen's wife has turned her house into a little court. She will have only French or Italian cooks to dress her meat and scorns her poor husband who thinks he has done very well in engaging the Lord Mayor's cook to prepare her a banquet. When three sucking pigs, fattened on muscadine and costing twenty marks apiece, are set on the table she waves them away as not good enough for her. Her husband expostulates with her on her extravagance, reminding her of earlier days when

> *you wore*
> *Satin on solemn days, a chain of gold,*
> *A velvet hood, rich borders, and sometimes*
> *A dainty miniver cap, a silver pin*
> *Headed with a pearl worth threepence, and thus far*
> *You were privileged and no man envied it:*
> *It being for the City's honour that*
> *There should be a distinction between*
> *The wife of a patrician and plebian.*

But now with her 'Hungerland bands and Spanish quellio ruffs' his wife will be as fine as a Court lady: she spends forty pounds on a nightgown and when she receives her gossips after lying-in has the baby in a rich canopied crib like a young prince. The dramatists usually saw to it that such proud ladies ended humble and penitent, well content to go back to their miniver caps, velvet hoods and threepenny pearls.

Massinger's *City Madam*, like Chapman and Marston's *Eastward Ho* a generation earlier, developed, with modern trappings, the time-honoured theme of the over-proud woman. But a new element was introduced into the treatment of city wives by the younger generation of dramatists. The citizen's wife is now not merely pretentious, but anxious to show her quality by having a lord for a lover. This was not difficult to manage because the young sparks at the Court were – the dramatists of the thirties are wonderfully in agreement on the subject – very willing to seduce a citizen's wife so that they might get their hands into her husband's coffers. The first step was usually to smuggle her into the gallery at a Court masque and make love to her in the dark.

A city beauty of this kind, Alice Saleware, in Brome's *The Mad*

Couple Well Match'd (*c.*1638), sits in her husband's shop 'more glorious than the Maidenhead in the Mercer's Arms, the Non-pareil, the Paragon of the City, the Flower de Luce of Cheap-side . . .' She has several Court admirers and she cleverly persuades her doting husband that if he wishes to appear like a gentleman he must not hang over her all the time or even share a room with her – 'that were most uncourtly'. Her plans are, however, brought to nothing by an unexpected turn of events. Her Court lover becomes virtuous.

The reputation of King Charles's Court and of elegant society in general is somewhat ambiguously reflected in these plays. Prynne's attack on the morality of the stage and his supposed reflection on the Queen in *Histriomastix* (1633) caused both Brome and Shirley to come to the defence of their own profession and of the innocent amusements of the Court. Prynne had de-clared 'delight and skill in dancing a badge of lewd lascivious women and strumpets'. Several of Shirley's plays seem designed to do little else but prove the contrary to be the case, and even Brome, who was far less favourable to the Court than Shirley, introduced a scene into his *Sparagus Garden* (1635) with the sole purpose of defending the reputation of the Court.

Sparagus Garden was an expensive pleasure ground on the south bank of the river, where asparagus and fresh strawberries were served, with sugar and wine, at exorbitant prices. The place had walks, lawns and arbours, and private rooms could be hired in the adjoining eating houses. The Garden had a dubious repu-tation but was patronized by some of the Court. Brome in his play brings the usual gang of tricksters, gulls and citizens' wives to this resort. They are at once much impressed to see three Court ladies – 'Every lady with her own husband: what a virtuous, honest age is this'. Shortly after, the Court party reappears; they engage in dull conversation, and dance a stately measure 'to help digestion'. The dance ended, one lady priggishly cries out that she sees some 'wicked ones' approaching, to which her virtuous gallant replies:

> *May the example of our harmless mirth*
> *And civil recreation purge the place*

> *Of all foul purposes . . .*
> *We seek not to abridge their privilege*
> *Nor can their ill hurt us; we are safe.*

If Brome had depicted any more of the Court's 'harmless mirth' in this style he would soon have brought it into ridicule, but this type of scene – which is apparently intended seriously – does not recur.

Shirley, a more consistent defender of the royal reputation and policy than Brome, offers a well-deserved compliment to the King and Queen in his *The Lady of Pleasure*. His heroine, congratulating a courtier-rake on his reform, attributes it to the truth and innocence

> *which shine*
> *So bright in the two royal luminaries:*
> *At Court you cannot lose your way to chastity.*

This high opinion of the Court was not shared by the Londoners in general. It must be remembered that most of the eulogies of King Charles's Court, with which we are familiar, were written after the King's death when its virtues shone all the more brightly by comparison with the disorders of the exile and the Court of Charles II. This posthumous reputation makes it difficult to form a dispassionate estimate of the opinion in which contemporaries held it, but comedies, especially Shirley's, throw an interesting light on the question.

Many of these comedies turn on the misinterpretation or slandering of innocence. This is a time-worn theme, but when it was used by the playwrights of an earlier generation the innocent person was almost invariably the victim of a plot – like the unfortunate Hero in *Much Ado*. In plays of the 1630s, on the other hand, the innocent have only themselves to blame: they persistently conduct themselves with an indiscretion that cannot but cause comment, and indulge in the most dubious manoeuvres. The young people of *The Ball*, *The Lady of Pleasure*, *Love in a Maze*, all behave with the utmost freedom and pour scorn on the malicious comments of a censorious world.

Celestina, the young widow in *The Lady of Pleasure*, takes a house in the Strand and announces her intention of leading a gay but virtuous life. She encourages admirers and when one of them ventures on a dishonourable proposal she magnificently turns the tables on him in a scene plagiarized from that between Bertram and Diana in *All's Well*. She suggests that he should sell his coat-of-arms and when he indignantly refuses, declares that her honour, like his, cannot be bought and sold:

> *think, think, my lord,*
> *To what you would unworthily betray me,*
> *If you would not, for price of gold or pleasure,*
> *(If that be more your idol) lose the glory*
> *And painted honour of your house.*

In *The Gamester* an unfaithful husband is reformed by being deceived into a belief that his virtuous wife has been unfaithful too. She herself is a cheerfully consenting party to this deception which goes on for several acts. The plot is an adaptation from a story in *The Heptameron*, but Charles I himself seems to have suggested it to Shirley for a play and he was delighted with the way in which Shirley had handled it. In Brome's *The Damoiselle* an impoverished knight advertises a raffle of his daughter and sells tickets at twenty pounds apiece. This unspeakable conduct turns out to be an ingenious trick to collect a dowry for her while making her beauty and innocence shine the brighter.

The theme which emerges from all these complicated intrigues is simply that virtue and innocence are to be judged by the inward intention, not by the outward appearance. This idea was the foundation of the practice of Platonic love which had recently come from France and was fashionable at Court. In Davenant's *Platonic Lovers*, which makes light-hearted fun of the convention, the avowed Platonic lovers, Theander and Eurithea, are allowed to be in each other's company at all hours unchaperoned without giving rise to scandal because they are

> *lovers of a pure*
> *Celestial kind, such as some style Platonical,*
> *A new court epithet scarce understood:*

> *But all they woo, sir, is the spirit, face,*
> *And heart: therefore their conversation is*
> *More safe to fame.*

Platonic love was all very well at Court where the conventions were accepted, but it made a very different impression outside the charmed circle, and the Queen's willingness to be the central star in this whole planetary system of courtly love gave rise to a great deal of groundless gossip and malicious scandal.

On the stage, at least by the conventions of the time, the innocent had only to declare themselves for all slanders to vanish away. In real life it was not so, and the misunderstandings which thickened about King Charles, his Queen and his Court during his personal rule played their part in undermining the position and power of the Crown.

The extravagance of the Court was another cause for complaint. Courtiers were not noted for punctuality in meeting their obligations, and the special privileges which protected them from arrest for debt were very unpopular. A similar privilege, protecting members of Parliament came to be hated no less bitterly after 1640. Davenant set his play *The Unfortunate Lovers* in an imaginary Italy, but the experiences, and the conversation, of the gay young courtier Rampino belong none the less to Whitehall. In the first act, he shows some visitors over the palace, asking them to walk boldly and not slink about or they will be taken for city spies trying to collect debts. Later, when he cannot pay his tailor, Friskin, he offers to get him court preferment, and perhaps a rocker's place to the next young prince or princess for the sempstress to whom he also owes money. The tailor, a man of ambition, is delighted with this and begins at once to boast of the future glories of the House of Friskin.

It was a serious weakness in King Charles and in some of his advisers – notably the Earl of Strafford – not to realize that a bad reputation, however undeserved, and a scandal, however baseless, can be dangerous to the government. They persistently tried to suppress criticism, where they should have removed its causes.

The King, and his father before him, had always striven to prevent their subjects from indulging in 'idle talk', in loose or scandalous speeches. But Charles appears to have believed that the ordinary tendency of human nature to speculate on public affairs, or on the private affairs of public men, could be stifled by stopping up the sources through which the public gained its information. Without news, he calculated, there could be no gossip about public affairs. When criticism of his foreign policy became too vocal, he accordingly prohibited the importation of the foreign newsletters, the *corantoes*, out of which his people gleaned their knowledge of what went on in the great world. (With a far clearer understanding of human nature, Cardinal Richelieu at the same time in France took charge of the press and fed it plentifully with such news as he wished the people to have. King Charles only learnt this trick during the Civil War when he began to publish an official newspaper, *Mercurius Aulicus*, at Oxford.)

The prohibition of the *corantoes* and the discouragement of newspapers generally are several times mentioned in contemporary plays. Lucina, in *The Ball*, declares scornfully that people with nothing better to do will fall back on private scandal 'when *corantoes* fail'. Thomas Heywood, in the prologue to *The Late Lancashire Witches* excuses himself for taking up this domestic and local theme, because of the lack of more significant subjects –

> *Corantoes failing, and no foot post late*
> *Possessing us with news of foreign state.*

That the news in the *corantoes* was inadequate and often false was generally known – Ben Jonson had mocked at them in an earlier generation – but they provided a contact with the outside world, they fed the public interest in the fate of the Protestant Cause in Europe and they were extremely popular. Therefore they continued to be smuggled into the country and were supplemented by handwritten sheets, circulated by enterprising newsmongers. Some of the sources used by these underhand journalists were moderately reliable; most were not. Shirley declared that your professional journalist 'will write you a battle in any part of Europe at an hour's warning, and yet never set foot out of a tavern'.

Davenant devoted the sub-plot in *News from Plymouth* to discrediting the newsmonger. Sir Solomon Trifle, a Justice of the

Peace, supplements his income by compiling a newsletter which he distributes through various agents, one of whom is a Puritan called Zeal. When his creatures call on him, he explains his manner of business to a friend:

> They come for news; man's nature's greedy of it.
> We wise men forge it, and the credulous vulgar,
> Our instruments, disperse it . . .
> News of all sorts and sizes, I have studied hard
> And from the general courants and gazettes,
> Public and private, letters from all parts
> Of Christendom, though they speak contraries,
> Weigh'd and reduc'd them to such certainties
> That I dare warrant 'em authentical
> Under my hand and seal . . .

His authentical news follows:

> Rome is taken
> By the ships of Amsterdam, and the Pope himself
> To save his life turn'd Brownist . . .
> . . . The Spanish fleet
> That anchor'd off Gibraltar, is sunk
> By the French horse . . .
> . . . From the Low Countries
> Antwerp is plundered, Brussels burnt, the cannon
> Brought before Lovaine, and the Prince of Orange
> Stands to be Emperor.

At this point the sceptical listener interrupts:

> The Emperor lives!

Not in the least put out, Sir Solomon continues:

> But is to die the tenth of October next,
> And he has it in reversion. From France:
> Rochelle recovered by the Huguenots,

And the fifth July last, yes, 'tis the fifth,
The Cardinal Richelieu as he slept in his tent,
Had his head cut off with an invisible sword
By the Great Constable's ghost.

This monstrous newsmonger is very properly arrested in the last act for holding unlawful intelligence with foreign princes. Less properly, he is threatened with the rack to divulge his sources of information.

James Shirley as well as the courtier playwrights and most of the university amateurs – Davenant, Mayne, Cartwright – supported the royal policies in so far as they mentioned them at all. Massinger and Brome on the other hand could be critical, Massinger sometimes so broadly – as in the case of the King's demands for money mentioned before – that the offending passage had to be deleted. Brome in *The Court Beggar* took up the abuse of monopolies and patents, which was one of the King's most fruitful ways of raising money during his unparliamentary rule. The satire is conceived in general terms and owes a great deal – as Brome usually does – to his master's, Jonson's, treatment of a similar subject in *The Devil Is an Ass*. The Parliament of 1624 had made monopolies illegal, but they had crept in again under the transparent disguise of patents. Monopoly rights were granted to those who claimed to have some special process or invention or some interesting experimental scheme for trade or industry. Projects, as they were called, were put forward in great numbers by hangers-on of the Court. In Brome's play a country knight, Sir Andrew Mendicant, comes to London and wastes his fortune trying to procure a grant of this kind. The Court is represented as being surrounded by sharks who will, for a consideration, suggest hopeful schemes to men like Sir Andrew and share the proceeds with him, if he can get a grant to operate them. These 'projectors', who follow Sir Andrew about in a babbling chorus, have plans which they assert will bring in fifty thousand pounds a year to them, twice as much to Sir Andrew, and £64,783 7s 9d to the Crown. When one of them is asked to change a shilling for two sixpences he has no ready money about him. This, to an audience who still had the gravest suspicion of all credit transactions, was proof positive that the fellow was a fraud.

Among the projects suggested to Sir Andrew is a monopoly of wig-making in the interests of the nation's health, an imposition of a fourpenny tax on any gallant wearing a new fashion on the first day he puts it on, and the establishment of a floating theatre on barges in the Thames so that the watermen may get back some of the custom recently lost to hackney coachmen and the carriers of sedan chairs.

Brome covered himself for this attack on one aspect of the royal policy by strongly defending another part of it in his play. The King in 1632 had issued a proclamation forbidding country gentlemen to come to London except on business. Sir Andrew Mendicant, who is one of these absentee landlords, is upbraided by his daughter for having abandoned his rural seat:

> *Your aim has been to raise*
> *Your state by court suits, begging as some call it,*
> *And for that course you left your country life*
> *To purchase wit at Court . . .*
> *And for the exchange of a fair mansion house,*
> *Large fruitful fields, rich meadows and sweet pastures,*
> *Well cropped with corn and stocked as well with cattle,*
> *A park well stored with deer too and fish ponds in't,*
> *And all this for a lodging in the Strand . . .*

Shirley, with considerable eloquence, in several comedies depicts the folly of country gentlemen and their wives who waste their fortunes in London. But though he can write persuasively of the pleasures of the countryside, he knew the other side of the question. Lady Bornwell, newly arrived in London with her husband, exclaims:

> *I would not*
> *Endure again the country conversation*
> *To be lady of six shires! The men*
> *So near the primitive making they retain*
> *A sense of nothing but the earth; their brains*
> *And barren heads standing as much in want*
> *Of ploughing as their ground. To hear a fellow*

> *Make himself merry and his horse with whistling*
> *Sellenger's Round! To observe with what solemnity*
> *They keep their wakes and throw for pewter candlesticks!*

To leave the boredom of the country was one thing, but there was no need to run to the other extreme, and Lady Bornwell's husband complains with some reason of

> *Your charge of gaudy furniture, and pictures*
> *Of this Italian master and that Dutchman,*
> *Your mighty looking glasses, like artillery*
> *Brought home on engines . . .*
> *Fourscore pound suppers for my lord your kinsman,*
> *Banquets for t'other lady aunt and cousins,*
> *And perfumes that exceed all: train of servants*
> *To stifle us at home, and shew abroad*
> *More motley than the French or the Venetian*
> *About your coach . . .*
> *I could accuse the gaiety of your wardrobe*
> *And prodigal embroideries, under which*
> *Rich satins, plushes, cloth of silver dare*
> *Not show their own complexions . . .*

The lure of the town sometimes reached the rich yeoman. In Brome's *Sparagus Garden* the foolish Tim Hoyden from Ta'anton arrives with 'four hundred pounds, sir, I brought it up to town on purpose to make myself a cleare gentlemen of it'. He falls at once into the hands of the decayed knight Moneylack who, under pretence of teaching him the ways of the world, removes most of it. Starvation on what he is assured is court fare provokes a spirit of rebellion in Hoyden: 'Marry, I feel that I am hungry, and that my shrimp diet and sippings have almost famished me and my purse too; slid, I dare be sworn, as I am almost a gentleman, that every bit and spoonful that I have swallowed these ten days, has cost me ten shillings at least.'

Crosswill, the captious country gentleman in *Covent Garden Weeded*, gets off more lightly. His humour being always to cross everyone, he came up to London because 'the Proclamation of

Restraint spurred him on'. But he was very well able to take care of himself when he got there.

The theme of this play is a direct imitation of Ben Jonson's *Bartholomew Fair*, modernized and made topical by being transferred to the new and much talked of region of Covent Garden. Cockbrayne, a Middlesex Justice of the Peace, who describes himself as a near relation of Justice Overdo of *Bartholomew Fair*, disguises himself and mingles with the inhabitants of Covent Garden in order to discover and reform their sins. He meets with much the same adventures and misfortunes as did Justice Overdo at *Bartholomew Fair*. Brome's play falls behind Jonson's in every respect, but it has a bustling liveliness and is full of topical allusions. In the first scene Justice Cockbrayne admires the new buildings:

I, marry sir! This is something like! These appear like buildings! Here's architecture expressed indeed! It is a most sightly situation and fit for gentry and nobility! . . . Yond magnificent piece the Piazzo, will excel that at Venice, by hearsay, (I ne'er travelled). A hearty blessing on their brains, honours and wealths that are projectors, furtherers and performers of such great works . . . The Surveyor (whoe'er he was) has manifested himself the master of this great Art. How he has wedded strength to beauty, state to uniformity, commodiousness with perspicuity. All, all as't should be.

The inhabitants, however, are not all as they should be and Justice Cockbrayne's expedition among them does little to improve them. Although the nobility and gentry hastened to take houses in Covent Garden as soon as it was built, so did the fashionable ladies of pleasure. Soon the new Covent Garden rivalled the Strand as the place where richly dressed young women, alluringly seated on balconies could

> *angle up*
> *The gay peripatetics of the Court.*

The setting of comedies in recognizable places was obviously an attraction to audiences, especially no doubt to those who either could not afford, or did not like, to venture in such places themselves. From the opening scene of *Covent Garden Weeded* it is clear that the buildings must have been represented on the stage – 'these appear like buildings'. No doubt the walks and arbours of *Sparagus Garden* were also fairly well imitated on the stage for that play too, so that citizens who could not afford the prices charged at such a resort could get a very good idea of what it was like for their sixpenny or twelvepenny seat at the theatre.

Shirley attempted great realism in his representation of a race meeting in his play *Hyde Park* (1632). The runners in the foot race – one of whom is called by the name of a famous Irish champion – actually cross the stage twice. Although Shirley could hardly do the same when it came to a horse race, he contrives in the dialogue to give a wonderfully vivid impression of the mounting tension as the race is run. The audience could hear the seventeenth-century equivalent of the cry 'They're off!' and listen to the shortening odds shouted by excited gamblers as the race was run. The excitement spreads to a group of ladies in the front of the stage who begin to lay bets among themselves –

> *What odds against my lord! –*
> *Silk stockings –*
> *To a pair of perfum'd gloves? I take it –*
> *Done. I'll have them Spanish scent –*
> *The stockings shall be scarlet. If you choose your scent I'll choose*
>   *my colour.*

Gambling ladies were probably not approved of by the majority of the audience but that would merely add spice to the scene. Incidentally, Shirley has another gambling lady in his play *The Example* (1634). The representation and the description of extravagant and fashionable pleasures are a marked feature of these plays which, in taste as well as time, stand midway between the Elizabethan and Restoration drama. Restoration drama is directed to a society audience which itself indulged in expensive pleasures, took them for granted and needed no explanations. But the public of the 1630s was still the mixed public for which Shakespeare had written. The explanatory character of some of the descriptions in Shirley, Brome, and others suggests that in their time it was a popular function of the theatre to provide the humbler members of this mixed audience with glimpses of a 'high life' which was something of a mystery to them and of which they already in some measure disapproved.

Another fashionable craze, more innocent than gambling and racing, which figures in the comedies, was that of collecting. The serious interest in antiquarianism of the later sixteenth and early seventeenth century had by this time spread to less scholarly enthusiasts, who fell an easy prey to fraudulent pedlars of antiques. Veterano, in Marmion's *The Antiquary*, was such a one, although he begins sensibly enough with the statement that ancient things 'are the registers, the chronicles of the age they were made in, and speak the truth of history better than a hundred of your printed commentaries'. He talks like a good book but behaves like a fool; on being offered a very dilapidated manuscript he recognizes it at once as one of the lost books of the *Republic* penned by Cicero's own hand.

Cartwright introduces an antiquary into *The Ordinary*. He has been deeply infected with the current passion for Anglo-Saxon studies and uses such phrases as 'I ween' and 'Waes hale' in his conversation. From his lips comes the faked folk rhyme which of recent years has been a popular subject for poker work in Olde Tea Shoppes, being – who knows? – perhaps taken for the genuine article.

> *St Francis and St Benedight*
> *Blesse this house from wicked wight*
> *From the Nightmare and the Goblin*
> *That is hight good fellow Robin.*
> *Keep it from all evil spirits,*
> *Fayries, Weezels, Rats and Ferrets,*
> *From Curfew time*
> *To the next prime.*

These comedies are light, frivolous, essentially ephemeral stuff and their charm lies in the incidental intelligence that they give of the things of everyday life in this period of calm before the Civil Wars.

Those who lived through that epoch were in later life to look back on the halcyon days before 1642 with much the same nostalgia that some now living feel for the legendary time before 1914. The survivors of the Civil Wars, of whatever party, could not but feel that those lost years, which had in truth been restless, depressed and rather unhappy, had been infinitely sweet. In retrospect the inestimable blessing of peace made that whole epoch bright. 'God Almighty send us a happy end of all our troubles and peace in this poor kingdom again'; Sir Thomas Knyvett writing in the midst of the Civil Wars uttered the prayer that was in the hearts of most honest Englishmen.

Something of this feeling about the interlude before the Civil War inevitably communicates itself to the historian. That epoch has the air of heightened peace and stillness which belongs to a time immediately preceding catastrophe. We know that there was much amiss, that there was distress and unemployment, trouble over enclosures, persecution of the Puritans, a bad run of plague in London and much else to darken those years. But there was also much poetry, much singing, wakes, whitsun ales and harvest festivals, jollity in taverns, learned talk in common rooms; crops ripened and were garnered in peace and the housewife and husbandman need fear no enemies save the weather and the gypsies. Life went on normally from day to day with no more than the ordinary anxieties and pleasures. England was by no means all a sunlit garden but there was a kind of truth in Marvell's poignant cry:

> Oh thou that dear and happy isle
> The garden of the world erewhile
> Thou Paradise of the four seas
> Which heaven planted us to please . . .
> Unhappy! shall we never more
> That sweet militia restore,
> When gardens only had their towers
> And all the garrisons were flowers,
> When roses only arms might bear
> And men did rosy garlands wear?

The beauty of these plays is that they fix, in phrase after phrase, the vivid ephemeral details of that time, the ordinary pleasures which became so sweet in retrospect simply because they were ordinary: the holiday expeditions to 'the city outleaps', Islington, Newington, Paddington, Kensington, to eat prunes and cream; the busy bustle of Hyde Park on a summer afternoon with a milk-maid leading round her red cow to offer drinks to the ladies, and the gentlemen sending their pages hurrying to 'Grave Maurice's Head' for ale; the 'booths and bagpipes upon Banstead downs' – though these we have still; the country bumpkins throwing for pewter candlesticks; the citizen's wife bringing her baby home from nurse with her coach stuffed with hampers of fruit and cheese cakes; the common hangings on the walls, The Prodigal Son and the Story of St Joseph; the thumbed copy of Foxe's *Martyrs* on the country gentleman's hall table for his tenantry to read while waiting. Out of the comedies we can hear the long-silenced voices talking of everyday things; laughing at the new portable chairs – 'the hand-barrows, what call you 'em? – Sedans; marvelling at the handsome pocket watches – 'you have not a gentleman that's a true gentleman without one'; the worldly ladies shopping in the Dutch shops of the New Exchange; the godly ladies trooping to church each with her prayer-book in its green dimity bag.

Take away the improbable intrigues and the ingenious entanglements, and a whole society with its pretty pleasures and preoccupations starts into life from the pages of these comedies. It is their real claim on our remembrance; the best that can be said of them was said by Alexander Brome, writing commendatory verses to the plays of his namesake Richard during the Commonwealth:

> *we may be glad*
> *To see and think on the happiness we had*

1955

Reflections on the Great Civil War

I. Edgehill, October 23rd, 1642

Edgehill rises sharply out of the rural uplands of Warwick-shire, commanding, from the neo-gothic tower which absurdly crowns its height, one of the loveliest and most typical views in the country. Below the steep summit stretching away from the smooth lower slopes on which Prince Rupert's cavalry champed in line, lies, distance beyond distance, the green park-like expanse of Warwickshire irrelevantly scored with quick-set hedges and narrow lanes, scattered with compact woodlands, starred here and there with those single magnificent trees which are so particular a feature of our countryside. I know of no part of England which the autumn visits with a more splendid glory, where the tenuous October sunlight touches more exquisitely the varying gold and green and brown of tree and hedgerow and field. It is a few miles only from Shakespeare's country, in the very heart of England.

The Battle of Edgehill was fought on an autumn afternoon, on 23 October 1642. It is not generally regarded as an important battle; text-books dismiss it as indecisive, and indecisive in a sense it was. For eighteen months before, the differences between King Charles I and his Parliament had slithered with disastrous rapidity from argument to defiance and from defiance to declared war. After a summer spent recruiting, the King had more or less de-cided to march on London, whence in the previous January he had fled, leaving Parliament in triumphant occupation. So here he was in the mild October weather riding disconsolately across the Midlands at the head of an army. As usual, painfully racked between two alternatives, he contemplated sometimes the forcible occupation of the capital and the silencing of the Commons and at others a compromise settlement. At Edgehill he found himself suddenly faced with the alternative in all its shocking nakedness. Here was, from the military point of view, the big opportunity. Prince Rupert, his nephew, who had turned out quite by chance to be a born general, had outflanked the Parliamentary army under Essex and installed the King's troops on the summit of Edgehill in a position to deliver a shattering blow. The Parliamentary army, at that time even more amateurish than the King's, lay sprawled in the uneven country below; if it could be put out of action the road to London would be comparatively clear. The Civil War would be over by Christmas.

But Rupert and the few other professional soldiers on either side had failed to understand the extraordinary nature of the conflict in which they found themselves engaged. At that time only a minority on either side wanted to deliver a smashing blow at anyone. The greater number were still uncertain whether they wanted to fight at all, and a considerable proportion had not even made up their minds conclusively as to which side they were on. The King's standard-bearer, Sir Edmund Verney, was in a typical state of anxiety and doubt: his eldest son was sitting in Parliament at Westminster. He was not the only one whose family had been torn in pieces by the war, for it was a period at which men's consciences were highly individual and uncomfortably active.

The King had reproduced the uncertainty in his own mind by dividing the command of his troops. Rupert, theoretically Lieutenant-General of the Horse, was in active command only on the right wing. The left was under Wilmot, a pleasant, indolent young man with a smattering of military experience and a fairly evident desire not to annoy Parliament too much, lest Parliament should win. The commandership-in-chief, so far as there was one at all, was supposed to belong to an elderly soldier of fortune, Patrick Ruthven, who, in the days before he became stone deaf, had been quartermaster-general to Gustavus Adolphus.

The battle therefore lacked any coherent plan. Rupert's initial charge drove the Parliamentary left wing off the field, but there was considerable delay in re-forming his newly recruited and untrained troops, and meanwhile the infantry in the centre, commanded with equal courage and almost equal inefficiency on both sides, were locked in a life and death struggle. Rupert's return relieved the situation, but although a few of the Royalist officers argued that a new attack on the exhausted and half-scattered enemy would be decisive, the majority felt that there had been enough fighting for one day. The occasion once lost never recurred. The battle of Edgehill was thus not so indecisive as it appeared, for never again was the King to have so evident an opportunity of ending the war at a stroke.

Edgehill was the first important engagement in a struggle which was to last intermittently for ten years, and was to fire and crystallize those rival theories of government which had been locked in bloodless conflict for the last quarter of a century. The ideas involved were fundamentally simple: absolutism against representative government. Was Parliament to develop as the legislative body of the kingdom, or was it to be transformed into a mere advisory committee with no coercive power? The issue has been confused by those writers who have recently pointed out that King Charles was on the whole an enlightened and benevolent ruler (making allowance for the occasional ear-croppings of his Court of Star Chamber), while Parliament, far from representing the people, was a fairly close oligarchy of the landed and monied class. The exercise of the representative principle in 1642 meant the representation of propertied men by a number of their own magnates and a hand-picked selection of their younger sons.

The Civil War was certainly no struggle of the people against the Crown; it was in a different tradition from the national and proletarian revolts of the nineteenth and twentieth centuries. Yet the principles involved are fundamental to government, as fundamental now as then. The struggle may not have been in the modern sense 'democratic', yet had it not happened or had it ended differently, the history of democracy in Europe, and far beyond Europe, would have changed. For this war saved the principle of representative government, and saved it in that very country whose language and whose people were to be one of the great vitalizing forces of the New World. It was at this period, the period when men in England thought it worth while to fight for the representative principle, that the New England colonies were being founded, by the fathers and sons and brothers of the men fighting in England.

Had King Charles won the war in that first campaign, would the principle have survived? It is dangerous to speculate on might-have-beens, yet the survival of effective representative government after a Royalist victory would have been improbable, and if the principle had gone under in England, as it did in so many other European countries at about this time, what might not have happened on the far side of the Atlantic? It is instructive to compare the history of the Spanish and the French Empires in America with that of the English colonies. These became a nation through rightly interpreting the political principles which the mother country had established a century earlier, and which, owing to the drag of certain reactionary forces, she had illogically failed to extend to her children.

Much then may have depended on this unfinished and indecisive battle. At the close of the day when the Royalist commanders were discussing the possibility of a renewed attack, the casual Henry Wilmot argued that quite enough had been done: and it was time to pause and 'enjoy the fruits thereof'. In a sense of which Henry Wilmot never dreamed, men unborn and lands unknown were to enjoy the fruits thereof.

In our rather shamefaced attempts to advertise our country to the foreigner, we make too little of the Civil War. It happened of course a very long time ago – though not so long ago as Joan of Arc or William the Silent, who are, or were, emphatically honoured in their own countries; and not nearly so long ago as the proto-German Arminius. It happened, perhaps unfortunately, at a period whose fashions in dress lend themselves to romantic treatment, so that in the popular mind this Cavalier-and-Roundhead business has degenerated into a clashing-sword accompaniment to many a stirring love drama. It even went abroad in this form and in the nineteenth century reached the Italian operatic stage in *I Puritani*. Measures of counter-action do not seem to have been strong enough. It is true that English historians have treated the conflict with dignity and at length and that the text-books have built it firmly and, on the whole, correctly into the fabric of constitutional development. But there, as far as the general public are concerned, it remains – fossilized, an antique.

Yet its very antiquity is all the more cause for admiration. Is it not worthy of comment that the English contrived to fight so remarkably *adult* a war at a time when no other people in Europe seem to have been, politically, more than adolescent? Compare this struggle with the pointless horror of Germany's coeval Thirty Years War, with the *mesquineries* of the Fronde, with the spasmodic, unconstructive separatist outbursts in contemporary Spain and Italy. The English Civil War is set apart from these by the more adult consciousness of the participants. Men that 'made some conscience of what they did', Cromwell said; but the description fitted many of the Royalist soldiers, no less. Chillingworth wittily deplored the fact that all the scribes and pharisees were on one side, all the publicans and sinners on the other; but it was a half-truth only, for pharisees and sinners there will always be in all conflicts. What distinguishes the English Civil War is the astonishing prevalence of plain sincerity on both sides. Moreover, the combatants never wholly lost sight of the purpose of the war; they were fighting for the better governance of England, and they never forgot that they must learn to live in peace hereafter with the men who were ranged against them. It would be absurd to pretend that there were no savage incidents, no persecution of the defeated, no acts of vengeance. There were all these. But they never became ends in themselves, never submerged the higher purpose of both parties.

Any detailed study of the combatants, any inquiry into their private lives, reveals the absurdity of those theories which explain the Civil War as a blockish alignment of class or interest. Men followed their beliefs with an independent fidelity; no class, no group, no family that was not split along the line of personal conviction. The 'money-power' in which some recent writers have tried to mask the parliamentarian party simply did not exist as a united political unit. Its representatives are to be found both at the King's right hand and tub-thumping with the Levellers. There were of course the usual number of time-servers, scoundrels, profiteers, yes-men and fools on both sides. Nor were the motives of any man or any group above suspicion. Self-interest was a powerful motive force. When has it not been? It was as much to the King's interest to maintain his own power as it was to that of the English gentry in Parliament to stand out for theirs; naturally. Yet the Civil War was not a selfish struggle for supremacy. Government not *of*, but *for*, the people was the ultimate end of the best men in both parties. They had, deeply ingrained, a saving sense of moral responsibility.

Ten years of fighting and nearly twenty years of unrest may seem a high price to have paid for the Restoration of King Charles II and a working compromise the virtues of which became only gradually apparent. War is always an uneconomic price to pay, although it may be the only one. Yet whatever its outcome the Civil War broadcast among the people theories, experiments, ideas and suggestions some of which were to germinate for a later harvest. It produced in the Agreement of the People a document which is the first modern charter of democracy – and an admirable one it is.

Those who first challenged the King's right to govern without Parliament, those who first raised the representative against the absolutist principle, may have conceived of Parliament as a body of propertied men chosen by propertied men. But they had set a train of action moving which they could not themselves stop, and they were to find among their own number before the end of the war those who saw the true bearing of the principle. 'I think,' said Thomas Rainborough, colonel of artillery and Member of Parliament for Droitwich, 'I think that the meanest He that is in England hath a life to live as well as the greatest He: and therefore, truly sir, I think it clear that every man that is to live under a government ought, first, by his own consent to put himself under the Government.' He meant manhood suffrage and was not alone in meaning it.

For the time being the men of property carried the day, though perhaps only because Thomas Rainborough was killed in a scuffle at Doncaster. It was to need another two and a half centuries until the 'meanest He that is in England' (let alone the meanest She) got a voice in the Government. But the foundation had been laid: the words had been spoken.

1942

II. John Hampden

'We had catched each others' locks, and sheathed our swords in each others' bowels, had not the sagacity and great calmness of Mr Hampden, by a short speech, prevented it.' The scene in the House of Commons thus recorded by a sitting member happened three hundred years ago when the locks of MPs were of a length to be 'catched' by angry opponents, though sheathing swords in each other's bowels was not, even then, an English custom. Otherwise Mr Hampden's short speech would not so easily have prevented it. A few months later, it is true, civil war between King and Parliament had broken out and Englishmen were slaughtering each other – but at least they were doing it *al fresco*, not among the benches of the House of Commons.

Hampden's typical intervention to still the rising passions of his fellow members came into my mind when I recollected that on 24 June of this year three full centuries had passed since 'John Hampden, the patriot' (as old histories used to call him) died at Thame of the wound he had received six days before during the skirmish on Chalgrove Field. Much water has flowed under the bridge since then; time has swept this and that way, submerged a great number of reputations and cast up others upon its banks as swollen, unrecognizable corpses. Only a few remain, and Hampden's, if a little battered, is still among them.

'With great courage, and consummate abilities, he began a noble opposition to an arbitrary court, in defence of the liberties of his country; supported them in Parliament, and died for them in the Field': thus a lapidary tribute chiselled midway between his time and ours, but after the poet Gray had aptly turned him into a household word with his 'village Hampden that with dauntless breast the little tyrant of his fields withstood'. In his own time opinions were divided. 'A man of that prudence, judgment, temper, valour and integrity, that he hath left few his like behind him,' wrote his Parliamentary obituarist; but the Royalist Clarendon attributed to him 'a head to contrive, and a tongue to persuade, and a hand to execute, any mischief'; and the authoritarian Strafford said sourly that he was one of those 'whose nature leads them always to oppose all that authority ordains for them'.

That is the crux of the matter, at least as far as we are concerned, for we have come again to that recurrent political cross-road which John Hampden and his contemporaries knew. We have changed our patter and brought our methods up to date, but the political labyrinth is the same, seeming larger perhaps and more crowded, but with the same dead-ends and by-roads. The problem of 1643 is the problem of today, only more vast, complex and insoluble; you cannot dispense with authority, but you must not let authority dispense with you. 'Now, *here*' – as the Red Queen said – 'it takes all the running *you* can do, to keep in the same place.'

Not that we are in every respect in the same place as John Hampden. Evidently not. His world was smaller and simpler than ours, and his problem by that much the more straightforward. The national issue could be kept apart from the international as it cannot be today, and Englishmen in his time had few responsibilities outside England. But no country can escape its past, least of all a country like our own with a political tradition exceptionally self-consistent. Hampden and Hampden's problem belong to us for good, and the division from us in time is no division from us in understanding. Much of our cultural and historic heritage is the same: we share with him for instance Queen Elizabeth, Shakespeare and Magna Carta, though we have got the Industrial Revolution, Enclosure and the British Empire as well. The average living Englishman has more in common with John Hampden – dead three hundred years – than he has with Gandhi or with Stalin.

When Hampden refused to pay Ship Money solely because the King had imposed the tax without consulting Parliament, his conduct was *comprehensible* to the generality of his compatriots, whether they approved it or not. But it amazed the Venetian envoy: 'They stick to their laws', he wrote home, 'and allow legal proceedings to be taken, solely to make it known that the laws are violated, and that they are compelled to pay by force.' Hampden was no demagogue and no idealist; he believed that the rights of man would look after themselves if the rights of Parliament were secure. He stood out – as a German historian has expressed it in a slightly puzzled way – 'not for a shining ideal, but for a statutory right' – the statutory right of Parliament to control taxation. In outline the story is not heroic. A very rich man refused to pay 20s towards the expenses of the navy, which was in the direst need, because the King had not formally submitted his plan to Parliament. No martyr's stake was involved, no concentration camp, merely expensive legal proceedings and possible detention at the

King's pleasure, which – for a wealthy man in the seventeenth century – did not mean prison in our sense of the word at all.

Why did he do it? The wealthy Parliamentarian leaders have been much mocked of late. They acted, we are told, from self-interest, to defend their influence as a class. The 'money-power' feared that the Crown would usurp its own particular right of exploiting the people. Talk of ancient English liberties was, it is said, mere eye-wash. Well, there is something in that too, though I think it would have distressed and astonished Hampden. But it is not in the nature of men to act ideally, and we know today that the nearest we can, any of us, get to sincerity is perhaps a genuine self-deception.

The significance of an act is not to be measured by its heroism or even by its sincerity. When Hampden refused to pay Ship Money he put up his hand like a policeman at the most dangerous cross-road in our history and firmly diverted the traffic. And there is no doubt whatever which way the traffic was going. A period of disorder and transition, the preceding century had caused all over Europe a terrifying increase in authority. The practice of representative government, quietly developing through the Middle Ages, had broken down under the joint pressure of Renaissance and Reformation. Machiavelli had codified *Realpolitik* and Divine Right had endowed despotism with a *mystique*. Dictatorship alone seemed capable of solving the problem of social order.

There was much to be said for it, as there always is. How easy it would be if the enemy held no trump cards! But the authoritarians have always held a good hand: they offer benefits dismayingly real and quickly to be had – order, peace, security, national greatness. You have only to open your mouth and shut your eyes and the benevolent despot will pop a sugar plum between your lips. For nine people out of ten this is gag enough, and for the tenth there are other methods. So the monarchies grow absolute, and the dictators rise, and there follows, at best, lethargy and corruption, at worst, gangsterdom and international war.

1943

III. Government by Consent

Ten days after the anniversary of Hampden's death the historical calendar records an anniversary which does not need the special circumstance of a tercentenary to secure its due observance – Independence Day.

The juxtaposition is a happy one, for we cannot too often recall our common heritage with the people of the United States. Doctrines of government, established during the English conflict of the seventeenth century, were faithfully preserved across the Atlantic, and the American colonists seceded for that very principle of government by consent – or, in detail, of no taxation without representation – for which Hampden had stood, and which indeed without his timely intervention might have perished among the Anglo-Saxon people as it did elsewhere.

It is very old indeed, this principle of no taxation without representation, very old, very simple and very important. Unfortunately also, it is a principle which can easily be ridiculed and misinterpreted, for it is not precisely a beautiful or an uplifting idea. Practical and business-like, it has remained – and will remain, as long as money is the sinews of the State – the most essential of the political rights of man, but it has not, baldly stated, power to inflame the heart. It was claimed before this war that nobody could be expected to go out and fight for a mere 'standard of living', nor have men perished in the field or on the scaffold for the unadorned principle of no taxation without representation. They have died for it wholeheartedly when it has been called the Will of God or the Rights of Man. We cannot do without these expansions and adornments, these slight disguises.

Later, of course, retribution falls on the coiners of fine phrases, when some of their descendants, prying into cause and effect, discover (with rather ingenuous surprise) that our ancestors were no better than ourselves, and that their noble ideals concealed motives which were sometimes personally and almost always politically self-interested. With unconcealed *Schadenfreude*, these debunkers tumble the economic skeleton out of the cupboard and warn us against being deceived by words alone.

Undoubtedly it was blindness in our forefathers – though one from which they derived nothing but strength – that they underestimated or concealed their more selfish motives. But their principles, now seen to be so heavily involved with loss and gain, do not thereby become of less importance to the welfare and even the freedom of mankind. No one with any real knowledge of political development in western Europe can doubt that the general tendency towards absolutism which set in about the time of the Renaissance was, in spite of any incidental benefits, a bad and a dangerous thing. No amount of special pleading for this dynasty or that monarch, no revelations about Hampden's investments, can radically alter this fact. No group, no party has ever acted with motives entirely pure, and it is well to remember that all of us are, in the words of Belloc, 'pretty nearly all day long doing something rather wrong'. This goes for Left and Right, Whig and Tory, Communist, Liberal and Fascist, and is not – as is generally believed – a monopoly of the 'other side'.

With these limitations, we may accept the *bona fides* of the seventeenth-century conflict and respect the virtues and the theories of our ancestors with no more reserve than did their American descendants in 1776. The consanguinity between the champions of Parliamentary Government in England and the founders of American democracy is exceptionally clear. There are, of course, changes of fashion and outlook to be reckoned with. Morality, in 1776, has nature for its framework and not religion; we feel the physiocrats behind the Declaration of Independence as we feel the sectarians behind so many of the political utterances of the English Civil War; Divine Providence has replaced that menacing individual 'the Lord', and 'the laws of nature and of nature's God' the specific mandates of Holy Writ. The Declaration of Independence is a wider and more spacious document belonging to a more spacious epoch. But the spirit of the Parliamentarian conflict is there: the same emphasis on legal as well as on moral justification, the same insistence on the reconstitution of accepted, rather than the establishment of new, rights. The salient points of the Parliamentarian case re-emerge clause by clause – the appointment of judges, the control of armed forces, the prevention of dictatorial interference with the legislature, the strengthening of the representative assembly, and the root principle of no taxation without representation.

The Anglo-Saxon contribution to the political evolution of mankind is thus exceptionally consistent and practical. It is also of immeasurable value. But it is not the only solution of the problem of government; it is a solution within a particular framework and by a particular group of peoples. Writing in the middle of the nineteenth century, Bancroft, the historian of the United States, could speak without further definition of the 'immutable principles of morals', of the 'unchangeableness of freedom, virtue and right'. We cannot speak so today; even our imperfect knowledge of the remote and complex civilizations which have lived, and which still live, on the surface of the globe, even the primitive researches of anthropologists and psychologists reveal variations on the theme of morality and government which reduce or reverse the authenticity of principles once thought of as absolute. 'The heart of Jefferson in writing the Declaration, and of Congress adopting it', says Bancroft, 'beat for all humanity.' For the negro slaves? for the Russians? for the Chinese . . .? 'All humanity' is an elastic phrase and has been used to cover as vast a number of races and peoples as a single mind can imagine, or, with equal sincerity, to indicate a section of the educated classes.

Between Hampden and Jefferson, the human landscape had opened out. Between Jefferson and ourselves, it has grown almost too gigantic for the single brain to master its variety. Nevertheless, abused or not, 'humanity' is an ennobling concept; to think of 'humanity' and to think for 'humanity', however narrowly the bounds are drawn, is an achievement for the limited mind of the individual man, the greatest achievement which civilization has to its credit and the object, in the end, of all civilization.

1943

Falkland

————⟨⟨⟨⟨⟨◇⟩⟩⟩⟩⟩————

Personalities which defy time are usually spectacular: a lively, rather than a placid, charm has survival value, and those figures whose immortality rests on *being*, not on *doing*, are on the whole rare – an occasional beauty, an occasional wit, an occasional 'character'. In politics they are fewer still, for in this field little save achievement commands immortality, unless it be a noble failure. Yet there are exceptions, and among the most notable perhaps that 'fine flame' of the Caroline age, Lord Falkland, who, on 20 September 1643, rode headlong into a rain of musketry fire at the Battle of Newbury and was shot dead.

He was not the only distinguished Royalist to fall in the criss-cross of skirmishes among the square hedged fruit gardens and vegetable plots which ringed the market town of Newbury. It was a bad day for the peerage; the young lords Carnarvon and Sunderland were lost. Carnarvon is nothing now but one of those young men in dazzling satin from Van Dyck's family group in the double cube room at Wilton – he was Lord Pembroke's 'monstrous great ward' (meaning his fortune not his person) and had been married to his guardian's stodgy daughter. And Sunderland, who was not painted by Van Dyck, is less even than that; at twenty-three he had had no time to make his name, and, a victim of treacherous September weather, he met his death unromantically with a heavy cold in the head. 'Pray bless Popet for me,' he had written to his wife on the previous day – 'Popet' was his daughter – and excused himself from further correspondence because 'I do nothing but sneeze'.

These two share a monument with Falkland on the field of Newbury; but he alone has a place in history. Why, one wonders, for he *did* very little. Can it be that he owes his immortality to the chance of his friendship with Clarendon which got him so large a place in the *History of the Great Rebellion*? Or can the 'incomparable young man', little as he achieved, stand on his own merits?

Small, unprepossessing, with a high, grating voice, Falkland's natural sweetness, his intelligence and good nature had the power to make anyone and everyone forget his extraordinary physical defects. Son of the Lord Deputy of Ireland, grandson and heir to the wealthy Lord Tanfield, educated in Dublin, he inherited at an early age an independent estate, married, to his father's apoplectic rage, the dowerless young woman whom he loved, and spent the blissful decade of the 1630s in keeping open house for the intelligentsia. In Parliament, however, he stood out as an enthusiastic defender of law in the State and liberty in the Church, yet sought – perhaps too late – to prevent the final breach with the King. Appointed, to his dismay, Secretary of State by Charles I, he followed his master loyally through the opening campaigns of the Civil War until his death at Newbury.

Not a great life, certainly; nor, on closer inquiry, a great intellect. Clarendon, with the partiality of affection, speaks of his 'prodigious parts of learning'; but they did not go beyond a good intelligence and an assiduous industry. He lacked originality. But he was analytically inclined, a careful and impartial critic with whom poets, philosophers and scholars could profitably discuss their work. At his house at Great Tew, conveniently near to Oxford, 'the most polite and accurate men of that university' were constantly to be found in fluent and informal session. So also were poets from the Court. There was something a little Russian about these unannounced week-enders, for their host himself frequently did not 'know of their coming or going, nor who were in the house, till he came to dinner, where still all met'. It sounds like something in Tchekhov.

These unending house-parties, with their flowing talk and friendly arguments, were no preparation for the crisis between King and Parliament so soon to arise in England. Yet if Falkland was unprepared and indeed unfitted for the harsher times to come, he was no escapist. Not for him to emulate the eccentric Lord Herbert of Cherbury, who refused the call to arms 'because I am newly entered into a course of physic', and remained pottering over his experiments at Montgomery. The underlying integrity of his character forbade such excuses; his sense of duty and his love of justice alike compelled him, the most tolerant of men, to take sides even in a quarrel he could not condone. Small wonder that, among the unreasonable clamours of war, 'dejection of spirit stole upon him', that he grew 'very sad, pale and exceedingly affected with the spleen', and at length sought the only way out by riding to certain death at Newbury.

Even in small things he had been oddly unfitted to the lawless exigencies of war. He abhorred spies and informers to such an extent that he would never use their services, which, for a Secretary of State in the seventeenth century, was to condemn himself to a perpetual working in the dark. Nor could he bring himself in any circumstances to the ungentlemanly act of opening other people's correspondence: intercepted treasonous letters accumulated on his desk with seals unbroken. Yet the impolite atmosphere of the camp – so different from that at Great Tew – had been brought home to him very early in the war when Prince Rupert, on the eve of Edgehill, busy with cavalry dispositions, had refused to receive him. 'In neglecting me, you neglect the King,' protested Falkland. But that indeed was the order of the day; law and hierarchy were suspended, and the King himself had become an interfering civilian to be disregarded. *Inter arma silent leges* – and *reges* too, if the arms are to be successfully carried. It was because Charles would not put his army first that he lost his war – not to Parliament, but to Parliament's army.

All these things were beyond the experience and understanding of Falkland, nor was he to live to see the end. He belonged to that gentle preceding decade, that time of quietude and contemplation, of talking and thinking, of poetry, and music; the decade of George Herbert and Nicholas Ferrar, of Milton's *Comus* and Herrick's *Hesperides*, of Inigo Jones and Anthony Van Dyck, of William and Henry Lawes – in every sense except the political, the halcyon decade of the seventeenth century. His personality, fixed by Clarendon, has become almost symbolic of it, and his brief, unhappy experience in politics and war represents the attempt to fuse what could not be fused, to apply one set of values to another set of circumstances, the genius of peace to the demands of war.

1943

Some Contemporary Accounts of
the Great Civil War *

That amiable old cavalier Sir Ralph Hopton remarked of his country's predicament in the midst of the Great Civil War that it was not to be thought of 'in good English'. But the contemporary documents of the Great Civil War, the letters, diaries, despatches, reported speeches, note-books, journals, news-letters and official papers which are scattered over these years as thick as leaves in Vallombrosa are for the most part – judged at any rate by our present degenerate standards – in good English.

By the middle years of the seventeenth century the language, as it was spoken and written by educated men, had become expressive and flexible, but had not yet lost the freshness, the occasional impulsive awkwardness, which is as much the charm of a young language as it can be of the young human being. It could be used well, of course, or used badly; it could be teased into whimsies or flattened into tedium; it could be overcharged with ponderous epithet or drawn thin with circumlocution. It had already its commonplaces and vulgarities.

It must have been at some time towards the outbreak of the Civil War that Dorothy Osborne's crusted uncle, as she tells us, 'threw the standish at his man's head because he writ a letter for him where, instead of saying as his master bid him that he would have writ himself but that he had the gout in his hand he said "that the gout in his hand would not permit him to put pen to paper". The fellow thought he had mended it mightily and that putting pen to paper was much better than writing.'

The mannerisms and conceits of contemporary literary fashions sometimes intruded a little grotesquely into other kinds of writing. King Charles I complained that, as a Secretary of State, the

* Lecture given at the Royal Society of Literature, 1948.

elegant stylist Lord Falkland left much to be desired: he drafted his minutes 'in so fine a dress' as positively to disguise the meaning they were intended to convey. Yet in general the ordinary language of this epoch is vivid and explicit. The words and phrases in current use still have the weight and value of a new coinage, unworn by too much use. The adjectives ring true and apt; the idioms are fresh; words and phrases briskly play their part without that lassitude of utterance, that hedging and blurring, which weakens the character and corrupts the meaning of the spoken language today. There is diffused through all the writing of the period, unprofessional or professional, conscious pleasure in the words themselves.

It is still in the first place a spoken language, a language for the tongue and the ear: not as it has since become in great part, with the spread of silent reading, a language for the eye. It is a language to be sung and shouted and bandied about, a language to come easily off the tongue, with fluency, with virtuosity even; not at all a language of understatement, reticence and silences: a language indeed in which it is a calamity to be like poor Lord Fairfax or the King himself, 'of a bad elocution'. Indeed there is hardly one influential man of this epoch who is not, in one way or another, a powerful speaker. There is hardly one of whose manner and tone we are not informed by contemporary witnesses – the elaborate and splendid oratory of Strafford, the solid close-packed argumentation of Pym, the insinuating tones of Hampden, the fervent manner and untunable voice of Cromwell, the pyrotechnics of George Digby, the expository methods of Edward Hyde, the exclamatory monosyllables of Rupert, the persuasive slow rhythm of Montrose – all these were recorded by men to whom the manner of a speech was as significant as its matter.

The King's English had come into being at the Inns of Court and in the Universities as the common interchange of a widely recruited and widely varied educated class. It provided a gradually accepted standard of grammatical usage and a general vocabulary, but regional variations were permissible still to educated men and regional accents, not too broad, varied the rhythm and enriched the texture of the language. The effect is sometimes distantly conveyed to us across three centuries by the personal variations of their spelling. It adds not a little to our sense of personalities, of situations, and even of political conflict, to recollect the colour and contrast of these ways of speech.

The historian cannot select his sources for their literary merit, reject this writer as tedious and that as trivial and turn away from the dismaying bulk of another. The task which compels him to examine, in so far as it is humanly possible, all the evidence relative to his subject, has its compensations in moments of literary pleasure the more precious for being unexpected and unsought. With the Great Civil War he is exceptionally blessed. An epoch which has for its chief historian a writer like Clarendon, who stands high among the masters of English prose, and which counts John Milton among its leading pamphleteers, evidently starts with an advantage. But it is, over and above this, an epoch in which the natural qualities of the language frequently produce an unconscious literature, so that in the most unlooked-for quarters the historian will come upon passages of heart-moving grace or inspiriting vigour, a scene vividly described or a character sharply projected, or some felicity of phrase no less exquisite for being accidental.

So much in introduction to my subject. The accounts and the documents bearing directly on the Great Civil War are innumerable. This was an epoch of a great unloosing of tongues, in which letter-writers and diarists were active, newspapers and newsletters came off the press in their thousands, and a considerable number of public men set out to record what they had lived through. In this necessarily brief account I can speak only of a few of these accounts, the choice being directed by nothing more significant than personal caprice – which after all usually plays a large part in our literary judgments.

The lucid, massive, incomparable Clarendon must come first, with a side-glance at his feebler Parliamentary rivals, Thomas May and Bulstrode Whitelocke. Then there is the vindication of the indignant Denzil Holles, the general record of bland Philip Warwick, the Reverend George Wishart's account of the campaigns of Montrose and Patrick Gordon's vehement counterblast, lastly the Diary of Richard Symonds, gent, of the King's Lifeguard.

Edward Hyde, later Earl of Clarendon, began to write the work which was to become the *History of the Rebellion* in draughty quarters in the Scilly Isles during the blustering March of 1646. At the time he was attending the fugitive Prince of Wales, while the already defeated Charles I was vainly trying to come to terms first with the Scots, then with Parliament, finally with the Army. While the King thus perilously slithered down the last fatal declivity to his destruction, the faithful Edward Hyde sought, by timely warning, to arm the prince against his father's mistakes. The *History of the Rebellion* was first conceived as a work of instruction in politics for the young prince and, in a lesser degree, for the ministers who surrounded him. This admonitory exposition of events was brought down to the beginning of the year 1644, that is to within three years of the time at which Hyde was writing. It was then abandoned for a quarter of a century. During that time Hyde became Earl of Clarendon, attended Charles II with devoted and not always welcome advice throughout his long exile, accompanied him back to England, and continued his first minister until his disgrace in 1667. After his disgrace, when he was living abroad cut off from most of his papers, Clarendon composed between 1668 and 1670 an autobiography which was in fact a vindication of his career and conduct, and finally in the last years of his life he took up once again the record of the war which he had written in his earlier exile, and by piecing it together with the autobiography converted it into the *History of the Great Rebellion* as we know it.

This patching and cobbling together of two works written at different periods and for quite different purposes makes the *History of the Rebellion* of rather uneven historic value, and gives it here and there an appearance of irregularity, disproportion and inconsistency. Yet in spite of these failings Clarendon's history in its entirety presents us with a unique and magnificent panorama of the causes and course of the war. The panorama is seen at first from the floor of the House of Commons by the young and frankly pushful Edward Hyde. To this period belong the vivid pictures – it is tempting to use the cinematic term *sequences* – of the opening months of the Long Parliament, the trial of Strafford, the King's repeated attempts to trim his sails to the wind and ride out the civil storm.

Although Clarendon for the dignity of history writes in the third person, referring to himself punctiliously as *Mr Hyde*, we look upon the whole scene through his eyes, and are in his entire confidence as to his hopes, opinions and fears. With him in the soft spring of 1641 we tread the pleasant walks of London's most fashionable pleasure-garden at Piccadilly and discuss the impending fate of Strafford and the dark future of the kingdom:

In the afternoon of the same day Mr Hyde going to a place called Piccadilly, which was a fair house for entertainment and gaming, with handsome gravel walks with shade, and where were an upper and lower bowling green, whither very many of the nobility and gentry of the best quality resorted, both for exercise and conversation, as soon as ever he came into the ground the Earl of Bedford came to him: and after some short compliments told him 'He was glad he was come thither, for there was a friend of his in the lower ground, who needed his counsel.' He then lamented the misery the kingdom was like to fall into by their own violence and want of temper in the prosecution of their own happiness. He said, 'This business concerning the Earl of Strafford was a rock upon which we should all split, and that the passion of the Parliament would destroy the kingdom. . . .'

Hyde and his noble friend continued in this anxious vein while they strolled through the fashionable crowd to find the Earl of Essex on the lower bowling green. It was against this implied background of the open air and the spring scents, and the distant rattle of the dice from the gaming tables, that Essex pronounced his own relentless verdict on Strafford: 'Stone dead hath no fellow.'

With the passing over of Hyde to the King's side and his association in Charles's government his angle of vision shifts. We see the deployment of the war from the royal headquarters at Oxford, and become partners not so much in the risks and anxieties of the field as in the factious bewilderment of the council table. In the last stages of all, after the King's defeat, the English scene is viewed wistfully from the exiled Court of Charles II. The book ends with the sudden uprushing of the English landscape to meet the reader, as Clarendon puts it, in 'one continued thunder of canon' – Dover, Canterbury, Rochester, London – as the restored King makes his joyful progress to his capital. Even the sage Clarendon here permits himself a discreet smile at the jests of his royal master.

> In a word the joy was so unexpressible and so universal that His Majesty said smiling to some about him 'he doubted it had been his own fault he had been absent so long, for he saw no body that did not protest he had ever wished for his return'.

Clarendon's *History* is sometimes incorrect in detail and chronology. It is often weak and rather uncomprehending on military matters, but as a general exposition of a great political upheaval, as the thoughtful and considered unfolding of causes and effects, policies and counter policies, of the interplay of individuals and events it is unparalleled. The characters which Clarendon drew owe not a little to the contemporary literary fashion of drawing and describing set types. But each is touched with personal observation. The most famous and the most moving is the description of Falkland, to whom he was profoundly attached. Inserted as a parenthesis after the Battle of Newbury it is too long to quote, but the opening sentences set the note for the whole:

> In this unhappy battle was slain the Lord Viscount Falkland, a person of such prodigious parts of learning and knowledge, of that inimitable sweetness and delight in conversation, of so flowing and obliging a humanity and goodness to mankind and of that primitive simplicity and integrity of life that, if there were no other brand upon that odious and accursed civil war than that single loss, it must be most infamous and execrable to all posterity.

Clarendon's more usual style in describing a character is less generous. With many talents, much industry, much perspicacity, he lacked the greatness of heart easily to recognize or to accept greatness in others. He writes of men critically and a little cautiously. Thus Strafford, who was to become for a later and more romantic age nothing less splendid than the Archangel of the Apostasy, is reduced by Clarendon from Satanic to domestic proportions – an arrogant, able, ambitious man, with too little tact. After briefly recapitulating his rapid rise to power, Clarendon continues:

> These successes applied to a nature too elate and haughty in itself ... made him more transported with disdain of other men and more contemning the forms of business, than happily he would have been, if he had met with some interruptions in the beginning, and had passed in a more leisurely gradation to the office of a statesman.
>
> He was, no doubt, of great observation, and a piercing judgment, both in things and persons; but his too great skill in persons made him judge the worse of things: for it was his misfortune, to be in a time wherein very few wise men were equally employed with him and scarce any whose faculties and abilities were equal to his; so that upon the matter he relied wholly upon himself; and discerning many defects in most men, he too much neglected what they said or did. Of all his passions his pride was most predominant: which a moderate exercise of ill-fortune might have corrected and reformed; and which was by the hand of heaven strangely punished, by bringing his destruction upon him by two things that he most despised, the people and Sir Harry Vane.

Clarendon's *History* appeared only a generation after it was completed, in 1702. The massive, persuasive power of this great work was immediately recognized, and there was a not unnatural attempt on the part of Whig writers and critics to set up a rival account of the Civil War from the Parliamentarian point of view. They resuscitated, or tried to resuscitate, for this unequal struggle Bulstrode Whitelocke, a solid intelligent Cromwellian whose *Memorials of English Affairs*, or *An Historical Account of what passed from the beginning of the reign of King Charles I to King Charles II his Happy Restoration*, was composed shortly after 1660 and had been published some years before Clarendon. Their second and even weaker candidate was Thomas May, the official historian of the Long Parliament whose book had appeared, as open government propaganda, during the war itself.

Neither as history nor as literature could either of these writers sustain comparison with Clarendon. Whitelocke's book is a collection of public documents strung together with a dry chronological narrative destitute of all attempts to arrange or present a comprehensible political picture and bare of reflections. It is the rather fragmentary raw material for a history rather than a history. Yet it conveys here and there something of the atmosphere of the home counties in the anxious moments of the war and gives some details without which we should be the poorer. Thus for instance in November 1642, when, in Milton's phrase, 'the assault was intended to the city' and the royal army had already stormed and taken Brentford – the nearest they were ever to get to London – Whitelocke in his terse dry way gives the story of the defence: very Cockney, very unspectacular, very typical.

The City Bands marched forth very cheerfully under the command of Major General Skippon, who made short and encouraging speeches to his soldiers which were to this purpose: 'Come my boys, my brave boys, let us pray heartily and fight heartily; I will run the same fortunes and hazards with you; remember the cause is for God.' Thus he went along with the soldiers, talking to them, sometimes to one company, and sometimes to another, and the soldiers seemed to be more taken with it than with a set, formal oration.

Beyond Hammersmith in a lane were placed the great guns ready to be drawn up as there should be occasion, and a little beyond that were the carriages, in a field close to the high way, placed with great guards about them for their defence. The whole army was drawn up in battalia in a common called Turnham Green about a mile from Brentford.

The General Essex likewise took great pains in the field, and accompanied with the Lords and Commons with him, rode from regiment to regiment encouraging them, and when he had spoken to them the soldiers would throw up their caps and shout crying, 'Hey for old Robin!'

The City goodwives and others mindful of their husbands and friends sent many cartloads of provisions and wines and good things to Turnham Green, with which the soldiers were refreshed and made merry; and the more when they heard that the King and all his army were retreated.

Clarendon's second rival, Thomas May, was a professional writer, an inferior poet and playwright who was generally supposed to have been set against the Court because he had been passed over for the laureateship in favour of Davenant. He can be given the benefit of a considerable doubt on this score, and his political views may have been formed quite independently of his disappointment. He composed, however, with the approval of Parliament, a one-volume history of the Long Parliament in Latin and English, which appeared shortly after the conclusion of the first Civil War. This little work is a brisk and competent summary of public affairs from the Parliamentarian point of view, but it is no more to be compared with Clarendon for breadth or depth or understanding than is the flutter of a London sparrow to the flight of an eagle 'wing-wide on the air'.

A Parliamentary writer of a different kind, less reliable and infinitely more vigorous, is Denzil Holles. Holles wrote his memoirs when he was in exile in Normandy immediately after his expulsion from Parliament in 1648. They are not so much memoirs as a vindication of his own conduct composed with a whirlwind vehemence so that the book gives the impression of having been written all in one singeing breath of indignation. Holles, who lived to be a respected elder statesman and to die old and honoured twenty years after the Restoration, had enjoyed – enjoyed I think in every sense – a noisy career. He had been one of the members of the House of Commons imprisoned in 1629 for pinioning poor Speaker Finch in his chair during the uproar which concluded the session. In the Long Parliament he had been active in opposition to the King with voice and hand until the inevitable split between the Presbyterian party (to which he belonged) and the Independents. With the ascendancy of the Army and Cromwell's party Holles was expelled the House and fled the country immediately afterwards. 'He was faithful and firm to his side,' Burnet wrote of him, 'and never changed through the whole course of his life. . . . He had the soul of an old stubborn Roman in him. He was a faithful but a rough friend and a severe but a fair enemy.'

A rough friend no doubt he was, and a severe enemy, but a fair one . . .? Burnet seems to have gone astray here or at least to have neglected the evidence of Holles's own memoirs. They have qualities and charms but fairness is not among them. Holles blackens with impartial brusquerie everyone who had got the better of him. The dedication set the tone:

221

To the unparallell'd couple, Mr Oliver St John His Majesty's Solicitor-General and Mr Oliver Cromwell the Parliament's Lieutenant-General, the two grand Designers of the Ruin of three Kingdoms. . . . Gentlemen, as you have been the principal in ministering the matter of this Discourse and giving me the leisure of making it by banishing me from my Country and Business, so is it reason I should particularly address it to You. You will find in it some representation of the grosser Lines of your Features, those outward and notorious Enormities that make you remarkable, and your pictures easy to be known.

His intention thus made unmistakably plain Holles proceeds to demolish the character of Cromwell, who, by his account, disgraced himself in every engagement he took part in, was led trembling off the field at Marston Moor, hid behind a hedge at Basing House, and never turned up at Edgehill at all, 'impudently and ridiculously affirming the day after' – so Holles says – 'that he had been all that day seeking the army and the place of fight'.

Holles a fair enemy? No, I hardly think so. But he sweeps the reader into the wake of his break-neck indignation, tearing through his sentences, leaping commas like hurdles, tying grammar into knots, and then slashing it through with a change of subject and never drawing breath for two or three pages at a time. Here he is on Sir Arthur Hazelrig, another Cromwellian whose personal courage he doubted –

. . . and Sir Arthur Hazelrig could come up to London, and into the House of Commons, all in beaten buff, cross girt with sword and pistols as if he had been killing his thousands when, tis more probable, if there was any danger, that he had been crying under a hedge, as he did at Cherrington fight, bellowing out 'Ah woe is me, all is lost! we are all undone!' in so much that a great officer, a Scotchman, finding him in that tune, wished him to go off the field and not stand gudding there (a Scotch term for crying) to dishearten the soldiers: but in the House of Commons he feared nothing, none so fierce and valiant . . .

The antithesis of the furious Denzil Holles is the benign Philip Warwick. No vindictive thought could lodge in the kindly, woolly intellect of this amiable courtier. 'I have no mind to give an ill character of Cromwell,' he begins his description of the Great Protector, and for a devoted Royalist who had suffered imprisonment in the Commonwealth to have no mind to give an ill character of Cromwell shows an uncommon degree of restraint.

His book was written late in life, by his own account 'from a frail memory and ill-digested notes'. Warwick had no great political perspicacity and no great skill in plumbing human nature, but he had been in personal attendance on the King both at Oxford at the height of the first war and in the anxious months at Hampton Court and Carisbrooke. He has an easy, genial, rambling style, an eye for the trivial details which more solemn observers do not think worth recording, and an ingenuous interest in men's outward manners and outward dress which gives a delightful freshness to his pictures. It is from him we learn of Prince Rupert's unfortunate manners at the Council table where he made too many enemies 'by seeming with a *pish* to neglect all another said and he approved not'.

His often quoted description of Cromwell derives, I think, its peculiarly vivid character from the fact that what had evidently most impressed Warwick was the Protector's final triumph over his sartorial shortcomings:

I have no mind to give an ill character of Cromwell; for in his conversation towards me he was ever friendly . . . The first time, that ever I took notice of him, was in the very beginning of the Parliament held in November 1640, when I vainly thought myself a courtly young Gentleman: (for we Courtiers valued ourselves much upon our good cloathes). I came one morning into the House well clad, and perceived a Gentleman speaking (whom I knew not) very ordinarily apparelled; for it was a plain cloth-sute, which seemed to have bin made by an ill country-taylor; his linen was plain, and not very clean; and I remember a speck or two of blood upon his little band, which was not much larger than his collar; his hatt was without a hatt-band, his stature was of a good size, his sword stuck close to his side, his countenance swoln and reddish, his voice sharp and untunable, and his eloquence full of fervor. . . . I liv'd to see this very Gentleman, whom out of no ill will to him I thus describe, by multiplied good successes, and by reall (but usurpt) power: (having had a better taylor, and more converse among good company), appeare of a

great and majestick deportment and comely presence. Of him therefore I will say no more, but that verily I believe, he was extraordinarily
designed for those extraordinary things, which one while most
wickedly and facinorously he acted, and at another as successfully
and greatly performed.

Warwick gives us also one of the rare moments when the royal
self-command of King Charles I came near to breaking-point. It
was during the last hopeless negotiations in the Isle of Wight
before the great axe fell:

I never saw him shed tears but once, and he turned presently his
head away; for he was then dictating to me somewhat in a window
and he was loth to be discerned; and the Lords and gentlemen were
then in the room, though his back was towards them: but I can
safely take my oath they were the biggest drops that ever I saw fall
from an eye; but he recollected himself and soon stifled them.

It is to Scotland that we must turn for a certain epic quality in
the writings about the war: Scotland where spontaneous, heroic
poetry was not wholly dead, where ballads – like 'The Bonnie
House of Airlie' – still sprang from the events of the time and
where indeed, but in another language, the bards still sang. Thus
Ian Lom Macdonald, the bard of Keppoch, was seen standing
aloof while his clansmen charged on the Campbells at the Battle
of Inverlochy. On being urged to do likewise he asked with proud
logic who, if he were killed, would sing the victory of his people?
But I am not competent to speak of the Gaelic sources for the
war.
The 'Annus Mirabilis' of Montrose, the astonishing sequence
of his victories, in wild country and against stupendous odds from
1644 to 1645, could hardly fail of a chronicler. The task was
accomplished in Latin by his erudite chaplain Dr George Wishart
and the book, published in The Hague in 1648, immediately ran
into three editions and made Montrose, rather to the annoyance of
some of the other Royalists, a popular and almost an international
hero. The authorship of the English translation which appeared
at about the same time and in the same place is uncertain. Here
and there the resemblance of the wording is very close to that of

Montrose's own despatches. Yet it would be unwarrantable to assume that Montrose had more to do with the translation than a little supervision. The style in general is laboured and a thought clerical with some seeking after humour. Argyll comes in for a good deal of scorn, although the author's respect for the fighting qualities of the Campbells reflects the often expressed opinion of Montrose himself. Wishart's translator writes:

Of the enemy were slain fifteen hundred among whom were many gentlemen of the Campbells who were chief men of the family . . . who fighting but too valiantly for their chieftain, had deaths answerable to their names and fell in Campo Belli, in the Field of War, I cannot say the bed of honour. Their fortune Montrose extremely lamented and saved as many of them as he was able, taking them in to his protection, whiles Argyll himself being gotten into a boat and rowed a little way off the shore, securely looked on whiles his kindred and soldiers were knocked on the head.

Yet there are moments where Homeric actions strike sparks from this sober style. Thus the astonishing sword play of the gigantic Alastair Macdonald at the Battle of Auldearn is described:

For Macdonald being a valiant man but better at his hands than his head (being overhasty in battle and bold even to rashness) disdaining to shelter himself behind hedges and shrubs whiles the enemy vapoured and provoked him with ill language, contrary to orders, upon his own head, advanceth toward the enemy . . . And he did it to his cost, for the enemy overpowering him both in horse and foot, and having many old soldiers amongst them, routed and repulsed his men. And certainly if he had not timely drawn them off into a close hard by, they had every one of them together with the King's standard been lost. But he made amends for that rash mistake in his admirable courage in bringing off his men for he was the last man that came off; and covering his body with a great targe which he carried in his left hand, descended himself against the thickest of his enemies. Those that came closest up unto him were pike men who with many a blow had struck their spearheads into his targe which he cut off by three or four at once with his sword which he managed with his right hand.

The same story is told in language of a more heroic resonance by the other and rival authority on the campaigns of Montrose, Patrick Gordon of Ruthven, in a book called *A Short Abridgement of Britain's Distemper*. In his account, however, Macdonald is rescued by the Gordons just as he is at his last gasp. He has breath left to cry out when he sees them coming, 'Now those are indeed the valiant Gordons and worthy of that name which fame hath carried abroad of them.'

Patrick Gordon's book was written as an answer to and an attack on other accounts. But his quarrel is not with Montrose. He asserted, not altogether without justification, that the services of the Gordons in the campaign had been disgracefully under-estimated. The truth was that the Gordons were unfortunate in their chief, the Marquis of Huntly, a vain man extremely jealous of Montrose, who withdrew his clan at more than one crucial moment. Patrick Gordon, their apologist, was not personally present at the battles he assiduously describes, but he evidently knew many of the people concerned and had his details from eye-witnesses. None the less in his laudable endeavour to glorify his chief and his chief's three sons, Lord Gordon, Lord Aboyne, and Lord Lewis Gordon, he ascribes prodigies of wisdom and valour to them on all occasions. The historical accuracy of the account is thus not always of the highest, but much can be forgiven a writer of such unmistakable fervency, so rich a vocabulary and so many quaint, cantankerous opinions.

A Highlander and a gentleman, Patrick Gordon had the lowest opinion both of lowlanders and of the common people, but his ascription of men's qualities to their diet is typical of his individual outlook. Thus he writes of the valour of the Scots:

> The commons in the north are found by experience to be more courageous and martial than those of the south; but this is to be understood of the common people, who naturally and by continual custom are born slaves and bondmen; their ordinary food also of peas and beans, heaving them up with flesh, fat and gross humours, as they are heavy lumpish and unwieldy. The commons of the north being fed with the lenifying substance of oats and barley, hath greater bones and are lean of flesh and therefore their blood hath in it more spirit and consequently more courage and greater action; although in

our gentry only consisteth the strength and valour of our nation and hardly hath there been found in all Europe a people more fierce, more daring, more full of courage and true valour, than the gentry of Scotland.

There is a flavour of heroic anachronism about much of Patrick Gordon's book which has in it faint persistent echoes of the 'Chansons de Gestes' and old ballads. All the men are handsome, valiant, chivalrous and rather larger than life; all the women are exquisitely beautiful; the troubled and complicated political background of Scotland is seen in terms of love, hate, envy, honour and chivalry between the principals.

A Royalist lady married to a husband of doubtful fealty is 'a sweet charming nightingale that did never cease powerfully to agent the justice of the King's cause with her husband'. When Lord Lewis Gordon, a very bad young man, took advantage of his elder brother's absence on the King's service to secure for his own the heiress who had been betrothed to his elder, Patrick Gordon showers on his calculating conduct all the most lyrical epithets.

> To this end he makes choice of one of the most beautiful ladies of the kingdom; she was daughter to Sir John Grant of Freuchie, laird of Grant, one of the greatest barons of the kingdom. . . . This rare and matchless piece of divine beauty he made choice of before he went to his travels and her fair idea was of such enchanting force as it had strongly maintained the possession of his soul against all the bewitching allurements of all home-bred and foreign beauties whatsoever.
>
> Therefore of her only he makes choice to marry. Nor would he defer the time, but making a visit to her mother's house he proposes the match. Nor was it long concluding. Only the consent of his father was wanting, on which he had not the patience for to stay, so powerful were the charms of her eyes, but he obtained it soon after for there was no disparagement to his dignity to be preferred to the marriage of her whom his elder brother should have married.

If Patrick Gordon is not an authority or a stylist of faultless merit, he certainly introduces a mixture of lyricism and of unconscious comedy which is irresistible.

So far the accounts I have considered are all, in some degree, set pieces, books written as books for a public. To end I would like to recross the border into England and discuss an account of the Civil War, or at least of part of it, which was written for no public except the author himself: 'The Diary of Richard Symonds.' Symonds, an Essex gentleman who served in the King's lifeguard, is by no means one of the great diarists of English literature. He was not so much a diarist as an indefatigable taker of notes on any subject that caught his fancy. He was interested in the effigies on tombs, the coats of arms in old churches, the names and incomes of the local gentry, the more striking phenomena of the landscape and any oddity, human, natural or ornamental, that he came across. Thus, 'the parson's wife of Fladbury, a young woman often carrying a milkpail on her head in the street, so far from pride'. Or, 'This night I saw a rainbow within a mile of Denbigh at five in the morning, and the moon shined bright: twas just against the moon'.

The 'Diary' is in two parts and is described by its author as recounting 'the marchings and movings' of the King's army. This title is not exactly misleading, for Symonds, in spite of some odd errors in his calendar, does give a valuable day-to-day account of the army's movements. But on the whole it was the churches and the fine houses which engaged his attention, and the fighting is rather in the nature of an interruption to his assiduous sight-seeing. Yet he can describe it in a confused, telegrammatic style which has its own vividness. Thus the siege of Plymouth:

Tuesday. At twelve o'clock both the armies of foot marched with drums beating and colours flying and took possession of the ground near the works under the mercy of the enemy's cannon which played upon them as they went.

Wednesday. Kept the same ground. In the morning the King sent one of his own trumpets with propositions of treaty whom they kept that day.

At night the King sent a drummer for the same purpose.

Thursday the return of those two was expected. At night the trumpet returned much abused, and they would have taken away his horse and told him they would hang him if he came again.

Saturday. In the night our soldiers gave the enemy strong alarms and cried Fall on, fall on the enemy. Shot thousands of musket and many pieces of cannon. Between 6 and 7 in the morning his majesty's army etc with drums beating and colours flying marched off. . . .

The rogues followed our rear . . . little or no hurt, only the basest language.

That for Symonds is a comparatively sustained attention to military matters. He writes with far more detail when he is describing the monuments in churches. He gives about twenty times the space to Salisbury Cathedral that he gives to the Battle of Naseby – a circumstance which indicates a refreshing sense of proportion. When the King's army conveniently spent nearly a week resting in Exeter, Symonds could really devote himself to the Cathedral which he describes as 'Much abused by the rebels when they tyrannized in Exeter'. He notes with great pleasure such details as 'a fair neat chapel, in the south side, a bishop fairly and costly entombed'.

Another monument in the north cross aisle between the body of the church and choir, of a bishop consumed to skin and bones like a skeleton. The east end of the choir is painted very curiously with a temple, Moses, Aaron etc. In the steeple is one of the biggest bells in England. The rebels when they had this city digged up a monument in the south chapel where Bishop Carey lies, and they found a coffin of stone with the bones of a man whole together. Upon the breast lay a silver chalice, which they took away.

He was not always lucky with his sight-seeing. The war frequently intruded; thus at Ramsbury, where the King's lifeguard arrived late one night, to leave early the next morning, Symonds only managed a tantalizing visit to the church in the falling dusk. His 'Diary' reads:

In the chancel lies a flat stone, in the midst a demy picture of a priest, two shields, and the inscription is circumscribed in old French; dark at night, could not read it.

The cheerful inconsequence of this diary and the author's interest in everything else as well as the war gives it its unique charm. His account of the final catastrophe, the quarrel between the King and Prince Rupert and the resignation of the leading officers, drifts away between an excellent description of Leominster Church, a copy of a rather inferior love duet between Daphne and Strephon, a recipe 'for the bellyache in a horse', some notes on the meaning of slang words and a way of curing corns by applying a piece of lean veal to the affected part. Perhaps it is best that it should do so, that the historian, always too prone to notice only the surface tragedies, should be thus reminded of the immense and various trivial stream of life which flows on all the while beneath and round them.

While a King is defeated and a whole social order falls into bewilderment and anarchy, while armies march and fight, and soldiers and statesmen face death in the field or on the scaffold, the parson's wife of Fladbury has just slipped out for the milk, her pail on her head, and perhaps, at five on a moonlit morning a mile from Denbigh a rainbow hangs in the sky.

1948

Two Painters

I. Sir Anthony Van Dyck

Sir Anthony Van Dyck died in England in December 1641, where, for nearly ten years, he had made his home. It was that gloomy winter when the tension between King and Parliament had all but reached breaking-point and Van Dyck's death appositely underlined the close of a period.

It had been an interlude for gracious action and diffused intellectual endeavour, when Inigo Jones designed the royal masques and Wenceslas Hollar etched the capital and taught the royal children to draw, when William and Henry Lawes composed their delicate airs and the number of young poets self-consciously writing was probably greater than at any time until our own. The young men whose attenuated faces Van Dyck had painted would improvise no more verses in the gardens of Whitehall, would experiment no more in their private laboratories with alchemy and magnetism, nor stroll on the lawns at Compton Wynyates or Great Tew talking of philosophy and the constitution. The bitter flood of political conflict, dammed up for ten years, was soon to obliterate the precocious flowers of the Caroline Renaissance.

Van Dyck had settled in London in 1632 and had been from the outset the darling of the Court, the King having a special landing stage constructed the more conveniently to reach his studio from the Thames. The painter lived beyond the precincts of the Puritan and disapproving City, in Blackfriars, a district wealthy, cosmopolitan and just a little disreputable. His elegant house, soon a rendezvous of society, was at one time ruled by the handsome demi-mondaine Margaret Lemon, at another by pretty Anne Carlisle, the miniaturist. The King himself gave a kind of left handed approval to this attachment, since he once presented Sir Anthony and Mrs Carlisle with five hundred pounds' worth of ultramarine for their joint use. Afterwards the painter decided to settle his affairs more suitably, and laid all but successful siege to a nobleman's widow, Lady Stanhope, only to lose her at the last by ungallant insistence on payment for her portrait. Soon after the Queen selected from her household a nobly born but suitably impoverished bride, Mary Ruthven. But this was towards the end of Van Dyck's career, when the informality of his earlier days – he had once made a habit of asking sitters to stay and dine with him so that he might study and sketch expressions as they talked and ate – had given place to the business-like methods of a fashionable practitioner. Sittings in his last phase were for an exact hour, at the end of which Sir Anthony courteously bowed the client to the door, while efficient servants cleaned his brushes and brought out the canvas and special palette for the next sitter.

Van Dyck's English period was the most prolific in his career: a century later Walpole declared that his 'works are so frequent in England that the generality of our people can scarce avoid thinking him their countryman'. Since Walpole's time the collection of paintings in public galleries and of facts in reference books has dispelled this genial intuition. No one today thinks of Van Dyck as an Englishman. We compare him learnedly with Rubens in whose studio he worked as a young man; we pursue the development of his style and distinguish between the first and second Flemish periods, the Italian period and his last, declining, English period. Yet if we assess him the more justly as a painter we miss one aspect of the truth. The fashionable portrait painter stands next only to the diarist as the recorder of a period; and in Van Dyck's age there was no diarist to compete with him. His, above all, was the imaginative sympathy which created our nostalgic vision of that lost decade.

Born of prosperous middle-class parents in Antwerp, highly trained in the professional technique of his art, Van Dyck would not at first seem to be the most sympathetic interpreter of the aristocratic dilettantism of the 1630s. But he had the successful portrait painter's essential gift, and saw men, with few exceptions, as they liked to see themselves. In Italy he had transformed the effete members of a stagnant society into figures solid with the consciousness of great traditions: in Flanders he gave an air of prosperous resolution to anxious statesmen and hard-pressed burghers. So in England, in the entr'acte of the great constitutional drama, he painted the nobles and their ladies with the gracious serenity of a land lapped in unending peace. The inhibited, adenoidal face of King Charles, unflatteringly rendered by Mytens, was transfigured by Van Dyck's hand with indefinable spiritual grandeur. The pompous Arundel became an elder statesman, the harassed Strafford a fortress of power, the crafty Pembroke a wise Ulysses, and eligible young peers – Carnarvon, Wharton, Digby – achieved a grace that flesh alone could never simulate.

Van Dyck, as an eighteenth-century writer expressed it, 'was the first painter who e'er put ladies' dresses into a careless romance'. But 'careless romance' was the mood of all his sitters, men and women alike: one recalls the artfully tangled curls of Lord Wharton, the clothes, all slashings and slits, of Lord John Stuart, through which lawn and lace profusely tumble, the trailing sashes, the lace-edged breeches, the wrinkled boots of soft leather. Did fashion ever more accurately mirror a period of grace and fantasy, of talk and postponement?

Yet it is in the rendering of a face or the choice of an attitude, rather than by details of dress, that Van Dyck built up our vision of the period. How far is this picture true? It can be modified by comparison with the work of other painters, with the etchings of Hollar and Faithorne, with the monumental sculpture of our churches. It must be modified in the light of history, for these gentle-faced sitters, Cavalier and Roundhead alike, were soon to face each other in uncompromising war: they always had it in them to be what they became in the next disastrous decade. The tranquillity of England in the 1630s, like that of the 1930s, was self-imposed illusion. Van Dyck enshrined the illusion for posterity.

II. The English Tintoret

At Oxford, opposite St Mary's Church in the High, with its new porch on barley-sugar columns and Our Lady in a baroque attitude, the painter William Dobson improvised a studio during the noisy years of the Royalist occupation. Sociable, gifted, extravagant, the painter flickers briefly across the darkening scene of England's Civil War, the most striking of Van Dyck's followers and the most talented English painter of the seventeenth century. Elevated to the courtier's rank as groom of the privy chamber, he had succeeded his friend and discoverer Van Dyck as sergeant-painter to King Charles I. As Van Dyck has fixed for after ages the visual graciousness of the Cavalier summer, so it was Dobson who recorded their stormy sunset. His is the harassed King, with thinning hair and sagging features, dictating, buff-coated, to the stout and unperturbed Sir Edward Walker seated at a drum for a table. His is the sensitive, saturnine Rupert, handsome, haughty and strained. His is the upward-tilted head of Montrose, the oblique studio light striking downwards on open forehead and obstinate jaw.

Temperamentally the painter was not unsuited to the uncertain time which saw his brief apogee. He came of the hanger-on class, poised always uncertainly between opulence and bankruptcy. His father, a St Alban's man of some little fortune, had been a favourite of Francis Bacon and a dilettante of the arts, or at least of architecture, for Aubrey tells us that Bacon's house at Gorhambury, that 'most ingeniously contrived little pile', was built with his advice and help. Bacon rewarded him with a civil service sinecure, the mastership of the Alienation Office. The post availed the luxurious Mr Dobson little, for as Aubrey concludes 'he spent his estate upon woemen' and thus 'necessity forced his son William Dobson to be the most excellent painter England hath yet bred'. Necessity was apparently for once the mother not merely of invention but of genius.

William Dobson was born in 1610, but it was not until the later 1630s that he began to attract attention. The facts of his early career rest on hearsay. He seems to have been at one time a pupil of a German artist from Mecklenburg who worked in England under the Italianate name of Francesco Cleyn and was employed by Charles I to design tapestries for the Mortlake factory. Posterity has almost totally forgotten Cleyn, a neglect which would have surprised him for he held himself in high esteem. 'Il famosissimo pittore, miracolo del secolo' appears as the legend to his self-portrait. But Dobson did Cleyn justice, for one of the few authentic records we have of him is his admission of indebtedness to the German master. Far better known was his subsequent employer and teacher the fashionable engraver Robert Peake for whom he appears to have done hack-work for some years.

The pleasant legend has it that Van Dyck, loitering one day among the print and picture dealers on Snow Hill, was struck by a painting exhibited for sale, inquired the artist's name and discovered Dobson in the proverbial garret. Whether the facts of their meeting were quite so fortuitous we may doubt. Dobson can hardly have lost touch altogether with the world of patronage in which his father had moved and the artist population of London in the 1630s was not so large but that the meeting of an evidently talented and interested young man with the all-conquering Van Dyck would be a matter of time. It was Van Dyck at all events who recommended him to the King, encouraged him in his work and presumably got him the entrée to the Royal collections which, with their notable examples of the late Venetian masters, were to have so strong an influence on his style.

King Charles, with one of his rare gracious phrases, called him the 'English Tintoret'. This is over-praise, but Dobson's dark, muscular style echoes far off the Italian master; less inventive, less powerful, more limited in colour and range, the English painter yet has an individuality which is unmistakably his own and which puts him outside the circle of Van Dyck's mere imitators. His fierce and virile touch was suited to the period in which he gathered his brief harvest, among the alarums of war. With what insight he fixed the features of this lost generation against the dark background, of these young soldiers who carried assurance on their brows and defeat in their hearts, of this whole doomed society which maintained to the last its interrupted culture, while the green college quadrangles were trampled bald by drilling feet, and Rupert's squadrons wheeled and formed in Christ Church meadows. Three winters and four summers he played his social and sociable part in the thronged city. He discussed archaeology with John Aubrey for whom he sketched the ruins of Osney; debated styles and techniques of painting with inquisitive Richard Symonds of the King's Lifeguard; caught his distinguished, hurried, military sitters as they came and went; until the hoarse gun on Magdalen Tower could make no more answer to the enemy guns drawing in from Marston, drawing in from Iffley, and the King's standard was hauled down from Christ Church and one day in June of the year 1646 the war, for Oxford, was ended.

Money had all the time been Dobson's difficulty. He is alleged in the troubled years at Oxford to have begun the practice of asking sitters for half the price in cash before he started. The precaution, which seems out of character with all we know of his feckless nature, did not help him much. Soon after the extinction of the King's cause he was in a London debtors' prison. An admirer bought him out, but his friends and his world were alike destroyed, and the ravages of consumption, unchecked by the unhealthy climate and too hectic life of Oxford, had gone too far. He died in the autumn of 1646, at about the same time as the Scots sold his most distinguished sitter to the English Parliament for two hundred thousand pounds.

1941

King Charles I
and the Protestant Cause *

E
nglish history in the seventeenth century is dominated by
the civil war between King Charles I and his Parliament.
The principal historian of this epoch, the late Samuel Rawson Gardiner, called this violent interlude the 'Puritan Revolution'. Gardiner's monumental work is now fifty years old and, in
the passage of two generations, has been attacked both in general
and in detail, although hitherto nothing comparable has appeared
to replace or supersede it. The modern tendency is to devote more
attention to the social and economic background of the war and
to turn away from its religious aspects. We seek for its causes today
in the economic changes, in the position of the gentry and in the
financial and trading interests of the wealthy Puritan city men.
Fifty years of research has produced interesting results and added
much to our general knowledge of English society and life at the
time of the war. But Gardiner had two advantages over most of
those who have come after him and over many of his critics. He
had been brought up in one of the more austere dissenting sects
so that he had a deep understanding of the Puritan outlook. And
he approached English history from a wide knowledge of European
history. These two factors enabled him to appreciate the strength
and fervour of English Protestant – and more especially of English
Puritan – opinion, and to gauge the extent to which it was outraged by the foreign policy as well as the home policy of Charles I.

Since his time English historians, deeply concerned with the
rich and fascinating details of the politics, economics, social life,
literature and philosophy of a vital and enthralling period of
English national history, have paid less attention to Continental
politics or their effect on England. As a result our knowledge of
the internal structure of the country has been enriched, but the

* Lecture delivered to the Huguenot Society of London, 1954.

generally accepted picture of the Civil War as something which was very much the private and insular concern of the English is, I submit, very misleading. Many people in the British Isles during the civil wars themselves and almost all European politicians saw the Great Rebellion as an integral part of the Continental wars of religion.

It is my intention to examine the truth of this belief. The religious policy of King Charles within the British Isles was a policy of uniformity. Archbishop Laud's attempt to break up the Walloon and Dutch communities which had settled in England in the time of Queen Elizabeth fitted into this general pattern. But this home policy was associated with a persistently pro-Catholic, pro-Spanish policy abroad, a foreign policy which intensified the bitterness and distrust felt towards the King not only by those who can properly speaking be called Puritans but by the majority of his Protestant subjects. This was, I think, a major reason, possibly the principal reason, why a conflict which might have been confined to parliamentary argument became in the end an open war.

About the year 1630, when King Charles I was beginning his personal rule, religious wars had been raging for upwards of eighty years in Europe. The Habsburg dynasty had constituted themselves the champions of Catholicism. They controlled Spain, the Netherlands, Austria and all of Hungary that was not in Turkish hands; they were also, as Emperors, overlords of Germany. Both their dynastic power and their crusade for Rome had suffered serious checks in the sixteenth century with the revolt of the Netherlands and the establishment of either Lutheranism or Calvinism as the official religion of at least three important German states – Saxony, Brandenburg and the Palatinate; various privileges had also been extracted by the Protestants of Bohemia.

Between 1620 and 1630, however, the Habsburg dynasty, in the most spectacular way, retrieved some of these disasters. The Spanish (southern) Netherlands reopened hostilities on the Protestant Dutch of the northern Netherlands and, among other successes, re-took the important key fortress of Breda. A Protestant revolt in Bohemia precipitated a war in Germany in which the Habsburg forces were almost universally successful. Protestantism was stamped out in Bohemia and in the so-called Upper Palatinate, a Protestant region on the Danube which was handed over to Catholic Bavaria; the imperial forces swept northwards as far as the Baltic, and in 1629 the Edict of Restitution restored to the Church the secularized lands in all the reconquered regions.

King Charles thus began his reign, had his first quarrels with his Parliaments and embarked on his absolute rule against a background of unparalleled disasters for the Protestant Cause in Europe. His own interventions in the European war had been singularly unfortunate, and I need not recapitulate here the dismal tale of the English expeditions to Cadiz and to the relief of La Rochelle. It is enough to say that by 1630, when the King decided for financial reasons to avoid further European wars, he had already caused grave anxiety among many of his subjects by the inefficiency with which he had allowed military and naval operations to be conducted.

The King's principal anxiety when he embarked on a period of non-parliamentary government was to secure for himself adequate funds for the necessary expenses of Court and State. The peace treaty with Spain in 1630 was of paramount importance in securing him some measure of financial independence. The Spaniards were anxious to find some safer way of transporting money to pay their troops into the Spanish Netherlands as the sea-routes were increasingly dangerous owing to the growing power of the Dutch. By the treaty of 1630 King Charles agreed to receive Spanish silver in the mint and to transport the minted money to the Spanish Netherlands in English vessels which, being neutral, were immune from Dutch attack. In return he was to have a percentage of each cargo of silver.[1] This plan was, naturally enough, not widely published, but it was well known to the City and to all those who had any dealings with the Dutch. The Dutch complained bitterly of it, asserting that it did them more harm than an open declaration of war would have done. Undoubtedly informed Protestant opinion in England was profoundly disturbed by the existence of this scheme by which the King's independence of Parliament was underpinned by Spanish silver. (It is hardly too much to say that there is a close parallel here with the situation which arose under Charles II when he received subsidies from Louis XIV.)

The Puritan–Protestant tradition of English foreign policy evolved in the time of Queen Elizabeth had satisfied at once the expansionist ambitions of the English and their religious fervour and had imprinted in their minds the idea that Spain was the natural enemy. The rightful place of England in foreign affairs was, they believed, among the supporters of the Protestant Cause.

The general dislike of Charles's policy was further sharpened by the existence of an attractive and sentimental figurehead for the Puritan point of view in the person of the King's own sister, Elizabeth, Queen of Bohemia. This princess had married Frederick V, Elector Palatine, who, in 1619, had accepted the Crown of Bohemia from the insurgent Protestants of that country. The revolt in Bohemia seemed to many English Protestants to be very like the Dutch revolt of the previous century; the similarities – which were in truth not many – were underlined for them by the fact that the Elector Palatine was the grandson of William the Silent while the Catholic ruler against whom the revolt was directed was the godson of Philip II. English volunteers poured out to the assistance of the Protestant Queen of Bohemia and her husband but there was no effective official intervention made. The rising was crushingly defeated and Elizabeth Stuart with her husband had to take refuge in the Netherlands. For strategic reasons Spanish forces occupied the Rhenish Palatinate while the Danubian Palatinate was handed over to the Duke of Bavaria. The exiled and dispossessed Elector Palatine died in 1632 and his widow, with her large family, seemed thereafter to the Puritans to be the living witnesses of the wrongs inflicted by the pro-Catholic, pro-Spanish policy of King Charles. When, in 1636, for purely practical reasons the name of the exiled Queen of Bohemia was dropped from the Prayer for the Royal Family, Puritans regarded this as a deliberate insult;[2] in fact, her name had only been omitted because, with the birth of the King's children, she had ceased to be heir presumptive to the throne.

The spectacular advance of Catholicism in the Empire set in motion a new flood of Protestant refugees, chiefly from Bohemia and the Palatinate. No official encouragement and very little help was given to these unfortunates if they came to England. We find individual Puritans offering help and protection to some – the

Providence Company gave one of them a chaplain's post in their new colony[3] – but there never seems to have been any question of permitting them to form communities in England. Evidently these refugee ministers were not unfamiliar figures in London for we have a case of an English out-of-work parson pretending to be a Palatinate refugee in order to raise alms from the charitable. But in general the official discouragement that they received contrasts unfavourably with the treatment of Protestant refugees in the previous century.

To the honour of the Church of England clergy it must be said that many of them did what they could to help the victims of the Counter-Reformation. The religious views of Archbishop Laud were shared only by a minority of the Anglican clergy, although his policy dominated all official action. I need not here enlarge on his unceasing efforts to destroy the French-speaking Protestant church established at Canterbury, or the Dutch at Austin Friars, or on the attack made by Bishop Wren in accordance with the same Laudian policy on the community at Norwich. Archbishop Laud in his strenuous effort to unite and purify the Anglican church and to suppress all kinds of dissent from it, whether native or foreign, was particularly hostile to the influence of the Netherlands. He not only disliked the communities already established in England but he complained to the Prince of Orange that English theological students, ordained in the Calvinist Netherlands, were coming back to England and, with the help of Puritan patrons, infiltrating the Church.

It is, however, fair to admit that although the Archbishop suspected and disliked the Calvinism of the Dutch, he was not altogether happy about the King's foreign policy. He, with his colleague in temporal affairs, Lord Wentworth, wanted the King to pursue a policy of neutrality in Europe because they felt that peace was essential to the security of the King's government. They were neither of them enthusiastic about the strongly pro-Spanish appearance of the King's policy. Both of them, and the Archbishop especially, would have liked to see the King counterbalance it by adopting, in home policy, an attitude of approximately equal severity to *all* who stood outside the fold of the Church of England – to Roman Catholics as much as to Protestant nonconformists. The King, however, under the influence of the Roman Catholic Queen and in direct opposition to Laud's advice, continued to treat English Roman Catholics with far greater leniency than English Puritans. The persecution of the foreign Protestant communities was thus in sharp contrast to the wide privileges allowed to Roman Catholic ambassadors or official visitors who freely brought in priests (often English priests) and opened their chapels to all who liked to come. While Laud harried the pastor of Canterbury, the Franciscans had re-established themselves in England, Catholic priests were openly proselytizing in London and Mary Ward, the founder of a new order of nuns, the *Englische Fräulein*, found it possible to return to Yorkshire with a small band of Sisters. The King's leniency to Roman Catholics thus made Archbishop Laud's policy of uniformity appear to be exclusively anti-Protestant.

The King again went against the Archbishop's politic advice in trying to force religious conformity on the Scots without adequately preparing the ground. In July 1637 he imposed a new Scottish prayer book, drawn up by Scottish bishops in conformity with the English model; this provoked resistance which very soon assumed the proportions of a national rising. Scotland, especially south-eastern Scotland, had connections with the Protestant Netherlands which were both commercially and intellectually even closer than those of the English. The principal legal adviser to the rebellious party in Scotland, Sir Thomas Hope, was the son of a Dutch mother. It is not surprising therefore that the Scots revolt followed in outline much the same course as the Netherlands revolt against Philip II seventy years earlier. The nobles became the leaders of the revolt in much the way that the Netherlands nobles had done, and, as in the Netherlands, the earlier part of the struggle was conducted in resolutely legal terms; formal protests and supplications to the Crown preceded the famous National Covenant of February 1638 which became the manifesto of the rebellious party.

Since Charles had no intention of yielding to the Scots rebels he had no choice but to make war on them. To do so the more effectively he entered into negotiations with his friends in the Spanish Netherlands to supply him with arms and to release any of his English subjects who were serving as volunteers in their armies. The Scots, with their Dutch connections, naturally bought equipment from the northern Protestant Netherlands.

Soldiers of fortune from the British Isles, who were serving abroad, returned home to take part in the struggle. Naturally all of those who joined the Scots were from the Protestant armies in Europe – chiefly the Swedish and Dutch forces. Of those who joined the King, a very high proportion were Roman Catholics, English, Scots or Irish, who had been employed in the Spanish forces. In this way the European conflict seemed in a manner to be simply transferring itself to British soil.

The first war against the Scots was a fiasco and ended in what was virtually an armistice, while both sides prepared for a second and graver trial of arms. In the summer and autumn of 1639, however, some startling developments took place in King Charles's relations with Spain. The capture of Breisach by their enemies had cut off the overland route by which the Spaniards sent troops to the southern Netherlands. King Charles therefore agreed to allow troops as well as money to be carried in English ships. The Dutch, disregarding English neutrality under this final provocation, stopped some of these troopships in the Channel. Charles therefore agreed to let the Spaniards shorten this dangerous journey by marching across England. During the course of the summer of 1639 about five thousand Spanish soldiers landed at Plymouth, marched across the country and were re-embarked at Dover.[4] The presence of Spanish troops actually on English soil, when the King was already at war with some of his Protestant subjects, gave rise to the rumour that Charles intended to crush all his critics with armed Spanish help. This unhappy impression was strengthened by the famous Battle of the Downs. A Spanish fleet, carrying large forces, had taken refuge in English waters where the Dutch under Martin Tromp blockaded them. Charles made arrangements for billeting the Spanish mariners and troops in Deal and Dover should they be driven inshore by storms or other disasters; he also supplied the ships with additional gunpowder from his arsenals. The Dutch refused to leave and, after some weeks, decided to disregard English neutrality, attacked and almost wholly destroyed the Spanish fleet. The scene was watched with enthusiasm from the shore by many of the inhabitants and the pastor of Canterbury composed a hymn of thanksgiving to celebrate the occasion.[5] Protestant opinion in England welcomed the destruction of the Spanish armament and refused, in this instance, to be outraged by the shocking violation of English territorial waters by the Dutch.

The King, on the other hand, was indignant with the Dutch and at one moment it was even suggested at Court that proceedings should be taken against the commander of the English fleet for not having intervened to prevent the battle – which meant, of course, for not having intervened on the Spanish side. This folly was fortunately dropped, but the King, in the teeth of public opinion, continued to increase his Spanish commitments. He needed money to ensure his victory over the Scots rebels in the second war for which he was preparing throughout the winter of 1639–40. Negotiations were opened with Spain by which he was to provide thirty-five ships of his navy to convoy Spanish transports through the Channel. Something also appears to have been said about the possibility of offering bases to the Spaniards in southern Ireland.[6]

These negotiations were cut short by the action of the Dutch who made it clear that they would declare war if the treaty were concluded. King Charles saw that he could not risk a Dutch war and the agreement with Spain was called off. But it had done irretrievable harm to his position at home.

In the summer of 1640 the King made his second and wholly unsuccessful war on the Scots. Defeated, he was compelled to call Parliament which reversed his religious policy, impeached Laud and forced the King to agree to the execution of Wentworth. Furthermore, it compelled him to pass legislation which progressively weakened the constitutional position of the Crown – to abolish the prerogative courts and to consent to triennial Parliaments. This political revolution, grave as it was, might still have run its course without an appeal to arms, had it not been for the King's foreign policy and the doubts it had engendered.

In October 1641 revolt broke out in Ireland. It was a revolt of the native Roman Catholic Irish population against Protestant English and Scottish settlers. Armies had to be raised to put down this revolt. That at once brought up the vital question: who was to control the armed forces, the King or Parliament? In view of the King's past record in foreign policy it was essential that Parliament should control the armed forces. A king who had been in close alliance with the principal Roman Catholic power – Spain – a king who had been suspected of wishing to land a Spanish army in England, a king who had certainly taken Spanish money and Spanish arms to help him against his own people, and who had even considered the possibility of giving the Spaniards bases in his dominions could not possibly be trusted with the task of putting down a Roman Catholic rebellion in Ireland. The Irish rebels themselves claimed that they were the King's friends and had risen to help him against his Puritan Parliament. The actual extent of Charles's connivance in the rebellion will always be doubtful, but, in view of his earlier policy, it is not surprising that many intelligent Puritans believed him to be involved in it, and saw the rising as an integral part of Spanish–Roman Catholic strategy in Europe.

Parliament insisted therefore in curtailing the King's authority over the armed forces to be raised for Ireland. The King would not accept this new infringement of his rights. In the spring and summer of 1642 both parties began to organize troops in accordance with their own conception of their rights and thus automatically produced a state of civil war in England.

NOTES

[1] The particulars and effects of this treaty are fully discussed in Feavearyear, *The Pound Sterling*, Oxford, 1931, pp. 82 ff.

[2] Prynne, *News from Ipswich*.

[3] A. P. Newton, *The Colonising Activities of the English Puritans*, Yale, 1914, pp. 120–1.

[4] *Calendar of State Papers, Domestic Series*, June 1639, *passim*.

[5] ibid. 1639–40, pp. 33, 35, 45; Cross, *History of the Walloon Church*, pp. 97–8.

[6] *Calendar of State Papers, Venetian*, 1670–2, pp. 44–5; Scottish Register House, Breadalbanc MSS , letter of 2 June 1640.

The Battle of Rocroi

In the hot August of 1936 I visited the battlefield of Rocroi. Time was short and the autobus service erratic, so that in the end I chugged out from Mézières in a station taxi. The driver, catching something about a battlefield, was very unwilling to go to Rocroi: there were battlefields of more recent memory closer at hand. If anyone had ever fought at Rocroi, he protested, it was very long ago. Very long ago indeed: on 19 May 1643.

Three miles on the French side of the Belgian frontier the little eminence of Rocroi dominates the accidented plain with its sparse woods and trickling streams. Within Vauban's massive fortifications, the village seemed grey and wizened, too small for the armour of its mighty prime, and in the grassy dip which once divided the inner from the outer wall, among nettles and food-cans, rusted a roll of wire from a later war. The apathetic girl at the *estaminet* brightened for a moment as she poured out an apéritif; Rocroi, she predicted, would soon be more lively – '*on nous à promis une garnison*'. The shadow of the coming war was the dawn on her horizon.

On the great lichened gate-post an inscription recorded the triumphal entry of the young Condé after his victory over the Spanish army in the plain below. Besieged by the Spaniards in the spring of 1643, Rocroi was relieved in a campaign which settled not only its own fate but that of Spain's power in Europe. About a mile to the south-west of the village, on a slope as innocently green as any in France, marking the centre of the Spanish position stands a small grey monolith: the inadequate gravestone of a nation. Here, backing narrowly line by line under the murderous onslaught of Condé's cavalry, perished the Spanish infantry, the hitherto unbroken shield of that dropsical monarchy whose destruction made way for the greatness of France. Here under the green turf their bones still lie – veterans of many campaigns, or young men newly trained to the greatest fighting tradition in Europe: soldiers from Spain and the Spanish provinces, from Castile and Aragon, from the plain of Milan and the uplands of Lombardy, from Flanders and Brabant, Luxembourg and Franche Comté, the picked troops, the *Panzerdivisionen* of a great authoritarian Power.

The struggle between the French and Spanish monarchies for the domination of Europe had lasted more than a century before France, emerging from the long night of her religious wars, began under the consolidating genius of Richelieu to gain the advantage. Not that her final victory was sure: far from it. Her armies were still undisciplined, ill-organized, without tradition, and caring more for appearances than war – 'all in bright armour and great feathers, wonderful beautiful to behold'. Only a few years before Richelieu himself had seen Paris nearly taken by a joint attack of the Spaniards with their Austrian and Bavarian allies. When in the spring of 1643 Don Francisco de Melo, Governor of the Spanish Netherlands, invaded France, the outlook for her defenders had seldom been more clouded. Richelieu had died in the preceding winter, and now the King himself lay dying, leaving as his heir a child of five, the future *Roi Soleil*. In command of the army sent to repel the Spanish invasion was the King's cousin, the Duc d'Enghien, a young man of twenty-three. Three older generals had been appointed to control his actions, Senneterre, Gassion and l'Hôpital. But Enghien – who was soon to be known as the great Condé – needed no such control: he was a soldier of genius.

In Paris the King, uneasily dozing on his deathbed among a crowd of courtiers, opened his eyes to see Enghien's father close beside him, and murmured feebly, 'I dreamt your son had won a great victory.' This was on 13 May, a little before he died, and the French army had not as yet engaged the Spanish in the plain below Rocroi.

Don Francisco de Melo was not much perturbed by the approach of the French army. Thinking it better to surround and overwhelm them in their entirety, he had let them advance unmolested through the sparse copses and defile into the open plain.

He had the superiority of numbers, though not by so wide a margin as he supposed, for his scouts had been baffled by Enghien's dispositions. When at about six o'clock on the evening of 18 May Senneterre ill-advisedly began the attack, Don Francisco was ready for him, and only the rapid intervention of the young Enghien prevented the destruction of Senneterre's cavalry and enabled the chastened general to extricate his men under cover of night.

The next morning broke fine and warm. On the French side Enghien and Gassion had the right wing, Senneterre and l'Hôpital the left. Facing them, with their backs to the beleaguered fortress, was the Spanish army, cavalry on the wings, infantry and guns in the centre, with German and Flemish reserves in the rear. Enghien's daybreak attack on the opposing cavalry took them by surprise; after a brief resistance they broke and fled. But on the far wing Senneterre was again in trouble. He had the worst of the ground, boggy, and the slope against him. Hard pressed by Melo's superior forces he had all but abandoned the field when Enghien, throwing textbook tactics to the winds, streaked through the centre of the Spanish position, cutting between the Spanish infantry and the reserves, and crashed in on Melo's rear. That finished the Spanish cavalry. Remained the infantry in the centre bereft of all support. They held the position with desperate courage until ammunition began to fail for their twenty-four great cannon and their musketeers. Then the white flag went up. In vain. Enghien advanced to parley, but, mistaking his move for a new attack, someone fired. With cries of *Trahison!* the French surged forward to final and ruthless victory.

Such was the battle of Rocroi, the first laurel wreath to adorn the infant brow of Louis XIV. He had been King for five days. But laurel wreaths are out of fashion, and it is not for its sake that Rocroi is to be remembered now. Rather because this battle dates – if such things can be exactly dated – the beginning of the long ascendancy of French influence in Europe. There may not have been very much to choose, politically, between the French monarchy and the Spanish; soon those minor Powers who had assisted France to overthrow her rival were leagued as bitterly against France herself. Nor is this surprising, for French kings fought Spanish kings not because they disapproved of one Power dominating Europe, but because they wanted themselves to be that Power. International politics, by and large, are a depressing study.

But whatever the political outcome of Rocroi, Europe gained something by that victory which had nothing to do with power politics or rival dynasties, and without which the history of the Continent, even of the world, would have been the poorer. For without the political victory of France the great and vital influence of the most civilized of European peoples would never have achieved its full expansion. Three centuries have passed, and at the close of them the greatest disaster in the recorded history of France. What has become in these last years of the sad girl at the *estaminet*, the garrison which was promised? What strangers have gazed and with what feelings at that lonely monument? Who in France on this 19th of May, 1943, will remember Rocroi? But let us here remember it, not as the first beam of glory from the *Roi Soleil*, but rather as the first ray of that quickening and benevolent sun which, from the genius of the French people, streamed over Europe for close on three centuries, and for lack of which we feel the cold today.

1943

Art, Truth and History

The connection between art and truth, that is the apprehension of truth and its communication by means of art, is the central problem of every writer and of every creative artist. All writers are confronted with it, and take their own ways to solve it with greater or lesser success. Many writers have committed themselves to opinions about it in private letters or public statements which in their turn become the subject of further analysis and discussion by ensuing generations of writers and critics. The subject is inexhaustible. It presents questions which are of the utmost importance to the practising writer, and of scarcely less interest to the practising reader, that is the reader who takes his reading seriously and finds his pleasure enhanced by the sharpening of his critical faculties.

While it is true that the greatest art is to conceal art, and few admire writers who allow the mechanism behind their achievement to become visible, it is equally true that some appreciation of the technical skill of the artist deepens and enriches our pleasure. At the first impact of a beautiful poem or a great work of art we do not want to divert our minds by considering the ingenuity of vocabulary, the sensibility of hearing, the subtlety in the association of ideas which have brought together certain effects of sound, and stimulated certain trains of thought to create in us a spontaneous reaction of delight; so with a great picture we do not want consciously to notice at the first instant the deliberate touches by which the balance and harmony of line and colour have been produced; but at a second and third examination these things enhance our pleasure, because by recognizing the details of craftsmanship we make ourselves at second hand partners in the act of creation. Moreover, apart from this subtle self-flattery in which all critical readers secretly indulge, the education of the ear, the mind and the eye to detect and value the finer points does actually enhance the initial impact that a work of art has on us, because we are enabled to react more quickly and more fully to the writer's or the painter's intention.

For the historian, the relationship of art to truth is a particularly exacting one; it may even seem rather a narrow one. What more is there to be said but that the historian has to tell the truth? At least that is ideally what he is supposed to do, and some would say that art does not come into it at all. But art *does* come into it, for within the limitations of our human condition, truth is not apprehensible nor can it be communicated to another person without the help of art. To pass on any piece of information intelligibly requires a feat in the arrangement of words and ideas. Art may come in at an earlier stage, before that of communication. Simply to apprehend a fact intelligently and intelligibly requires a degree of art.

Benedetto Croce has equated art with intuition and argued that we cannot *know* anything until we have given it a name, that is – formalized it in our minds, and that this formalization, or naming, is essentially a creative art. His English disciple, the philosopher and historian Collingwood, said that an historic fact only has meaning for us, in so far as we can re-think the thought that created it. The historian, according to Collingwood, has to make the creative act himself in the first place in his own mind. On the intensity with which he can make it depends the depth of his understanding of it. That is the first move: the first creative act. Only afterwards comes the second creative act of communication. On the skill with which he can communicate his thought depends his power to convey the meaning to others. They are two separate things and there is art in both.

This is not really any different from the processes of thought of any writer dealing with reality. It is what happens with the novelist or at least with those who deal in life as it is: not of course with the writers whose quality is a heightened imaginative power, the allegorical or the romantic, who illuminate life by lifting it into another atmosphere. But the creative writer, the novelist who aims at giving us life as it is, faces the same problem as the historian – the problem of reading the meaning of an incident and conveying it to the reader. Virginia Woolf wrote thus of Jane Austen:

> She makes us wonder why an ordinary act as she describes it becomes so full of meaning . . . Here is nothing out of the way. It is midday in Northamptonshire; a dull young man is talking to a rather weakly young woman on the stairs as they go up to dress for dinner, with housemaids passing. But from triviality, from commonplace, their words become suddenly full of meaning and the moment for both one of the most memorable in their lives. It fills itself; it shines; it glows; it hangs before us, deep, trembling, serene for a second; next, the housemaid passes, and this drop in which all the happiness of life has collected gently subsides again to become part of the ebb and flow of ordinary existence.

The incident comes from *Mansfield Park*. Edmund Bertram and Fanny Price are going upstairs on the eve of the ball given for Fanny; Edmund had only a few hours before planted in her bosom the seeds of anguish and ecstasy by coupling her and Mary Crawford as the 'two dearest objects I have on earth' and now in this incident on the stairs he assuages her agony by indicating that he has serious doubts of Mary Crawford's suitability as a wife.

But it is not only this moment, it is the whole extremely commonplace love story of Edmund and Fanny that Jane Austen irradiates, with never a false tone, simply by seeing the truth about these two dull virtuous young people with an artist's integrity and intensity. We cannot be amused and delighted by Fanny as we are by Emma Woodhouse and Elizabeth Bennett, because poor Fanny was not amusing or delightful, but we *know* her as if she were a living person, because Jane Austen has perfectly created and perfectly projected her. Fanny's experience first became a part of Jane Austen's experience and then a part of ours.

The historian has to do very much the same thing, with this difference; that the novelist is free to adapt and invent provided that the material is that of authentic and living experience. The historian, on the other hand, is dealing with events which once occurred independently of him and which he seeks to describe, or, if he is a pioneer, to re-establish accurately. But although everything about which the historian writes had at one time a separate existence in itself, it exists for him in the present only as he is able to re-think it. Thus the quality of our understanding of the past depends on the quality of understanding its interpreters have brought to it. The French Revolution was, at the time, a series of terrifying and present realities. Today it is a number of ideas and traditions, right or wrong, vague or vivid according to the intensity or accuracy with which the evidence has been examined and the ideas interpreted or transmitted.

The creative process of the artist in history is obvious enough in that kind of history which is generally called literary history – that is in history which is frankly designed to be read as literature. Literary history is concerned, and legitimately concerned, with conveying the writer's view of events to the reader with the greatest intensity. Many historians in the last two centuries have shown that history of this kind can also contain scholarship of great value. Several major works which were conceived and undertaken as works of literature and designed to appeal to the educated public as a whole were also works of significant and sometimes pioneer research. Gibbon's *Decline and Fall* embodies the most extensive scholarship; Motley's *Rise of the Dutch Republic* involved laborious and exhaustive work in the Dutch archives; Froude was the first historian to realize the necessity of consulting the Spanish archives and to penetrate into Simancas.

All histories conceived as literature have this in common; that they are written about subjects of general interest. They deal with people and principles which are generally understood, with incidents interesting and dramatic in themselves. But there are many subjects which have to be studied and which ought to be studied, but which no historian could or should wish to turn into literary history. The underlying mechanism of administration, the slow development of institutions, the intricate interlocking of economic and social facts, which must of necessity be studied in meticulous detail and infinite variety unless we are to be misled by facile generalizations – all these things are of the greatest importance in the study of history, but very few of them can be adequately or even honestly treated in an essentially literary manner. Writing about them is none the less an art, and a very difficult one; and some works on these highly unliterary subjects are most certainly literature.

Frederick Maitland is by some considered to be our greatest historian; certainly no one would deny him a place on the heights. Quite apart from what he wrote about, he wrote a clear, spare, lively English which is a pleasure to read. But when in his great book *Domesday Book and Beyond* he set out to trace and delineate the legal ideas which bound together the rural society of England in the eleventh century, he was writing for the students of medieval history and of law to whom his ideas were originally delivered in the form of lectures; and he was writing for the same kind of public outside the lecture hall – for specialists, for people who had professional reasons to learn about such things. He was not thinking about the general reader, and he could not do so, because that would have compelled him to simplify too much and to explain things that, with his students, he could take for granted. But his book, all his books, are works of art, both for the vision which forms them and the lucid manner in which they are written.

In 1888 in a lecture at Cambridge, Maitland regretted that no history of English law had ever been written; the 'great man for the great book' had not yet appeared. In fact he had appeared; he was born in 1871, was a schoolboy at the time of Maitland's lecture and his name was William Holdsworth. His majestic *History of English Law* came out between 1903 and 1938 and is the most important book on English history to appear in this century. But Professor Holdsworth did not expect the literary world to receive his book with raptures (he would have been embarrassed if they had done so) and he did not design it to be read with effortless delight by the general reader. If he had done so he might have written a brilliant essay on English law, but it would not have been the great and authoritative book that it is, the mine for all future historians to dig in.

There are innumerable historical themes too detailed, too vast, too abtruse, too specialized to be suitable for literary treatment in the generally accepted sense of the word. Yet any book on such a subject, if it is to be valuable at all, must be a work of art. There must be behind it a strong and clear apprehension of reality, and there must be the power to convey it to the readers for whom it is intended.

This has more to do with form than with style. The distinction between style and form is not always clearly made in practice. Style is the surface manner of presentation, the use of words, the shaping of sentences and paragraphs; form is the structure underlying the ground plan and conception of the book. It is certainly better if a historian has both, but he can, and often does, do without style. He cannot do without form, for if his writing is formless his book ceases to be art and ceases to be history – it becomes a mere catalogue of statements, dry insignificant bricks without mortar.

It is a pity, of course, to do without style because even with the most abstruse subjects clarity and crispness are a help to presentation. Maitland was a master of the cool short sentence, and, unobtrusively, of the right choice of adjectives when adjectives were called for. Because of the closely knit argument and the nature of his subject matter it is not very easy to take out a single paragraph for quotation as an example. But here he is summing up, at the end of a passage on land tenure and legal terminology at the time of the Conquest. First he utters a few significant but not over-weighted general principles:

> We must not be in a hurry to get to the beginning of the long history of law. Very slowly we are making our way towards it. The history of law must be a history of ideas. It must represent, not merely what men have done and said, but what men have thought in bygone ages. The task of reconstructing ancient ideas is hazardous, and can only be accomplished little by little. . . . Against many kinds of anachronism we now guard ourselves. We are careful of costume, of armour and architecture, of words and forms of speech. But it is far easier to be careful of these things than to prevent the intrusion of untimely ideas . . .

If, he elaborates, we introduce anachronistic ideas –

> we shall be doing worse than if we armed Hengist and Horsa with machine-guns or pictured the Venerable Bede correcting proofs for the Press; we shall have built upon a crumbling foundation. The most efficient method of protecting ourselves against such errors is

that of reading our history backwards as well as forwards, of making sure of our middle ages before we talk about the 'archaic', of accustoming our eyes to the twilight before we go out into the night.

The effect of the extremely simple metaphor at the end is very striking, because he uses metaphor so sparingly that it comes with a shock of novelty, though in fact his figure of 'going out into the night' is straightforward, even commonplace, in itself.

Surface style is something which strikes the reader immediately; it is what attracts us to, or repels us from, a writer in the first place. It played a foremost part therefore in the now ancient controversy between the academic and the literary historians. Both sides put too much emphasis on style (as though this was the only place in which a historian displayed his art) and this caused a misapprehension of what was really meant by art, and the consequent revolt of scholars against art at the close of the last century. History they claimed was a science pure and simple.

The ire of the academic historians was aroused by the personal idiosyncrasies, the charm, the wit, the passion, the sheer individual energy displayed by the great literary historians. They noted with disapproval the evident prejudices of Macaulay or Froude, and with – possibly – a certain *schadenfreude* the weakness in technical knowledge which caused Carlyle, for instance, in his *Oliver Cromwell* to be taken in by some outrageously faked documents. They rather illogically ascribed the errors which they detected in these historians to the treatment of history as art, by which they meant nothing more than attention to style.

J. R. Seeley, who was still Professor of Modern History at Cambridge when the young Trevelyan was a student, spoke sternly to him, as he tells us in *Clio: A Muse*, on exactly this point. Art, asserted Professor Seeley, had nothing whatever to do with history. He was conscientiously anxious to eradicate any misapprehension on this point from the mind of the young student who, being a great-nephew of Macaulay, might well have a dangerous family inheritance.

Professor Seeley applied his anti-art attitude with some vigour to his own style which is aggressively unpleasing; he dammed the flow of his sentences with obstructive subsidiary clauses; he made no attempt at clarity or cleanness of phrase, so that often his sentences have to be read several times before their meaning is clear, and he mixed up abstract and concrete ideas, a slackness to which historical writing is all too subject – as for instance: 'The Counter-reformation broke out' as though the Counter-reformation were a wild beast in a cage.

Yet Seeley's two major historical works, *The Growth of British Policy* and *The Expansion of England* are still, if not generally read from end to end, at least frequently consulted, and the ideas which he put forward in them played an influential part both in the interpretation of our history and on our political ideas. This could not have been so unless he had been in some degree also an artist, whether he knew it or not. And undoubtedly he was, because he had a powerful sense of form. His style most certainly does not flow, but his ideas do, and once the reader has surmounted the surface difficulties he will find that Seeley's books have great persuasive power; because the facts are related to each other with discrimination and vision. It is not necessary to agree with his ultimate conclusions in order to admire the skill with which he amasses and arranges his knowledge to arrive at them. While vigorously repudiating the use of art as unfit for the science of history, he showed a high degree of artistic skill in his own treatment of his material.

I never had the honour to meet the late Sir William Holdsworth, the great historian of English law, but I should imagine he was not a man who had much patience with the airs and graces of literary history. Yet in the marshalling of his facts, the shaping of his argument, the interplay of narrative and analysis, the vision with which he relates the small particular incident to the general argument, the skill with which he distinguishes and analyses the many different forces at work in the shaping of English law, he is a major artist.

Those who proclaimed that history was a science pure and simple did no damage to literature but they did some damage to history. Writers are tough, and writers who wished to write history were bound to go on writing, whatever the academics said to discourage them. The damage was done not by discouraging writers, but by encouraging those who had no aesthetic gifts at all to believe that they could do very well in history in spite of this deficiency. But the card index is not knowledge. It is only the beginning of knowledge, and the accumulation of facts is useless until they are related to each other and seen in proportion. Historical material cannot be intelligently understood without a certain aesthetic sense. Sir John Neale, who writes with equal success in both kinds of history – the literary and the academic – has said in one of his essays 'All facts are not born free and equal', and indeed they are not. There is a hierarchy of facts. To arrange them rightly, to distinguish the important from the trivial, to see their bearing one upon another, requires a skill which is very comparable to that of the painter giving significant form to the objects before him, judging the values of light and shade, or the spatial dispositions of shape and colour.

The good historian, whatever his theme, must be an artist. Without art there may be accumulations of statements, there may be calendars or chronicles, but there is no history. Any way of thinking about, or looking at, historical facts, which has any value at all, must be an exercise of the imaginative and discriminating faculties. History in any intelligible form *is* art.

But if history is *art*, in what way does the historian's attitude to art and truth differ from that of the essentially imaginative writer? Very profoundly. It is the privilege and indeed the function of the creative artist to use, that is to manipulate and to intensify, the truth about life as he sees it. The bare truth is not enough in itself. 'Realism by itself is fatal,' said Turgenev, and, in another passage on the same subject, 'Truth is the air without which we cannot breathe, but art is a plant, sometimes even a rather fantastic one, which grows and develops in this air'. It is self-evident that these are two statements that no historian should make, or even think. Realism is fatal? But the historian laboriously strives after the whole unvarnished truth. 'Art is a plant, sometimes a fantastic one' – but the pedestrian historian cannot allow anything fantastic, except of course when the vagaries of human nature do really – as they sometimes do – produce a fantastic effect.

The letters and commonplace books of writers are full of indications of the way in which experiences and incidents from life can be and must be adapted, expounded, telescoped, or amalgamated to make novels and stories, to make *literature*. Henry James evolves a situation from a fragment of conversation overheard at a tea party; Joyce Cary describes the face of a woman seen on a boat-trip, a visual memory, which was later vitalized by the fragment of a half-heard anecdote and from which grew a story which was only very tenuously related to the chances which inspired it.

The work of creative imagination is *controlled* by experience; it has to spring from knowledge and understanding of life, but the writer is free to use and reject what he wants, to present a heightened or simplified picture; he is not subservient to the facts he has accumulated or the observations he has made. They are his material to be freely used as his art directs, and he can invent or discard as it suits him.

The historian cannot do this. He can only use what he has before him. He cannot invent and – this may be even more difficult – he cannot reject except within very cautious limits. The novelist – and this goes for the historical novelist too – can reject those parts of the material which for one reason or another seem to add nothing to what he wishes to project. Indeed selection of essentials is an important part of his art. The historian can only select in a much more limited manner; naturally he *does* select and reject because everything cannot be included in an intelligible book. There must be some theme or theory, and there must be some parts of the historical material which are adjudged not relevant. But over-selection, over-simplification are major causes of misrepresentation in history, and the historian cannot ask with the novelist: does this fact add anything to the pattern of my novel as I see it? to the projection of this character or this situation as I intend it? He has to ask: does this fact add anything to my knowledge and understanding of this incident, of this situation, of this epoch? And he must be very sure indeed that it adds nothing before he decides to pass it over.

The historian has to decide whether an apparently irrelevant fact is truly irrelevant. He also has to find a place for the awkward fact which does not fit with the pattern of development or the scheme of events as he had at first seen it. This is often a strain on his patience and his conscience. He has to find a place for new evidence which will make sense when added to the existing evidence, whether or not the result fits in with his own theories. If his theory is destroyed by new evidence, he must abandon it and start again. It is never safe and it is usually impossible to insert new material into the texture of an older theory. The attempt to do so produces a result like that picture of the Gerbier family which was begun by Rubens during his visit to England in 1630. Gerbier, an engraver, a go-between in the traffic in works of art, who was under the patronage of Charles I, had a handsome wife and a family of pretty, plump children whom Rubens painted when he was staying in their house. But the lady was very fruitful and had many more children later; new pieces of canvas were attached to the picture at one side and additional little Gerbiers, not by Rubens, were introduced. The effect is very strange, not only because the picture has an extra foot or two that does not fit, but because the original fluid and beautifully placed composition by Rubens has been thrown out of balance.

New material, new evidence, additional historical facts are very like the little Gerbiers. They should not be added on. A new picture has to be painted, a new composition thought out, which will include all the children, or all the facts, in a new relationship to each other.

But although the pattern, from the very nature of things, has frequently to be altered, there must be a pattern for the historical process to be apprehended at all. G. M. Young has said of the historian:

> Movement and continuity are the conceptions with which he works and what aesthetic writers claim a passionate apprehension of form to be to the painter, a passionate apprehension of process is to the historian.

This is true, but like all obsessions, the obsession with process can become dangerous. For when a highly satisfactory pattern of process has been worked out by the historian he is very unwilling to let it go; yet he may have to let it go if facts come to light which gravely modify it. Almost any theory about historical process could be sustained, almost any pattern could be worked out, if the historian allowed himself the freedom of other creative writers to eliminate what he does not wish to see. Being human, most historians do, to some extent, fall into this error, and some much more seriously than others.

The historian's sense of form should never be so strong that he cannot modify the shape into which he has cast his material when new evidence compels him to do so. It should never be so strong, but often is; and there are occasions when historians behave far more like writers of fiction than they either admit or know. There can be very few who have not at some time or other made an unconscious excision or elimination; or turned a blind eye to details which did not suit their books. It is a price that has to be paid, because without the sense of form there can be no capacity to relate facts, to analyse them, to compose or to sustain an argument. G. M. Young is right when he talks of the passionate apprehension of process; without passion in this sense who would undertake or carry through the backbreaking, eye-aching business of research, and count a hundred hours well spent if they produce one fragment of evidence, or one long-desired clue? Without passion there might be no errors; but without passion there would certainly be no history.

To raise once more the old question – is History an Art or a Science? Or is it as some have argued a hybrid between the two? The best answer is to turn the question inside out. All sciences are devoted to the quest for truth; truth can neither be apprehended nor communicated without art. History therefore is an art, like all the other sciences.

1958

The Conversion of Malta

━━━━━━◀◀◀◆▶▶▶━━━━━━

Two Englishwomen, middle-aged and soberly clad, each with a large, corded trunk, embarked on a Dutch ship at Leghorn early in the year 1659. They booked their passage with the Captain as far as Alexandria, where, they told him, it was their mission 'to preach the Gospel of Christ to the inhabitants'. Whatever he thought of their prospects, he made no comment.

They were West Country women of the sober, fearless, respectable middle class; their names – already known to several irate magistrates of England – were Katherine Evans and Sarah Chevers. For some years now, leaving home and kindred, they had travelled preaching together, facing the stocks, the whipping-post and furious objurgations from the Bench with that limitless brave innocence which was the characteristic of their faith. They were of the Society of Friends.

They had been storm-tossed and sea-sick on the long journey from London to Leghorn, and although they looked undismayed on the swarthy people, and the evidences of idolatry in churches with more towers, turrets and bells even than the 'steeple-houses' of England, they had evidently been glad to fall in with kindly merchants of their own faith at Leghorn. Now they were setting out for unknown territory, leaving the strange coast of Italy, with its foreign architecture and unfamiliar vegetation, for lands even more unimaginable. The honest timbers of their Dutch vessel were the last link between them and the comprehensible, Protestant north. Not that, moving trance-like at the guidance of the Lord, they would have paused to admit such feelings. They were, among Papists or Infidels, in Italy or Africa, always in the hands of God.

Women of character and courage, versed in the Scriptures and in little else, Katherine had the readier and the sharper tongue,

Sarah had the louder voice for preaching and the greater persistence in what she undertook. Both, like many Englishwomen before and since, were indifferent to ridicule. They would do as they thought right, whether they should be mocked by rude boys or burnt alive.

Not far out from Leghorn, their ship changed course, to have the companionship of another vessel, in the pirate-infested seas, as far as Malta. When the Captain informed his English passengers of the new plan, they knew at once, by revelation, how fateful Malta would be to them and Katherine was moved of the Lord to cry out: 'Oh we have a dreadful cup to drink at that place!'

Their first sight of the island confirmed both their faith and their fears. Standing on the deck, they saw with wonder the crowded, scrambling city, its walls and windows alive with a dark-faced, strange humanity. Unused to Mediterranean crowds they took this for a phenomenon peculiar to the day of their arrival and immediately went to their cabin to pray. It had become clear to them that Alexandria was not to be. Malta – the island on which Saint Paul had been shipwrecked – was their appointed place.

While they were below, the English Consul came on board to see the Captain. He left for the English ladies an invitation to his house, possibly in the hope of restraining whatever activities they had planned. The island, which was ruled over by the Grand Master of the Knights of St John of Jerusalem, was a stronghold of the Church militant and the Inquisition was active.

Neither Knights nor Inquisition daunted Katherine and Sarah. On the following day, each carrying a bundle of tracts, they set off for the Consul's house. Over light refreshments he introduced them to two or three Jesuits. He made no secret of the fact that his sympathy was with the government and official religion of Malta – he could hardly otherwise have maintained himself as consul – but he evidently hoped to carry off the situation by treating the newcomers as diverting eccentrics. The sharp eyes of Katherine and Sarah saw through him at once, though they accepted his invitation to visit his sister, a nun, on the following day. In the nuns' parlour their simple manners and the novelty of their conduct made a pleasant break in the dull routine of convent life, but there was temporary embarrassment when, on being shown over the buildings and chapel, they not only refused to bow to the altar but profited by the occasion to deliver a short lecture on the evils of idolatry.

Meanwhile their ship had sailed, and since they insisted on staying, trunks, tracts, and all, the Consul – by this time acutely anxious – thought best to continue his hospitality, if only to supervise their conduct. The Inquisition was not an institution to be lightly challenged and he could not have Katherine and Sarah jeopardizing the good reputation of the English colony. His plan had some effect for, in spite of his guests' inclination to rise up and prophesy in and out of season, more especially at open windows, fifteen weeks went by before the Inquisition made its deadly pounce. When it did he was not sorry to lose them; he had given them fair and repeated warning.

The Maltese Inquisition, which was the Roman, not the Spanish, Inquisition was strict in suppressing heresies, but had not the gruesome and highly regulated methods of Spain. The two women seem to have been confined in the ordinary prison, their examination and conversion being entrusted almost wholly to the English friars in the place. The small English colony, mostly converts, took the liveliest interest in them; the more obstinate did Katherine and Sarah become, the more did it grow to a point of honour with their compatriots to bring them back to the Mother Church. It was almost as if their conversion were to be a symbol of the return of the whole erring motherland.

Katherine and Sarah found themselves at first shut into a small inner room with 'two little holes in it for light and air'. They were much tormented 'with flies called muskatoes', nor were these the worst they had to suffer; they had no means of washing, no fresh air, their hair began to drop out, their skins grew rough as 'sheep's leather', and they had to lie down and breathe through the door chink from time to time so as not to be stifled.

In this horrible den they were constantly visited by the friars, and here, day after day, feverish, unwashed and unafraid they defied their interlocutors, triumphantly capping every quotation from Holy Writ and scornfully dismissing arguments from other sources. Their Bibles were soon taken away: vain precaution, they knew them by heart. More than usually exasperated by Sarah's pat, decisive answers one friar declared 'he saw an evil spirit in her face'. With unexpected personal vanity, she was indignant; she thought he meant the ravages of the 'muskatoes' on her complexion.

Katherine, meanwhile, was comforted by a vision in the night and soon after, extracting pen, ink and paper from her precious trunk, indited a letter to the chief Inquisitor. 'To the Lord Inquisitor (so-called),' she headed it, and went on: 'Men's persons I cannot admire; they that do admire and respect any Man's person, do it because of advantage.' After this preamble she called him to order in the name of the Lord. Pen and ink were shortly after removed from her.

The prohibition seems to have been relaxed or evaded later, for both women wrote letters home and Katherine composed a continuous stream of reflections, prayers and hymns. Captivity and daily arguments were not soothing to her soul and the thought of the Day of Judgment gave her grim comfort:

> Then some shall howl and some shall mourn
> The rest shall wish they'd ne'er been born
> For Pain and Torment Day and Night,
> Because they have despis'd the Light. . . .

Yet to consign all Malta and the friars to perdition was not primarily her intention; she would gladly have saved them. At every possible opening in the examinations both she and Sarah reversed the order of proceedings and began to convert their converters.

Not for some months did their captors take the obvious step of separating them. Perhaps they had no other cell vacant before, since the new cell found for Sarah was not, from their point of view, a happy choice. It gave on an alleyway leading from a court of justice to a church. Never a procession went by but she would be at her window loudly – and in English – exhorting the worshippers to repent. Soon after a fleet of twenty sail assembled off Malta to go against the Turks and the city was full of soldiers and sailors, both French and Italian. 'Go not forth to murder, nor to kill one another,' cried Sarah from her window to the troops pouring into the church to pray for victory. It was no use; the fleet sailed, the Turks were defeated and to Sarah's grief 'there was great triumphing and glorying in Blood'.

The determination of the English friars to make converts, not martyrs, of the Quaker women, must have been the chief factor in preserving their lives. But in the early days of their imprisonment they were in real danger and constantly threatened with torture and burning. Katherine and Sarah, both doubtless well primed from childhood with atrocity stories of the Inquisition, never doubted the validity of the threats. And indeed it must remain something of a mystery why none of them was carried out; neither in its course nor in its conclusion was the case a typical one.

Cut off from all intercourse with people of their own language (except the friars), locked up without hope of release, expecting daily their final martyrdom and trembling with fear every time a loud Mediterranean brawl occurred within earshot – which was often – the two women, alone or together, in sickness or in health remained unshaken. They held fast not only to their religious tenets but to all the other peculiar rulings of their faith. They would take no oath, they would borrow no money, they would bow to no authority; they would not even say in advance when or what they would eat, lest the Lord should command them otherwise at the last minute. They were proof against threats and against temptation; when attempts at conversion took on a different form and they were coaxed with tales of how much they would be cherished by the whole English colony, and indeed all Malta, if they gave in, they were unmoved. The Inquisitor, hearing that Katherine was by this time really ill, sent her a present of two plump fowls. She refused them saying firmly that she would live only of her own, and Sarah, whom they next tried to trick into cooking them behind Katherine's back, was equally emphatic.

Both women had so far paid all their expenses punctually, but at the end of one year and seven weeks their stock of money was exhausted. From this time onwards, the Inquisition having lost all but a theoretical interest in them, they were allowed to go among the other prisoners, and soon found means both to pay their way and to introduce an air of middle-class respectability into the gaol, by knitting stockings and neatly darning clothes for their companions. When not preaching they were gentle, kindly and efficient creatures and seem to have been liked, although they provoked derision when from time to time they dishevelled their hair, cast dust on their heads and did loud penance for the sins of Malta. Greater misgivings were expressed when they washed the dust out of their hair by dipping their heads into buckets of cold water. But, as Katherine triumphantly observed, vindicating English habits of personal cleanliness, 'they caught no cold, nor had so much as the snuff in their Noses'.

Spasmodic efforts were by this time being made for their release. A new English Consul, more sympathetic than the last, assisted by the English Captain of a passing vessel, prevailed so far with the authorities that Katherine and Sarah could have sailed back to England at once if they would have consented merely to kiss the crucifix. (This at least was what they understood the condition to be.) Valiant and exasperating women, they utterly refused. Thinking that 'idolatry' was their chief trouble the patient Consul tried again, and this time procured their release on condition that some reputable citizen would go bail for their staying away from Malta. Neither Katherine nor Sarah would hear of it: it made them debtors to a third party. Besides the Lord had made his will known to Katherine and it was not yet his will that they should leave.

The new Consul gave it up. His embarrassment was increased by the arrival, soon after, of a Quaker minister named Daniel Baker whom the Turks had expelled from Smyrna. No sooner was he landed than he wrote to the prisoners, 'Dear Lambs, Peace be unto you,' with several pages more of spiritual consolation. For the rest he contrived to talk to them through the prison grating and to utter a certain number of home truths about the spiritual darkness of Malta before the harassed Consul hustled him on board a ship for England. He was not a popular passenger, for at Gibraltar, on Holy Thursday, he slipped ashore, marched into a local church, strode up the aisle and after derisively watching the priest for some minutes, turned his back on the altar, rent his garments, sprinkled a handful of dust on his head and in resonant biblical English called on the worshippers to repent. They must have taken him for more of a lunatic than a heretic, for no one touched him, though the Captain of the ship left Gibraltar in a hurry and, as Baker wonderingly noticed, 'spake bitter Things against him'.

By this time, however, George Fox himself was anxious that
something should be done for the prisoners at Malta, and George
Fox had a powerful streak of common sense. Evidently the only
way in which the two women could be unconditionally released
was by the direct intervention, not merely of a higher but of the
highest authority. Someone must approach the Pope.

A possible intermediary, the London Quakers suggested, was
the King's cousin, 'Lord d'Aubenay'. This gentleman, whose
name was Ludovic Stuart, was a cadet of the royal family, and had
been brought up largely in France, where he had taken orders and
become a canon of Notre-Dame. In spite of his priestly office he
had quietly assumed the title of his elder brother, George Lord
d'Aubigny, when the latter was killed fighting on the King's side
at Edgehill. Since George left a voluble widow and a son, the
family thought poorly of Ludovic's conduct, but the subsequent
accession of the real Lord d'Aubigny to the Dukedom of Rich-
mond had, so to speak, evened out the honours.

Ludovic Stuart, whatever his greed for worldly titles, had
gracious manners and a not unkindly heart. The Quakers found
him 'a well-temper'd Man . . . notwithstanding he was a Priest in
Orders belonging to the Romish Church'. Besides being 'well-
temper'd' he had through his royal connections the necessary
personal influence. With surprisingly little delay, in July 1662,
the Vatican gave orders for the unconditional release of the two
prisoners at Malta.

Even so Katherine and Sarah distinguished clearly between the
will of Christ's Vicar ('so-called') and the will of Christ. There
was a moment's painful anxiety for the English Consul while they
awaited the Inner Light. It came: they might leave their prison.
They packed their deplenished trunks, took care to tip their
gaolers and stepped forth into freedom, not forgetting to kneel
down once more on the prison threshold and implore the mercy
of Heaven on their persecutors.

The weeks which elapsed before a suitable boat was found for
their homeward journey were uncomfortable for the Consul with
whom they stayed, and whose wife and servants, they sadly noted,
became less and less civil daily. Katherine composed a manifesto
and all but smuggled it out of the house; Sarah fasted for a week
in sackcloth and commanded the Consul to make God's will known

to the Grand Master, to call Malta to repentance. The Consul refused to pass the message on, and when, sure enough, a thunderstorm caused an explosion in the arsenal and a serious fire Sarah could hardly be blamed for recognizing in this the awful consequence of disregarding a heavenly mandate.

In the late summer they were at length taken on board the *Saphire*, Captain Samuel Titswell, who agreed to carry them home. The rest of his passengers were four and twenty Knights of Malta, very fine, aristocratic and condescending. One of them was the Inquisitor's brother and so like him Katherine could have singled him out anywhere. It was, on the contrary, he who singled her out, amused and impressed, perhaps, by the story of her astonishing obstinacy. He led her on to argue, nodded sympathetically and dismissed her with a good-natured platitude: there were many ways to Heaven, he said, but they would all meet there in the end. She had not been three years in prison to let so gross an error pass. 'There is only one way to Heaven,' she said tartly.

Their trials were over, but their visions were not. The vessel touched at Tangier, recently handed over to the English by the Portuguese and alive with English troops, whose language and conduct appalled them. They complained to the Governor, and might have preached to the soldiers had their attention not been diverted to the even greater need for redemption of the wild Moorish tribes in the neighbouring hills. Nothing would content them but they must go forth to enlighten the heathen. The Governor curtly refused permission, and the *Saphire* carried the protesting pair rapidly out of the Mediterranean.

Beyond the Pillars of Hercules the story fades away, though now and again across the years their names recur in the long martyrologium of the Quakers, striking as dauntless against the Anglican, as against the Roman, error. It was perhaps Lord d'Aubigny who voiced the respect which transcends doctrine, when in his courtier-priest's rich lodging he received their thanks (for they were grateful). 'Good women,' he said, 'for what service or kindness I have done you, all that I shall desire of you is that when you pray to God, you will remember me in your prayers.' It was the tribute which from time to time the world will pay to Faithful and Valiant for Truth.

1946

The Common Man in the Civil War

It is a good rule for the inquirer who wants to know about the people of a past epoch that he should 'go on reading until he hears them talking' – a graphic phrase which I learnt from Mr G. M. Young. We do not know an age until we are at home with its ways of thought and manner of expression, until we can recognize its essential idiom, the commonplaces of its daily vocabulary, its special tone of voice.

But whose voices does the historian hear? He may read widely and wisely in official and unofficial papers; he may ferret through diaries and newspapers, private letters and public statements, Acts of Parliament, plays, poems, sermons, account books, wills, laundry lists, inventories – all the multifarious survivals from his chosen epoch which his single brain can absorb. After all this, whom does he hear talking? It is obvious that the loudest and clearest voices will be those of the more articulate members of society, the well-educated, the well-born, the well-placed. It is easier to pick up the ideas of the college common room than of the skittle alley, of the lawyer's study, the squire's dining room and his lady's parlour, than of the yeoman's fireside, the alehouse, or the laundry. This is true even of an epoch as richly documented as the English Civil War. We have a clearer visual image of the lives and personalities of the rich than of the poor. Some of their houses still stand, more of them at any rate than of the cottages of the poor; we can see, sometimes still in use, some of their furniture and hangings. We know their faces and the fashion of their clothes from surviving portraits. We have to reconstruct much more laboriously our picture of the home, the possessions, and the daily life of a labourer – the one- or two-roomed cottage, the earthen floor, the rough table and stool, the bench fixed to the wall, the spinning wheel and wash tub, the straw palliasse for sleeping, the earthenware pots and leather bottles.

The further we go back in time the more difficult is it to distinguish the voices of ordinary people, and the more do we have to rely on literature (when it exists) to fill in the gaps left in the records. Chaucer, Langland, and Shakespeare can sometimes help us. We can discover the economic conditions in which humbler people lived from their wills and the inventories of their goods, but the sound of their voices reaches the records chiefly when they are in trouble – in collision with the law, or petitioning for relief in time of distress. The impression that we get of the life and fate of the common man in past ages is therefore often more gloomy than it would be if we knew more of his behaviour when he was not in the courts or on the parish.

The middle years of the seventeenth century are particularly interesting because, in the voluble clash of opinions which was stimulated by the disorders of the Civil War, the voice of the common man becomes for the first time clearly distinguishable. Isolated voices had of course been uplifted before from time to time, but in the war years, the religious fervour which had in part caused the war, and the physical upheaval which accompanied it, gave a release and outlet to inquiring, uneducated minds. The hundreds of pamphlets composed by simple people in the Thomason Collection in the British Museum represent only a very small part of what was going on; for one man who could write a pamphlet there were ten who could stand on a tub and preach to their neighbours and a hundred who could debate ideas, cite Scriptures, and talk politics. For every preacher and self-appointed prophet there must have been hundreds more who exercised their wits in ale-house arguments or as they worked at the bench or rested in the fields.

The source of their inspiration was the book that they knew best, the Bible, strongly backed by the book they knew second best, Foxe's *Book of Martyrs*. It is not easy to estimate the degree of literacy among the poor, but working people usually left their young children at the petty school while they were at work, at least until the children were old enough to be helpful. These schools were kept by someone who plied a sedentary trade, often a cobbler, and could overlook the children while he did so, and impart after a fashion the letters of the alphabet to those who wanted to learn. Those who could not read got their Bible by ear, and later, when the pamphlet war was raging, picked up the ideas and arguments set forth in print by hearing them read aloud. Their memories, on the average, would be a great deal better than ours, for few human faculties can have declined more than memory with the spread of books and printing.

It is easy enough to mock at the strange fantasies which uneducated people conjured out of their Biblical studies. Dryden, an Anglican and later a Roman Catholic, expresses at the latter end of the seventeenth century, in his *Religio Laici*, only a sad contempt for these illiterate prophets:

> *The Book thus put in every vulgar hand*
> *Which each presumed he best could understand,*
> *The Common Rule became the Common Prey*
> *And at the mercy of the rabble lay.*
> *The tender page with horny fists was gaul'd*
> *And he was gifted most who loudest bawled.*
> *The Spirit gave the doctoral degree*
> *And every member of the company*
> *Was of his trade and of the Bible free . . .*
> *This was the fruit the private spirit brought*
> *Occasion'd by great zeal and little thought . . .*

Great zeal, certainly, but Dryden is wrong in accusing his humble compatriots of 'little thought'. They may not have thought very well, having no training, but they thought a great deal, and the crime of most of these prophets in the eyes of the educated and privileged was chiefly that people of their kind were not supposed to think at all, or at least not about such matters as these. King James I had deliberately published the *Book of Sports*, permitting his subjects to play games on Sunday, because if they were not so occupied he feared they would speculate on religion and politics, which was not fit for them to do. George Thomason, who put all seventeenth-century scholars in his debt by amassing throughout the Civil War every printed pamphlet on which he could lay hands, frequently writes across the title page of some religious outpouring the statement that the author is 'a comfit maker in Bucklersbury', a hay-trusser, a cobbler, or some such; he evidently thought the exercise of such a profession sufficient warrant for putting the views of the writer outside serious consideration. No one was more fierce in condemning these low-born prophets than John Taylor, the Water-Poet; he was himself a Thames lighterman, and had established himself as a favoured eccentric in the 1630s by writing doggerel verses and travellers' tales. The vindictive rage which begins to appear in his writing when hundreds of other uneducated men also set up for authors is comic, but a little saddening.

Much of the preaching and prophesying was, naturally, very silly, often hysterical, sometimes a little mad. In the Thomason Collection there are records of strange hallucinations; a little girl had a vision of angels, about the bigness of turkeys, and with the sweetest faces she ever beheld; a troop of wretched beggars were arrested one of whom claimed to be the Woman Clothed with the Sun and the Princess All Glorious Within. There had always been such aberrations, but they multiplied enormously during and immediately after the War, and while their folly is often distressing, the quantity and quality even of these crazy imaginings suggest the extent to which a new light had broken through into the drab and limited lives of the very poor.

For some, religious speculation was never more than an outlet for splendid imaginings which had hitherto nothing on which to feed, or for an egoism which had been starved in the narrow conditions of ordinary life; but with others religious ideas rapidly acquired a practical and secular tinge. Doctrines from the Bible were held to justify social, economic and political changes. Something of the kind had happened often enough before; the late Dr Schenk in his excellent book on *The Concern for Social Justice in the Puritan Revolution* showed that many of the Leveller doctrines had a respectable pedigree in medieval religious–political ideas. But never had speculation been so widespread, so imaginative, and so formidable as it was to become in the later 1640s. It is as though the common man, who in earlier centuries had hardly been able to get a word in edgeways, had for a brief interlude come to dominate the scene.

Among the multitude of voices, that of John Lilburne was

certainly the loudest. He was admittedly rather an uncommon common man, since genius is always uncommon, and he certainly possessed genius. He came in fact of very small gentry, and being a younger son was early apprenticed to a trade, but he had a knack of identifying himself with almost every predicament and almost every demand of the common man in the middle years of the century. In his innumerable pamphlets he frequently assumes the part of what we might call the common man, for he is very fond of a title which suggests that he is standing out as a representative of 'man' in general, and symbolizing in his person the wrongs and suffering inflicted on him by the hand of government, whether King or Parliament or Corporation. He calls himself – to give a specimen handful from the titles of his works – the Christian Man, the Just Man, the Oppressed Man, the Resolved Man, the Innocent Man, the Upright Man, the Afflicted Man. And indeed, as these titles imply, he packed an immense amount of trouble into a life of little more than forty years.

In the 1630s, before the Civil War, he was in trouble with the King's Star Chamber for distributing unlicensed literature; released by the Long Parliament, he enlisted, was taken prisoner at Brentford, tried for high treason and narrowly escaped hanging at the King's hands; subsequently he was exchanged; distinguished himself in the fighting; was wounded; withdrew from the Parliamentary army because he would not take the Covenant which was imposed after the alliance with the Scots; next he was in trouble for unlicensed printing (he was concerned with a whole series of clandestine printing presses during the Civil War); for libelling the Speaker, for libelling the Earl of Manchester and others; he was constantly in and out of the Tower; trying to reform the government of the City of London, trying to break down the monopoly of the Merchant Adventurers in the wool trade; organizing the outcry in the New Model Army against Parliament; then the mouthpiece of the Leveller movement; constantly up against Cromwell, who he believed had betrayed the cause of liberty for which the war had been fought; twice acquitted to loud popular acclamation; sent into exile, he returned and was shut up by an exasperated government, and in 1655 became a Quaker only a year or two before his death. It is a temptation to anyone discussing the common man in the Great Civil War to let John Lilburne steal the show. But it is not really my intention to say very much about the Levellers with whose republican–egalitarian views he is chiefly associated or to discuss the outburst of democratic theories which marked the end of the Civil War. These things have already had their fair share – and perhaps rather more than their fair share – of attention from historians.

What I want briefly to consider are the facts – or some of them – behind these theories; the hard and humble facts about the lives of ordinary people in the war, and the way in which their practical experience stimulated their ambitions and loosened their tongues. In a necessarily brief and partial summary many of my points may seem very obvious, and yet in the analysis and discussion of history the obvious is often overlooked simply because it *is* obvious. Theories and speculations can exercise a greater charm over students of history than bread-and-butter facts, but the truth, or something approaching the truth, in the reconstruction of the past can only be achieved by the constant association of theories with the facts out of which they must, in great part, grow. This is especially important in the epoch of the Civil War, many of the ideas that it generated are so interesting in themselves that we are tempted to study them in isolation, and so to acquire a misleading perspective of what actually happened.

The Civil War was in many ways a disaster. Three hundred years later we still mourn the destruction it wrought; noble houses like Chipping Campden blown up by the Royalists to prevent it falling into enemy hands; or Basing House razed by the conquerors; majestic Pembroke Castle reduced to a shell; the massive walls of Corfe laboriously and vindictively blasted into fragments; and the cathedrals – the shattered glass at Canterbury, the burnt manuscripts at Winchester, the fury of destruction which swept Hereford, Worcester, Rochester, the siege works which blew the central spire of Lichfield to the skies; the fine silver plate melted down for money, and sometimes not even melted but crudely stamped out into ill-shaped coins. Neither the long-term nor the immediate destruction was comparable to what was done at the same time in Germany's Thirty Years War, but it was none the less distressing. The destruction of growing crops, the seizure of livestock and goods, the exactions of the armies in cash and kind were not comparable to those of the much larger and more ruthless armies at that time fighting in Europe, and more especially in Germany; but they were none the less to be deplored and they caused much acute, if temporary, distress.

But there were compensations, and if I appear to emphasize these it is not because I underestimate the suffering caused by the war, but simply because its relieving features have been less frequently considered and are less familiar. I do not mean to preach the soothing doctrine that all was for the best, or the platitudinous one that you will gain on the roundabouts what you lose on the swings. But there was some gain to be had out of the disordered conditions of the war, and the common man, in and out of the armies, had his share of it.

Consider for example the city of Leicester, stormed, taken, and plundered on the night of 31 May 1645 by King Charles's men, so that, as Captain Richard Symonds of the Royal Life Guard informs us, by one in the morning there was 'scarce a cottage unplundered'. This was extremely unpleasant for the citizens of Leicester, but enjoyable for the King's Welsh infantry who had never before had so much wealth in their pockets. A fortnight later when the Royalist infantry surrendered at Naseby, the Parliamentary soldiers relieved them of what was left of their spoil. This was saddening for the Welsh infantry, but enjoyable for the East Anglians and the Londoners who rifled their waggons and knapsacks.

Plunder is an ugly word, said to have come to England from Germany with General Lesley's troops in the Bishops' War of 1640. I do not condone the practice. But at least in a civil war the losses by plunder are a little mitigated by the fact that property is changing hands between citizens of the same country. It is not being carried out of the country altogether by conquerors. We should guard against the modern fallacy of assuming that the common man will be nothing but a victim in times of public disaster. In the accounts of the borough of Leicester, for instance, are many small payments to messengers sent out to gather news of what was happening in the neighbourhood: six shillings to a man who rode to Coventry to find out what had happened at Kineton fight, as they called the Battle of Edgehill. There was someone six shillings better off for the kind of employment that is much in demand in a war. Such payments are frequent in the parish and town records of the period. Archdeacon West in his delightful and informative book *Rude Forefathers* gives extracts from the accounts of a village constable near Newark. Two shillings and fourpence is paid for repairing some armour; a shilling is paid to carters hired for transport by Prince Rupert, and they are given free beer for the journey as well. These small repeated expenses came heavy on a small village, but carters, blacksmiths, and odd-job men were earning more money. If the war checked and hampered some kinds of industry it stimulated other kinds. No doubt it stimulated chiefly the unproductive kinds, but its immediate effect was often to absorb unemployment and to put more money into the ragged pockets of casual labourers.

The war brought anxiety, expense, and loss above all to the yeoman and the petty tradesman, to those who had worked and saved to maintain their small property and their place in the world. Take for instance a typical inventory of the possessions of such a man at this time, a yeoman in Essex: he possessed a great joined table and eight stools, one little joined table and chair, a cupboard and settle with three boxes on it; two dozen pewter saucers, a salt cellar; two feather beds with curtains and bolsters, besides two trundle beds with blankets, coverlets, and pillows, eight pairs of sheets, ten napkins, and one tablecloth; three brass pots, three brazen candlesticks, one large kettle, and one middling kettle; a horse valued at two pounds; wearing apparel and a purse of money together valued at sixty-two pounds. Such a householder as this was in constant anxiety during the Civil War. He was subject to a weekly assessment imposed for the support of the armies; he was quite likely to have his horse seized or stolen by passing troopers; his household goods might be damaged by soldiers quartered on him, or plundered if they got out of hand, as they very frequently did. Both parties quite shamelessly raised money by driving off grazing cattle and selling it back at a price to its indignant owners. A market of this kind was regularly held in the great quadrangle at Christ Church, Oxford, and there are many other examples.

Resistance and revolt against the soldiers came in the end from farmers, not from the very poor. The Clubmen who in 1645 banded themselves together against both parties in the West Country were for the most part yeomen, who found leaders among the local lawyers and clergy. They disappeared when the superior discipline of Parliament's New Model Army put an end to plunder and, temporarily at least, lightened the burden against which they had risen to protest. Self-government and self-help were traditions long established in the English village; though there are plenty of examples of men, women, and children taking refuge in woods and ditches for a night or two while fighting was actually going on in their native place, there was no tragic problem of a permanently displaced and fugitive civilian population. Villagers and citizens stayed in their homes and grimly faced the additional problems that the war brought with it. Many were seriously impoverished, a few utterly ruined. Parish accounts at this time frequently record the giving of alms to families who showed certificates to prove that they had once been in better circumstances but had been ruined by the wars, or to wounded men, or to the widows and children of soldiers. Even allowing for a percentage of forged certificates and hard-luck stories there is evidence enough from all over England that the war years were a time of distress.

But there is another side to this. If the laborious tradesman, or yeoman, or respectable artisan who had built up his little business, or husbanded his acres, looked upon the war with anxiety and dismay, his sons, in whom the sap of life was rising, might feel very differently. Richard Baxter reports censoriously that the villages in his part of the country, near Kidderminster, were much quieter after the King's army had passed through in the early months of the war because all the bad young men were swept into it. Bad they may have been; high-spirited they certainly were, and the army offered, to young men impatient of the narrow horizon within which they had been born, an opportunity to see something more of the world.

If in the Civil War the voice of the common man begins to make itself heard to some purpose in English politics, this is in part because so many of them had, during the war, broken away for the first time from the rigid local and traditional pattern into which they had been born.

The use of modern terms in describing the society of another epoch can be misleading. It is convenient to use the word 'class', and hard for anyone born in our century to do without it. Indeed I have used some clumsy circumlocutions in the foregoing pages in order to avoid it. But 'class' in our sense is a nineteenth-century word and suggests a society stratified laterally as ours now is. There was, of course, some lateral stratification in the seventeenth century, and there were social groups which can be described as 'classes' although they did not use the word themselves. The nobility, the larger gentry, the smaller gentry, merchants, yeomen, and so on down to the landless labourer – such stratification of society certainly existed. But the key-word in the seventeenth-century social pattern is not 'class' but 'degree', which suggests not the lateral grouping of society that we know, but a pyramidal society rising step-by-step from lowest to highest. That is precisely what existed not only in the wider national sense – the Kings-Lords-and-Commons of seventeenth-century political theory – but in thousands of smaller regional groups, in town and village, throughout the country. Society was made up of small local communities in which each man had and knew his degree, had certain limited means of rising from one degree to the next, and had moreover certain obligations to those above and below him. The dominating loyalties and interests of Englishmen at this time were not class loyalties and interests, but local loyalties and interests within an accepted hierarchy.

A contemporary writer declared that there were as many wars in England as counties, and the war began with a series of disconnected local clashes between men of influence trying to gain control, either for King or Parliament, of the local reserves of arms. At the very outset of the trouble in January 1642, after the King's unsuccessful attempt to arrest the Five Members, the tenants of John Hampden marched into Westminster from Buckinghamshire, a thousand strong, offering to live and die for Parliament. The incident has an oddly feudal flavour. All over the country in the early months of the war the relationship of mutual obligation between landowner and tenant, or between the man of influence and the 'meaner sort' was what chiefly counted in creating the earliest alignments. Anthony Wood records that in the villages round Thame the lesser gentry and clergy were so much obliged to the Hampdens and the Ingoldsbies that they naturally adopted their politics. The obligation could work the other way: for instance Fairfax attacked Wakefield in the spring of 1643 because he was compelled by the outcry of the poor to secure some Royalist prisoners for purposes of exchange; several hundred of his men had been taken and their womenfolk were making such a clamour for their redemption, and were becoming such a burden on the community since their men had gone, that he had to act. Fairfax was wise to yield to this pressure, or to fulfil this obligation.

Lord Derby, the greatest landowner in Lancashire, can serve as an awful warning of what could happen to a man who failed to fulfil his duties to the common man. After a very brief experience of his methods the respectable young men of the Lancashire villages hastened to enlist in the nearest Parliamentary garrisons in order to avoid being seized on by Lord Derby's officers and compelled to fight without pay and without proper arms. His unpaid troops lived by plunder and he made himself so hated in Lancashire that his defeat at Whalley Abbey in the spring of 1643 was one of the few incidents in the Civil War which resembled a Jacquerie. As soon as the cottages round about saw that Derby was getting the worst of it, they came surging down the hills armed with scythes and flails to wreak vengeance on his detestable robber bands. The shortcomings of his methods were again visible at Marston Moor when his Lancashire men threw down their arms, crying that they were pressed men and did not want to fight.

An unpopular landowner could be, in this way, disastrous. A popular one on the other hand might create – as some of the Cornish gentry did – an extraordinarily effective local force. But regiments raised by a single magnate tended to have little interest in the war beyond loyalty to their leader; the splendid Cornish infantry went to pieces when Sir Bevil Grenville and four or five other active and popular leaders were killed within a few weeks of each other in the summer of 1643. On the Parliament side, the regiments of Denzil Holles and Lord Brooke fought with great courage in the first campaign of the war, but Holles got tired of fighting and Brooke was killed, whereupon their regiments also disappeared.

The influence of the powerful magnates was important in creating the armies on both sides, but it was by no means the only force at work. Coats, boots, and pay were a powerful incentive at the beginning of the war to the unemployed of London, which had been badly depressed for the last year, still more of East Anglia where the weavers were suffering from a prolonged economic crisis. This explains the ease with which Parliament first put an army in the field and the remarkably poor quality of many of the troops. They joined to get a living and a little amusement; and who shall blame them? They had been having a very bad time in the palmy days of peace. As the army of the Earl of Essex marched across the Midlands, the men broke down park railings, killed the deer, pilfered what they took a fancy to, and broke up the churches (in proof of their godliness). Their officers were mostly too inexperienced, or too much afraid of them, to impose any discipline.

Indeed the extraordinary lack of discipline on both sides is a vivid proof of the rather tense relationship brought about by the war between the common man and his rulers. Both sides badly needed troops; both sides found it hard to keep them regularly paid; and the leaders on each side knew very well that deserters from their ranks would be welcomed by the others. There were, of course, exceptions; soldiers with religious principles who refused to desert their cause – like the Parliamentary prisoners taken at Cirencester, many of whom stood up to a great deal of ill-treatment by the Cavaliers in Oxford rather than agree to serve the King. But in general in the early days of the war the rank and file were not very well informed as to what it was all about. The Parliamentary garrison at Banbury went over to the King after Edgehill; many of the Royalists captured at Alton in December 1643 re-enlisted with Sir William Waller for Parliament; the Parliamentary force which surrendered to Rupert outside Newark in March 1644 was disarmed and given leave to march away, but quite a number preferred to join the conquerors. Consequently generals who wanted to prevent their troops deserting were chary of imposing unpopular discipline.

Fairly severe military regulations were of course issued by both sides, and there were intermittent efforts to put them into force. Men were hanged now and again for plunder as a deterrent to others; but the two great volumes of Prince Rupert's correspondence in the British Museum, and the fairly extensive correspondence of Fairfax, Waller, and other Parliamentarians, as well as the indications in contemporary diaries and memoirs, all convey the impression that the first anxiety of every commander was to keep his troops from deserting at whatever cost. The Earl of Essex wrote a letter of almost apologetic courtesy to call back to their duty the men whom he politely described as having 'gone to visit their friends' after Edgehill. A year later, we find the Lord Mayor of London strongly objecting to the search made in the City for the deserters – of whom there were hundreds – from Sir William Waller's army. He said they were better employed pursuing their civilian avocations and he would not answer for the good order of London unless the search was called off – which it was. As late as the spring of 1644 an officer under Fairfax in Yorkshire complained that his men 'have disbanded themselves and are following the plough and from thence they will not be drawn'. Another difficulty with troops who had strong regional attachments was not merely that they refused to march too far from their villages, but that they put the interests of their wives and children first and insisted on returning home to look after them if enemy troops should happen to be anywhere in the neighbourhood.

All this would seem to suggest that the common man, as common soldier, had a fairly good idea of how to look after himself. There were, of course, some compelled and unwilling men in both armies (more in the King's than in Parliament's) but it would be as grave a mistake to regard the soldiers on both sides as, in general, bullied victims as it would be to think of them as convinced and conscious champions of regal authority or of parliamentary government.

It was a major problem with these armies to create some feeling of corporate loyalty; and this applied as much to the better kind of volunteers as to the pressed men and those who came in merely for plunder and sustenance. It was shown over and over again that men would fight very bravely out of personal loyalty to a good commander, or out of local pride – to show that Cornish men were better than Devon men, or that the men of Halifax were superior to the men of Leeds. But this kind of feeling evaporated when the commander was withdrawn or when circumstances failed to strike a chord of local pride. On the King's side, Charles himself worked extremely hard to create a personal bond between himself and his army. 'Your King is both your case, your quarrel, and your captain. Come life or death, your King will bear you company,' he said to his officers before Edgehill. He was meticulous about attending to his military duties at Oxford, regularly going the rounds in person, and when he was on campaign with his armies on several occasions he marched all day on foot with the infantry, a commendable gesture at a time when it was quite usual for infantry officers to ride, leaving their men to slog through the mud. But such personal attachment as Charles could inspire by his actual presence was necessarily limited, and the conception of loyalty to a more or less remote King was not enough to hold an army together; loyalty to individual commanders in the end became one of the chief stumbling blocks in the way of a united Royalist force.

The Parliamentary side might appear at the outset to have much the same difficulties. Cromwell, recruiting in the Fens, called upon the young men to rise for 'religion and the laws of the land', but it was said, no doubt with truth, that they really enlisted because they hoped, obscurely, that they would get their Fens again out of the clutches of the enclosers. The surge of determination to defend London when the King marched against it after Edgehill in the autumn of 1642 was essentially an expression of civic indignation; the city, deeply divided in its politics, was brought together by the threat of military conquest. In the following August there seems to be something rather more like a sense of national emergency in the enthusiasm with which the London regiments marched to the relief of beleaguered Gloucester, but here again the printed accounts of that gallant business make it very clear that regional pride was involved: the London apprentices were showing the men of Gloucester what one great city could do for another.

Cromwell said, several years later, that he had seen as early as the Battle of Edgehill that what was needed was a change of spirit, and the recruiting of the right kind of men. He was only partly right in this, and what he actually said at the time shows that he subscribed to the general view that the solution of the problem lay in having good officers. 'If you choose godly, honest men to be captains,' he said, 'honest men will follow them,' and he was one of the first who had the courage and good sense to offend the social hierarchy by appointing on merit officers of humble origin. Cromwell's success showed that there was something in his theory, but good captains were not enough: more was needed to create the sense of corporate unity in the army and a real and conscious belief in a Cause.

Here the Parliamentarians had for a start an enormous advantage over the Royalists. The chaplains who marched with their armies held varying theological views but as Puritans they all believed in preaching: that is, they believed that the first duty of a minister of God was to establish, by expounding the Scriptures, a contact with, and a hold over, his parish, or his congregation, or in this case, the men in his care. His first duty was not to tag along after the officer-in-command doing any paper-work that was necessary. Many Puritan chaplains did of course act as secretaries, and many Royalist chaplains preached good sermons and were concerned for the moral welfare of the troops. But it is none the less true, from a very early stage in the war, that the tendency of the Royalist chaplains was to devote more of their time to serving the interests of the commanders than to preaching the word of God to the troops. They were moreover handicapped by the fact that the Prayer Book, which they were chiefly fighting to preserve, allows no latitude for extempore prayer. The Parliamentarian chaplain could, if he wished – and he usually did – make his prayers as well as his sermons a constant instruction to the troops. The effect of such preaching and praying in creating a corporate belief in a righteous cause can hardly be overestimated. It was strongly assisted by officers like Cromwell, and Philip Skippon of the London Trained Bands, who had himself composed a small manual of devotion for the use of the troops.

In the autumn and winter of 1644–5 both the King and Parliament reorganized their armies in the interests of greater efficiency. The King's reorganization was a failure because he could not impose any real unity; there was no unity of spirit or understanding on which to build. There were only sectional loyalties. Parliament's reorganization created the famous New Model Army, and unity of counsel and command was successfully imposed because already there was a foundation of unity in spirit and understanding on which to build. The ordinary soldiers of the New Model were in process of becoming a new political entity.

But to turn from the effect of the war on the soldiers to its effect on civilians: their condition certainly does not seem at first sight to be very enviable. I have already pointed out that there were certain advantages in the war – the absorption of unemployment and the creation of additional (if not very productive) work for the casual labourer. But this is not very much to put in the balance against the day-to-day inconveniences, the constant financial pressure and the more occasional heavy suffering which the war imposed on the ordinary man and woman.

A nation-wide system of taxation was gradually created by Parliament. It took two forms: the Excise, a purchase-tax at first imposed on less essential goods but steadily extended, and the weekly assessment. The amount of the assessment was fixed by Parliament for each county, but the County Committees (which were really responsible for local government during the war) fixed the sum to be paid by each region. On top of this weekly burden, the commanders of the armies assigned certain quarters to their troops who collected their support from them in cash or kind. The King's commanders did the same, and when the King summoned the loyalist members of Parliament to Oxford they imitated the financial methods of Westminster, and imposed an Excise and assessment in the King's name. It thus quite frequently happened that regions were alternately paying out to the King or to Parliament, according to which was at the moment in control, but although there was plenty of country that was under disputed authority, especially in the Midlands, it was as far as I know unusual for any village to be paying dues to *both* parties at once. When all the surviving minute books of the various County Committees come to be edited, we shall be able to form a much clearer picture of what actually went on during those difficult years. Those that have been examined reveal (in spite of a certain amount of vindictive personal squabbling between the gentry of both parties) a surprising degree of fairness in assessment and competence in collection.

Apart from these hard but regulated exactions, the common

man in the small towns, villages, or open country was subject to a good deal of casual annoyance and plunder. The Cavaliers (and for anything I know to the contrary the Parliamentarians as well) in the early days made a practice of 'sweeping the commons' for horses – in other words driving off any horses that people had been foolish enough to put out to grass on the common land. Sir Ralph Hopton, as he advanced from Cornwall in the spring of 1643, took advantage of a market-day to raid Totnes and drive off all the horses he found in the town. In the critical time when the King was advancing on London in the autumn of 1642 the Parliamentarians, being very short of waggons and draught-horses, waylaid the carriers on the roads into London and commandeered their carts. The problem of feeding an army on the march was always difficult, and it was quite usual for the men to drive off cattle and sheep to supply their wants; the soldiers of Essex, as they approached Newbury in the wet autumn of 1643, were driving about a thousand sheep.

The ballads of the day reflect the resentment of pillaged farmers and over-taxed citizens; one of them puts into the mouth of a Parliamentary tyrant the reflection:

> *Oh we shall have, if we go on*
> *In Plunder, Excise and Blood*
> *But few folks, and poor, to domineer o'er*
> *And that will not be good.*

But a London barrister called Greene whose brief diary jottings have survived makes a reflection which, in our times as well, the ordinary citizen has sometimes discovered to be true: 'We begin now to see', he writes, 'that a Kingdom according to human discourse is not so easily ruinated and will commonly hold by stronger roots than we imagined; we may hold out, if God has not determined otherwise, two or three years longer at this rate – only grow poorer and poorer.'

He wrote this in the winter of 1642–3; the first Civil War lasted another three and a half years; the assessments continued until the Restoration, and the system of taxation which John Pym and his party initiated – apologetically and with great assertions that it was a temporary measure only – was the beginning of regular national taxation in the modern manner.

But there were mitigating elements in all this, elements which writers of popular ballads, or men and women petitioning against oppression, or seeking to have their assessments reduced, naturally did not emphasize. England was not, to either party, an enemy country; politically it was the aim of Parliament and of the King not to crush or conquer but to win the confidence of the people. Each side emphasized in its propaganda that law and order reigned in the regions it controlled, that citizens would not be plundered and farmers could attend the weekly markets without fear. These statements were not true, but they represented a genuine intention. Quite apart from the political aspects of the matter, neither money nor food for the troops would be forthcoming unless the life of the country was allowed to proceed as far as possible in a normal manner. The King for instance wanted to cut off the trade of London, and he was fairly successful in blocking the roads from London to the West with his great outposts at Donnington Castle and Basing House, but he could not effectively prohibit trade to London until he had an alternative outlet to offer to merchants. This occurred when Prince Rupert took Bristol in July 1643, and the King's attempt to build up Bristol as a rival to London is an interesting side-issue to the war.

Royalist recruiting in North Wales and the fighting in the North Welsh marches very seriously disturbed the cattle-droving on which the economy of the country depended; it also interrupted the Shrewsbury wool trade and turned Shrewsbury in two years from a relatively loyal and friendly into an extremely hostile town, whose citizens in February 1645 joined with the attacking Parliamentary force to capture, kill, or drive out the Royalist garrison. It was naturally the aim of both parties to avoid this kind of thing. Sir Thomas Fairfax, in the West Riding of Yorkshire, made enormous, though unsuccessful, efforts to gain control of the whole region of the four great wool towns, Wakefield, Bradford, Leeds and Halifax, because so long as the Royalists held one half of the West Riding and the Parliamentarians the other, the natural economy of the region was fatally choked, and it became very difficult for either party to draw sustenance from it.

It is therefore true to say that both sides were acutely conscious of the need to preserve the economic life of the country, and on the County Committees soldiers and civilians consulted together in what they hoped would be the best interests of both.

Commanders found it extremely difficult to maintain discipline and prevent the troops from plundering, but there is a great difference between the effects of casual plunder and a deliberate 'scorched earth' policy. In the war in Scotland both Montrose and Argyll deliberately laid waste the country of the opposite party, but in England there were no such clear divisions and the deliberate wasting of country in order to prevent the enemy occupying it hardly occurs at all. On the contrary both sides as far as possible tried to prevent the destruction of young corn and fruit-bearing trees. Parliament was unfortunately driven to be reckless about timber because Newcastle was Royalist and therefore had to be blockaded to prevent the King raising money by the sale of coal. London was therefore completely cut off from its normal coal supply and had somehow (and very inadequately) to be provided with fuel by felling trees for thirty miles round, beginning with those in the royal park at Windsor.

There was one other important mitigating factor in the Civil War. The troops, with very few exceptions, were English; they were not alien to the civilian population. The armies did not have time to become professionalized; they were still, up to the end of the war, essentially citizens in arms. There was therefore no irreconcilable hostility between them and the civilian population. They were not, as the professional armies abroad were, an entirely separate order of people at natural enmity with the peasant and the tradesman. We know from contemporary European literature and pictures, from the works of Grimmelshausen, the paintings of Wouvermans, the engravings of Callot and Stefano della Bella, as well as from direct documentary evidence, how furious and how bitter was the division between the professional soldiers and the peasantry on whom they had to live, and whom they regarded as natural victims.

There was nothing, or very little, to be compared with this in England. Naturally a good deal was made of the indiscipline of the troops by the propagandists of the opposite party, but it was in fact ridiculous to compare the brief and more or less accidental plunder and burning at Brentford or Birmingham with the deliberate sacking of Magdeburg and Prague. Occasionally noncombatants were killed defending their goods from plunder, or during the capture of a town, but this was exceptional and was usually deplored by the commander responsible; or if he did not deplore it he would find it necessary to explain that he had, for one reason or another, absolutely no choice in the matter. The accidental killing of civilians was never taken for granted.

When all the mitigating circumstances have been considered, the war can only be thought of as a time of suffering, anxiety, and loss for the majority of the population, at least in their physical and economic condition. It was, as Hugh Peters in a sermon vividly expressed it, a 'blessed change . . . to see the highways occupied again; to hear the carter whistling to his toiling team; to see the weekly carrier attend his constant mart; to see the hills rejoicing, the valleys laughing'. But the very troubles and disorders through which the country had passed had created the mental and moral atmosphere favourable to changes and questionings more disturbing than the physical distresses through which they had come.

The war had begun in 1642 as a constitutional struggle between King and Parliament – that is, between the King and what was in effect the ruling class. Both parties believed, sincerely enough, in governing for the good of the people, but neither had any idea of giving the people any say in the government. Five years later, in 1647, there came the violent collision between 'the people' – or the New Model Army calling itself not unjustly 'the people' – and the *Grandees*, the men of property, the triumphant commanders and Parliament men who had originally challenged the King.

This was the obvious outcome of the war. In the last five years great numbers of ordinary Englishmen had seen a world outside their town or village and learnt to think in larger terms of a nation, or a people, as a whole. They had also been encouraged to act in a manner wholly foreign to the rigid social code of their time. In the heat of action they were as likely to see the gentry at a disadvantage as at an advantage. They had fired on their betters, pulled them off their horses, seen them in the ugly humiliations of pain and fear and defeat – the Marquess of Worcester without hat or cloak, helplessly watching the soldiers tear his possessions in pieces, the officers of the defeated garrisons and their wives going out with saddened, straightened faces between the lines of their conquerors. Those who had seen such things might well reflect on how the great were brought low. The war was not six months old when one of the Parliamentary captains (it was young Hotham, later to be executed for treachery) predicted that 'the necessitous people', having once learnt the joys and advantages of soldiering, would not hesitate to 'cast the rider' and 'run like wildfire through all the counties of England'. They did not in the end succeed in 'casting the rider', but some of them certainly tried.

They had no doubt made other experiences as well. Young men who had never seen anything but, at best, the parlour of some small squire's house, now entered as conquerors some of the greatest houses in England, stared with wonder, or envy, or austere disapproval at the stately splendours of Welbeck, or Bolsover, or Raglan Castle, or Latham House. Disapproval was, I imagine, more frequent with them than envy; there is relatively little trace of vindictiveness of the poor against the rich in anything they said or did. But they had gained a new experience and a new perspective; they had learnt that, in time of war, Jack was as good as his master, and sometimes better.

The egalitarian political theories which spread at the end of the war among the soldiers of the New Model Army were the creation of men with intense and logical ways of thinking, and they had a pedigree that ran back to the Middle Ages. There is nothing startlingly original in the basic claim that all men are equal. But the fervent plea of John Lilburne for the under-privileged and the rapidly spreading doctrines of the Levellers were received with enthusiasm and intelligence because the common man, or common soldier, had in the last five years crossed frontiers of space and of experience which led him to understand that there were interests which united men from Yorkshire, from Staffordshire, from Essex, indeed from all the counties of England. He had learnt to question the authority of the great and to believe in his own capacity. It was one of the great, though accidental, achievements of the English Civil War that it gave the common man a chance, briefly, to taste the possibility of power and to speak his mind.

1957

Literature and the Historian*

The modern historian is compelled by all the influences of the time to approach literature with a certain diffidence. On the one side he hears the echoes of those warnings uttered by scholars against the delusions of fine writing and the cultivation of history as an art. He may uneasily recall the statement of that great and human scholar J. B. Bury that 'history is a science, neither more nor less', or the dictum of Professor York Powell in his inaugural lecture at Oxford in the 1890s that 'style has no more to do with history than it has with law or astronomy'.

On the other side he may feel the silent reservations of his fellow writers, the poets, the novelists, the literary critics, and sometimes of the public. For history, by comparison, appears uncreative, the fruit rather of study than of inspiration. Dr Johnson declared that 'in historical composition all the greatest powers of the human mind are quiescent . . . there is no exercise of invention. Imagination is not required in any high degree.'

The historian can, however, take heart from the undeniable fact that history had a secure place among the muses from classical antiquity, which was not seriously questioned until after the scientific revolution of the seventeenth and eighteenth centuries: a revolution which, in western Europe, so thoroughly shook up men's ideas and values that equilibrium has never fully been regained.

If he has the good fortune to write in English he can further seek reassurance in contemplating that long alliance between history and literature which has been, and still is, one of the glories of the English-speaking peoples. The tradition stretches back five centuries past Gibbon, Clarendon, Bacon, Raleigh, to the Berners translation of Froissart: it has been upheld and renewed in the twentieth century on both sides of the Atlantic.

* Presidential address to the English Association, 1956.

It is a tradition distinguished by writing of many different kinds – vivid narrative and lucid exposition, dramatic projection of character, or reflective analysis. The English language has many moods and the historian makes use of them all.

I should like to call a few passages to mind, but with this warning – that of all prose, historical prose lends itself least well to this process of selection. History being the record of human action is a richly variegated material, and it is not easy to give a true impression of the stuff by snipping off an inch or two for a pattern.

Here none the less are some passages. First a piece of direct narrative from Berners's translation of Froissart describing Wat Tyler's march on London – surely one of the best accounts of a popular rising ever written, so fearful in its straight simplicity.

In the morning on Corpus Christi day, King Richard heard mass in the Tower of London, and all his lords, and then he took his barge with the Earl of Salisbury, the Earl of Warwick, the Earl of Oxford and certain knights, and so rowed down along the Thames to Rotherhithe whereas was descended down the hill a ten thousand men to see the King and to speak with him. And when they saw the King's barge coming they began to shout and make such a cry, as though all the devils of hell had been among them . . . And when the King and his lords saw the demeanour of the people, the best assured of them were in dread; and so the King was counselled by his barons not to take any landing there but so rowed up and down the river. And the King demanded of them what they would, and said how he was come thither to speak with them, and they said all with one voice: 'We would that you should come a-land and then we shall show you what we lack.' Then the Earl of Salisbury answered for the King and said: 'Sirs, ye be not in such order or array that the King ought to speak with you.' And then the King was counselled to return again to the Tower of London and so he did.

And when these people saw that, they were inflamed with ire and returned to the hill where the great band was, and there showed them what answer they had and how the King was returned to the Tower of London. Then they cried all with one voice, 'Let us go to London', and so they took their way thither; and in their going they beat down abbeys, and houses of advocates and men of the court, and so came into the suburbs of London which were greater and fair and there bear down diverse fair houses . . . There were many within the city of their accord, and so they drew together and said 'Why do we not let these good people enter into the city? They are our fellows, and that they do is for us.' So therewith the gates were opened and then these people entered into the city and went into houses and sat down to eat and drink. They desired nothing but it was incontinent brought to them, for every man was ready to make them good cheer and to give them meat and drink to appease them.

Now, to leap the centuries, and try a different manner and a different subject, here is Macaulay's dramatic portrait of Thomas Wentworth, Earl of Strafford:

But Wentworth – whoever names him without thinking of those harshly dark features, ennobled by their expression into more than the majesty of an antique Jupiter; of that brow, that eye, that cheek, that lip wherein, as in a chronicle, are written the events of many stormy and disastrous years, high enterprise accomplished, frightful dangers braved, power unsparingly exercised, suffering unshrinkingly borne; of that fixed look, so full of severity, of mournful anxiety, of deep thought, of dauntless resolution, which seems at once to forbode and to defy a terrible fate, as it lowers on us from the canvas of Van Dyck? . . .

He was the first Englishman to whom a peerage was a sacrament of infamy, a baptism into the communion of corruption. As he was the earliest of that hateful list, so was he also by far the greatest; eloquent, sagacious, adventurous, intrepid, ready of invention, immutable of purpose, in every talent which exalts or destroys nations preeminent, the lost Archangel, the Satan of the Apostasy . . .

Differences in style reveal differences in temperament; after the generous heat of Macaulay the cool irony of Edward Gibbon:

It is a very honourable circumstance for the morals of the primitive Christians, that even their faults, or rather errors, were derived from an excess of virtue. The bishops and doctors of the Church, whose evidence attests, and whose authority might influence, the professions, the principles, and even the practice of their contemporaries, had studied the scripture with less skill than devotion and they often received, in the most literal sense, those rigid precepts of Christ and the apostles to which the prudence of succeeding commentators has applied a looser and more figurative mode of interpretation. Ambitious to exalt the perfection of the gospel above the wisdom of philosophy, the zealous fathers have carried the duties of self mortification, of purity and of patience, to a height which it is scarcely possible to attain, and much less to preserve in our present state of weakness and corruption. A doctrine so extraordinary and so sublime must inevitably command the veneration of the people; but it was ill calculated to obtain the suffrage of those worldly philosophers who, in the conduct of this transitory life, consult only the feelings of nature and the interest of society.

To come to the present century, here is G. M. Trevelyan in the mature manner of his social history, which never approaches the cynicism of Gibbon. He is describing the manners of the early eighteenth century:

It was the privilege of all gentlemen, from a Duke downwards, to wear swords, and to murder one another by rule. As soon as men were well drunk of an evening they were apt to quarrel, and as soon as they quarrelled they were apt to draw their swords in the room, and if manslaughter was not committed on the spot, to adjourn to the garden behind the house, and fight it out that night with hot blood and unsteady hand. If the company were not wearing swords, the quarrel might be slept upon and forgotten or arranged in the sober morning. The wearing of swords, though usual in London, as being like the full-bottomed wig a part of full dress, was fortunately not common in the depths of the country among the uncourtly but good-natured rural squires, whose bark was often worse than their bite. And even at Bath, Beau Nash employed his despotic power to compel the fashionable world to lay aside their swords when they entered his domain: in this he did as good service to the community as in teaching the country bumpkins to discard their top boots and coarse language at the evening assemblies and dances. During his long supremacy as Master of the Ceremonies, nearly covering the reigns of Anne and the first two Georges, Nash did perhaps as much as any other person even in the Eighteenth Century to civilize the neglected manners of mankind.

Last of all, here is another portrait in the grand manner, from a living writer:

There now appeared upon the ravaged scene an Angel of Deliverance, the noblest patriot of France, the most splendid of her heroes, the most beloved of her saints, the most inspiring of all her memories, the peasant Maid, the ever shining, ever glorious Joan of Arc. In the poor remote hamlet of Domremy, on the fringe of the Vosges Forest, she served at the inn. She rode the horses of travellers, bare back, to water. She wandered on Sundays into the woods, where there were shrines and a legend that some day from these oaks would arise one to save France. In the fields where she tended her sheep the saints of God, who grieved for France, rose before her in visions. St Michael himself appointed her, by right divine, to command the armies of liberation. Joan shrank at first from the awful duty, but when he returned attended by St Margaret and St Catherine, patronesses of the village church, she obeyed their command. There welled in the heart of the Maid a pity for the realm of France, sublime, perhaps miraculous, certainly invincible . . .

That, of course, is from Sir Winston Churchill's *History of the English-Speaking Peoples*.

The literary achievement is splendid, but in spite of all, the chill of scholarly criticism strikes to the bone. It cannot be denied that the literary historians are open to criticism for failures of perception and failures of scholarship which can at times be traced directly to their literary technique. Macaulay's denunciation of Strafford is noble in sound and volume, inspired in its range of images. But, by striking off so splendid a phrase as 'the Satan of the Apostasy', Macaulay introduced a Miltonic grandeur into our vision of the man and the epoch, which makes it hard to bring the mind down again to the sober and pedestrian level on which alone historical inquiry can be safely pursued, and just estimates made of persons and things.

I would not willingly forgo Macaulay's splendid phrase, but a great power over words and images can and does intoxicate, and the historian has chosen a branch of literature in which the utmost sobriety is usually advisable. It is not quite always advisable because there is the delicate and subtle problem of historic imagination: the power to move, or to give the impression of moving, from one epoch into another, the capacity to feel and think the thoughts of another time. This is a gift of literary imagination, and at its highest it sometimes resembles a state, if not of intoxication, then of possession. Thomas Carlyle is more frequently and more strenuously possessed by this kind of imagination than any other British historian. He ceases to be a recorder of the scene and becomes himself an actor, or more truly a disembodied spirit, restlessly moving from the mind of one character to another. He makes nothing of travelling two hundred years on the thunderclouds of his imagination to give a helping hand to Cromwell and his men at the Battle of Dunbar.

The night is wild and wet . . . the Harvest Moon wades deep among clouds of sleet and hail. Whoever has a heart for prayer, let him pray now, for the wrestle of death is at hand. Pray, – and withal keep his powder dry! And be ready for extremities, and quit himself like a man! . . . the hoarse sea moans bodeful, swinging low and heavy against those whinstone bays; the sea and the tempests are abroad, all else asleep but we, – and there is ONE that rides on the wings of the wind.

About four o'clock comes order to my pudding headed Yorkshire friend, that his regiment must mount and march straightway . . . Major Hodgson riding along heard, he says, 'a Cornet praying in the night'; a company of poor men, I think, making worship there, under the void Heaven, before battle joined; Major Hodgson turned aside to listen for a minute and worship and pray along with them; haply his last prayer on Earth, as it might prove to be. But no . . . the Heavens in their mercy I think have opened us a way of deliverance! – The Moon gleams out, hard and blue, riding among hail clouds; and over St Abb's Head, a streak of dawn is rising . . . The Scots too . . . are awake; thinking to surprise us; there is their trumpet sounding, we heard it once; and Lambert who was to lead the attack is not here. The Lord General is impatient; behold Lambert at last! The trumpets peal, shattering with fierce clangour Night's silence; the cannons awaken along all the line: 'The Lord of Hosts! The Lord of Hosts!' On, my brave ones, on!

It is difficult to be sure whether the Lord General, who leads these praying troops to victory at the first streak of dawn after a stormy night, is in truth Oliver Cromwell, or a renegade Scot called Thomas Carlyle. The imaginative leap is complete. Carlyle has written himself and thought himself into the very heart of the scene. Without this extraordinary achievement of personal projection, English history as well as English literature would be the poorer for what is, by and large, a masterly interpretation of the Puritan mind in general and of Oliver Cromwell in particular.

But such imaginative fervour can be very unsafe; the slightest slip in scholarship makes it at once appear ridiculous. It is the measure of Carlyle's greatness that, although he did make mistakes, he emerges none the less as one of the great masters. But the dangers of his method, in these days of more searching scholarship, are apparent. The writer who trusts too deeply in his imaginative powers to re-create the past falls into an error as dangerous and more ridiculous than the writer who resists the imaginative impulse altogether.

Exuberance of imagination, whether about words or phrases or the interpretation of the past, can betray the writer into exaggerations and errors when he is working within the strict limits of history. On the other hand, the measured and restricted manner, the urbane, well-bred style of Edward Gibbon for instance, is not fitted to illuminate the darker or the higher reaches of the human spirit or to give more than a brilliant surface account of their manifestations. The *Decline and Fall* is the great masterpiece of historical writing in the English language; there are moments at which that clear, emphatic, and witty style stands between the author and the full interpretation of his subject. Gibbon's style, which reflects his mind, forces him to make light of things too complicated and too illogical or too sublime to be accommodated in the balanced framework of his sentences. But much of history, and much of human thought, is complicated and illogical, and some of it is sublime.

There is no literary style which may not at some point add to or take away something from the ascertainable outline of truth, which it is the task of scholarship to excavate and re-establish. The ability to light upon a splendid phrase, the imaginative power to breathe life into the names and actions of people long dead, may be misleading in one way; the clear, logical, and moderated manner, the epigrammatic, the concise, and the witty, may be as misleading in another.

It was partly, though not entirely, because the literary historians could sometimes be shown to have sacrificed the demands of scholarship to the demands of style that an open antagonism to literary treatment grew up among historical scholars in the later nineteenth century. Hence the dictum that style has no more to do with history than with law or astronomy. A gentler compromise was reached by Sir Charles Firth when he argued that the clear presentation of history is a necessary part of the historian's work; some art, he declared, was essential to this task and should be cultivated. History could not stand alone as a pure science. This point of view, modified by the temperamental leanings of individuals towards science or towards art, is now fairly generally held by academic historians.

The relationship of science to art in history is admitted; but the exact nature of that relationship remains undefined and possibly indefinable. Is literature the constant helpmeet and partner of scholarship, or is it the poor relation asked down for a few days once a year to assist at some necessary social occasion and help to hand round the drinks? Is the literary presentation of his work something which only begins to concern the historian when the work of scholarship is done, or is it something always present to his mind?

This problem can best be answered by negative arguments. The reaction against literature was mistaken and harmful, but it was not unreasonable or causeless. The great popular success of certain works of history which were, and are, also works of literature created a popular demand for history which was satisfied – had to be satisfied, the laws of supply and demand being what they are – by writers and historians of lesser value than those who had created the demand. The genius of a Macaulay, the vision of a J. R. Green are not given to everyone. Moreover it is a commonplace in all the arts, not in literature alone, that the style of a master, copied, diffused, ultimately parodied by imitators, can damage the reputation of the master and the art in question. Macaulay was well aware of this: 'My manner, is I think, and the world thinks, on the whole a good one,' he wrote, 'but it is very near to a bad manner indeed, and those characteristics of my style which are most easily copied are the most questionable.' The same could be said of

Gibbon, whose manner, badly imitated, had a stultifying effect on English historical style for generations. In our own time, in the narrower field of biography, the imitators of Lytton Strachey managed by their smart-aleck antics to obscure for a long decade what was really valuable in the new approach to biography.

When bad popular work came flooding in to fill the demand created by good work it was not remarkable that the more austere and conscientious historians revolted against the popular treatment of history, and came not to distinguish very clearly between popular history and literary history. The revolt against the literary treatment of history was really a revolt against popularization, in which writers of vision and power were indiscriminately condemned, along with their inferior imitators.

Furthermore, history has followed the same curve during the last two to three generations as many other branches of knowledge. First a great increase in available information and evidence led to the development of new and more precise techniques of research. Then technical advances and ever-widening fields of inquiry led to over-confidence in man's capacity to attain exact knowledge. This was followed by the dismaying discovery that men know less by knowing more. A profusion of evidence means conflicting evidence. By and large, over the whole field, doubt and uncertainty increase with the increase of information. The flow and meaning of events, the relation of cause to effect are no longer clear. Historians have dug out information about the structure of society or its economic foundations, the physical conditions or the spiritual preoccupations of our forefathers, which modify or revolutionize, or merely confuse, the once accepted versions of the past. Scholars of great perception and integrity disagree fundamentally on the construction to be put on the always increasing evidence available. What we once thought was progress, we are now constrained to regard as regress. In the interpretation of certain epochs, and indeed in our attitude to the whole story of man, we scarcely know any more if we are coming or going. When a philosopher–historian of the scope and vision of Professor Toynbee arises to suggest an overall pattern, the specialist scholars, who are writhing like Laocoön in the toils of their more detailed research, wrench themselves free of their devouring doubts for just long enough to shoot him as full of arrows as Saint Sebastian.

Historical thinking is slowly and painfully going through very much the same process of questioning, destruction, and ultimate enlightenment that fell upon the natural sciences three hundred years ago. The old certainties are gone, the new are uncreated.

When so much is to be done and so much seems at stake – for we all have to believe that our own particular interest is of great importance to the world – is it to be wondered at that the mere creation of literature, this apparently irrelevant additional element in the historian's task, should seem of lesser importance to the research student, and the exact relationship of literature to history be left undefined?

It is only fair to the historian of today to remember that he thinks and works against the background of shifting values, of fluid knowledge and fluid opinions. This is very different from the atmosphere of more definite opinions, more rigid moral standards, and much more limited historical knowledge against which the classics of literary history were produced in the past.

The reaction against literary history was not causeless. Scholars had some grounds for thinking that historians with a strong literary gift were betrayed at times into sacrificing exactitude of statement to beauty of language, to minimizing or enhancing the historic picture by the qualities of individual style.

This is true. But the converse is not true. The historian who cultivates literary style can make mistakes, but there is no opposite guarantee that the historian with no literary style will make none. That is the great fallacy. Good writing is no guarantee of good scholarship; but neither is bad writing. The austere instinct which prompted the historians of fifty years ago to concentrate exclusively on discovery and regard the cultivation of writing as irrelevant, was a wrong instinct. There have been scholars of great distinction and valuable influence, who were bad writers. But they are rare. The sense of form, the capacity to weigh and to use words correctly, the shaping of sentences, and the structure and presentation of a scene, a fact, or an exposition are the natural concomitants of the clear, inquiring, disciplined, and imaginative mind which is needed for historical research. But most talents are the better for cultivation. The scholar who cultivates – as he must – the patience, the self-discipline, the spirit of inquiry, the open mind, the exactitude, and the strong but controlled imagination which are all necessary for research, will almost certainly find some of these qualities – equally important for the writer – reflected in his handling of the English language when he comes to set down his conclusions. In the same way, the writer who cultivates these qualities in his writing will find his perceptions sharpened and his ideas clearer when he turns to research.

J. B. Bury, who so sternly proclaimed that history was 'a science, neither more nor less', wrote himself with lucidity, ease, and distinction. The gritty, awkward and disjointed manner which marred a good deal of serious historical writing in the early years of this century frequently reflects the slow-moving, awkward, and short-sighted approach of the writers, not only to the beauties and possibilities of the English language but to the possibilities and beauties of historical inquiry. The close relationship between clear thinking and good writing is illustrated time and again by the work of the great scholars. This fact has been obscured by the common confusion between literary history and popular history. Properly speaking, all history which is written with style and distinction belongs to English literature; it need not necessarily be 'popular' in the sense that millions can read and understand it. In other branches of literature, the universal genius who speaks to all hearts and all ages, who does not become obscure by reason of contemporary allusions or turns of phrase that reflect passing fashions, is very rare – a Shakespeare, a Tolstoy. But no one would expect millions to read and appreciate the poems of John Donne, or the prose of C. M. Doughty. These are more specialized tastes; but such writing belongs none the less to the great heritage of literature.

In history alone the term 'literary' has associations with the idea of popularity. It is assumed that good writing in history will occur most often, if not exclusively, in history which is directed towards a large public. But this does not follow. Much of the best historical writing of the last fifty years – and that in spite of the self-denying ordinance against literature passed by some of the practitioners themselves – has come from scholarly specialists, with little or no interest in reaching a large public or being acclaimed as literary figures. For the expressive, explicit, and exact use of words you would go far to find the equal of F. W. Maitland writing on the development of English law and institutions fifty years ago; and in this field today the great scholars, medieval or modern, Sir Maurice Powicke, Sir Lewis Namier have a precision, elegance, and clarity in the exposition of their themes which make many popular historians look slapdash and slipshod.

Anyone interested in modern English style would do well to turn, from time to time, away from the avowedly literary works, be they novels or criticism or literary history or that great field for fine writing so popular today, the travel book, and look into the pages of the learned periodicals. The subjects may be unappealing to the general reader but the manner in which they are treated is often an example of good style – cool, clear, reflective, and economical – in striking contrast to the average of modern popular writing, with its slack structure, careless and inattentive use of metaphors and images, and vocabulary corrupted by the stale-picturesque.

The practice of the finest scholars bears out the thesis that literature and scholarship, so far from being radically opposed to each other, are natural allies. Literary sensibility and literary technique are something more than pleasing additional graces to be cultivated by the historian if and when he has time. They are valuable to him not only in his final task of communicating his thoughts to the reading public, but from the very inception of his work; they will guide, help, and illuminate the whole process of historical inquiry.

The literary treatment of history is not a superficial thing; it goes to the root of the subject. Admittedly, it has its superficial aspects. For instance, the literary historian will often take note of superficial details which are irrelevant to the march of events and which would be rightly disregarded by a scholar dealing with, say, the evolution of ministerial responsibility or the fluctuations of wages in the fifteenth-century woollen industry. The literary historian will almost automatically make a note of any authentic details he can discover which are likely to enhance the reality of what he is describing or help the inward eye of the reader: the colour of a general's cloak or a woman's hair, the brightness or dullness of the weather, the hangings on the wall, the flowers in the garden – all things of very little consequence in themselves. In this respect the literary treatment of history is indeed merely an innocent and pleasing additional elegance. But this elegance can be used with wonderful skill and imagination, as for instance in Lytton Strachey's famous account of the dying Queen Victoria.

Yet, perhaps, in the secret chambers of consciousness, she had her thoughts too. Perhaps her fading mind called up once more the shadows of the past to float before it and retraced for the last time the vanished visions of that long history – passing back and back, through the cloud of years, to older and ever older memories, to the spring woods at Osborne so full of primroses for Lord Beaconsfield – to Lord Palmerston's queer clothes and high demeanour, and Albert's face under the green lamp, and Albert's first stag at Balmoral, and Albert in his blue and silver uniform, and the Baron coming in through a doorway, and Lord M. dreaming at Windsor with the rooks cawing in the elm trees, and the Archbishop of Canterbury on his knees in the dawn, and the old King's turkey-cock ejaculations, and Uncle Leopold's soft voice at Claremont, and Lehzen with the globes, and her mother's feathers sweeping down towards her, and a great old repeater watch of her father's in its tortoise-shell case, and a yellow rug, and some friendly flounces of sprigged muslin, and the trees and the grass at Kensington.

Here the details are accurate visual details assembled from many sources; slight in themselves, they have been selected, organized, and related to the story of the dying Queen in such a way as to illuminate what the author felt to be the essentials of her life and personality. Strachey's treatment can be compared with another closing passage, equally famous, written sixty years earlier – Motley's last lines on William the Silent.

He went through life bearing the load of a people's sorrows upon his shoulders with a smiling face. Their name was the last word upon his lips, save the simple affirmative with which the soldier who had been battling for the right all his lifetime commended his soul in dying 'to his great Captain, Christ'. The people were grateful and affectionate, for they trusted the character of their 'Father William', and not all the clouds which calumny could collect ever dimmed to their eyes the radiance of that lofty mind to which they were accustomed, in their darkest calamities, to look for light. As long as he lived, he was the guiding star of a brave nation, and when he died the little children cried in the streets.

This passage from Motley's *Rise of the Dutch Republic* illustrates a further, and more significant, stage in the marriage between literary and aesthetic sensibility and historical inquiry. In the passage about the death of Queen Victoria, Strachey has selected from the thousands of small background details that he had accumulated about his subject a striking few that light up, here and there, the personal experiences of the Queen's lifetime. He is giving us here not history but conjecture based on historical knowledge; he is making, with considerably greater discretion and restraint, the imaginative leap that Carlyle made at the Battle of Dunbar.

Motley does not depart from the stricter historical treatment of his theme. He conjectures nothing as to the state of William the Silent's mind in his last moments; he tells the facts and he sums up the impression objectively from contemporary evidence. Yet his summing up, like Strachey's more frankly imaginative flight, has the effect of poetry, the effect of striking through the surface facts to some deeper, less expressible truth about life and death and politics and the human heart.

The secret of Motley's great passage lies most of all in that last sentence: 'As long as he lived, he was the guiding star of a brave nation, and when he died the little children cried in the streets.' The first part of the sentence is almost rhetorical, a sentence very well fitted to the old-fashioned idea of the dignity of history with its 'guiding star' and 'brave nation' – fine words but generalized and not particular to Motley or to the occasion; it is the last sentence, with its entirely simple statement of fact – 'and when he died the little children cried in the streets' – which like a sudden beam of sunset light through clouds, streaming over the landscape, illuminates the whole of the preceding passage and tells us more about William the Silent as a ruler and as a leader than many piled-up paragraphs.

It has this effect because it is not a *rhetorical* phrase but an *historical* phrase; by the time the reader has got so far with Motley's *Dutch Republic* he knows his author well enough to understand that this is no flourish but a documented fact. He need not even consult the footnote to be reassured that these children were actually seen by someone walking in the streets of Delft at the time.

But – and this is the crux of the matter – this particular detail in a contemporary letter *might* have been missed by an historian less sensitive than Motley to aesthetic and literary values. The documentation of the epoch is very rich; there is a great deal to read and to digest; and in the mass of material it is not easy to hit upon the significant detail. By the significant detail I mean something much more than the picturesque detail. It is a superficial gift, though a useful one, to be able to pick out the vivid additional stage directions that may be found among the evidence – the picturesque touches. But it is a gift of a deeper kind to seize unfailingly on the kind of detail which illuminates to the core of an event. This is in part a literary gift, or rather it arises from the sharpening of perception which comes from literary training and the study and appreciation of literature.

It is not only in detail that the study and appreciation of literature, and the constant practice of history as an art, can be helpful to history as a science. The writer who approaches his task with some conception of the value and significance of form in writing or – more elementary still if you like – some idea of the sequence and flow of words and thoughts, some natural feeling for the relationship of words to form, will not fall into the danger of heaping up facts, and making a narrow, dry, unilluminating catalogue instead of an interpretation of his subject. If he has always in his mind a consciousness of the necessity of linking his material together, he will be a better historian as well as a better writer, for the problem of historical interpretation is largely a problem of finding out and establishing the correct relationships between facts; of restoring sequences of cause and effect whether in the lives of individuals or in much broader connections. In all this, the sense of form and structure, which has to be cultivated by the writer, is of equal importance to the historian.

The contention is one which cannot perhaps be proved except by negative evidence. History which is unimpeachable as scholarship should have lasting value regardless of its quality as writing. But when we look at the great works of scholarship which have lasted it is astonishing how rare it is to find one that reveals a writer devoid of literary skill and judgment.

Style in history is an index to the mind, and the great scholar, whether he cultivates it or not, is rarely without the natural gift. Fine writing may be the business only of the historian who has chosen to write of wide themes for a wide public. But good writing is almost the concomitant of good history. Literature and history were joined long since by the powers which shaped the human brain; we cannot put them asunder.

1956

Captain Hind the Highwayman

There was a noisy arrest one November morning in 1651 at a barber's shop opposite St Dunstan's Church in Fleet Street. The news spread quickly through the neighbouring alleys so that Captain Hind the Highwayman had a large public when he was brought out, manacled, thrust into a waiting coach and carried off to the Council of State at Westminster. Highwaymen did not, as a rule, command the attention of the Government and I like to think that the dapper little man, as he entered on the last phase of his notorious career, had the gratification of knowing that he had achieved something.

The highwayman proper, as distinguished from the ordinary robber, foot-pad and the other minions of the moon known to Shakespeare, was new to the annals of English crime. The word itself, significantly, begins to occur only during the general relaxation of law and order which accompanied the outbreak of the Civil War in 1642. The armed horseman whose method was to force the wealthy traveller at the pistol's point to hand over his money was perhaps a natural outcome of that time. The highwayman needed steady nerves, firearms and a good horse, all things which a deserter, a cashiered officer, might very well possess. Highwaymen were not, however, all of this class; indeed relatively few of them were, but the new technique which rapidly became as popular as it was effective was probably learnt from pioneers who had once been soldiers. Sometimes they operated alone, more often in gangs. Many, if not all of them, pretended to a sort of Robinhoodishness. The only prey worth their while were the rich but they made a kind of virtue of this necessity and for that reason, perhaps, were popular, in theory at least, among the poor.

James Hind was one of the first to mark the profession with the strong imprint of his character. His gaiety, his daring, his Royalist sympathies and elegant manners were the familiar talk of inn-keepers and ostlers on every main road. He had 'pranced the road' from London to York, was well known to Gloucestershire, the Fens and the Thames valley and had, with his gang, at one time, levied almost regular tribute on the travellers who came to London by way of Barnet Heath.

Fame is not healthy for a highwayman and after a few years Hind fled the country, lurked in the Netherlands, dodged across Ireland and arrived in Scotland just in time to be presented to the young Charles II – who had a weakness for clever scoundrels – and to enlist in the Royalist army as it set out to invade England. He saw action at Warrington and Worcester and after the King's defeat went to earth in the rabbit warren of London's most disreputable quarter.

Hind had ridden as a trooper in the King's army, but his public would not believe that their hero had played so small a part. It was widely rumoured that he had been Scoutmaster-General and, when the young King eluded the pursuit of his enemies, it was to the skill and daring of Jemmy Hind that popular opinion attributed his escape.

The flattering rumour was Hind's undoing. Because they thought he might lead them to the King, the Government spared no pains in tracking him down. It was not Captain Hind the Highwayman but James Hind the Royalist whom the Council of State wished to see. The fugitive trooper from the King's defeated army would have been safe enough in London had he not trailed with him into his new profession those tell-tale clouds of glory from his past. His interview with the Council of State was a dis-appointment to both parties; he turned out to be of no importance to them at all.

Yet it hardly seemed sensible to release a public hero who had also been, in his time, a fairly considerable public nuisance. Direct evidence of his robberies was hard to come by, so he made his appearance at the Old Bailey about a month later on a charge of high treason.

Jemmy Hind was small and personable, with a confidence that did not overflow into swagger and gave him the easy air of a gentleman. A large audience had come to see and hear, hoping for some of his famous jests. The hearing, however, gave him few favourable openings for his wit and it was only at the end that he raised a laugh. Squinting down at his heels as he left the dock – 'A plague on these great jingling spurs!' he said, and gave his irons a shake. Outside the crowd pressed upon him with lugubrious sympathy, asking him if he was to be hanged. 'No, no, good people,' he said, 'they are not in such a hurry to hang true folk.'

The fact was that they were not in such a hurry to hang a common thief on the distinguished charge of high treason. Evidence had come to light that, during his operations in Berkshire, he had once killed a man in a brawl; he was transferred to Reading and the charge was altered to manslaughter.

Under a medieval statute not yet repealed it was possible for any man who could read to avoid hanging for manslaughter by pleading benefit of clergy; this reduced the penalty to a formal branding in the palm of the hand. Captain Hind in the dock at Reading was the same civil, witty, confident gentleman that he had been in London. But he had not realized that he would have to prove his right to benefit of clergy. He was utterly taken aback when a book was handed to him and he was told to read a paragraph. The gallant, play-actor's mask of gentility fell from his face: he could not read a word.

It was an eccentricity almost, for even in the humbler class from which he came, illiteracy was unusual. His father was an honest saddler of Chipping Norton who had wanted to make a scholar of his son; Hind had been two years at school but his incorrigible 'waggishness' had prevented him from learning anything at all. Later he had been apprenticed to his father, and, when that did not please him, to a butcher; at the age of about eighteen he borrowed forty shillings from his doting mother and ran away to London.

Here he had fallen in with Allan, the boldest highwayman of his day, who used to disguise himself as a bishop, bowling along in his coach with outriders and servants. Once on a lonely stretch of road, off came the episcopal disguise, the coach was hidden behind a hedge and the gang took up their action stations. When, a little later, the bishop and his train reached the next town, they would listen with sympathy to the story of the robber band which had held up so many travellers that day and thank Heaven that the rogues had not molested them.

Young Hind learnt his profession and his good manners as gentleman usher to Bishop Allan and when Allan 'went to heaven in a piece of string' he set up on his own. The country was still disordered with echoes of civil war. Hind – one of the first gentlemen of the road to do so – adopted the title of Captain and permitted a general belief that he had served in that capacity for the King. His political views were, however, genuine; he robbed Parliament men for preference and once, when he had robbed a poor Cavalier in error, he not only gave him his money back, but dined with him at the next inn on the road, riding off at first light after paying the reckoning for them both. This was an act at once delicate and generous; Hind was a rogue but he was nature's gentleman.

There had been traces of grace and gallantry on the roads before Hind's time, but he was the first who made it a prevailing fashion. He never robbed without a jest and he always, with a little flourish, handed back to his victim a few shillings expenses money for the rest of his journey. In return he expected courtesy from his clients and when a traveller, for whom he had laid an ambush, came dawdling up at a foot pace, he whacked him smartly with his cane and cried 'Have I nothing to do all day but wait for you?'

His quick wits and resourcefulness gave rise to hundreds of tales. When he nipped a bag of gold out of a gentleman's coach at Hyde Park races, he got his booty safely through the London suburbs by waving it in the air as he galloped past, shouting, 'I've won my wager; I've won my wager'. The crowds made way for the jubilant victor and long before the pursuit came up with him, he had vanished.

Another time, when some of his victims were pelting along a dark highway after him, he ran into a happy, drunk parson, coming home from a wedding. Hind pressed his loaded pistol into his hand, breathlessly explaining that highwaymen were after him. Fire, he told the parson, and they'll away. The parson fired wildly, the pursuers took him for their robber, overpowered him and carried him off to prison, while Hind was already safe in the woods. The parson was, of course, a vile Puritan interloper; Hind the Cavalier would not have played such a prank on a priest of the Anglican church.

True or false, the stories sprang from a genuine personality – the gay, civil gentleman who, in the dock at Reading, crumpled so pathetically into the saddler's truant son.

But life was to end more nobly. While he waited for the hanging, Parliament passed an Act of Oblivion to cover crimes of violence committed during this disorderly epoch of the war. Hind was reprieved. But the authorities would not let so dangerous a thief escape. They revived the charge of high treason and transferred him from Reading gaol to Worcester. Here at the next assizes he was tried and sentenced to be hanged for taking up arms for the usurper Charles Stuart. So, at last, on 24 September 1652, Jemmy Hind the saddler's son joined the distinguished band of martyrs, knights, esquires and peers of the realm who had mounted the scaffold for their King. He died if not exactly the death of a gentleman, yet a death that many gentlemen had not been ashamed to die.

1956

The German Myth

❯❯❯❯❯❮❮❮❮❮

A ll normal human beings are interested in their past. Only when the interest becomes an obsession, overshadowing present action and future conduct, is it a danger. In much the same way healthy nations are interested in their history, but a morbid preoccupation with past glories is a sign that something is wrong with the constitution of the State. It is found among scattered and broken peoples, among the declining and impoverished, among the parvenu or recently restored. I am not here speaking of a merely learned preoccupation with the past, but rather of that romantic concern with ancient splendours which is expressed by the resuscitation of forgotten and long out-dated customs, the injudicious reproduction of ancient architectural styles, the creation of unnecessary monuments, and the prostitution of historiography to modern 'patriotic' purposes.

Most nations have passed through periods of this kind. History, in spite of the occasional protest of historians, will always be used in a general way as a collection of political and moral precedents. But there is a distinction in the methods by which it is so used, a distinction between argument and statement. There is an important difference between the deduction of a principle from certain given facts, and the emotional prejudice which endows the facts themselves with preternatural significance. Few nations can safely cast stones in this matter. But in no European country has the tendency been so marked as in Germany. The preoccupation of the German people with their past, their bewildered reverence for it, their clumsy and repeated attempts to endow their confused political story with symbolic meaning, are symptoms of profound national ill-health.

The traveller in Germany sees on every side evidence of a

romantic–symbolic 'let's pretend' attitude to national history. This misunderstanding of the past is combined with a sometimes crafty, sometimes ingenuous, attempt to blend it with the present. German history lacks outward unity. All the greater, therefore, is the desire to endow it with mystic oneness. Hence the emphasis on *Einheit* – unity – in German patriotic literature and in German text-books. The most improbable places have been found for blazoning this lesson: as for instance on the sword-blade of the gigantic statue of Arminius, erected on the dubious site of his victory over the Roman legions in the Teutoburgerwald. The figure of the ancient Teutonic chief, 186 feet high from the base of the arched substructure to the tip of the upraised sword, dominates the landscape and brandishes in the face of heaven the inscribed legend:

> *Germany's unity, my strength,*
> *My strength, Germany's strength.*

The conception is a nineteenth-century one, as indeed is the whole Arminius legend in its present form.

He is a strange figure, this Arminius, typical of the confused thinking which has gone on round German history. One of the many quarrelsome barbarian chieftains in the partially conquered lands beyond the Rhine, he had the intelligence to realize that he could only make a stand against the Romans by persuading his fellows to enter into alliance with him. He had also the necessary force of character and military skill to hold the ephemeral alliance together long enough to bring the Romans to decisive battle. The achievement was a considerable one, though not as stupendous as the German legend has made it. This grand old Germanic figure unhappily perished in the grand old Germanic way: not long after his victory he was murdered by other jealous chieftains. The main source of the story of Arminius is in Tacitus. It was here that Ulrich von Hutten found it early in the sixteenth century; he was the first German propagandist to see its possibilities, but he saw them through the eyes of a sixteenth-century anti-clerical as much as of an early German nationalist – indeed at that time the two were closely knit. Arminius represented to him the native *secular* force of Germany. Not until very much later does the Arminius legend again creep into the political field, this time with a purely nationalist bearing. With the revival of the German language and the revolt against foreign fashions in the later eighteenth century, enterprising publicists were bound to exploit Arminius yet again. One writer in a macabre fantasy called *Besuch um Mitternacht* conjured up the pure-bred barbarian chief to reproach a German prince impatiently waiting for his Italian mistress.

Nevertheless, Arminius missed fire as a popular figure. He was too uncouth perhaps, too remote from the complicated, stuffy world of the eighteenth and nineteenth centuries. Kleist's play about him, for instance, although written in 1808, was not printed before the author's death, and did not reach the stage until after the Franco-Prussian War. It has held it more or less ever since, but one suspects a dutiful rather than a spontaneous response from the generality of the public. Arminius in fact continues to be a text-book, rather than a genuinely popular, national hero, although where he does touch an occasional faithful heart, he certainly evokes an extravagant devotion. The sculptor who designed his monument spent nearly forty years on this labour of love, and died within a few months of its unveiling: life had no more to offer.

A yet more confusing example of German historical mythification is presented in the well-known Barbarossa legend. This is a real piece of folk-lore, ancient and very widespread, long before Rückert's poem and the nineteenth-century imperial revival gave it its text-book currency. There seems to be all over Europe, and for all I know beyond it as well, a kind of necessity for national heroes to retain a dim, sleeping immortality in the secret places of the mountains, ready to return when their time shall come. Several mountains in Germany – one of which is significantly near to Berchtesgaden – dispute the honour of being the resting place of Barbarossa. Traced to its foundations, however, this legend, too, shows a tendency to resolve itself into meaningless fragments. In the first place, the original legend had nothing to do with the immensely solid, foursquare, unspiritual figure of Barbarossa. It was whispered first of his grandson, Frederick II, that extraordinary man with his incomprehensible scientific interests, and his oriental morals, who caught the popular fancy of western Europe by his recapture of Jerusalem. It mattered little to the Germans that he had spent only a small part of his reign among them, and done nothing whatever for their development as a nation. Nobody at that time cared very deeply about nations as such. The struggle was between Papacy and Empire, between the claims of the spiritual and the universal, and the material and particularist; it reached its dramatic height under the leadership of this brilliant, ruthless giant. To half Europe, Frederick was Antichrist, to all he was *Stupor Mundi*, and when he died, all the dark and secret and primitive beliefs of Germany, the forces of past paganism and future anarchy, were gathered up in the cult of his immortality. So firmly was it believed that he would come again, that once or twice he even conveniently appeared – until the imposture was discovered.

It is evident from this that some transformation of the legend was essential before it could be used for nationalist purposes. The transformation began early in the sixteenth century. The gradual solidification of nationalist sentiment rapidly put the international, extremely un-German figure of Frederick II out of fashion. Naturally, almost imperceptibly, Barbarossa slid into the vacant place. There was no denying that Barbarossa had all the solid German virtues so evidently lacking in his grandson: he had been a brave, bluff soldier, a strong ruler, a determined leader, and he had been intensely, and even consciously Germanic. Moreover, he was a sympathetic figure, undeniably '*gemütlich*', which could not be said of Frederick II. Rückert's too easily memorized – and, once memorized, unforgettable – quatrains have riveted him in the minds of generations of school-children.

But it is not in the selection and interpretation of national heroes alone that the German preoccupation with their past is most evident. It is recognizable in the too-careful preservation, the fossilization almost, of their ancient cities; it is flaunted in Hamburg's huge Bismarck statue, regarded by patriotic citizens as the nineteenth-century equivalent of the ancient figures of Roland, which were the guardians of the old Hansa towns; it appeared in romantic guise in the lavishly restored or wholly rebuilt castles of the Rhineland; it shrieked in sheer madness from the pinnacled height of Neu Schwanstein. But all this is harmless and pleasant enough. No one with a taste for the bizarre can regret Neu Schwanstein and the faked castles have become as much a part of the landscape as the faked ruins of English eighteenth-century parks.

The danger comes only with the marriage of this innocuous play-acting, this national Bovarism, to the high technique of German scholarship. The Germans who have allowed themselves to be so bewitched by the romantic and the symbolic in their history also, and by an entirely separate process, gave birth to the most scholarly school of historians. The public mind is not very subtle; it cannot be expected to distinguish between attractive fable and actual fact. Still less can it do so if it is, as in Germany, desperately anxious that the fable should be fact, and generally befuddled by undiscriminating respect for authority and the printed word. German historical scholarship has gained, rightly, a very high reputation. The fruits of that reputation have been gathered in Germany by propagandists and irresponsibles. Rosenberg reaped where Ranke had sown.

The romanticization of German history has become a moral necessity for the maintenance of national self-respect. Light-hearted burlesquing of historical figures is rare and unpopular: the 'de-bunking' of time-honoured heroes, which was no more than a refreshing exercise in other countries, was regarded with distaste and apprehension by the German public, so that historians and journalists who indulged in it gained more publicity than their research often deserved, and have many of them later paid for their disregard of national feelings in a manner out of proportion to the triviality of their work. It was significant of this same desperate preoccupation with their picture of the past that the Nazi Government made it an offence to 'traduce' the heroes of German history. German history, the sad and straggling tale of missed opportunities, division, frustration and defeat, varied by outbursts of desperate self-assertion, has got to be moulded into an image which is beautiful, coherent and *convincing*. One at least of the mad King of Bavaria's castles was designed, not by an architect, but by a scene-painter. At the risk of falling myself into the typically German fault of arguing from symbols, I am tempted to see in this a parallel to the weakness of German history as seen by the Germans. It is not founded squarely on fact and built for daylight; it is not architectural, but scenic.

1942

Oliver Cromwell and the
Elizabethan Inheritance*

I n this the first of the Neale lectures I take my opening cue
from Sir John Neale's great work on *Elizabeth I and her
Parliaments*, namely that passage in the second volume in
which he describes the most famous of all her speeches to her
faithful Commons, the so-called 'Golden Speech' on November
1601. She made this speech, with her matchless sense of political
necessity and political timing, when she saw that she must yield
to the clamour of Parliament against the gross abuse of monopolies.
Having to yield, she did so in such a manner as to turn her surrender into a triumph, by making it the occasion of proclaiming
her love for her people in terms which were to become famous.

This speech, Neale tells us, was 'printed time and again in the
course of the seventeenth and eighteenth centuries at crises in the
nation's history'. I remember that it deeply moved a London
audience in the darkest time of the last war when Dame Edith
Evans spoke it from the stage, and phrases from it in William
Plomer's libretto of the opera *Gloriana* written for the Coronation
of Queen Elizabeth II have been carried to the opera houses of the
world in Benjamin Britten's music.

But my concern is with the seventeenth century. The Golden
Speech was twice reprinted during the conflict between Charles I
and Parliament. The first time was in January 1642. King Charles
had just made his ill-conceived attempt to intimidate Parliament:
he had gone down to the House of Commons in person to arrest
his principal opponents. Had Queen Elizabeth I, unimaginably,
found herself constrained to take such a course, we may be very
sure that she would have avoided any possible risk of failure. Not
so King Charles. There he was in the House of Commons with
his martial train just outside the door – only to find that in his own

* The Neale Lecture delivered at the University of London, December
1970.

phrase 'the birds had flown'. The Five Members whom he had planned to seize by force had already left the House and escaped by the back door. 'The attempt without the deed' confounded him utterly. He had passed the point of no return on the road to disaster.

Very soon after this incident a version of Queen Elizabeth's great speech came from an anonymous printer, garnished with an unusually seductive portrait of the Queen. Citizens of London, already wrathful against the King, were reminded of the memorable phrases uttered by her forty years earlier: 'God hath raised me high,' she had said, 'yet this I account the glory of my Crown that I have reigned with your loves.' And she had concluded: 'Though you have had and may have many mightier and wiser princes sitting in this seat, yet you never had nor shall have any that will love you better.'

It was very clear in 1642 that King Charles was neither a mightier nor a wiser prince and did not love them better. He had fled from his capital. He had made it clear to the envoy of the Prince of Orange that he would subdue London by raising forces in the North, while his Queen was about to enlist any foreign aid that she could get to assist him in his plan.

Six years later, after the defeat of the King in the Civil War, the Golden Speech was issued again in March 1648. Charles was by that time a prisoner in the Isle of Wight. He had none the less contrived to organize a renewal of the English conflict, coupled with an invasion from Scotland. On the eve of a second Civil War, the reprinted words of Queen Elizabeth I significantly underlined the most obvious of all the sovereign's duties – namely the protection of the subject. Elizabeth had thanked God that she had been the means to keep her people in safety – 'to preserve you from danger, yea, to be the instrument to deliver you from dishonour, and from shame and from infamy, to keep you from out of servitude, and from slavery under our enemies, and cruel tyranny and vile oppression intended against us'.[1]

Thus the Golden Speech of Elizabeth I, by which she had strengthened the links of loyalty which bound her subjects to her, was used by the opponents of King Charles to emphasize that ideal of monarchy from which he had so lamentably departed.

There were of course many men and women in England (whose active life extended into the Civil War) who could recall vividly the days of Elizabeth, vividly if not always quite accurately. Thus the venerable minister of St Ann's, Blackfriars, William Gouge, preaching in 1644, the year of Marston Moor, on 17 November, the anniversary of Queen Elizabeth's accession, recalled his youth: 'Through God's blessing I spent eight and twenty years of my days under her reign: and I have often blessed God that I was born and so long brought up in that blessed time.'[2]

Memory may have gilded his recollections of his youth. The eight and twenty last years of Elizabeth's reign had not been a wholly blessed time for Puritans whose disruptive aspirations to reform the Church had been ruthlessly quelled by Archbishop Whitgift. But it would seem that even those Puritans who had adult recollections of the reign of Queen Elizabeth had tacitly agreed, by the second quarter of the seventeenth century, to forget about this awkward aspect of her policy, and to remember only that the great Queen's handling of internal and external affairs compared very favourably with that of King Charles. He had neither won respect abroad nor preserved peace at home, and his attempts to quell the Puritans had been virulent without being effective.

Among the principal opponents of King Charles in the Long Parliament of 1640 only John Pym could truly be said to be Elizabethan born and *bred*. He was nineteen when the great Queen died and may therefore have formed his ideas by that time. John Hampden was eleven in 1603; Oliver Cromwell not quite four. In so far as accurate information is available, it would seem that the King's opponents were slightly older – a little more Elizabethan – than his supporters.[3] But the distinction, in times which were so much more conservative and traditional than our own disturbed epoch, is probably not very significant. The great majority of those who were old enough to sit in Parliament in 1640 would have been brought up and educated by Elizabethan parents, guardians and schoolmasters, and this would apply to both parties alike. Indeed, by laying a different emphasis on the achievements of Queen Elizabeth, her reign could be used as propaganda by both sides. As effective propaganda it was, however, largely used on the Puritan-Parliamentary side, a development which might well have surprised the great Queen herself.

Elizabeth's reign of forty-five years, during a period of great dangers and great changes, both in national and international life, could in retrospect be idealized in several different ways, according to interest, temperament or belief. For many, and for Puritan sympathizers above all, she was honoured first and foremost as the Protestant saviour, 'that glorious Deborah' who had been miraculously preserved by divine Providence to lead her people out of the Babylonish captivity of Rome.

Closely connected with this was the glorification of her as the champion of oppressed Protestants in Europe and, during the latter part of her reign, the acknowledged leader among European Protestant princes. But there was no need to have strongly Protestant, let alone Puritan, sympathies, in order to glorify the Queen as the victorious defender of England against foreign enemies, and Spain above all, or to magnify the naval glories of her time.

In the years that closely followed her death the emphasis was, however, on the peace and prosperity of her reign, rather than its glory. It was not until humiliation and defeat set in that Elizabethan glory replaced Elizabethan peace as a dominating element in the picture. Elizabeth as the dedicated ruler who had preserved her people from civil war, from the ambitious rebellions of over-mighty subjects and the lethal religious conflicts that divided other nations – this was the ideal set forth in Cranmer's speech over the infant princess in the last scene of Shakespeare's *Henry VIII*:

> *In her days every man shall eat in safety*
> *Under his own vine, what he plants; and sing*
> *The merry songs of peace to all his neighbours . . .*

The view echoes the speech of Sir Walter Mildmay in the Parliament of 1584, at a time when Elizabeth, with consummate skill, was still managing to keep England out of dangerous and expensive military commitments in Europe:

Moreover, through the goodness of Almighty God by the ministry of this our gracious Queen we have enjoyed peace now full twenty-six years, the like whereof so long together, hath not been seen in any age: the commodities whereof may appear sufficiently by comparing the blessedness of this our happy peace with the miserable state of our neighbours, long afflicted with cruel wars. We possess in all freedom and liberty our religion, which is the chief; our lands, lives and goods, our wives and children. They on the other side, through civil and intestine troubles are bereaved of all those good things that we enjoy, in danger to fall at the length into the grievous yoke of perpetual servitude.[4]

This view of Queen Elizabeth's reign certainly chimed in well, in the early years of the seventeenth century, with the peace-loving policy of King James I.

Elizabeth as an opponent of the Puritans was conveniently forgotten by the critics of the Church policies of King James and King Charles. Indeed King Charles on at least two critical occasions in his later years proclaimed, quite truthfully, his intention of preserving the episcopal Church of Queen Elizabeth. It was significant that her name, used by him in this context, had no persuasive magic at all.

Elizabeth's parliamentary record was also subject to the modifications of time and memory. The irate King James quite correctly cited her effective control of the Commons when he dissolved the recalcitrant Parliament of 1621 for encroaching on the rights of the Crown and presuming to dictate foreign policy in a manner wholly unknown 'in the blessed reign of our late predecessor that renowned Queen Elizabeth'.[5]

The opposition read the record differently. Eight years later Sir John Eliot, the most reckless leader the Commons had yet known, was to occupy his imprisonment in the Tower by composing a work on recent parliamentary history that he did not live to finish. Its purpose was to show the decline of English government in the quarter of a century that had passed since those days of perfect harmony between Crown and Parliament in Elizabeth's time. 'That great councell of Parliament', he wrote, 'was the nurse of all her actions; such an emulation of love was between that senate and this Queen, as it is questionable which had more affection, the Parliament in observance unto her or she in indulgence to the Parliament.'[6]

The tension between the Stuarts and their Parliaments, as Eliot saw it, was caused by their unwillingness to allow the Commons, in his pleasing phrase, to be 'the nurse' to their royal actions. So the facts appeared to him and to a growing number of his contemporaries, though what Queen Elizabeth would have thought of the idea that Parliament was her 'nurse' may be left to the imagination.

Accuracy of memory, or a just assessment of facts, have never had much to do with those popular ideas about the past that carry weight in political arguments. Recollections of 'Queen Elizabeth of famous memory' became hazier and feelings stronger as she receded in time. I need hardly emphasize to this audience that, on his accession in 1603, King James was not subject to those highly unfavourable comparisons with the great Queen that later came into fashion. Indeed, the French envoy at the time, the veteran Villeroy, who had lived through many changes of reign in France, commented on what he called the 'strangely barbarous and ungrateful' behaviour of the Londoners who lit bonfires for the new King on the very evening of the day on which they learnt of Elizabeth's death. But nothing in 1603 could have been more disastrous than a hiatus in the succession and it may reasonably be assumed that the bonfires were a demonstration of solidarity in support of the Queen's proclaimed heir rather than a sign of indifference to her death.[7]

The auguries for King James were favourable. He had shown skill in maintaining his authority over the notoriously high-spirited and disunited Scots. There was no obvious reason why he should prove less skilful in England. The introduction to the Journals of the House of Commons in 1604 refers to his 'eminent virtue and experience in government' which is not, in view of his past performances, an unduly exaggerated estimate. Furthermore, what a contemporary called 'his masculine virtue and fair progeny' gave assurance of a safe succession. It was over a hundred years since any sovereign of England had been the father of sons at the time of his accession. James had two and his wife was still young. The succession was more secure than at any time within living memory.

This was, or appeared to be, a great blessing to the subject.

Paradoxically it was to prove less of a blessing to the Crown. Once again I quote Sir John Neale on the peculiar position of Elizabeth: 'The symbol of the Virgin Queen is more than a curiosity: it is a transcendent clue to the age' – to Elizabeth's age.[8] She was unique. The lack of an heir of her body had been for years a nagging anxiety and a threat to the future of the nation. But it immensely enhanced her position as the sole guarantor of her people's welfare without a partner in her responsibilities, without a competitor at her Court. It was a different matter for a King with a sturdy son at his side, an acknowledged successor, the possible head of faction. Discontented courtiers and disgruntled politicians would be looking towards the dynamic Prince Henry before the boy was fifteen.

In 1603 this danger lay ahead. King James held an exalted view of his own authority; it was in effect much the same view of royal authority that Queen Elizabeth had held, but King James spoke about it much more, and even wrote books about it. Yet, in spite of his insistence on the God-given nature of his office, he was of a jovial disposition, less dignified and more approachable when he first came to England than Queen Elizabeth had been in her later years. He was by no means personally unpopular, although the English resented the multitude of Scots who followed him southward and mightily increased the scramble for Court preferment and profits. But in the early years of his reign, while Robert Cecil remained his minister and his guide, major errors were usually avoided.

It is time that I turned my attention to the other name in my title, that of Oliver Cromwell. I must plead guilty to having used his name a little loosely. A more exact title might have been 'The English Revolution – or The Civil War – and the Elizabethan Inheritance'. But men of his breeding and his generation shared much the same conceptions or misconceptions about the immediate past and, at least in the early stages of the conflict, were influenced by their ideas towards the same ends.

We have no evidence at all of what Cromwell's childish views may have been, but it is probable that his first impressions of the new epoch were favourable. His mother, Elizabeth Steward, came of a Norfolk family who claimed to be related to the new dynasty.

His rich uncle, Sir Oliver Cromwell of Hinchinbrooke, entertained the King lavishly on several occasions. But he was disappointed of any reward for his hospitality, and his debts compelled him to sell Hinchinbrooke, thus reducing the fortunes and the standing of the Cromwell family in the county. Whatever effect these sad consequences may have had later on young Oliver's opinions, it seems at least probable that he enjoyed, and was impressed by, the pageantry and banqueting of the royal visits in his early childhood.

He was educated with a strong Protestant bias. His ideas of recent history like those of many of his contemporaries would have been drawn from Foxe's *Book of Martyrs*, with its powerful emphasis on the Protestant mission of the English and on Elizabeth I as the saviour of her people from Popery. In Foxe's lively account she appears as a heroine akin to the Jewish prophetess Deborah. She is represented as a princess saved from mortal danger and the plots of her enemies through 'the gracious and favourable Providence of the Lord' so that she might rescue her people from idolatry. This conception of Elizabeth was followed by other contemporary historians whose works were generally available; by John Stow in his *Annales*, by Camden in his Latin history of Elizabeth's reign, by John Speed in his *History of Great Britain*.[9]

As Cromwell grew up, the early popularity of King James declined. Cecil's death and the increasing domination of Court favourites undermined respect for the Crown. A faction began to grow round Prince Henry, whose popularity was rather an indication of discontent with King James than evidence of any exceptional virtue in the young Prince. When he died in 1612 it was a noticeable fact that in the elegies devoted to him, as in the poems addressed to him in his lifetime, his most lauded virtue was his aggressive and warlike temperament. Sir William Alexander compared him enthusiastically to the Black Prince. Drummond of Hawthornden regretted that, since this paragon had to die, he had not died in battle while victoriously scaling the walls of Rome.[10]

This is significant. When Queen Elizabeth died, the most praised virtue of her reign, its greatest achievement, had been the peace and safety of her people. King James had made peace with

Spain soon after his accession, a pulling out of European commitments which was judicious and indeed necessary at the time. Eight years later, when Prince Henry died, the King's claim to be '*rex pacificus*' was no longer so popular and the ideal recollection of Elizabeth was growing steadily more glorious. By the middle years of King James's reign, Bishop Goodman records, the memory of the old Queen was 'much magnified, such ringing of bells, such public joy and sermons in commemoration of her, the picture of her tomb painted in many churches, and in effect more solemnity and joy in memory of her coronation than was for the coming of King James'.[11]

By the time Cromwell reached Cambridge in 1616 King James had committed himself to a peace policy based on a grave miscalculation of his power. He believed that, in a Continent threatened by religious war and by the dynastic ambition of the Spanish–Austrian Habsburg, he could hold the balance by marrying his daughter to a leading Protestant prince and his son to the Infanta of Spain. The Protestant marriage had been achieved without difficulty and Princess Elizabeth had become the wife of Frederick, Elector Palatine of the Rhine, the youthful head of the Union of Protestant German princes. He was also a grandson of William the Silent, the pre-eminent Protestant leader of a previous generation.

This alliance had been popular at the time but ill-feeling grew in the country as James embarked on the second part of his plan, the project of a Spanish marriage for the Prince of Wales began to take shape, and the Spanish ambassador gained an obvious ascendancy over the King. The last voyage and the death of Raleigh stirred up confused and angry memories. Meanwhile a Protestant revolt in Bohemia set up a chain reaction that was soon to arouse a storm of emotion in England.

The Czechs had risen against their Habsburg King, Ferdinand. He was a godson of Philip II whose mission as a champion of Catholicism he had espoused with single-minded fanaticism. The Bohemian rebels offered the crown to the Protestant Elector Frederick. As leader of the German Protestant Union and son-in-law of James I, they believed he would be able to rally strong support. And they did not overlook his own hereditary commitment to the Protestant Cause as a grandson of William the Silent. Would the Bohemian revolt be to Habsburg power in central Europe what the Dutch revolt had been to Hapsburg power in the Netherlands?

It worked out otherwise. Frederick got no support from his fellow princes in Germany or from his father-in-law. By going to Bohemia, he left his lands on the Rhine unguarded. They were occupied by troops from the Spanish Netherlands who thus gained a threatening strategic advantage over the Dutch. Frederick was totally defeated; Bohemia was ruthlessly restored to Austrian dominion and the Catholic Church. The remainder of his German lands were given to the Duke of Bavaria who speedily extinguished Protestantism there also. Thus the precarious religious and political balance in Europe was shifted emphatically in favour of the Counter-Reformation and the Spanish–Austrian power.

Feeling in England ran high. The Commons in a petition to the King in December 1621 referred to 'the strange confederacy of the Princes of the Popish religion aiming mainly at the advancement of theirs and the subverting of ours and taking the advantage conducive to that end on all occasions', and named the King of Spain as 'the chief of that league'. The language was a thought melodramatic, but their reading of the situation was right – or at least a great deal more right than King James's. He persisted in his delusion that the Spanish marriage would restore the balance and solve all problems. Enraged at their presumption in seeking to dictate on foreign policy he enlisted the shade of Queen Elizabeth as his ally. He began his answer to them with a quotation from the quelling speech she had made to the 'insolent Polonian ambassador' who presumed to read her a lecture on how she should act in foreign affairs: 'Legatus expectabamus, heraldum accepimus.'[12]

Circumstances alter cases. The King might think himself Elizabeth's equal in his desire to avoid involvement in a European war for as long as he could, but *her* policy had been based on a shrewd assessment of realities; *his* was based on a delusion. The Spaniards were not, as he fondly hoped, willing to evacuate the lands of his son-in-law for the questionable advantage of placing an Infanta on the throne of England.

I need not here recapitulate the dismal story of the ensuing years during which the Protestant Cause in Europe fared ever worse. The Dutch were thrown on to the defensive, while in Germany the Habsburg counter-thrust against the Protestants reached the Baltic. The peace policy of King James was abandoned in total ruin and was succeeded in his last unhappy year, and in the reign of his son, by intervention in Europe of the most lamentable ineptitude. King Charles's reign opened with an expedition against Cadiz that made England a laughing stock. Spinola, the greatest general in the service of Spain, is reported as saying: 'The English thought they could take all Spain with 12,000 infantry and a few horsemen. The only prudence they showed was in retiring as speedily as possible with great losses and disgrace . . .'[13]

This was followed by the failure to relieve the Huguenots at La Rochelle. 'Since England was England she received not so dishonourable a blow,' wrote Denzil Holles, an angry member of Parliament, and a wit wrote a bitter epigram on the Duke of Buckingham, who had led the expedition:

> *Charles, would ye quail your foes, have better luck:*
> *Send forth some Drakes and keep at home your Duck.*[14]

'Some Drakes' . . . there was not one Drake. Now in these years of dishonour while England became a mockery in foreign affairs, the image of Queen Elizabeth, the champion of Protestant Europe, the patron of great sailors and English sea-power, assumed full splendour as the symbol of national greatness; the Gloriana image, not the Deborah image. Thus she appears in ballads and broadsheets and on the lips of speakers in the House of Commons.

When Cromwell entered Parliament in 1628 this image was foremost. It was in this Parliament that Cromwell would have heard the febrile Sir John Eliot denounce the mismanagement of recent foreign enterprises by calling to mind

that princess, that never to be forgotten excellence Queen Elizabeth, whose name, without admiration, falls not into mention with her enemies. You know how she advanced herself, how she advanced this kingdom, how she advanced this nation in glory and in state;

how she depressed her enemies, how she upheld her friends; how she enjoyed a full security, and made them our scorn, how now are made our terror.[15]

After further eulogy of Elizabeth's handling of foreign affairs he denounced the present policies of the Crown as so far contrary to the Protestant and national interest that they might have been forged by the arch-fiends of Spain themselves.

A year later, when Charles had dissolved Parliament and let it be generally known that he would never willingly call another, Sir John Eliot shifted the emphasis of his praise for Elizabeth to her greatness as a parliamentary ruler:

No age can parallel the love between her Parliament and her, when harmony and concord seemed to hold emulation with the spheres, where no string jarred, but all parts answered in a general symphony of the whole. What was the condition of the kingdom when her government did leave it is well known to all men. What it is now, this labour will express . . .[16]

We cannot grudge poor Eliot his illusions as he slowly died in the Tower. But he had conveniently forgotten quite a few jarring strings in this harmony of the spheres, including at least one member of Parliament, Peter Wentworth, a patriot of rather his own colour, who like him had died in the Tower.

Meanwhile, deprived of parliamentary subsidies, King Charles made peace abroad, and especially with Spain, in a manner which was both opportunist and servile. Asserting his neutrality in the European conflict, he entered into an agreement for the transport of Spanish bullion across southern England. This bullion was of course for the payment of Spanish troops in the long war against the Dutch; and by avoiding the greater length of the Channel the danger of interception by Dutch ships was confined to the short passage from London to Antwerp. As his difficulties increased, King Charles undertook that Spanish troops as well as Spanish silver could go overland through the south of England. Only a few actually did so, yet enough to make a sinister impression on his English subjects. Just before the collapse of his personal government a scheme was even mooted for the English navy to convoy Spanish transport in return for a subsidy of four million ducats.[17] Small wonder that in these years his name was held in contempt by both sides in the European conflict.

During this time, the memory of Queen Elizabeth was kept green by further editions of Stow's *Annales* as well as by the English translations of Camden's Latin history of England which enjoyed considerable popularity. Not that the translators of Camden perceived the potential danger to King Charles inherent in the cultivation of Elizabeth's memory. The book was after all a loyal and patriotic work in itself. One translator was himself a chaplain to Archbishop Laud, and the other dedicated his work respectfully to King Charles as 'the story of her who, whilst she lived, was the joy of England, the terror and admiration of the world'.[18]

On the record there was no inherent reason why the Queen should become, posthumously, a danger to the Anglican King. Elizabeth had not been a Puritan Deborah fulminating out of the Old Testament. Far from it. She had established the Episcopal Church in which Charles believed and had driven the Puritans into the wilderness. Both James and Charles took their stand on the Elizabethan settlement against the Puritan attack in and out of Parliament. Charles saw himself, truly enough, as 'constant for the doctrine and discipline of the Church of England as it was established by Queen Elizabeth', and he defended his position vigorously against critics in the Long Parliament with the declaration that his intention was 'to reduce all matters of religion and government to what they were in the purest times of Queen Elizabeth's days'.[19]

Elizabeth, the Episcopalian Queen, was historically the more correct vision. But it lacked popular appeal, and the total disregard of this aspect of her reign by her Protestant-Puritan admirers in the half-century after her death provides a striking example of the way in which men will take and use what they want from the past and blankly overlook what does not suit them.

The anniversary of Queen Elizabeth's accession, 17 November, fell just a fortnight after King Charles, driven to the wall by the Presbyters' revolt in Scotland, opened the Long Parliament in

1640. The two ministers chosen to preach before Parliament on that day, Cornelius Burgess and Stephen Marshall, geared their sermons to the idea of a covenant between the nation and God. The allusion was clearly to the example of the Presbyterian Scots who had initiated their revolt by the signing of the National Covenant in defence of their religion, an oath to God against the King. Both these English preachers cited Queen Elizabeth as though she had approved, or would have approved, such a Covenant. Thus Stephen Marshall declared: 'This day eighty-two years agone, the Lord set up the Gospel among us and took us to be a nation in Covenant with him.' Burgess called attention to the new dangers which now assailed England fourscore years after 'our late royal Deborah . . . began a new resurrection of this kingdom from the dead', and prayed that the 'door of hope by her set open this day be not again shut for want of a Covenant'.[20]

It is hardly to be wondered that, against such obstinate blindness to the facts, King Charles cited the actual record of Queen Elizabeth in vain. Yet there were other aspects of her policy which, at an earlier time, he might have exploited to some advantage, had he been gifted with a tenth part of her political touch. Neither Charles nor his father before him had ever cared very much for the conception of Elizabeth as 'the joy of England, the terror and admiration of the world'. But in making propaganda for his naval building programme financed out of the levy of Ship Money, a few references to Queen Elizabeth would hardly have come amiss. King Charles preferred to invoke the memory of the Saxon King Edgar, surnamed the Peaceful, whose somewhat remote naval record though interesting to antiquarians could hardly be expected to fire the imagination of English seamen or the citizens of London.[21]

This was only a minor error in public relations, and probably nothing would have made the King's ship-building a popular enterprise so long as he continued his pro-Spanish foreign policy. It is at least arguable that the refusal of John Hampden and others to pay Ship Money would not have commanded so much sympathy had the levy been combined with intervention for the Protestant Cause rather than with underhand support of Spain. In any case when the Long Parliament summed up the King's errors in the Grand Remonstrance of 1641 they scornfully dismissed Ship Money as being 'taken upon *pretence* of guarding the seas', and they placed high among their accusations his treaty with Spain.

In propaganda of the popular kind Queen Elizabeth continued to be the ideal of an English ruler. An anonymous doggerel pamphlet published on the eve of the Civil War invoked her almost as a patron saint, called her 'blest Eliza . . . with Saints inroul'd'. Another pamphlet, more ambitious and better informed, offered a rapid sketch of English history showing how wicked foreigners, French as well as Spanish, but chiefly the Spaniards, had entangled England in sinister plots. Renowned Elizabeth had outwitted all their machinations; King Charles had fallen an easy victim.[22]

It is now more than half a century since A. P. Newton in his *Colonising Activities of the English Puritans*[23] demonstrated the close connection between the governors of Providence Company with their interests in the Caribbean and the leaders of the Parliamentary opposition to King Charles. The anti-Spanish interests of this relatively small but influential group were specialized. Behind them was a much more general and popular fear of Spain in Europe, fear of resurgent Catholicism, a genuine concern for the endangered Protestant Cause, a genuine sympathy for the refugees from persecution who had fled from Bohemia, from the occupied Palatinate, from other regions of Germany overrun by imperial and Spanish armies, and some of whom had found refuge in England. It was against this background of present danger to what they thought of as 'true religion' that many Englishmen impotently and angrily resented the servile neutrality to which their King had bound them. Looking back to the recent past, they idealized the vision of Elizabeth, blessed, renowned and 'of famous memory'. By 1640, she had become Deborah and Gloriana all in one: the Protestant saviour of her people, the Protestant champion abroad and the symbol of that national honour which England had now lost.

I am not suggesting that these memories of Elizabeth were among the causes of the Civil War. Only that they were an element, and an important one, in the climate of opinion which made a civil war possible and which enhanced a sense of historic and God-given mission in bringing down the government of King Charles. For the older generation, those of Cromwell's age, those who were men and not mere boys in 1640, this sense of Protestant mission was strongly associated through Foxe's book, and its echoes in other popular works, with the providential accession of Elizabeth. It was this sense of mission, intensified by the events of the Civil War, which Milton put into his famous words: 'When God is decreeing some great work of Reformation to be done, what does he then but reveal himself as his manner is first to his Englishmen . . . ?'

It was thus in the logic of events that (after the defeat and death of the King who had betrayed the reforming mission of the nation) issue should finally be joined with the Spaniard: as Cromwell did in 1655 of course. It was too late by then for the Protestant Cause in Europe, which, by the intervention of France, had emerged battered but surviving from the Peace of Westphalia in 1648. But there was still the desire for an English foothold in the Caribbean, though the religious mission was not here quite so obvious. Cromwell's policy differed fundamentally from that of Elizabeth in the nature of its organization and its purpose. It was aggressive, not defensive, and it aimed at an extension of English commerce and power at the national level in a manner unimaginable fifty years earlier.[24]

But Cromwell certainly and naturally invoked Elizabeth as his forerunner in this holy war. In the manifesto published to justify the declaration of war, composed by Milton, much was made of the past century's history, of Spanish attempts to destroy Queen Elizabeth and to 'subdue this whole island in the year 1588'. Much was also made of the opportunities which now lay before the nation 'of promoting the glory of God and enlarging the bounds of Christ's kingdom' by driving the Spaniards out of the West Indies.[25] The connection between the two was clearer to them than it is to us.

In his speech to Parliament Cromwell himself recalled how 'Queen Elizabeth of famous memory' had been the object of murderous attempts inspired by Jesuits, Papists and Spain, and linked recent attempts on his own life to these – as all part of the same continuous plot against the English nation and the Protestant interest. 'If Pope and Spaniard and Devil and all set themselves against us . . . ,' he concluded, 'yet in the name of the Lord we should destroy them.'[26]

Cromwell's speeches, unlike those of Queen Elizabeth, were not works of art. They contain passages of great practical good sense interspersed with confused graspings towards ideas that are felt rather than expressed. But certainly from this one there emerges a conviction that national honour and a sense of religious mission go together and that, somewhere in the divine purpose of Providence, it all goes back to Queen Elizabeth. Indeed psychologists might trace in this speech evidence that he identified himself, in danger and glory, with her.

Cromwell's astounding success in his foreign enterprises, coming between the humiliations of the previous and the succeeding reigns, would cause him to be remembered and praised (if surreptitiously) within a few years of the Restoration of Charles II when English prestige again went into a steep decline. Inevitably he would be linked, as he would have wished to link himself, to the ever-receding glorious memory of the great Queen.

Thus in 1675, a satirical ballad attacks the government of Charles II in a doggerel dialogue between two horses – the bronze horse on which Charles I still rides at the top of Whitehall, and the marble horse from a statue of Charles II no longer extant. The marble horse, often deploring the decline of English affairs, says:

> *I freely declare it, I am for old Noll,*
> *Though his government did a tyrant's resemble*
> *He made England great and her enemies tremble.*

And on further questioning from the bronze horse, he appeals – if in a somewhat irreverent form – to the deathless name of Queen Elizabeth:

> *A Tudor, a Tudor! We've had Stuarts enough;*
> *None ever reign'd like old Bess in her Ruff.*[27]

1970

NOTES

[1] The versions of the Golden Speech published in 1642 and 1648 are in the Thomason Collection in the British Museum (E.200 and E.432). For information about other printed versions of this speech and for the most authentic text see J. E. Neale, *Queen Elizabeth I and Her Parliaments* (London, 1953, 1957), 2 vols, II, pp. 388–93.

[2] William Gouge, *Mercies Memorial* (London, 1644). British Museum, Thomason Tracts, E.23.

[3] D. Brunton and D. H. Pennington, *Members of the Long Parliament* (London, 1954), pp. 15–16.

[4] Neale, op. cit., II, p. 28.

[5] S. R. Gardiner, *History of England, 1603–1642* (London, 1883–4), 10 vols, IV, p. 268.

[6] John Forster, *Sir John Eliot* (London, 1872), 2nd edition, 2 vols, II, p. 386.

[7] G. Goodman, *The Court of King James I* (London, 1839), 2 vols, I, p. 9.

[8] Neale, op. cit., p. 421.

[9] William Haller, *Foxe's Book of Martyrs and the Elect Nation* (London, 1963), pp. 228–34.

[10] Drummond, *Poetical Works*, ed. L. E. Kastner (Manchester, 1913), 2 vols, I, p. 76.

[11] Goodman, op. cit., pp. 96–7.

[12] J. E. Neale, *Queen Elizabeth I* (London, 1934), p. 345.

[13] *Letters of Peter Paul Rubens*, ed. Ruth Saunders Magurn (Cambridge, Mass., 1955), p. 124.

[14] *Letters and Despatches of the Earl of Strafford*, ed. W. Knowler (London, 1739), 2 vols, I, pp. 41–2; Drummond, op. cit., II, p. 245.

[15] Forster, op. cit., II, p. 239f.

[16] ibid., II, p. 383.

[17] *Calendar of State Papers, Venetian*, 1640–2, pp. 44–5, 50, 53.

[18] Haller, op. cit., pp. 228–9.

[19] *Lords Journals*, IV, p. 142.

[20] Both sermons are in the Thomason Collection in the British Museum, E.204, 8 and 9.

[21] Thomas Haywood, *The Description of His Majesty's Royal Ship* (London, 1637).

[22] *The Humble Petition of the Wretched Commons of England to the Blessed Elizabeth of Famous Memory* (London, 1642), Thomason Tracts, E.108; *The Anatomie of the French and Spanish Faction* (London, 1644), Thomason Tracts, E.35.

[23] *The Colonizing Activities of the English Puritans: The Last Phase of the Elizabethan Struggle with Spain* (New Haven, Conn., 1914).

[24] For an illuminating comparison of Cromwell's Spanish war with Elizabeth's see Christopher Hill, *God's Englishman* (London, 1970), pp. 167–8.

[25] Wilbur Cortez Abbott, *Writings and Speeches of Oliver Cromwell*, 4 vols (Cambridge, Mass., 1937–47), III, pp. 890–1.

[26] op. cit., IV, pp. 261, 265–71, 278.

[27] *Poems and Letters of Andrew Marvell*, ed. H. M. Margoliouth (Oxford, 1952), 2nd edition, 2 vols, I, p. 195.

Edward Gibbon

I

When Edward Gibbon published the first volume of his *Decline and Fall of the Roman Empire* in 1776, it was hailed by the most eminent critic of his time as 'a truly classic work'. In the hundred and eighty years which have elapsed since then, that contemporary judgment has been confirmed. Gibbon's great book is still read for pleasure and information. The balance and form of his presentation is as gratifying to the mind as a noble eighteenth-century building to the eyes. The flow of his narrative, the clarity of his prose and the edge of his irony still have power to delight and, although seven generations of scholars have added to or modified our knowledge of the epoch, most of what Gibbon wrote is still valid as history.

Edward Gibbon was born at Putney, then a pretty suburban village a few miles from London, in the year 1737. His father was a gentleman of extravagant habits and comfortable means with interests in the City; in his youth he and his family had come under the influence of William Law and his two sisters are said to appear in Law's *Serious Call* as the frivolous Flavia and the devout Miranda. The devout Miss Gibbon continued to be Law's disciple and a pillar of his holy household until his death in 1761. It is strange that so close a link should exist between the great mystical writer and the highly rational historian.

As a child Edward Gibbon was small and sickly, easily bullied by tougher boys at Dr Wooddeson's school where he was sent at nine years old to learn Latin. Of the seven children born to his parents he alone survived, and his delicate mother died when he was ten, when he was handed over to the care of her sister, Catherine Porten. Nothing more fortunate could have happened to him, for this excellent woman combined all the qualities most necessary to his health and happiness. She was resourceful, energetic, practical, deeply affectionate, imaginative in her understanding of his intellectual needs and not unduly possessive. To ensure herself an independent income and to make a more cheerful home for her nephew, she set up a little boarding-house in London for boys attending Westminster – the school which Gibbon himself attended on the rare occasions when he was well enough to do so. He gained his real education from the wide general reading in which she encouraged him. In the autobiography which he carefully composed in later life he called her 'the true mother of my mind as well as of my health' and left a grateful description of her personality: 'Her natural good sense was improved by the perusal of the best books in the English language and if her reason was sometimes clouded by prejudice, her sentiments were never disguised by hypocrisy or affection. Her indulgent tenderness, the frankness of her temper, and my innate rising curiosity, soon removed all distance between us: like friends of an equal age we freely conversed on every topic, familiar or abstruse, and it was her delight and reward to observe the first shoots of my young ideas.'

In his twelfth year Gibbon describes himself as having fully developed that 'invincible love of reading, which I would not exchange for the treasures of India'. During the brief time that he was well enough to attend Dr Wooddeson's school at Kingston he read Cornelius Nepos whose lucid simplicity he later commended as an excellent model. More important was his discovery of Homer in Pope's translation which, he says, 'accustomed my ear to the sound of poetic harmony'. In his mature style the influence of Pope's fluent precision in the use of words can still be traced. He read in the next two or three years everything on which he could lay hands – poetry, history, travel and romance – until in his own phrase his 'indiscriminate appetite subsided by degrees in the *historic* line'. He was fourteen when he came upon the *Universal History* while on a visit to friends and he 'was immersed in the passage of the Goths over the Danube when the summons of the dinner bell reluctantly dragged me from my intellectual feast'.

When he was sixteen his health suddenly improved; the prostrating headaches from which he had suffered as a child vanished away and he was sent to the University to complete his education. Owing to his irregular schooling and wide but unconventional reading he arrived at Oxford in 1752 with 'a stock of erudition which might have puzzled a doctor and a degree of ignorance of which a schoolboy might have been ashamed'. But so slack was the tuition at Oxford at that time that no one took the least notice either of his education or of his ignorance. Teaching and discipline were equally lax and Gibbon, who was ardent to acquire knowledge, was bored and disgusted. Thrown back on his resources during what he was later to call 'the most idle and unprofitable' months of his whole life, he began to examine the religious controversy recently caused by the publication of Middleton's *Free Enquiry into the Origin of Miracles*. The startling result of his researches into the early history of Christianity was his conversion to Catholicism, and he was privately received into the Church of Rome in June 1753.

As the law then stood in England, his conversion meant that he had to leave the University, and since Roman Catholics were excluded from public employment, it put a stop to any hope of a political or legal career. Gibbon's father, who was distressed at this unconventional turn in his son's life, packed him off to Lausanne to complete his studies and reconsider his religious views under the care of the Protestant pastor, Pavillard.

Gibbon stayed in Switzerland for nearly five years and there he laid the solid foundations of his education. His conversion had not gone deep; at Christmas 1754 he was reconciled to the Protestant religion. During the ensuing year he perfected himself in Latin and French, and formed the habit of writing his copious diaries entirely in French. He read French and Latin historians, began to learn Greek, toured Switzerland and wrote for practice 'a very ample relation of my tour'. But his most valuable discovery was the important work on logic of the Abbé de Crousaz, which, he records, 'formed my mind to a habit of thinking and reasoning I had no idea of before'. He now began to exercise his critical faculties by writing essays or, as he preferred to call them, 'observations' on Plautus and Virgil. He corresponded with neighbouring *savants*, saw the plays of Voltaire, and began to compose, in French, his *Essai sur l'étude de la littérature*. He knew that he wanted to be a man of learning and a writer, but he aimed at criticism or philosophy rather than history.

In June 1757 he met Suzanne Curchod, a pretty, intelligent, well-read young woman, the only child of a neighbouring pastor. Suzanne had no fortune except her intellect and her charms but she was greatly sought after. Gibbon's entry in his diary is short and telling:

I saw Mademoiselle Curchod: Omnia vincit amor, et nos cedamus amori.

Gibbon himself was by no means unattractive. Although he was very small, his fresh colour and lively expression gave him charm and his conversation was fluent, witty and erudite; also he appeared to be a young man with a future. Mademoiselle Curchod, who had a good many admirers, was disposed to be coy. Gibbon pursued her. She held him off a little too long and by the time she decided to relent his own ardour was evidently cooling. But he could hardly admit that he had changed his mind, and when he left Switzerland in the spring of 1758, it was on the understanding that he would return to marry her. In his autobiography he gives a laconic and slightly disingenuous account of what next occurred. His father opposed the marriage and Gibbon, in his famous phrase, 'sighed as a lover but obeyed as a son'. He does not explain why, although he came home in May, he did not mention Suzanne to his father until August, nor does he tell of Suzanne's desperate letters, imploring him to be true to her.

Gibbon was not made for domestic life and he probably knew it. He had the egoism of the natural scholar and wrote of himself 'I was never less alone than when by myself'. This is not the temperament that makes an ardent lover or a good husband. In a moment of youthful impulse he had thought himself in love with an intelligent young woman, but it is clear that his love evaporated when he began to think about the responsibilities and commitments of marriage. The sigh that he heaved as a lover was a sigh of relief.

If Gibbon had the egoism very natural to scholars he had also an affectionate and grateful nature and his treatment of Suzanne is the only example of blameable personal conduct in his life. He was a good son although he had some cause for complaint of a father who never did much for him except squander his patrimony. The elder Mr Gibbon had married again while his son was abroad; and it is much to Gibbon's credit that, although naturally apprehensive at first, he soon became devoted to his step-mother and remained so to the end of his life. In all the ordinary exchanges of family and friendship Gibbon was kind, reasonable, well behaved and warm-hearted. But when it came to the stronger passions he failed, as scholars commonly do. Those whose first passion is knowledge justly fear the intrusion of any rival interest.

II

Gibbon was now twenty-one years old. He spoke and wrote French fluently – at this time more fluently – than he did English. He had fully determined to devote his life to scholarship and writing though he had not yet settled on a subject. But for the next few years family interests and patriotic duty kept him in England. He had seen little of his father as a boy and nothing at all since he left Oxford. An excellent relationship now sprang up between the two, for the older Mr Gibbon admired his son's erudition and enjoyed his company, and Hester Gibbon, the step-mother, who had no children of her own, was blessedly free from jealousy. In 1761 both father and son volunteered for the Hampshire militia. The Seven Years War was in progress and there were rumours of a possible French invasion. Nothing of the kind happened but Edward Gibbon spent the best part of two years marching about with the troops in Hampshire, living sometimes in billets and sometimes under canvas. Of this period he was later to say that 'the Captain of Hampshire grenadiers . . . has not been useless to the historian of the Roman Empire'. The part played by an English gentleman in local manoeuvres hardly seems on a level with the exploits of the great Roman generals and the ferocious barbarian leaders which Gibbon was later to describe. But the good historian should be able to use his own experience to illuminate that of others, and however absurd the comparison between eighteenth-century Hampshire and the battlefields of the fifth century must appear, however wide the difference between Captain Edward Gibbon of the militia and the thundering chiefs of the gothic hordes, there are certain unchanging elements in the soldier's experience which Gibbon learnt to appreciate.

He found much of the life very boring but he was young and strong enough to enjoy, in limited quantities, the rowdier amusements of his fellow officers. He did not however neglect his studies, went on steadily with his reading in all his leisure hours and completed the *Essai sur l'étude de la littérature* that he had begun in Lausanne. His proud father persuaded him to have this little work printed and when the King's brother, the Duke of York, came down to inspect the militia Captain Edward Gibbon, again to satisfy his father's whim, presented him with a copy. The Duke, sitting at breakfast in his tent, promised with conventional courtesy to read it as soon as he had time.

The little book is composed in correct but uninspired French, imitated from Montesquieu. Gibbon himself, looking back on it from the eminence of his maturity, found it 'marred by a kind of obscurity and abruptness', confused and badly put together. It is indeed difficult to make out exactly what thesis Gibbon was trying to prove. 'A number of remarks and examples, historical, critical, philosophical, are heaped on each other without method or connection,' said Gibbon disparagingly, and the description is accurate. But the book contains one or two pages which reveal the writer's intelligence and his gift for history. In an admirable passage he compares Tacitus with Livy and praises the former as the ideal of the historian–philosopher. In another, he considers the nature of historical evidence and the framework of historical cause and effect within which all the other sciences are contained.

Irksome duty in the militia ended, with the war, in 1763 and Gibbon, now twenty-six years of age, set out on a second visit to the continent of Europe. He passed through Paris whence he wrote home that he had enjoyed better company and conversation in a fortnight than eighteen months in London could supply. Early in 1764 he was again in Lausanne and was certainly taken aback when he encountered Suzanne Curchod during an entertainment at Voltaire's house. The unhappy business ended not too graciously. The poor girl, who was now an orphan and very poor, still hoped to marry him. She wrote him long letters, carefully and intelligently criticizing his *Essai sur l'étude de la littérature*. This was not perhaps the wisest way to win back a lover's heart but, even had she used more feminine wiles, she would not have succeeded. Gibbon was determined to escape her and, covering the shabbiness of his own conduct by an easy self-deception, he convinced himself that she was a shallow and calculating flirt. 'Fille dangereuse et artificielle,' he wrote censoriously in his diary. Suzanne implored Jean-Jacques Rousseau, then at Geneva, to see Gibbon and reason with him, but Rousseau replied that he liked nothing he had heard of Mr Gibbon and thought him unworthy of her love. Suzanne gave up hope and shortly after married the elderly banker Necker.

She had done very well for herself and soon she was inviting Gibbon to her house to prove to him that she no longer loved him and that she had made a better match. The procedure was natural; it was also, as Gibbon did not fail to note in his diary, rather vulgar. But time smoothed away all asperities. In later years these uneasy lovers enjoyed a pleasant middle-aged friendship, and the elderly distinguished historian was once, to his amusement, the object of a proposal of marriage from Suzanne's precocious little daughter, the future Madame de Staël.

Gibbon was by no means exclusively occupied with Suzanne during his second visit to Lausanne. He renewed his friendship with the Swiss scholar, Deyverdun, who had been tutor to several distinguished young Englishmen including Lord Chesterfield's heir, and he made the acquaintance of another travelling compatriot, John Holroyd, later Lord Sheffield; these two were to be his closest friends for many years. Meanwhile he went on with his studies and accumulated voluminous notes on the ancient monuments of Italy in preparation for his journey there in a few months' time.

He was by now fairly sure that he intended to write history but his mind still wavered between a number of topics. He had considered a history of the Third Crusade, or of the Renaissance wars of France and Italy; or a life of Sir Walter Raleigh; or of the

Marquis of Montrose; but by the summer of 1764 the principal subjects had reduced themselves to two: the Fall of the Roman Empire, or the Rise of the Swiss Republic.

About this time he visited the Court of Savoy, an occasion of which he has left a characteristically vivid description. He got on so well with the princesses of Savoy and 'grew so very free and easy that I drew out my snuff box, rapped it, took snuff twice (a crime never known before in the presence chamber) and continued my discourse in my usual attitude of my body bent forward and my forefinger stretched out'. Gibbon was a young man of twenty-seven, with only an obscure pamphlet to his name, but he already had the confidence and the tricks of speech and gesture of a much older and more established scholar. What made Gibbon different from other conceited young men was that he had something more than wide reading and a lively talent for conversation; he had genius, as almost everyone was able to see.

There was another difference. In spite of his assurance, in spite of the vanity which sometimes made him ridiculous, Gibbon had the inner humility of the scholar in the face of his material. He was more eager to learn than to teach.

In the autumn of 1764 he left Lausanne for Italy and by October had reached Rome, whence he wrote, in what for Gibbon is almost a bemused strain, to his step-mother:

> I have already found such a fund of entertainment for a mind some-what prepared for it by an acquaintance with the Romans, that I am really almost in a dream. Whatever ideas books may have given us of the greatness of that people, their accounts of the most flourishing state of Rome fall infinitely short of the picture of its ruins . . . I was this morning upon the top of Trajan's pillar. I shall not attempt a description of it. Only figure to yourself a column of a hundred and forty feet high of the purest white marble . . . wrought into bas reliefs with as much taste and delicacy as any chimney piece at Up Park.

The great conception already half formed in Gibbon's mind was taking shape, but he was able – and that is one of the attractive things about Gibbon – to remember that he was writing to a lady with no conception at all of what he was trying to describe; he brings it within the scope of her imagination, in the most natural way in the world, by comparing it to the carved chimney-pieces in a house she often visited.

Gibbon had thoroughly prepared himself for his visit to Rome by making careful notes of the topography of the classical city and the geography of Italy, and by mastering the science of medals which is of paramount importance in the study of Roman history.

The crucial hour was now at hand and he recorded it with due solemnity:

> It was at Rome, on the 15th of October, 1764, as I sat musing amidst the ruins of the Capitol, while the bare-footed friars were singing vespers in the Temple of Jupiter, that the idea of writing the decline and fall of the city first started to my mind.

Gibbon slightly dramatizes this great moment and it has been pointed out that his diaries show that the idea of writing something on the fall of Rome had been in his thoughts for some months before. But there is a considerable difference between his first foreshadowings of an idea and the moment at which a book takes shape and quickens within the author's mind. It is that moment which Gibbon, with his natural sense of the dramatic, has fixed and recorded.

But other interests still competed with the *Decline and Fall* and on his return to England in 1765 he turned once again from the vices of the Roman Empire to the virtues of the Swiss republic. He composed a long introductory section to a history of Switzerland, in French, and read it aloud to a literary society. By a rare stroke of good fortune, his listeners unanimously condemned it. 'The momentary sensation', writes Gibbon, 'was painful; but their condemnation was ratified by my cooler thoughts. I delivered my imperfect sheets to the flames and for ever after renounced a design in which some expense, much labour and more time had been so vainly consumed.' He had another reason for changing his mind. He did not know German and, although his friend Deyverdun was generously willing to help in this part of the research, he saw that to study the growth of the Swiss Confederation some personal knowledge of this 'barbarous gothic dialect' would be essential. About the same time, fortunately, he was persuaded to drop the curious vanity of writing in French.

So at last, about his thirtieth year, the stage was set for him to begin on his great book. He did not devote himself to it entirely but, in the intervals of his study, lived the easy social life of a cultivated gentleman, dining and conversing among the distinguished men of his time. He was for twelve years an almost entirely silent Member of Parliament and he held a minor government post as a Commissioner of Trade and Plantations, from which he derived a small additional income. This was welcome to him because his father, who had died in 1770, had not left him rich.

III

The first volume of the *Decline and Fall* appeared in 1776. It carried the story of the Roman Empire from the ordered tranquillity of the Antonine epoch through the intrigues, revolutions and disasters of the third century to the rehabilitation of the Empire under Diocletian and the establishment of Christianity as the official religion under Constantine: a hundred and fifty years of rapidly succeeding events and changing ideas. The opening paragraph of the great book immediately awakens interest, creates a remarkable and comprehensive picture of the age described, and reveals that air of learned and untroubled candour, and that sure and shapely style which was to be maintained throughout the whole gigantic undertaking:

In the second century of the Christian era, the Empire of Rome comprehended the fairest part of the earth, and the most civilized portion of mankind. The frontiers of that extensive monarchy were guarded by ancient renown and disciplined valour. The gentle but powerful influence of laws and manners had gradually cemented the union of the provinces. Their peaceful inhabitants enjoyed and abused the advantage of wealth and luxury. The image of a free constitution was preserved with decent reverence: the Roman Senate appeared to possess the sovereign authority, and devolved on the emperors all the executive powers of government. During a happy period (AD 98–180) of more than fourscore years, the public administration was conducted by the virtue and abilities of Nerva,

Trajan, Hadrian, and the two Antonines. It is the design of this, and of the two succeeding chapters, to describe the prosperous condition of their empire; and afterwards from the death of Marcus Antoninus, to deduce the most important circumstances of its decline and fall; a revolution which will ever be remembered, and is still felt by the nations of the earth.

Horace Walpole, prostrated by an attack of gout in the week of publication, sent round a note congratulating Gibbon on 'the style, manner, method, clearness, and intelligence' of his first chapter and added, 'Mr Walpole's impatience to proceed will give him such spirits that he flatters himself he shall owe part of his recovery to Mr Gibbon.' A few days later he was writing to a friend:

> Lo, there is just appeared a truly classic work . . . The style is as smooth as a Flemish picture, and the muscles are concealed and only for natural uses, not exaggerated like Michaelangelo's to show the painter's skill in anatomy. The book is Mr Gibbon's *Decline and Fall of the Roman Empire* . . . I know him a little, never suspected the extent of his talents for he is perfectly modest but I intend to know him a great deal more . . .

Walpole was wrong in imagining Gibbon to be modest, as he was later to discover. In every other respect his judgment has been fully confirmed by time.

The enthusiasm with which literary London received the book was not shared by the Anglican clergy. The first volume contained the famous Chapters XV and XVI devoted to the rise of Christianity and the treatment of Christians by the Roman Empire up to the time of Constantine the Great. Gibbon was not a militant anti-Christian; but he had acquired most of his philosophic ideas in the French-speaking part of Europe, and had come to accept the easy cynicism of contemporary French intellectuals as though it were universal. Their way of thought appealed naturally to his exact, unemotional mind. When he described his subject as 'the triumph of barbarism and Christianity', when in his autobiography he slyly drew attention to the same thing in concrete form with his striking picture of the ruins of the Capitol and the barefooted friars singing in the Temple of Jupiter, Gibbon was neither throwing out a challenge nor making propaganda against religion; he was stating what he felt to be the only accurate view of the matter. As the Church had gained in power, so Roman civilization had declined: that was the inescapable fact.

The violent attacks which were soon made on his treatment of Christianity astonished and distressed him. 'I was startled', he writes, 'at the first discharge of ecclesiastical ordnance,' and well he might be for not only were angry pamphlets written against him but he was twice made the object of special attack in a sermon. Most of the criticism was as trivial as it was passionate, but one cleric, the youthful Dr Davis of Balliol College, Oxford, accused him of misquoting his sources and plagiarizing other writers. These accusations Gibbon answered in a manner that exposed the presumption of his attacker. Gibbon was a thorough and careful scholar and he had a deep and comprehensive knowledge of the available material. It is one of the minor ironies of history that he quarried so much of his book from the source materials laboriously assembled in the previous century by the great antiquarian and scholar Tillemont, himself a devout believer, who, in his pertinacious gathering of the documents, had certainly never intended them to serve the purposes of a writer with so different an outlook on the Church.

Gibbon's treatment of Christianity is in truth more offensive in manner than matter. Sainte-Beuve, whose analysis of Gibbon in *Causeries du lundi* is particularly illuminating on this question, describes his writing as impregnated with a secret contempt for any feelings that he himself did not share. This contempt is all the more deadly for being cloaked in the guise of urbanity; as, for instance, in the famous paragraph in which he subtly discredits the initial miracles of Christianity.

But how shall we excuse the supine inattention of the Pagan and philosophic world to those evidences which were presented by the hand of Omnipotence, not to their reason but to their senses? During the age of Christ, of his Apostles, and of their first disciples, the doctrine which they preached was confirmed by innumerable prodigies. The lame walked, the blind saw, the sick were healed, the dead were raised, daemons were expelled, and the laws of nature

347

were frequently suspended for the benefit of the Church. But the sages of Greece and Rome turned aside from the awful spectacle, and, pursuing the ordinary occupations of life and study, appeared unconscious of any alterations in the moral or physical government of the world. Under the reign of Tiberius, the whole earth, or at least a celebrated province of the Roman Empire, was involved in a preternatural darkness of three hours. Even this miraculous event, which ought to have excited the wonder, the curiosity and the devotion of mankind, passed without notice in an age of science and history.

This attitude of ironical superiority towards believers still has the power to exasperate and provoke the devout. But Gibbon was not so much an anti-Christian as an agnostic. It was not religion that he disliked but exaggerated legends or meaningless rituals designed to captivate the multitude or make them amenable to the priest. Significant of this is his famous dictum: 'The various modes of worship which prevailed in the Roman world were all considered by the people equally true, by the philosopher, equally false, and by the magistrates, as equally useful.' This exact and careful statement, relating to a particular epoch, is frequently misquoted, and Gibbon is popularly credited with having said that 'All religions seem to the people equally true, to the philosopher equally false and to the magistrate equally useful'. Whether or not Gibbon would have agreed to so general an assertion, he did not make it. He was too good a historian to generalize widely or wildly and his comments were usually in strict relation to the epoch of which he was writing.

None the less his inability or unwillingness to sympathize with an attitude of mind not his own is a blemish in his great work. It closed his understanding to the irrational forces which can inspire men to wisdom as well as folly. As the fourth century, which principally occupies his first and second volumes, was one of the most deeply and vehemently religious epochs of European history, his blindness on this point can be as irritating to the student of history as it is offensive to the Christian.

The failing is part of Gibbon's character and outlook, that very character and outlook which give to the whole history its air of classic mastery. To wish Gibbon different is to wish the masterpiece unmade, and even while we regret the cynical pleasure which Gibbon evidently felt in demolishing the miracles and reducing the sufferings and the numbers of the Christian martyrs in the Diocletianic persecution we cannot but take pleasure in the sobriety of his argument and the poise of his style:

> After the church had triumphed over all her enemies, the interest as well as the vanity of the captives prompted them to magnify the merit of their respective suffering. A convenient distance of time or place gave an ample scope to the progress of fiction; and the frequent instances which might be alleged of holy martyrs whose wounds had been instantly healed, whose strength had been renewed, and whose lost members had been miraculously restored, were extremely convenient for the purpose of removing every difficulty, and of silencing every objection. The most extravagant legends, as they conduced to the honour of the church, were applauded by the credulous multitude, countenanced by the power of the clergy, and attested by the suspicious evidence of ecclesiastical history.

Gibbon goes on to investigate the statistics of the glorious army of the martyrs and to suggest that, after all, only a small number 'sacrificed their lives for the important purpose of introducing Christianity into the world'.

The arguments in this passage are unexceptionable. But the tone implies not only an unwillingness to accept false martyrs and invented sacrifices but a disparagement of the emotions which inspired genuine martyrs to make real sacrifices.

This weakness in the book is also its greatness. It is Gibbon's capacity for writing of passionate and desperate times with a cool mind that enables him to write in general with such untroubled objectivity. It was not his gift to understand the hearts of men, but it was his duty and pleasure to understand their minds. He took great pains not only to read essential contemporary sources, but to be fully acquainted with the literature and the other productions of the ages he studied. If he did not understand the heart of a Christian slave he understood the mind of a Roman senator. If he did not greatly value the human passions he set the highest possible value on the human intellect. His own mind had developed in the favourable atmosphere of a time which delighted to call itself the Age of Reason. As one of his most acute modern critics, Mr Christopher Dawson, has said, 'he stood on the summit of the Renaissance achievement, and looked back over the waste of history to ancient Rome, as from one mountain top to another. The tragedy for him is the dethronement of a noble and intelligent civilization by force and ignorance. It is the triumph of the illiterate and the irrational that he records and deplores.'

While he understood the minds and the calculations of the people about whom he wrote, he did not, like the romantic historians, throw himself into their hearts and try to share their feelings. The historic present – Carlyle's favourite tense – is practically unknown to Gibbonian grammar, a point of language which strikingly illustrates the change which the romantic movement wrought in the treatment of history.

But if Gibbon is not conventionally religious, neither is he indifferent to moral standards. He assumes that it is the right and duty of the historian to have a clearly defined moral attitude and he is exquisitely skilful in introducing judgment by way of implication. With what quiet contempt he deals for instance with the barbarian Ricimer, who, in the fifth century, elevated and destroyed puppet emperors at will. One of these, Majorian, was not only a man of strong and noble character but an old companion in arms. Majorian strove to revive the ancient discipline of the Romans; this did not suit Ricimer and he had to go. 'It was not perhaps without some regret', writes Gibbon, 'that Ricimer sacrificed his friend to the interest of his ambition.' In fifteen words he more perfectly exposes the baseness of Ricimer than he could have done in a paragraph of rhetoric. He carries on the story in the same tone:

> He resolved in a second choice to avoid the imprudent preference of superior virtue and merit. At his command the obsequious senate of Rome bestowed the Imperial title on Libius Severus, who ascended the throne of the West without emerging from the obscurity of a private condition. History has scarcely deigned to notice his birth, his elevation, his character or his death. Severus expired as soon as his life became inconvenient to his patron.

Gibbon's just and generous admiration is reserved for those who best display the classic virtues: justice, fortitude, perseverance, moderation. He greatly admires cleverness but never for itself alone. His morality, classical again in this, did not permit him to respect success unless it was allied with the virtues. He admires Diocletian, the hard-working self-made man who restored order to a distracted Empire, more than Constantine who succeeded to his work and whose sly calculations and mercenary attitude to religion he found contemptible. He admires the men who failed nobly, like Julian the Apostate, or Majorian who strove to save the tottering fabric, and he despises those who succeeded ignobly.

IV

Gibbon's reputation was established by the publication of his first volume which ends with the triumph of Constantine. He was now something more than an erudite man and a good *raconteur*. He was an established historian equal in fame to Hume and Robertson, the two great figures whom he had admired in his youth. His vanity grew with his fame, or at least became more apparent, but since his achievement justified it and he had with it so much genuine good humour, his friends were disposed to regard it as an engaging foible. When he told an anecdote or illustrated an argument he liked to be listened to, and the gesture he has himself so well described – the body bent forward and the forefinger extended – was designed to attract the attention that it commanded. But he was not a conversation-killer; he knew how to take part in a general discussion; and one of his younger friends, Lord Sheffield's daughter, was to leave it on record that he had a great gift for drawing out the opinions and ideas of the young people he met. This capacity argues a genuine interest in the ideas of others and a benevolence which counteracted the effects of his vanity.

But he did not like to be put out of countenance. Once at a dinner party he had told a good story and 'with his customary tap on the lid of his snuff box was looking round to receive our tribute of applause, when a deep-toned but clear voice was heard from the bottom of the table very calmly and civilly impugning the correctness of the narrative'. Gibbon defended his position, but the deep-toned clear voice, which was that of the youngest guest present, would not be silenced. Seeing defeat imminent, Gibbon hurried from the table and was found by his host looking for his hat and cloak. 'That young gentleman', said Gibbon, 'is, I have no doubt, extremely ingenious and agreeable but I must acknowledge that his style of conversation is not exactly what I am accustomed to, so you must positively excuse me.'

The young gentleman, twenty-one at the time, was William Pitt, who would be Chancellor of the Exchequer at twenty-three, and Prime Minister at twenty-four. In later life he came to value Gibbon's company as Gibbon did his. Gibbon's vanity made him like the sensitive plant; he wilted for a moment at an aggressive touch but he soon recovered and retained no malice.

In 1779, four years after the publication of his first volume, Gibbon brought out the second volume, devoted to the invasions of the barbarians and the Circus quarrels at Constantinople. The subject was not so much to the liking of the polite society of the eighteenth century as that of the earlier volume, and Horace Walpole, who had so deeply admired the first, was disposed to be critical, objecting that so much time and skill should be spent on so unrewarding a theme. Gibbon was highly offended. He seems to have taken with much more humour the reception he got from the King's brother, the Duke of Gloucester, to whom he presented a copy. 'Another damned thick book?' exclaimed the affable prince. 'Always scribble, scribble, scribble, eh, Mr Gibbon?'

With the fall of Lord North's government Gibbon lost the small post on which he had depended for part of his income. He decided therefore that he would be able to live more peacefully and more cheaply in Lausanne, and by the autumn of 1783 he transferred himself and his library to a delightful house which he planned to share with his old friend Deyverdun. The two scholars occupied separate parts of their pleasant mansion but met for dinner over which they discussed the problems and pleasures of their work, and entertained their friends from time to time. Lausanne society still abounded, as it had in Gibbon's youth, with intelligent and well-behaved ladies, and the two middle-aged scholars sometimes wistfully thought that a wife between them would not come amiss. 'Deyverdun and I have often agreed in jest and in earnest that a house like ours would be regulated, graced and enlivened by an agreeable female companion, but each of us seems desirous that his friend should sacrifice himself for the public good.' Each of them feared the obligations more than he valued the advantages of taking so momentous a step and they continued their bachelor existence. Gibbon knew how fortunate he was and wrote with a full sense of his blessings to Lady Sheffield describing his new library which commanded from 'three windows of plate glass, an unbounded prospect of many a league of vineyard, of fields, of wood, of lake and of mountains'. He concluded with satisfaction: 'An excellent house, a good table, a pleasant garden, here no contemptible ingredients in human happiness.'

Gibbon's common sense is one of his most attractive qualities. He did not want more than he had from life, and certainly he had everything that a scholar could want. But comfortable means and ample leisure do not content everyone and many writers have been as happily circumstanced as Gibbon without being so contentedly aware of the fact or so grateful for their blessings. Gibbon was firmly and rightly contemptuous of the delusion, shared by many eighteenth-century intellectuals, that the ignorant peasant, free from the anxieties and speculations of the educated and powerful, was much to be envied. Frederick the Great was reported to have said to d'Alembert, as they walked in the garden of Sans Souci, that a poor old woman whom they saw asleep on a sunny bank was happier than they. 'The King and the philosopher may speak for themselves,' wrote Gibbon, 'for my part I do not envy the old woman.'

It was Gibbon's pleasant habit to work in a small pavilion at the end of his garden and here he finished the last volume of his great work, a moment commemorated in a famous passage in his autobiography. 'It was on the day, or rather the night, of the 27th June 1787, between the hours of eleven and twelve that I wrote the last lines of the last page in a summer-house in my garden. After laying down my pen I took several turns in a *berceau* or covered walk of Acacias, which commands a prospect of the country, the lake, and the mountains. The air was temperate, the sky was serene, the silver orb of the moon was reflected from the waters, and all Nature was silent. I will not dissemble the first emotions of joy on the recovery of freedom, and perhaps the establishment of my fame. But my pride was soon humbled, and a sober melancholy was spread over my mind by the idea that I had taken my ever-lasting leave of an old and agreeable companion, and that whatsoever might be the future fate of my history, the life of the historian must be short and precarious.'

The quietude and peace of that scene is illuminating. Gibbon was a great writer, and his book meant everything to him, but he never seems to have had – indeed it is unthinkable that he should have had – that intense relationship for love, hate, and exasperation that many great writers have with their work. His attitude to it is well behaved and under control like his writing: 'an old agreeable companion'.

The *Decline and Fall* itself ends with a deliberately low-toned passage. Sainte-Beuve, with his usual perspicacity, has said that Gibbon finishes 'cette longue carrière comme une promenade', and at the moment of setting down his pen pauses to consider the view and to take his ease. The closing paragraph describes the gradual unearthing of imperial Rome from the rubble of the Middle Ages. There is just a suggestion, but only a suggestion, of the new dawn, after the six volumes which have discussed the long decay and the final collapse of anything resembling or carrying on the tradition of the Roman Empire:

> Prostrate obelisks were raised from the ground, and erected in the most conspicuous places; of the eleven aqueducts of the Caesars and consuls, three were restored; the artificial rivers were conducted over a long series of old, or of new, arches, to discharge into marble basins a flood of salubrious and refreshing waters; and the spectator, impatient to ascend the steps of St Peter's, is detained by a column of Egyptian granite, which rises between two lofty and perpetual fountains, to the height of one hundred and twenty feet. The map, the description, the monuments of ancient Rome, have been elucidated by the diligence of the antiquarian and the student; and the footsteps of heroes, the relics not of superstition, but of empire, are devoutly visited by a new race of pilgrims from the remote, and once savage, countries of the North.

That is the end of the book proper. Gibbon added a postscript, and after twenty years of work he could hardly have done less: he briefly summed up the story that he had tried to tell and concluded: 'It was among the ruins of the Capitol that I first conceived the idea of a work which has amused and exercised twenty years of my life, and which however inadequate to my own wishes I finally deliver to the curiosity and candour of the public.' To anyone acquainted with the sufferings and struggles of the writer, the exhilarations and frustrations and fallacious triumphs, or with the labours and problems of historical research, that phrase 'amused and exercised' must seem what perhaps it is – an understatement. Yet it may not be. The judicious use of exact but unexaggerated terms produces exact and unexaggerated reactions. Gibbon's style reflects and may also partly have shaped his character.

He came to England for the publication of his last three volumes, was given a splendid dinner by his publisher, attended the trial of Warren Hastings, and was made the object of a delicate compliment from Sheridan in his speech for the prosecution. 'Nothing equal in criminality is to be found,' said Sheridan, 'either in ancient or modern history, in the correct periods of Tacitus or the luminous pages of Gibbon . . .' Later he teased Gibbon by asserting that he had said not 'luminous', but 'voluminous'.

V

It was now 1788, a year before the fall of the Bastille. The political storms in which the century was to end were about to break and literary fashions were moving fast away from the detached manner of Gibbon towards the subjective and emotional manner of the romantics. In this year – 1788 – Schiller's play *Don Carlos* appeared as well as his passionate and vivid history of the Revolt of the Netherlands; Goethe's *Egmont* is of the same year. The turbulent reaction from the logic and order of French thought towards the exaltation of the passions and the ideal of a wild liberty was well on the way. Mirabeau, who had come to England shortly before the Revolution in search of radical inspiration in a country whose liberal institutions had been praised by Voltaire, looked about for English historians to translate into French. For Gibbon, the greatest of them all, he felt only disapproval. At a large dinner party he fixed an indignant stare on a fat little man who had been pointed out to him as the author of the *Decline and Fall*, and spent the meal rehearsing what he would say to him. 'You, an Englishman!' he would say. 'No, you cannot be. You, who admire an empire of more than two hundred millions of men not one of whom could call himself free. You who extol an effeminate philosophy which sets greater value on luxury and pleasures than on virtue; you who write in a style which is always elegant but never vigorous – you are not an Englishman but at most a slave of the Elector of Hanover.' His courage, perhaps fortunately, failed him, for the object of his angry glaring was guiltless of the *Decline and Fall*. Gibbon was in Lausanne at the time.

Mirabeau's view is unfair; like many other critics of Gibbon, he had not read the book. What Gibbon admired in the Roman Empire was not its expanse and power, still less its authority over the individual. What he admired was the spectacle of peaceful order which enabled the arts of civilization to be practised. He did not admire effeminate philosophies and luxuries, and he deplored the decay of democratic institutions while appreciating the craft with which successive Emperors had curtailed them. His admiration was reserved for the strong classical virtues, for reason and restraint.

If the reformers and revolutionaries, and the poor young *exaltés* of liberty who were soon to have such a rude awakening, found much to criticize in Gibbon's book its reception among the discriminating older generation surpassed even the author's by no means modest hopes. Adam Smith pronounced him 'at the very head of the whole literary tribe at present existing in Europe'. He was generally acclaimed as the greatest of English historians – a position from which he has not yet been dethroned.

On his return to Lausanne after his triumph in London he found things were no longer what they had been. His friend Deyverdun was dead. The romantic movement had launched upon the country a quantity of staring tourists, come 'to view the glaciers'. Gibbon was also perturbed by the 'furious spirit of democracy' which had been let loose by the French Revolution. His own political views are best summed up in the comment which he made at this time on the internal politics of Switzerland. Lausanne, long unwillingly subjected to the aristocratic government of Berne, was stirring uneasily. Gibbon had no patience with this nonsense: 'While the aristocracy of Berne protects the happiness, it is superfluous to inquire whether it be founded on the rights, of man,' he wrote.

Fascinated by the politics of the past, he was resentful of the politics of the present because they threatened his calm retreat. Lausanne was now full of refugees from the Revolution. 'These noble fugitives', he wrote, 'are entitled to our pity; they claim our esteem, but they cannot, in their present state of mind and fortune, much contribute to our amusement. Instead of looking down as calm and idle spectators on the theatre of Europe, our domestic harmony is somewhat embittered by the infusion of party spirit.' The comment is curiously insensitive, and Gibbon's public comments are indeed often out of key with the natural kindliness he showed in his personal life.

In the summer of 1793 his great friend Lord Sheffield was suddenly left a widower. His wife, reacting very differently from Gibbon, had fallen ill owing to long and strenuous hours of work on behalf of homeless French refugees in England. Gibbon, genuinely distressed at his friend's grief, hurried home to console him. He passed the summer between London and Lord Sheffield's country house and was able both to give comfort and to receive much pleasure from the company of Lord Sheffield's daughters and their young friends. He was only fifty-six and at the height of his intellectual power. A great edition of English medieval documents, of which he was to be the editor, was projected and he looked forward to the new work, declaring with confidence that he was good for ten or twelve more years of valuable work. But his friends had grown alarmed for the state of his health. His vanity prevented him from admitting that the hydrocele from which he was suffering had reached embarrassingly large proportions. At length, however, he agreed to an operation in the autumn of 1793. This was temporarily successful but the condition worsened again in January. Gibbon was now taking quinine every six hours and drinking five glasses of Madeira at dinner on doctor's orders. In the circumstances it is not surprising that the immediate cause of his death, on 17 January 1794, appears to have been cirrhosis of the liver.

English history lost a remarkable piece of editing when Gibbon died before he could begin work on the documents. But anything after the *Decline and Fall* would have been an anti-climax. His life's work is the one massive, incomparable book, and all the rest that he left behind him is interesting chiefly for the light it throws on the mind and the method behind the great history.

The *Decline and Fall* stands alone in English historical literature. Style and structure apart, its erudition still amazes; what other history has stood the test of seven generations of scholarship and criticism without being wholly superseded? Gibbon's views have been modified and added to; yet his book remains basically a standard work for the decline of Rome, at least, if not for the Byzantine empire.

Of the style and structure it is hard to speak briefly. His unique quality – unique, that is, among English narrative historians – is his exact control. Most English historians of any literary sensibility are given to passion; the quality is inherent in the calling. They become involved in the events they describe, are moved, excited, carried away. This makes for powerful writing and sometimes for a sharper insight into character, but it does not make for a steady, comprehensive vision, or for clear presentation.

The English as writers have a false conception of themselves. We do not think of ourselves as passionate, yet the great strength and almost all the faults of English writing arise from passion. We are among the most passionate and impulsive writers in the modern world. We commonly set more value on something called 'sincerity' – a word which often describes what happens when a writer loses control of his material – than on symmetry and order. We are the first to condemn a deliberate and perfected work of art as 'dead'. Sometimes this judgment may be right, but often it is no more than an angry prejudice arising from our own vehement and untidy minds. Consider for instance how few Englishmen are really capable of appreciating the flawless achievement of Racine. Shakespeare, the transcendent artist who broke all the rules, had left to his countrymen an unwritten charter to despise them.

Gibbon was not entirely without passion, for his love of learning and reverence for the intellect amounted to passion. But he kept it within bounds and when he wrote, his first thought was for the whole work of art. Each sentence performs its right function in relation to what goes before and after, each paragraph carries the narrative on at the necessary pace, or establishes a point in the exposition. Because of this attention to detail the massive volumes are always easy to read and never monotonous. The narrative passages are never clogged with too much imagination, and the expository paragraphs and chapters stand out with a fine static clarity. Gibbon's control of his material was so sure and his sense of form so strong that he seems to have been able, at least in his later volumes, to achieve his effects without rewriting. His plan was clear in advance and he would write his sentences in his head and commit them to paper only when he was satisfied of their completeness. In earlier times, when he still rewrote substantially, it seems to have been the form or order of each chapter rather than the shape of each sentence which gave him anxiety. Of his first volume he wrote to Lord Sheffield, 'The first chapter has been composed *de nouveau*, three times, the second twice' and he spoke of an intention to '*refondre*' or recast other important parts of the book.

Gibbon's style is highly cultivated and therefore artificial. It is also a dangerous style to copy and he has suffered badly from imitators who aped his mannerisms without understanding their purpose and without having the sensitive ear and varied vocabulary which made it possible for him to use them with effect. He had, for instance, a trick of pairing words; open the great volumes anywhere and you find phrases like this – '*The relaxation of discipline* and the *disuse of exercise* rendered the soldiers *less able* and *less willing* to support the fatigues of the service.'

This is not done merely to add a spurious weightiness to simple statements. It is done, almost always, with the express purpose of slowing down the narrative at those points on which Gibbon wants the reader's mind to dwell. He thus detains the reader's attention by the simple device of making him read more slowly. But he never exactly duplicates his phrases; the additions are artistically correct, because they add to or modify the meaning. In the hands of less skilful writers, who duplicated without art and without apparent reason, the trick which was widely copied became intolerable.

The chance by which the *Decline and Fall* came to be written looks almost providential; here was an English mind with the romantic bent of the English – evident in his early reading and tastes – carefully cultivated in the French tradition and saturated with French culture. He produced in consequence, in the most exact and expressive English, a history which is a model of lucid exposition and balanced form yet which never loses that undercurrent of feeling essential to great historical writing.

The *Decline and Fall of the Roman Empire* is an outstanding work of English scholarship and one of the great monuments of English eighteenth-century literature. This double achievement has had a profound influence on the whole tradition of English historical writing. The increasing complexity of techniques of historical research, and the ever more exacting standards of scholarly accuracy which began to prevail in the later nineteenth century, thanks to the massive and precise scholarship of the Germans, inevitably divorced history from literature. But in England this divorce never became complete and the reunion of history and literature in this country in our own time, may be traced in part to the influence of Gibbon. His method and manner and his splendid assurance may no longer be the models by which modern English historians work but he remains the presiding genius of our historical literature. The union of knowledge and style which he achieved is still the ideal of the English tradition.

1955

The Scientists and
the English Civil War

S ome time in the personal rule of King Charles I, as John
Aubrey records, the mathematician John Pell was invited to
dinner by John Williams, Bishop of Lincoln, 'for the freer
discourse of all sorts of literature and experiments'.[1] If Aubrey's
chronology is correct the occasion would have been after the
Bishop's disgrace, when he was no longer keeping open house in
his fine Huntingdonshire mansion of Buckden, where 'the choicest
and most able of both Universities came thick unto him'.[2] He
may even have been in the Tower at the time, where he continued
to entertain as generously as he could.

Pleased with the abilities of John Pell, the Bishop would have
offered him a benefice, but the mathematician, with remarkable
honesty, said that 'being no Divine and having made the Mathematics his main study' he did not think himself suitable for such
preferment. Williams, impressed by this answer but distressed at
the rejection of the only form of permanent help that it was in his
power to give, broke into a lament on the general lack of patronage
for the sciences: 'What a sad case it is that in this great and opulent
kingdom there is no public encouragement for the excelling in any
Profession but that of Law and Divinity. Were I in place, as once
I was, I would never give over praying and pressing His Majesty
till a noble Stock and Fund might be raised for so fundamental,
universally useful, and eminent a science as Mathematics.'[3]

Though Bishop Williams was never to be in a position where
he could influence the Crown to this excellent purpose, the first
decades of the seventeenth century did see the growing acceptance
by men of perception and learning of the importance of educating
the young both in mathematics and in the natural sciences. The
King had granted a charter to Sir Francis Kynaston in 1635 for a

modern school to be called Musaeum Minervae, where the scholars were to be instructed in physiology, anatomy, astronomy, optics, cosmography, arithmetic, algebra, and geometry, as well as music, fencing and dancing.[4] Though the older schools still neglected such subjects, the private study of them was increasing, certainly not before it was needed. The practical equipment with which some of the principal ministers of the Crown faced their increasingly complex duties was often lamentable; the Earl of Strafford, governor of Ireland and one of the King's ablest financial advisers, has left occasional scrawled figures among his papers which show him to have been ignorant of the technique of multiplication. A kinsman of his, William Gascoigne, who had become keenly interested in astronomy, in a correspondence with the famous mathematician Oughtred declared that 'he never had so much aid as to be taught addition at school', and that he 'left both Oxford and London before I knew what any proposition in geometry meant'.[5] Gascoigne's school was no doubt to blame, but he must himself have neglected the opportunities offered by Oxford and London, since Gresham College in London had been offering lectures in geometry since the end of Queen Elizabeth's reign, and Sir Henry Savile had founded the Savilian professorships in geometry and astronomy at Oxford in 1619. It is true that Sir Henry Savile's judgement may not always have been of the wisest, if the story later told by Seth Ward to John Aubrey has any foundation in fact. The geometry professorship at Oxford was open to mathematicians from any part of Christendom, and was accordingly applied for by Edmund Gunter who had been teaching at Gresham College; after watching him perform with his sector and quadrant 'resolving of triangles and doing many fine things, Sir Henry burst out "Do you call this reading of Geometry? This is showing of tricks, man," and so dismissed him with scorn and sent for Henry Briggs from Cambridge.'[6]

But comfortable places in colleges for mathematicians were very limited, and Bishop Williams was only too well justified in his lamentation, in the 1630s, that the branches of knowledge which led to reasonable security in the world were still almost exclusively Law and Divinity. Throughout the seventeenth century it remained usual for those interested in the sciences to pursue a subsidiary profession. The Church was the most usual, though for those principally interested in the natural sciences the medical profession offered a reasonable way of making a living. This accounts for the very high proportion of divines and physicians among the first fellows of the Royal Society.

Among mathematicians John Wallis was remarkable even in his own time for the variety of his gifts. Hearne, enumerating his talents, wrote: 'He was withal a good Divine, and was no mean critic in the Greek and Latin tongues. . . . He had good skill in the Civil Law . . . and 'tis frequently said that he would plead as well as most men, which can hardly be doubted if it be consider'd that he had an extraordinary knack of Sophisticated Evasion.'[7] But if a facility in so many branches was rather exceptional, a reasonable capacity in the exercise of a subsidiary profession was almost an essential for a seventeenth-century man of science. No doubt a talent for Sophisticated Evasion might also come in useful in the quest for patronage. Pell's honesty to Bishop Williams certainly lost him what might have been a safe and suitable livelihood, and twenty-five years later he did indeed take Holy Orders to maintain himself. On the perimeter of the respectable world of science would be found those who, having for one reason or another failed to qualify as divines or physicians got along – and indeed sometimes did very well – out of astrology, alchemy, or journalism.

Though at this stage in the history of scientific thought the era of specialization had not dawned, there was also strong financial pressure to add an accidental element of confusion by compelling thinkers to diffuse their energies. This would not be remedied until there were endowments available to enable men of science to pursue their researches unhampered by the necessity of earning a living.

Though there were vague motions towards a better organization of those concerned with the natural sciences and the new philosophy, nothing much happened in England beyond the friendly association of certain groups around country houses owned by generous patrons. England was a small country where communication and co-operation were not really difficult. As Archbishop Mathew has pointed out, in his study of England under Charles I, 'all serious students were comprised within a circle of correspondents and were to that extent well known'. Thus even William Oughtred, whose humble way of life as vicar of a small Surrey parish caused surprise to distinguished foreign visitors, was under the patronage of the Earl of Arundel, and must have known through him many of the Court virtuosi, certainly Sir Kenelm Digby and, at a later date, John Evelyn.[8] Gascoigne, who pursued his mathematical and astronomical studies in a distant Yorkshire manor house, was probably in touch with Sir Charles Cavendish, the patron of Hobbes, and was known by name to a surprisingly large circle despite his early death.

The King himself was more deeply interested in the arts than the sciences, though he shared the enlightened conviction of most of his fellow rulers in western Europe, that inquiry, so long as it did not interfere with religion or the State, was greatly to be encouraged. He placed the deer in his royal parks at the disposal of William Harvey for his researches into the mysteries of generation. He gave his royal patronage to Theodore de Mayerne who, if as a physician lacked any great originality of mind, had the perception to rescue from destruction and publish Thomas Moffet's *Theater of Insects*, one of the earliest significant works on entomology. And he encouraged such dilettanti in the sciences as Kenelm Digby and that inveterate inventor of hydraulic machines the Marquis of Worcester.[9]

The deceptive promise of King Charles's court as a centre of intellectual life was brought to an end by the outbreak of Civil War in the summer of 1642. It would be a delicate question to decide how far the war hampered and how far it stimulated scientific inquiry. In those spheres where war is usually stimulating – namely in the application of science to means of destruction – it was singularly barren. Though Prince Rupert, the King's nephew and cavalry commander, fancied himself both as chemist and mathematician, his hands were too full with day-to-day organization for him to give any time to the experiments which amused his later years. Thirty years on, he and others would be constantly drawing the attention of the Royal Society to the great benefits they might confer by improving the efficiency of fighting ships and cannon,[10] but while he commanded the King's troops his activities in this respect did not go beyond advice and a good deal of personal activity in mining operations – enough at any rate for a courtly poet to call him

At once the Mars and Vulcan of the war.[11]

During the war little or nothing was heard of the numerous inventions of the Marquis of Worcester, not even of the quick-firing devices for muskets and cannon of which his *Century of Inventions* was full.[12] Nor did anyone on either side, in England or in Scotland, resuscitate the burning mirrors and the primitive form of tank which the mathematician Napier of Merchistoun had evolved fifty years before 'for withstanding strangers and enemies of God's Truth and Religion'.[13]

Mathematicians were, however, in demand in other spheres, and in December 1642 John Wallis achieved fame by breaking a Royalist code in an intercepted letter. He remained for the rest of the war the head of Parliament's deciphering department, and used to boast long after the Restoration of King Charles II that he had decoded the King's correspondence taken at Naseby. In later years he would add that he had been careful to omit from his version things which he believed would seriously damage the King's cause. But this was another example of his talent for Sophisticated Evasion; nothing whatever in the King's captured letters escaped the eyes of his enemies.[14] At the end of the war his services to Parliament procured him the Savilian Professorship of Geometry at Oxford, in place of Peter Turner, a worse mathematician, but a better Royalist, who though well into his fifties had volunteered in the King's forces at the very outset of the war.

This volunteering led to some significant losses. William Gascoigne, abandoning his experimental studies in his Yorkshire manor, went with other loyal gentlemen to join the Royalist forces before Marston Moor and was among the four thousand dead who were left on that disastrous field. His experiments in the art of flying had achieved no more than two broken legs for the unfortunate boy whom he persuaded to try his method, but he had made interesting progress in perfecting the telescope and his fragmentary correspondence with Oughtred reveals a remarkable mind.[15]

There were other losses of a different kind, of which the most famous (or infamous) was the destruction of Harvey's papers. He had left London hurriedly when the Court fled, and his house was searched after he had gone by ignorant soldiers who took away the manuscript notes of his book *De Insectis*. Of this Harvey himself said that 'of all the losses he sustained no grief was so crucifying to him'.[16]

Once he had settled down in the King's headquarters at Oxford Harvey had leisure to pursue the studies that really interested him. It was here, during the war, that he inspected the heart of Lord Montgomery, a nineteen-year-old Irish peer who was active in the King's forces. Owing to an accident in childhood the young man's heart was exposed; he wore a silver plate to protect it. Harvey displayed the obliging young nobleman to the King 'that he might see and handle this strange and singular accident with his own senses, namely the heart and its ventricles in their own pulsation, in a young and sprightly gentleman, without offence to him'.[17] The King concluded the experiment with the melancholy observation to Montgomery: 'Sir, I wish I could perceive the thoughts of some of my nobilities' hearts as I have seen your heart.'[18]

Harvey found numerous friends and disciples in Oxford, and George Bathurst of Trinity College put his rooms at his disposal or rather at the disposal of the sitting hen whose eggs they opened daily in order to observe the progress of the embryo. From the arts of war he held himself aloof. His young friend, Charles Scarburgh, who had been excluded from Cambridge as a Royalist, and whose interests were somewhat divided between medicine and mathematics, became far too enthusiastic an artillery officer for Harvey's liking, and he urged him to 'leave off his gunning' and come back to his proper profession.[19] There was indeed as much need of physicians as of gunners in the war. Harvey was, himself, dragged out of his Oxford preoccupations to attend the King's nephew, Prince Maurice, stricken with a fever during the fighting in the West Country.[20] It was during the Civil War, too, that Richard Wiseman, looking after the wounded at the siege of Taunton, made certain observations on the insensibility of brain tissue which he was to publish many years later.[21]

It needed concentration of purpose and that remarkable serenity of spirit which Harvey enjoyed to resist the interruptions to which all study of whatever kind was subject in Oxford during the war years. In the University city all able-bodied civilians from sixteen to sixty, regardless of their social standing, were required to do one day's work a week on the fortifications (or pay someone else to do it, which was no doubt the usual solution found by men of learning).[22] The trenching and ditching threatened to undermine the Physic Garden founded only twenty years before.

The two Savilian Professors were each infected in different ways with war fever. Peter Turner, Professor of Geometry, had leapt to arms and been almost immediately captured. John Greaves, Professor of Anatomy, took over the running of Merton College, the Warden being in London with the Parliamentary party, to the great annoyance of the sub-warden. He did what he pleased 'of his own strength', and at the end of the war was in trouble with the victorious Parliamentarians for conveying away the money and possessions of the college goods for the advantage of the Court. He had also lent out goods to courtiers, presumably household stuff which was very badly needed in the overcrowded town. Worst of all, when the Queen lodged for the best part of a year in Merton College, Greaves had been far too familiar with her Roman Catholic suite. He had not only given the Queen's Confessor, Father Philip, leave to use the Library, but he had feasted her chaplains, 'sent divers presents to them, and among the rest an Holy thorn, an excellent instrument of idolatry and superstition at least: and the said Mr Greaves was observed to be more familiar with these Confessors than any true Protestants use to be'. Finally he had drawn up a petition against the absent Warden, 'inveigled some unwary young men to subscribe it' and so got him voted out of office and replaced by William Harvey.[23]

The Parliamentary Visitors at the end of the war, in the course of purging the University, purged Greaves out of his professorship. He managed, however, to exert some influence in the appointment of his successor, Seth Ward, whose politics were very moderate, and whose attainments and promise were infinitely more notable than those of Greaves. Though it is demonstrably unfair to align progress in the teaching of science during the seventeenth century entirely with the Parliamentary party, there is no doubt that Oxford, which gained Ward, Wilkins, and Wallis under the Puritan dispensation did very well out of it.

Cambridge, behind the Parliamentary lines in East Anglia, had been purged much earlier in the war. A flight of refugees came across to Oxford, where in spite of serious overcrowding they were, on the whole, generously received. They were, for the most part, scholars in law and divinity, though Charles Scarburgh, ejected from Caius College, was one of them. With the support of the energetic Greaves he was taken in at Merton. Seth Ward, his friend, who had joined him in the peaceful days before the war in propagating Oughtred's *Clavis Mathematica* at the University, was ejected at the same time from Sidney Sussex. If he had been resident at Oxford during the war years after his ejection he would probably have been too suspect to be acceptable for the Oxford professorship he got in 1648, so that it was fortunate that instead he sought tranquillity with his old friend and master, Oughtred, at Albury. Oughtred, who received him with the utmost generosity, was himself far from safe. His patron Arundel had very wisely left the country and was far away in Padua. It may therefore have been through Arundel's suggestion that the Grand Duke of Tuscany, Ferdinand II, at this point offered Oughtred a refuge in his dominions and a salary of £500 a year. But Oughtred was over seventy and in any case could not contemplate either changing or concealing his religion.[24] He stayed therefore in Surrey, though Parliament, in control of the county, was purging so-called 'scandalous ministers' and Oughtred, as a known Royalist and one who had given more attention to mathematics than to his parish, was an obvious target. Powerful protection was, however, forthcoming to prevent his ejection from his vicarage: or possibly there were Parliamentarians with the discretion to realize that the ejection of a venerable mathematician of international fame would do their cause no good.

Those who had the means to do so, dilettantes or serious thinkers, had mostly left the country. Hobbes had slipped away to Paris. The young John Evelyn, after a momentary thought of joining the King, very sensibly went abroad. John Pell, who had missed his preferment in the 1630s, was fortunate at this time in being called to the professorship of mathematics at Amsterdam, though after the end of the war he was tempted back by Cromwell with a salary of £200 a year. It was curious that having got him home again, the protectoral government proceeded to use him for diplomatic missions. Whether this diffusion of his talent and interruption of his work affected his powers of concentration, or whether he was cursed with a negative and delaying temperament (his own worst enemy), he came to be, in the latter part of the century, a tragic figure of non-fulfilment. 'To incite him to publish anything,' wrote John Collins, 'seems to be as vain an endeavour as to think of grasping the Italian Alps in order to their removal.'[25]

For peace, tranquillity, and the absence of political strain Europe was not far enough away. There may have been some talk, when the younger John Winthrop was in England on the eve of the war in 1641, of a group of experimental philosophers removing to America. But the story is not recorded until about a hundred years later, and the scientists whose names are cited, Robert Boyle and John Wilkins, are not very probable candidates, given the date of Winthrop's visit, when Boyle was only fourteen and abroad in any case, and Wilkins was satisfactorily placed as chaplain to the Elector Palatine.[26] Given Winthrop's interests, and his subsequent relationship with the Royal Society, there is at least nothing improbable in the idea, though the details are evidently wrong.

Robert Boyle and his next brother had been travelling to complete their education, and were caught by the outbreak of the war at Marseilles, whence they retreated judiciously to the theocratic republic of Geneva, where they stayed for two years unable to get any money and living precariously on credit. Though this must have been embarrassing they were well out of the war in Ireland, where their four elder brothers were vigorously and bloodily employed. By the time Robert Boyle got back to England in 1644 the King's cause was visibly declining, but the war looked likely to drag on indefinitely; in Ireland, where some of his patrimony lay, it did in fact continue for another six years.

In London in 1645, against a background of insecurity, political upheaval and the steady penalization of the defeated, began the meetings from which the Royal Society was ultimately to grow. It cannot be truthfully said that these meetings were in any direct way an outcome of the Civil War which provided their unhappy background. All through the 1630s, in a less deliberate and self-conscious fashion, such groups had existed, and the idea of a society of this kind was well known and had distinguished examples in Europe. Yet the conditions of the time gave a negative inspiration; the meetings of the Philosophical Society as its members called it were a silent protest against the irrationality of the times. 'Good God that reasonable creatures, that call themselves Christians, too, should delight in such an unnatural thing as war!' wrote the nineteen-year-old Boyle.[27]

He was asked to join their meetings in spite of his extreme youth about a year after they had first begun. The famous account of the first meetings, given some years later by John Wallis, is too well known to quote but it fixes the earliest date as 1645, the year when the King's defeat became inevitable, and when London had been virtually under martial law and suffering from grave difficulties over food and fuel for nearly three years. Milton, in *Areopagitica*, has left an unforgettable account of London during the heroic months of the war:

> Behold now this vast City: a city of refuge, the mansion house of liberty, encompassed and surrounded with His protection; the shop of war hath not there more anvils and hammers waking, to fashion out plates and instruments of armed Justice in defence of beleaguered Truth, than there be pens and hands there, sitting by their studious lamps, musing, searching, revolving new motions. . . .

It is a stirring vision, but anyone who has lived for long under war conditions knows that, though moments of elation occur, they are flanked by long stretches of drabness and doubt. By 1645 it was becoming apparent that though the war might end, the disturbances and disorders would not, and that a return to stability – especially to moral stability – was far off, and already seemed to many of the older generation an impossibility.

It was then against a background of weariness and gloom that Theodore Haak, a German exile who had been living in England working as a translator and general go-between in intellectual circles for the last twenty years, suggested the formation of a club for weekly meetings. Haak had been long associated with Samuel Hartlib, that indefatigable propagator of useful knowledge, and both of them were in touch with foreign scholars and foreign universities. It was Haak who had been instrumental in getting John Pell his professorship at Amsterdam, and he and Hartlib had, in the days before the Civil War, discussed with English virtuosi a plan for an international college. The meetings he now suggested must have seemed at the time a very much lesser substitute.

There was faint, but very faint, hint of grander patronage in the background. John Wilkins was chaplain to the Elector Palatine, then resident in London, and well known to Haak, Hartlib, and the intelligentsia of the capital. Eldest nephew of the King, and dispossessed from his own lands since the beginning of the Thirty Years War, he had come to London, as he claimed, with the intention of reconciling the King and his subjects, but in fact with the tacit hope that the Presbyterian party in the country might regard him as a more suitable King than his uncle.[28] The Elector's patronage was not very lavish because he had not the means, but he was genuinely interested and had given a good deal of help and encouragement to Wilkins, who dedicated to him in 1648 his *Mathematical Magic, or the Wonders that may be performed by Mechanical Geometry*.

At the meetings of the club 'We barred all discourse of divinity, of state affairs, and of news, other than what concerned our business of philosophy', Wallis recorded some years later.[29] The prohibition was essential. Although the political opinions of the earliest members were most of them moderate, inclining towards the current brand of English Calvinism (few of them after the Restoration were to find any great difficulty in rejoining the Episcopal Church in which Wilkins and Ward later became bishops), the situation in London was, during these first years, so tense and so troubled that only a strict adherence to the 'no politics' rule would eliminate all possible friction.

Thomas Sprat, twenty years later, summed up the situation in his *History of the Royal Society*: 'Their first purpose was no more than only the satisfaction of breathing a freer air, and of conversing in quiet with one another, without being engaged in the passions and madness of that dismal age. . . . For such a candid and impassionate company as that was, and for such a gloomy season, what would have been a fitter subject than Natural Philosophy?'[30]

The young Boyle, returning to England after the regulated calm of Calvinist Geneva, was shocked and distressed by the violence and changeability that he found – 'they esteem an opinion as a diurnal, after a day or two scarce worth the keeping'.[31] He built his hopes on his new friends as on a rock. 'The corner-stones of the *Invisible* or (as they term themselves) the *Philosophical* College do now and then honour me with their company,' he wrote, 'men of so capacious and searching spirits that school philosophy is but the lowest region of their knowledge . . . persons that endeavour to put narrow-mindedness out of countenance.'[32]

The story of the evolution of the Royal Society has been told so often that it has become hackneyed. It was, of course, in one sense a perfectly natural development and a mere imitation of the sort of learned bodies that had already come into being abroad and were to continue to do so throughout the century. But the Accademia del Lincei, Accademia del Cimento, the Académie des Sciences and others owed their being to powerful official or individual patronage and existed in countries which, if not precisely at peace, were at least held in a more or less static framework of religious and political convention. The Royal Society in its embryo stage, on the other hand, was the outcome of individual co-operation among men of science in a time of almost complete political and religious disintegration.

To 'endeavour to put narrow-mindedness out of countenance' in such an epoch, though it was not unique, was none the less heroic. The insistence of the members of the Invisible College on the secular character of the knowledge they sought, implicit in the refusal to discuss divinity, was really significant. For it did not emanate from men who had turned their backs on religion but, rather, from religious men who were ready to separate belief and doctrine from inquiry. Thus 'Mr Hobbes the Atheist' remained an unusual and slightly shocking figure among seventeenth-century scientists, and those who met in the Invisible College in the late 1640s were men of rather more than merely conventional religious faith. The devout Boyle was to give a great deal of his life and thought to the propagation of the Gospel among the heathen and none of them was indifferent to the ultimate shape that religion would take in their much-tried country. It was thus by implication an expression of a profound faith in the power and usefulness of knowledge that led these men to dissociate themselves for the prosecution of their work from the political and religious disputes in which they were all to some extent 'engaged'. Proud of the achievement, for he was always pleased with the triumphs of learning, John Aubrey was later to write: 'Experimental Philosophy first budded here and was first cultivated by these virtuosi in that dark time.'[33] But he did not altogether realize all the implications of that very remarkable achievement. It was neither an escape nor a revolt from current religious beliefs or political doctrines; but it was an emphatic statement that the pursuit of useful knowledge had a right to separate existence.

Meanwhile the oppressed, defeated and exiled, mostly of an older generation, found some solace in the return to their old interests. Hobbes's patron Charles Cavendish, back in England and much impoverished, went on with his mathematical speculations, but to what effect will never be known, since his executor's wife sold all his notes for waste paper.[34] Kenelm Digby, in exile in Paris, returned to his chemical experiments, but struck the critical young John Evelyn as nothing but an 'arrant mountebank' trying to palm off on him a quack cure for indigestion.[35] In England, in prison in the Tower or released on bail, the Marquis of Worcester collected his *Century of Inventions* and looked sourly towards the experimental station he had made at Vauxhall, which had been taken over, without much success, by the Cromwellian government.

Prince Rupert, in the intervals of commanding a fleet of English privateers and earning his living as a soldier of fortune with the French, the Savoyards, and the Austrians, associated himself for a time with the work of his gifted sister Elizabeth, the disciple and correspondent of Descartes, but later, reverting to the technical problems which always interested him more, worked out in association with Wallerand Vaillant the method of engraving to which Evelyn was to give the name mezzotint.[36]

It was in exile at Maastricht that Sir Robert Moray, after spending half his life as a professional soldier, became an enthusiastic amateur of the natural sciences, gave himself up for long months to the study of chemistry, and acquired the knowledge which was to make him a moving spirit in the ultimate foundation of the Royal Society. There was, moreover, a younger generation of nobles and courtiers coming on, better equipped to appreciate and understand the new advancement of learning. Charles II, and the Duke of Buckingham less attentively, studied mathematics with Hobbes. As a prisoner of Parliament in England the young Duke of York had had instruction in mathematics from Oughtred's pupil Jonas Moore.

Though the outburst of gaiety which followed the Restoration showed that the repressions of the 1650s had not suited all temperaments, there were certainly some among the younger generation who had profited by them. 'Persons of Quality, having no Court to go to, applied themselves to their studies,' wrote an observant French visitor in 1662, 'some turning their heads to Chymistry, others to Mechanism, or Natural Philosophy; the King himself has been so far from being neglectful of these things that he has attained to so much knowledge as made me astonished, when I had audience of His Majesty . . . the English Nobility are all of them learned and Polite.'[37]

The writer, Monsieur de Sorbière, was no doubt somewhat carried away by his reception, for he was squired about everywhere by Sir Robert Moray and introduced principally to his virtuoso friends, in or out of the nobility. But it was certainly true that the generation who had lived through the war and its aftermath could look forward, if not to the generous provision that Bishop Williams had once spoken of, at least to an epoch of expansion and encouragement.

1961

NOTES

[1] *Aubrey's Brief Lives*, ed. Oliver Lawson Dick, London, 1949, p. 230.

[2] John Hacket, *Scrinia Reservata*, London, 1692, Part II, p. 32.

[3] Aubrey, loc. cit.

[4] Rymer, *Foedera*, XIX, pp. 638–41; see also Weld, *History of the Royal Society*, London, 1878, I, pp. 19–23.

[5] Rigaud, *Correspondence of Scientific Men*, Oxford, 1841, I, p. 84.

[6] Aubrey, p. 268.

[7] Hearne, *Remarks and Collections*, ed. Dobell, Oxford, 1885, *seq*, I, p. 198.

[8] David Mathew, *The Age of Charles I*, London, 1951, p. 243; Aubrey, p. 223.

[9] At this date Worcester was known as Lord Herbert of Raglan, his father being still alive; in the Civil War he became Earl of Glamorgan, and on his father's death Marquis of Worcester. In the interests of simplicity rather than precision I have called him Worcester throughout.

[10] A. R. Hall, *Ballistics in the Seventeenth Century*, Cambridge, 1952.

[11] Anon, *Elegy on Prince Rupert*, London, 1682.

[12] Dircks, *Life of the Marquis of Worcester*, London, 1865, pp. 462ff.

[13] Napier never printed these inventions, thinking them too dangerous, but sent the MS. to Anthony Bacon, brother of Francis.

[14] Hearne, VIII, p. 394.

[15] Aubrey, p. 210; Rigaud, I, pp. 83, 84, 87.

[16] Aubrey, p. 128.

[17] Harvey, *Works*, ed. Sydenham Society, pp. 382–3.

[18] The anecdote occurs in a footnote under 'Mount Alexander, Earl of,' in G.E.C.'s *Complete Peerage*. Montgomery married, raised a family, and was created Earl of Mount Alexander for his services in the Civil War.

[19] Aubrey, p. 129; Aubrey says merely that Scarburgh 'marched up and down with the Army', but Harvey's reference to 'gunning' and Scarburgh's mathematical studies have led me to assume that he was in the artillery.

[20] Warburton, *Prince Rupert and the Cavaliers*, London, 1849, II, p. 307.

[21] Longmore, *Richard Wiseman*, London, 1891.

[22] Steele, *Tudor and Stuart Proclamations*, I, No. 2433.

[23] *Register of the Visitations of the University of Oxford from 1647 to 1658*, ed. Montagu Burrows, *Camden Society*, New Series, 29, London, 1881, pp. 252–3, 283.

[24] Aubrey, p. 224.

[25] Rigaud, I, pp. 196–7.

[26] Sir Henry Lyons, *The Royal Society*, Cambridge, 1944, p. 7.

[27] Boyle, *Works*, I, pp. xxvii.

[28] For the curious behaviour of Charles Louis, Elector Palatine, during the Civil War, see the present writer's *The King's War*, pp. 589–90.

[29] Weld, I, p. 36.

[30] Sprat, *History of the Royal Society*.

[31] Boyle, *Works*, I, p. xxiv.

[32] ibid.

[33] Aubrey, p. 238.

[34] Aubrey, p. 58.

[35] Evelyn's Diary, 17 November 1650.

[36] See a recent article (1960) by Orovida Pissarro in the *Publications of the Walpole Society*.

[37] Sorbière, *A Voyage to England*, 1662, pp. 32–3.

William Penn

I shall not easily forget the impact of my first encounter with William Penn. It happened in the pages of Besse's *Sufferings of the Quakers* which I was turning over in search of material on Nonconformity in the early days of Charles II. Taken unadulterated, Besse is gloomy reading, in spite of the lucid faith which shines from every page. Browbeaten, bullied, insulted, the Quakers struggled on, with the law closing in remorselessly against them. More than four thousand were in prison by 1662. The creed of non-violence always exasperates the violent; local persecution pursued them, justices of the peace delighted to make them the butts of coarse merriment, the Lord Mayor of London particularly disliked them. Patient, obstinate, equable and full of apt quotations from the Scriptures, the Quakers were not put out of countenance. They were simply shouted down.

Shouted down, evicted, expelled, carted off to prison . . . the Quakers' story seemed symbolic of the eternal helplessness of the innocent and the good in the struggle not with evil (for there the fight is open and equal) but with stupidity and ill-nature in high places. What could they do, these saintly shoemakers and country folk? What could they ever do?

At this moment in my reading and my thoughts appeared the marginal entry *Comitment of W. Penn*, and the youthful son of a choleric admiral (who had recently thrown him out of his house) strode into the picture and turned the tables on authority.

The reason? He spoke the same language. Trained in the law, he challenged them with retorts not from the Gospels but from their own law books until the maddened Recorder of London wished aloud for the powers of the Spanish Inquisition to quell him. To prevent disorder in the court he had him shut up out of sight in the baledock whose wooden walls were higher than the prisoner's head. Penn could still hear what was going on and, detecting a further irregularity, hoisted himself into view with gymnastic skill and loudly cited Coke's Second Institute. The jury acquitted him. The Recorder bade them think again. They still acquitted him. The Recorder fined them forty marks each. Penn's voice was instantly upraised. 'Take him away,' shrieked the Recorder. 'I can never urge the fundamental laws of England,' said Penn, 'but you cry: "Take him away".'

In the outcome the jurors brought and won an action against the Recorder; Lord Chief Justice Vaughan uttered his celebrated vindication of the freedom of juries and an important point was scored in constitutional law.

Triumph. But was it quite the triumph the Quakers wanted? Penn had vindicated the fundamental laws, not of God, but of England. The issue has subtly changed from faith to politics.

This is by no means to belittle William Penn; great courage and great faith are needed wilfully to compromise a hopeful career, to embrace a persecuted sect, to endure long imprisonment with equanimity. Yet the dazzling Inner Light of a George Fox or a James Naylor seems reduced in William Penn to the pleasant glow of a domestic lamp. We are sometimes called on to-day to admire Penn for his noble failures, his visions of universal peace and brotherly love; this too lofty view clashes inevitably with the Penn of history, the 'talking, vain man' whom Bishop Burnet knew, with the 'tedious, luscious way' he imagined to be persuasive. Impossible not to feel, watching this other Penn, that the bold perceptions of the young Quaker had later become embedded in layers of self-satisfied benevolence. Self-satisfaction went before disaster. His dabbling in politics was unsuccessful and some of the mud thrown at him for playing the courtier to James II stuck; estrangement from Friends followed, strife in Pennsylvania, debts, accusations, distrust. The overburdened mind found release in a return to childhood until a benign old gentleman vacantly ambling after butterflies was all that remained of William Penn.

His reputation had already declined when he wrote that little work *The Fruits of Solitude*, the 'sweet, dignified and wholesome book' in which R. L. Stevenson found 'so much honest, kind wisdom'. That it has certainly. In one incomparable phrase only does this manual of courageous common sense light up suddenly with the flame of an eternal truth – 'They that love beyond the World cannot be separated by it'. But for the rest, the honest, kind wisdom remains earthbound.

More than any other single influence Penn seems to have given to the Friends their reputation and their bent for practical Christianity, their orientation, as it were, away from mysticism to prison reform. (Penn's own views on prisons were astonishingly in advance of his time.) These are great things, but they are not the greatest, and the abiding strength of the Friends derives from a source nobler than utilitarian goodness.

Yet the first step towards the civilized State – the State whose object is the Good Life – must be the concrete admission of the dignity of the human soul. Without this the spiritual capacities of man are for ever frustrated. Penn abhorred, in his own words, 'Obedience upon Authority, without Conviction'. The human mind must be free to choose.

When it came to conflict with authority, his feet were as firmly on the ground as those of any lawyer in England. He saw to it that Magna Carta was printed in Philadelphia, thus bringing (along with Quaker doctrine) the fundamental laws of England to the New World. So, too, in England itself, he had defended God's word through the words of Sir Edward Coke.

We cannot, I think, put him among the greatest, not with those who, like Faithful, go 'with Sound of Trumpet, the nearest way to the Celestial Gate'. But without him and his kind, never a Faithful of this world but will be burnt at the stake in Vanity Fair.

1944

Aspects of Politics

I

'Unlimited power is apt to corrupt the mind of those who possess it,' said the elder Pitt. He was not, presumably, the first person to notice this phenomenon, and he was certainly not the last. Lord Acton's more epigrammatic version has become a cliché of our times. 'Power tends to corrupt, and absolute power corrupts absolutely. Great men are almost always bad men.'

Pitt's statement pleases me better if only because it does not so readily lend itself to quotation in and out of season. Lord Acton was too wise and too widely informed a man to have built as much on the quotation himself as has been built upon it since. He did not – if I remember rightly – suggest that power was the only corrupting influence, a suggestion which on the strength of his dictum we now hear inferred or asserted in the strangest quarters.

Yet surely the most cursory glance at the world about us shows that powerlessness is at least as demoralizing as power. More men are undermined by frustration than by success. 'Since we cannot attain to greatness,' wrote Hazlitt, 'let us have our revenge by railing at it . . .' We are more subtle today. How comforting is the smug reflection that since power corrupts, we, who have none, are not corrupted. But that is not what Lord Acton said.

The rise and fall in the popularity of certain quotations is an index to some of the currents in the thought of our time. Disillusion with, and suspicion of, power are not in themselves unhealthy things. Rather the reverse. But human associations of thoughts are never simple, and the overstated suspicion of power joins in our own time with another influential current – the suspicion of motive which has come to us with the diffusion of certain psychological truisms.

379

On the one hand we accept the dictum that power corrupts and is therefore bad (and add joyfully 'All great men are bad', for we shall never be great ourselves and this gives a kind of merit to our failure). On the other hand we accept a general, and in itself sound, theory that all motives are corrupt, springing from subconscious causes over which man's control is limited by his ignorance. But the human being is built with a curious inability to apply a general truth to his own case. Self-deceived and corrupted motives invalidate the actions of other people, or in politics, of the other party. They have nothing to do with our own.

These are overstatements, debating points if you will. Yet the presence of these two currents in the general thought of our day is undeniable and their confluence has produced a third and more important tendency. Suspicion of power and suspicion of motive, valuable if held in control, paralyse all human action if they themselves take control. They breed disillusion with that active and essential part of man's life which we call politics. And the politics of our time certainly give ground for this disillusion – though not more than the politics of many other times in the unquiet history of our race.

Wars and aftermaths of wars are not edifying; elections are not edifying; political trials are not edifying. Man as a political animal appears mean, vindictive, ambitious, self-interested and distressingly ingenious at shifting the blame. All over the world we see him parading his deplorable weaknesses, we forget how heroic a figure he cut – was it yesterday?

All this provides excellent excuses for disillusion. It becomes almost a virtue to dismiss politics with a shrug of the shoulder as a dirty business, a vulgar and self-interested scramble for power. Now is the time for all good men emphatically not to come to the help of the country. Now is the time for seclusion and the monastery.

At certain moments in the history of our civilization there has been a paramount need for this retirement of the good. Thus only did Saint Benedict and his monks among the crags of Italy preserve the moral code of Christendom from the collapse of the Roman Empire. But our state has not yet reached that extremity – not quite. Nor are the majority, if indeed any, of our disillusioned of the stature of Saint Benedict. It is absurd to confuse a gentlemanly distaste for the vulgarity of the political scene with a call to abandon the world.

The anti-politicals of our time have with few exceptions no intention of retiring to monasteries – or even to California. The lofty eminence from which they condemn the political world exists largely in their imagination, for they continue to live in and on that society which the politicians are doing their best to sustain or destroy. And in so far as they and we live in that world I do not see by what right we can dissociate ourselves from its political life. Corrupt motives are not the monopoly of politicians or businessmen – though reading the literature of disillusion would lead one to think so. Disillusion itself breeds corruption of motive, and men may withdraw themselves from the duties and responsibilities of their time for reasons no less corrupt than those for which other men shoulder them. The danger of the anti-political teaching of our day is that it encourages, in our tired and irreligious society, not saintliness but *fainéantise*. We forget in the smug condemnation of the political world that its standards depend, and always will depend, on the moral quality of the men who go into it. It is true that saints are rarely found in politics. But it does not follow that only scoundrels are.

'Power to do good', wrote Francis Bacon, 'is the true and lawful end of aspiring, for good thoughts, though God accept them, yet towards men are little better than good dreams except they be put in act; and that cannot be without power and place, as the vantage and commanding ground.' As a statement of the practical view of the political problem, that cannot be bettered, and to insist on Bacon's own too patent imperfections both as man and statesman, would be beside the point.

In an imperfect world we cannot afford to insist on absolute standards. Only very rarely have successful men positively disliked being successful and they have not always been better men on that account. Personally I should feel comparatively little confidence in a Prime Minister who did not evidently rather enjoy the job. No one pretends that enjoying power is good in itself, but it is a necessary concomitant of the temperament which seeks expression through action, that is through power. It is a weakness rather than a vice, and by no means the monopoly of the politicians.

Before the psychological fashions of our time had made everyone suspicious of motives, before all good men were shown up as bad men cleverly disguised, our grandfathers very properly believed that the desire to do good might be an important element in deciding a man on a political career. We have grown so clever today that we know this desire to do good is only a polite word for power lust, mere humbug.

Humbug which could abolish the slave trade, free America, reform the prisons, release the children from the mines and factories, and fight with dogged and often unrewarded persistence the hundred battles which are still going on to-day was not without value to the human race. Better perhaps a little humbug than a vast cynicism.

II

About fourteen years ago in a train in Russia I was informed by a young student that history did not begin until the French Revolution. The view was evidently a simplified one put forward for my benefit and has been as far as Russian doctrine is concerned very much modified of later years. Dmitri Donskoi and Ivan the Terrible – not to mention Peter the Great and several other heroes of recent Russian monster historical novels – were all a long way pre-Revolution. But let that pass; the grain of truth behind my Russian student's statement is one that we must reckon with in our time.

What happened at the Revolution was that the concept of 'the people' became for the first time vital. Earlier ages, it is true, can show a fair number of statesmen and thinkers for whom 'the people' did in fact mean something fully realized and understood; but as a political force the idea lacked reality. 'The people' figured for the most part as a catch-phrase, sometimes meaning only the upper class of society, sometimes an ill-defined and despised mob. Spasmodic popular risings there had always been, Jacqueries and Peasants' Revolts or such narrower outbursts as the Gordon Riots. But 'the people' (almost always 'the mob' when they expressed themselves in this way) exercised no sustained and hardly even a spasmodic influence on political events.

It is the undoubted and revolutionary contribution of the last century to have brought 'the people' – not as a mere concept but as a force – into a dominating place in politics. We live in a period in which democracy is for the first time a practical possibility. Cynics have pointed out that it is also the period in which a war fought to make the world safe for democracy was followed within a generation by its widespread disappearance.

But Fascism is the disease of democracy; therein lies its peculiar danger and the explanation of its virulence in our time. It appeared in its most violent forms among those populations which were least politically adult, that is, whose people had had least preparation for the opportunity when it came to them. It developed forms which, for all the general resemblance of the doctrine, had strongly marked characteristics derived from the nation wherein they grew. But the study of the peculiar national, political or economic conditions which gave rise to the particular forms which we have recently crushed in Europe must not be allowed to blind us to the fact that it is a disease to which every modern democracy is subject. The body politic of every democratic country is vulnerable.

The casual use of such words as despotism, dictatorship, tyranny – all of them dating from pre-democratic periods – confuses the issue. Fascism, though it leads in the old Machiavellian way by craft and conquest to the elevation of one man or one small group, can only succeed by first seducing 'the people'. The ingenious propaganda mechanism by which alone it survives is evidence enough of this. 'The people' may be silenced, intimidated and crushed, but they must also in large measure *believe*. *Credere, obbedire, combattere* as every other blank wall in Italy proclaimed. And it would have been an interesting experiment to count, during a short walk in any German town, how often the word *Volk* winked alluringly from the political hoardings.

The special constitution of a nation may be more or less subject to the Fascist disease but it is folly in the critical age through which we are living not to recognize that any democratic constitution provides by its very nature a breeding ground for its germs. Democracy, like the human organism, carries within it the seed of its own destruction. The defeat in arms of the two nations which were Fascism's prime advocates was a necessary operation, but does not in itself guarantee any other nation against an outbreak of the disease. If democracy is to survive we must diagnose the cause and find the prophylactic for Fascism.

The danger lies in the still incomplete conception of 'the people'. On Christian and liberal principles, the emergence of 'the people' as a political force was a great advance, although there were aesthetic by-products of oligarchic and aristocratic society which we shall never see again and which are a permanent loss to society. They would be too dearly bought back at the price of the *ancien régime*; that I suppose no liberal thinker can deny. Moreover, they could not at our present stage of society be bought back, for the choice is no longer between popular and aristocratic government, but between the rule of the people as we understand it in this country and the perversion of democracy which for lack of a better word we call Fascism. In politics it is impossible to undo the centuries and we must face the problems of our time as we find them.

The weakness from which democracy – the government of the people – suffers is a weakness of definition. What are 'the people'? The answer, thoughtfully given, is of course that they are the whole of society (not merely one class – a common error this), but – and this is more important – that they are a great number of separate entities, each one having a separate birth and death and an astonishingly large number of quite peculiar characteristics.

When politically conscious society was confined within small compass it would never have occurred to anyone to obscure the private entity of each of its members. It is because of the vastness of modern democracy that party and class have been given a higher value than the individual. Since 'the people' became a force in politics the individual has been progressively submerged; it is the natural outcome of the increase in the population of the political world. Our narrow imaginations cannot conceive of the mass in terms of individuals, and the first effect of giving every man his right to a say in his political fate has been the removal from him of his identity as a man. He becomes a party-member, a worker, an Aryan or what you will.

This is the subversive tendency which must be overcome in our time if democracy is not to perish. We must find means to extend our political imagination so as to reduce the necessity for simplification and grouping. We must above all find means to eradicate in men and women the primitive fears which make them seek refuge in groups and herds, preferring the cosy irresponsibility of the mass to the responsible loneliness of the individual.

European culture as we know it rests on respect for the individual. That respect has in our time dwindled until hardly even lip service to the old idea is left. If democracy is to survive, if the State is to be the instrument of man, not man of the State, respect for the individual must be imaginatively increased and extended as never before. Only in this way – and not by the organizing of parties and shouting of slogans – can the body politic be immunized against Fascism. But it is easier to diagnose than to prescribe and indeed the chief reason for the sickliness of most bodies politic is the failure of political theorists – even the most experienced and the wisest – to find the solutions to the problems they set forth.

The entry of the people into the field of effective government has altered the face of the political world and should alter it for the better. So at least the Levellers and the Idealists (of whom I count myself) have hoped for centuries. Meanwhile there is still the dangerous corner of Fascism, of the wholesale deception and enslavement of the people, to be turned. The person most to be feared in modern society is the Common Man. He is, like the Average Man, the Economic Man, and a host of his predecessors, a figment of the imagination. It does not make him any the less dangerous. Indeed, in some respects, it makes him, as an idea, even more dangerous.

The essential thing about each one of us is that we are unique. However mass-produced our fashions and ideas, however stereotyped our accents, no two human faces are exactly alike, no two human handwritings are indistinguishable, and – to the accurate listener – no two human methods of speech are identical – the word arrangement, the attack, the particular selection of threadbare idioms from the common pool remains individual. Different experiences differently accepted have differently shaped and carved each home-going face in the crowded train. 'I know nothing after all so real or substantial as myself,' said Lord Shaftesbury at a period when life, if more callous for some, was less exhausting for all. Under the pressure of our own times it is only this confidence in our own identity which enables us to navigate at all the rapids of our world.

But there is a parallel instinct which makes most of us, while propelling our little skiffs more or less inexpertly along, seek to join up for company with the thousands of other little skiffs shooting the rapids in the same direction. The success of the human being in negotiating these rapids depends on the success with which he can reconcile and combine the necessary egoism and the necessary desire to move with the herd. In different societies and at different epochs the balance between the two has been differently held; a smaller deviation will serve to make a man an eccentric to-day more than it did in the eighteenth century. (Is there perhaps something a little wistful in the prevalent vogue for studying the eccentrics of the past?)

But to come back to the Common Man. He does not exist in the flesh. And no one, I imagine, so interprets the phrase as to mean that in this century of the Common Man we are all to aim at a certain dead level of ordinariness. On the contrary, we all ought to know by this time that the Common Man is a fine fellow. Has he not just won the war against Fascism? And yet . . . When the great names are purposely omitted from a nation's expression of thanks to its saviours, there must surely have been a number of common men (without capitals this time) who paused to wonder whether Field-Marshal Montgomery had not perhaps contributed rather more to the total result than each of them.

This is in no sense to minimize the joint effort of a whole people, still less the countless personal efforts which added up (fantastic addition) to the united effort. The war against Fascism has been won – hitherto – by the Common Man as no earlier war in history has been so won. But what inspired these individual efforts? What kept the telephone operator at her task as the bombs whooshed down and nerved the bank clerk to tackle the incendiary bomb, and made thousands, even millions, of men and women carry for six years burdens of work and worry far beyond their strength? Surely it was something very different from a belief in the Common Man. It was the desire to be the Uncommon Man, or, call it by its old name, the hero.

Centuries of moral teaching have held up for our admiration certain high individual examples of conduct. The hero is a figure which it is still fortunately impossible to escape. He dominates our earlier literature, he prances across the old history text-books. He is still to be seen riding or meditating or gesturing in public squares. (True that investigation of his identity may be baffling. 'Sir Francis Hotchkiss, Bart., 1804–1882'; what can be made of that?) All the same the great man was – and is – there, to be respected, to be emulated, an example. And the Common Man rose, and rises, to the great occasion when it comes, because for centuries all the moral teaching he has had has taught him to aspire – not to ordinariness – but to greatness.

But the trend of moral and political teaching in our own time is away from individual greatness and example. Since the common people came into their own, emphasis on uncommon people has come to be regarded as bad taste. The tendency is a necessary part in the process of democracy, and without some temporary over-emphasis on 'the people' in the part of hero the balance, once too sharply tilted in favour of the individual, could hardly have been redressed. I do not myself forget the day when I stumbled on to those lines of Auguste Barbier on the Revolution of 1830 –

> *La grande populace et la sainte canaille*
> *Se ruaient à l'immortalité . . .*

and a flaming Red Dawn for some time afterwards blinded my eyes to any heroism other than that of 'the masses'.

But the balance can tilt too far, for on the whole crowds are rarely more admirable (and frequently less so) than individuals. If the Common Man becomes the exemplary type, all aspiration ceases and the Common Man will no longer be admirable. The saving grace, and also the danger, lies in the fact that no teaching and training can ever eradicate the desire to admire and to aspire which exists in every human being. It must find its outlet. And this brings the argument back to the starting-point; for if with the most laudable democratic intentions we play down the Great

Man, whether in our own time, or in the records of the past, something else will usurp that necessary place. The film star, naturally; or the types portrayed by the film star, the gangster and the gangster's moll. But all this, though significant, is not so harmful as the political outcome of this levelling of greatness. What standards of choice will be left to us? What kind of windbags and nonentities will be able to deceive us? If this is really to be the Century of the Common Man we may expect a flood of pinchbeck dictators.

For the truth is that men do not desire to be the Common Man any more than they are the Common Man. They need greatness in others and the occasion to discover the greatness in themselves.

1945

Shakespeare between Two Civil Wars*

When William Shakespeare was born, at Stratford-on-Avon in April 1564, nearly eighty years had gone by since King Richard III had died on Bosworth Field and King Henry VII had united the Red Rose of Lancaster to the White Rose of York and inaugurated an epoch enriched

> *with smooth-fac'd peace,*
> *With smiling plenty and fair prosperous days!*

At least – as in the concluding words of Shakespeare's play on King Richard III – there was general lip service to this theme of the peaceful Tudor times which had made England whole again after the long and bloody civil wars between the rival dynasties of Lancaster and York.

As a picture of the times, this was of course something of a simplification. England had not been lapped in unbroken peace and smiling plenty during the sixteenth century. On the contrary, the country had passed through the ravaging experience of the Reformation, with the economic upheaval and political risks involved. There had been numerous local uprisings, some, like the Pilgrimage of Grace, of considerable magnitude; there had been the attempt to set a rival sovereign, the prim, puritanical Lady Jane Grey, on the throne in place of Henry VIII's eldest daughter, the Catholic Mary Tudor; there had been, in the same cause, Sir Thomas Wyatt's ill-starred rebellion. There had been times when it looked – with the change of religion, with the ambitious intrigues of great families, with the uncertainty about the succession – as though there might be Wars of the Tudor Rose as bloody and as long as those of the White Rose and the Red. And all these political

---

* Lecture delivered at the Folger Shakespeare Library, Washington, USA, 1964.

and religious tensions had been worked out in a country which was undergoing a prolonged social and economic crisis owing to the unprecedented increase in population and the decline in the value of money. Yet there had been no irretrievable descent into a divided government, and for this there was gratitude to the Tudors – to the cautious cunning of King Henry VII, to the tyrannical strength of Henry VIII; most of all, in the years during which Shakespeare grew up, to the wary skill of Queen Elizabeth and her great minister William Cecil.

It is obvious how much the shadow of past civil wars and the fear and horror of internecine conflict inspire the history plays of Shakespeare. The division of the country against itself is the ultimate disaster. So, in *King John*, the bastard Faulconbridge rallies the spirits of his countrymen in the face of French invasion:

> *This England never did, nor never shall,*
> *Lie at the proud foot of a conqueror,*
> *But when it first did help to wound itself. . . .*
> *Come the three corners of the world in arms,*
> *And we shall shock them. Nought shall make us rue,*
> *If England to itself do rest but true.*

To herself but true – it is the division of England that breeds danger. Shakespeare, in common with most of his contemporaries, thought with dread of that kind of war in which men of one nation and one speech, who should have been bound by ties of sacred loyalty to one sovereign, turned their swords upon each other:

> *The brother blindly shed the brother's blood,*
> *The father rashly slaughtered his own son –*

conflicts in which such a scene of tragedy could take place as that which Shakespeare depicts in the third part of *King Henry VI*, when the unfortunate King, left alone during the Battle of Towton, at first muses on the happiness that might have been his in a quiet and pastoral life and is interrupted by the entry of two soldiers, each triumphantly dragging a newly slain foe; only to discover, the one that he has killed his father, the other that he has killed his son. This scene, which epitomizes the horror of civil war, as Shakespeare and his contemporaries saw it, is not easy to act on the modern stage; it seems too improbable a coincidence; but it must be taken as a formal and tragic pageant of civil war: we have the King, unseen by the combatants, standing in the midst, hearing all that they say, feeling that as King he is the author of all these woes; and, symmetrically arranged one on either hand, the young man who uncovers the face of the man he has killed only to discover the features of his own father, and on the other side, a graybeard warrior who recognizes his victim too late as his own son. But this dramatic simplification is given a realist explanation: Shakespeare tells us just how it came about. The son says:

> *From London by the King was I press'd forth;*
> *My father, being the Earl of Warwick's man,*
> *Came on the part of York, press'd by his master.*

A factual statement – the boy, perhaps an apprentice in London, has marched with the London men under the King's banners; but the father is a tenant of the Earl of Warwick and so bound to serve in the wars as his overlord serves, against King Henry, with the Yorkist side – a straightforward explanation immediately understood by Shakespeare's audience, showing how, in the structure of their world and society, a young man who has done no more than follow a necessary obligation finds that he has become a parricide.

Shakespeare, following a fashion in praise and gratitude of the Queen and her forebears, loved to describe the England of his time in terms of pastoral tranquillity. Thus, in the play of *Henry VIII*, words of prophecy are spoken over the infant Elizabeth:

> *She shall be lov'd and fear'd. Her own shall bless her:*
> *Her foes shake like a field of beaten corn,*
> *And hang their heads with sorrow. Good grows with her;*
> *In her days every man shall eat in safety*
> *Under his own vine what he plants, and sing*
> *The merry songs of peace to all his neighbours.*

This emphasis on peace is paralleled by passages – many of them – on the horrors of war. There is the Bishop of Carlisle's famous prophecy in *Richard II* of ruin if the usurper Henry is made King:

> *And if you crown him, let me prophesy,*
> *The blood of English shall manure the ground . . .*
> *And in this seat of peace tumultuous wars*
> *Shall kin with kin and kind with kind confound;*
> *Disorder, horror, fear, and mutiny*
> *Shall here inhabit, and this land be call'd*
> *The field of Golgotha and dead men's skulls. . . .*

Numerous other passages could be quoted from plays not necessarily about English history testifying to the intensity of Shakespeare's feeling on the horrors of war. Mark Antony prophesies over the dead body of Julius Caesar:

> *Domestic fury and fierce civil strife*
> *Shall cumber all the parts of Italy;*
> *Blood and destruction shall be so in use*
> *And dreadful objects so familiar*
> *That mothers shall but smile when they behold*
> *Their infants quartered with the hands of war,*
> *All pity choked with custom of fell deeds;*
> *And Caesar's spirit, ranging for revenge,*
> *With Até by his side, come hot from hell,*
> *Shall in these confines with a monarch's voice*
> *Cry 'Havoc!' and let slip the dogs of war.*

Where peace is concerned – or the peace of England, at any rate – does Shakespeare protest too much? In a way, yes, or at least the emphasis that he lays on the contrast between peace and war is essentially the emphasis of a man writing in an epoch when peace could not be regarded as the normal state of affairs; the order and tranquillity of society are something to be deeply thankful for, not something to be taken for granted.

England was, it is true, *internally* at peace, but from Shakespeare's twenty-fourth year until his fortieth, there was *external* war with Spain, and there was a formidable threat of invasion in the year of the Armada. In Scotland, the northern half of the same island, civil disorder seemed at times endemic, and there had been serious civil war in Shakespeare's youth. Just across the Narrow Seas, the Netherlands were the scene of fighting for almost the whole of Shakespeare's life, as the Dutch in a strenuous and painful struggle broke free of the Spanish yoke; and France was intermittently for many years plagued by an embittered and destructive war.

In the last act of *Henry V*, when after Agincourt the Duke of Burgundy plays the mediator between Henry V and the French king, Shakespeare puts into his mouth a plangent lament for peace, which has so long been absent from France, 'this best garden of the world'. All the fruits of the fertile land are destroyed:

> Her vine, the merry cheerer of the heart,
> Unpruned dies; her hedges even-pleached,
> Like prisoners wildly overgrown with hair,
> Put forth disorder'd twigs: her fallow leas,
> The darnel, hemlock, and rank fumitory
> Doth root upon, while that the coulter rusts
> That should deracinate such savagery.
> The even mead, that erst brought sweetly forth
> The freckled cowslip, burnet, and green clover,
> Wanting the scythe, all uncorrected, rank,
> Conceives by idleness and nothing teems
> But hateful docks, rough thistles, kecksies, burrs,
> Losing both beauty and utility.
> And as our vineyards, fallows, meads, and hedges,
> Defective in their natures, grow to wildness,
> Even so our houses and ourselves and children
> Have lost, or do not learn for want of time,
> The sciences that should become our country.

This in the play is meant for the France of 1415; it could stand as well for the France of the 1590s before the strong and healing hand of Henry of Navarre put an end to the divisions.

That such things had once been in England; that they still were in other less happy lands; that the threat of them was not altogether lifted but that by heaven's mercy and Elizabeth's skill they were held at bay; that they might come again: this is the unrestful political background of Shakespeare and his contemporaries.

And these things did come again in England: this is the meaning of my title, 'Shakespeare between Two Civil Wars'. Twenty-five years from Shakespeare's death the country was again to be split asunder by divided factions and divided interests, in a conflict the seeds of which were already sown in the reign of Queen Elizabeth I and had germinated fast under her successor, King James I. A conflict which, moreover, was to have its first pitched battle within a few miles, and almost within sight, of Shakespeare's home town of Stratford-on-Avon, just where the London road traverses the high escarpment of Edgehill. Here would be fought the first great battle between King Charles I and the forces of his Puritan Parliament. Along this road Shakespeare must often have travelled, must indeed sometimes have halted on that steep ridge on his way to London to look back over the fertile plain of Warwickshire; or on his journey home have greeted from here the familiar countryside of his childhood, looking across what is still one of the loveliest views in England. Here, soon after his death and in the lifetime of his daughter, Englishmen would fight Englishmen in deadly conflict.

The English Civil War, when it came, would be a war different in its causes and character from the dynastic feud which brought on the Wars of the Roses. It would have indeed more of the ideas that animate Shakespeare's Roman plays; conceptions of liberty and tyranny, of patrician and popular government, would be canvassed. Its avowed causes were the tension between Crown and Parliament and the mistaken efforts of the King to curb the Puritan movement, which had gone far beyond his, or anyone's, power to curb. Yet there would still be elements of the old feudal England in this later war of the seventeenth century. It would still have been possible – though I do not say that I have evidence of its actually occurring – that a young apprentice fighting for Parliament with the forces raised in London could have come face to face in battle with his father, a country gentleman whose loyalties had led him to follow the banners of some great landowner among the Cavaliers, maybe the Earl of Northampton from Compton Wynyates, who would be the greatest Cavalier landowner in Shakespeare's own region. There were certainly many examples of families divided against themselves in the civil wars of King Charles and his Parliament. We find the Countess of Denbigh, for instance, whose husband was slain on the King's side early in the war, writing to implore her son, who was in arms for Parliament, no longer to side with those who have been guilty of his father's blood. And there still survived into the Stuart epoch some of the picturesque accoutrements of the Wars of the Roses – the standards carried before the troops were often gay with the heraldic devices of their leaders. There would be many on both sides, both for King and for Parliament, who felt, as their forebears had done in the Wars of the Roses, that they fought out of loyalty to the interest or influence of a particular family – for the Stanleys, and therefore for the King, in Lancashire; for the Fairfaxes, and therefore for Parliament, in Yorkshire – rather than for any deeper issues of politics or religion.

The differences between the profound constitutional conflict of the English seventeenth century and the dynastic strife of the fifteenth are greater than the similarities. But there were certain resemblances. If we think of Shakespeare's life in the perspective of time between these two civil conflicts, we see why peace was to him and to his contemporaries a precious thing, a delicate equilibrium threatened by dangers and instabilities in the State and marvellously maintained by the great Queen.

The dangers of war and disorder that seemed nearest to Shakespeare and his contemporaries were not, of course – for they had not the gift of prophecy – quite of the kind which ultimately broke upon the country. They feared, and justly feared, difficulties over the succession to the throne when Queen Elizabeth died. During Shakespeare's early years as a playwright and in his young maturity, in the 1590s, the Queen was old, childless, and extremely touchy when asked to make provision for the succession. Yet think what a disputed succession could have meant to England, a Protestant country with a considerable Catholic minority, in a period when Europe was divided by the Counter-Reformation into two worlds, and when it would have been of inestimable value to Spain to have a friendly or even a satellite sovereign on the English throne. The dangers of Spanish invasion were not at an end with the defeat of the Armada in 1588. It was feared, and justifiably feared, that the death of Elizabeth might be the signal for disturbances in England – a disputed succession with the possibility of civil war and Spanish invasion.

In fact, when the great Queen died on 24 March 1603, there was no trouble at all. Thanks to the forethought and skill of Robert Cecil, a minister devoted to the Queen but devoted also to the best interests of his country, King James VI of Scotland, Elizabeth's cousin, Mary Stuart's son, became King James I of Great Britain with a minimum of disturbance. Cecil had long been in correspondence with him, unknown to Elizabeth, carefully grooming and training him for the part of England's King.

Although we sometimes get the impression from popular textbooks that the Tudors were good and the Stuarts bad, and that King James was a sad falling-off after the great Elizabeth, this was not what was felt at the time. In 1603 the great majority of responsibly minded citizens welcomed the Scottish king with genuine enthusiasm. He was not the rather absurd figure that he later became but an intelligent man in the prime of life who had made a success of the difficult task of governing the self-willed and much divided nation of the Scots. He was a married man with a sprightly and fruitful wife, the Danish princess Anne, and a young family. His coming solved the nightmare succession problem which had hung over England pretty well ever since Henry divorced Queen Catherine of Aragon.

For it was the succession problem which had caused the Wars of the Roses: the dispute as to which of two branches of the royal house had the legal right to reign in England. The House of Stuart came in on a firm legitimate right – no doubtful marriages, no children of the left hand, but a straight descent from King Henry VII; and, unlike any sovereign of England for nearly a hundred years, King James already had two sons. Is it a wonder that the people of England breathed more freely and poets were lavish of praise to 'our fruitful sovereign James'? To quote only one of the many poems of welcome:

> *Lo, here the glory of a greater day*
> *Than England ever heretofore could see*
> *In all her days! When she did most display*
> *The ensigns of her power, or whenas she*
> *Did spread herself the most, and the most did sway*
> *Her state abroad, yet could she never be*
> *Thus blest at home, nor ever come to grow*
> *To be entire in her full orb till now.*

This refers of course to the union with Scotland; the poet then goes on to praise the King:

> *Glory of Men – this hast thou brought to us,*
> *And yet hast brought us more than this by far;*
> *Religion comes with thee, peace, righteousness,*
> *Judgment and justice which more glorious are*
> *Than all they Kingdoms; and art more by this,*
> *Than Lord and Sovereign, more than Emperor,*
> *Over the hearts of men that let thee in*
> *To more than all the powers on earth can win.*

Those lines, I need hardly add, are not by Shakespeare. They are by Samuel Daniel. Shakespeare took no part in the rather excessive adulation showered on the new king by a great number of his contemporaries. He was not, of course, above including some fulsome compliments to King James in his plays. At the conclusion of the play of *King Henry VIII*, praises for King James are tacked on a little awkwardly after Cranmer's long speech of prophecy about the glories of Elizabeth's reign: like the phoenix, Cranmer declares, the ashes of Queen Elizabeth will create another sovereign:

> *As great in admiration as herself;*
> *So shall she leave her blessedness to one . . .*
> *Who, from the sacred ashes of her honour,*
> *Shall star-like rise, as great in fame as she was,*
> *And so stand fix'd; peace, plenty, love, truth, terror,*
> *That were the servants to this chosen infant,*

> *Shall then be his, and like a vine grow to him:*
> *Wherever the bright sun of heaven shall shine,*
> *His honour and the greatness of his name*
> *Shall be and make new nations: he shall flourish,*
> *And, like a mountain cedar, reach his branches*
> *To all the plains about him.*

And in *Macbeth*, the scene between Macduff and young Malcolm, the legitimate King of Scotland – in which Macduff persuades the young man to invade the country and dethrone the usurper who has murdered his father – that scene is full of courteous glances at King James. Thus Malcolm lists what he calls the 'king-becoming graces':

> *As justice, verity, temperance, stableness,*
> *Bounty, perseverance, mercy, lowliness,*
> *Devotion, patience, courage, fortitude.*

These are a group of virtues such as King James would have thought the ornament of good kings. For, though in his numerous and eloquent political writings James took the view that kings were God's viceregents on earth and could not therefore be questioned by their subjects however badly they behaved, yet he also held that the king's duties to God, if not to his people, required him to reign virtuously and to exercise just such king-becoming graces as Malcolm names – always allowing that when he speaks of 'lowliness' he means of course lowliness and humility before God and God alone, not any unkingly bowing to the will of his subjects, and by 'courage' the profounder virtue of moral courage, not mere physical courage, in which King James was notoriously deficient.

A further passage in the same scene refers to Malcolm's contemporary, the eleventh-century King of England, Edward the Confessor, with whom he has taken refuge. Edward, a gentle and holy king, is described curing his subjects of the illness known as the 'evil' by the sanctity of his touch. This miraculous healing quality of the royal touch was supposed to be inherited by English kings, and King James, after he ascended the throne, was pleased to exercise it; it ministered to his sense of the holy and God-given nature of kingship. Shakespeare in a short passage, usually omitted in modern stage productions, refers explicitly to it.

This whole scene between Malcolm and Macduff (barring only that great tragic passage in which Macduff hears of the murder of his wife and children by bloody Macbeth) is apt to be boring to modern audiences: it refers to political issues and ideas that are no longer of any live interest to us. Yet it contains one line and a half which are not only most beautiful and moving at the point where they come in the play but are striking to any historian interested in the decline of the English monarchy after the coming of the Stuarts.

When the young Malcolm at length ceases to temporize and declares that he is indeed ready and willing to come back to Scotland and liberate the oppressed nation from the tyrant Macbeth, he says to Macduff:

> *What I am truly*
> *Is thine and my poor country's to command.*

Now the phrase 'thine to command' was in the English of Shakespeare's time no more than a catchphrase, a very common signature to a polite letter, the equivalent of 'Yours sincerely' today. But Shakespeare's genius is sometimes most strikingly shown in a way he has of taking a phrase, which is a mere commonplace of speech, familiar to all, and, by the way he places it, giving it an extraordinary weight. In this case it is the spacing that does it: 'thine to command' becomes 'thine *and my poor country's* to command'. This is the King making his vow of service to his people, and I have heard that line given so that it brought tears to the eyes.

King James had a very high conception of the duties of the kingly office, although he also had a very high conception of his power; his son King Charles, who was to be the unfortunate protagonist of the war between King and Parliament, also felt deeply about his duties. Both these sovereigns would have agreed that they had under God a sacred obligation to their people and therefore were in a sense 'their country's to command'. But neither of these two Stuarts, nor, to be sure, Queen Elizabeth I, nor for that matter Shakespeare himself, would have thought of this as meaning that the sovereign was *answerable* to the people in a democratic or parliamentary sense. They conceived it their duty to do what *they* thought right for their subjects, having a charge, from God and from no one else, to govern them. And it is no doubt in this sense that Shakespeare puts the words into young King Malcolm's mouth: he will give his utmost – his life, if need be – to save his poor country from Macbeth and rule it as a just and virtuous monarch should.

But there has to be much practical wisdom as well as political theory in maintaining a monarchy such as that which the Tudors maintained. The first Stuart king, in an admittedly difficult political situation, was to show that in many ways, some of them rather simple and obvious, he had not the necessary wisdom. He lacked that sixth sense of what his people were thinking that had never failed Elizabeth, even in her last difficult and troubled years.

In *Measure for Measure* occurs a short, significant passage which is also thought to be a polite compliment to King James. The Duke, in the first scene, has just made over his power to the regent Angelo and is about to leave Vienna. Angelo not unnaturally suggests that he escort the Duke out of the town with due honours and attendance. To which the Duke replies:

> Give me your hand.
> I'll privily away. I love the people
> But do not like to stage me to their eyes.
> Though it do well, I do not relish well
> Their loud applause and aves *vehement*;
> Nor do I think the man of safe discretion
> That does affect it.

This is a side reference to the new king's notorious aversion to crowds. King James had psychological excuses for this. No man who had been as often manhandled and kidnapped as poor King James had been by his turbulent Scottish subjects in his youth would have been willing to expose himself to crowds. But Shakespeare in this passage seems to be praising this attitude in the King.

He will not be a demagogue; he will not 'stage himself', that is, play the actor, before the people's eyes. But is this conduct altogether wise in a ruler and did Shakespeare think it so?

Now what Shakespeare did or did not think about politics is a subject which has given scope for wide speculation; and it is part of Shakespeare's universal genius that we can always find in him a line of thought which is akin to our own. And therefore I do not claim to be proving anything about Shakespeare's way of thinking, but if we look at his attitude to rulers and to people there are certainly indications that he knew and understood very well – as how should he not? – the sensitive balance that must be maintained between the successful ruler and his people. And he knew also that those who shrink from contact with the rude multitude are not, generally speaking, the most successful in maintaining law, order, and their own authority.

Take *Richard II* – this is a study of marvellous subtlety showing a king who lives in a world of his own elegant and intellectual conceptions. Faced with the ultimate crisis, he plays his defeated part with undefeated authority. He confronts the successful rebel Bolingbroke:

> *We are amaz'd; and thus long have we stood*
> *To watch the fearful bending of thy knee,*
> *Because we thought our self thy lawful king;*
> *And if we be, how dare thy joints forget*
> *To pay their awful duty to our presence?*
> *If we be not, show us the hand of God*
> *That hath dismiss'd us from our stewardship.*

Later in the tragedy of the deposition scene, the broken, powerless, degraded Richard makes the victorious Bolingbroke and all his faction look like a gang of vulgar bandits. Inevitably – in the longer perspective of history – one is reminded of the equally dramatic performance put on by King Charles I at his trial in 1649. But Richard cannot regain his crown by words, any more than King Charles could. We know that, whatever his just right to the throne, Richard lacked one vital thing that Henry Bolingbroke had – the popular touch. It is again part of Shakespeare's extra-

ordinary genius that he first plants in our minds the idea of Bolingbroke's attraction for the multitude by letting Richard, in his days
of power, describe it with scornful derision. He and his favourites
have been watching and mocking at Bolingbroke as he goes by:

> *Ourself and Bushy, Bagot here, and Green*
> *Observ'd his courtship to the common people:*
> *How he did seem to dive into their hearts*
> *With humble and familiar courtesy;*
> *What reverence he did throw away on slaves,*
> *Wooing poor craftsmen with the craft of smiles. . . .*
> *Off goes his bonnet to an oyster wench;*
> *A brace of draymen bid God speed him well*
> *And had the tribute of his supple knee,*
> *With 'Thanks, my countrymen, my loving friends'.*

The dramatic irony of this scene is that King Richard does not
realize that he is laughing at the very quality in Bolingbroke that
is – for him – no laughing matter. Bolingbroke will be carried to
the throne of England in part at least on the plaudits of the people;
and Richard, the mocking, refined, out-of-touch Richard, will be
murdered at Pomfret Castle.

So also King Henry VI, who lives in his studies and his prayers,
cannot establish the relationship with the people that comes easily
to such a bluff, brave wencher as his rival, King Edward IV. It is
not, in the case of poor King Henry VI, for lack of trying. The
recent revival of interest in this sprawling early trilogy, the three
parts of *King Henry VI*, has introduced us to many subtleties in
what was once a much neglected group of plays; and in seeing
recent productions of them I have come to regret that Shakespeare
worked on this subject before he had reached the height of his
powers. For in Henry VI himself there is a sketch for a figure
potentially as tragic as that of Richard II – a king whose impulses
are all towards virtue, unselfishness, piety, and compassion, who
only wants to do his duty as a king but is temperamentally unfitted
for his part. This is his tragedy – that he means so much better
towards his country than any of his rivals; but he shrinks, first behind his uncle regent, the good Duke of Gloucester, under whom

things do not go too badly, and then behind his wife, Margaret of Anjou – the most horrible female character in all Shakespeare, not excepting Lady Macbeth – and everything goes very badly. But always he is completely remote from his people and can only wring his hands over their misfortunes:

> *Woe above woe! grief more than common grief!*
> *Oh, that my death would stay these rueful deeds!*
> *Oh, pity, pity, gentle heaven, pity! . . .*
> *Was ever king so griev'd for subjects' woe?*

Had Shakespeare drawn Henry VI with all the power of his maturity, the King would be one of his great tragic creations.

In King Henry V, on the other hand, Shakespeare gives a picture of a king who has the common touch to perfection. We may not nowadays feel quite that sympathy with King Henry's aggressive militarism that the Shakespearian audience felt, but here is a ruler who exerts authority, commands loyalty, and inspires devotion because he can speak to the very hearts of his subjects. The young man who in his wild youth had kept company with Jack Falstaff and knew the taverns and back streets of London grows into the king who on the night before Agincourt can walk from tent to tent speaking as a friend and equal with his men, and who can rouse them on the day of battle with that great speech which through over-use and over-recitation has come to sound rhetorical to us, but which is in essence a very simple message of unity and encouragement to men whose only hope in a tight place is to stand together and fight hard:

> *We few, we happy few, we band of brothers;*
> *For he today that sheds his blood with me*
> *Shall be my brother. Be he ne'er so vile,*
> *This day shall gentle his condition;*
> *And gentlemen in England now abed*
> *Shall think themselves accurs'd they were not here,*
> *And hold their manhoods cheap whiles any speaks*
> *That fought with us upon Saint Crispin's day.*

This is Shakespeare's idea of how Henry V would have spoken at Agincourt in 1415, but it is a speech which breathes the spirit of the Elizabethan age, when, in time of national peril, the sovereign, though a woman, showed herself among her people, claimed that she had the heart of a king and was also proud to describe herself as 'mere English'.

In many other plays, besides the English history plays, we find Shakespeare noticing the importance for the successful leader – in politics or war – to have an understanding of the people, to be able at least to command their love. Thus Claudius says irritably of Hamlet after the murder of Polonius:

> *How dangerous is it that this man goes loose!*
> *Yet must not we put the strong law on him.*
> *He's loved of the distracted multitude.*

This is Hamlet's danger to the King – that he has the love of the people, which Claudius has not.

In *Coriolanus* – well, nobody can say that Shakespeare gives a very sympathetic picture of the Roman populace in that play; but the uncompromising *unwillingness* of Coriolanus to make the slightest attempt to understand or to get into contact with them is the political cause of his downfall. The theme of this great play is human pride rather than politics, but we notice again Shakespeare's awareness of the necessity of contact between ruler and the ruled. (The two tribunes of the people, incidentally, are such very unattractive characters because one senses in them that they are exploiting the people for their own ambitions; the true feeling of human relationship between the two hostile parties in Rome – plebs and patricians – is indicated in the small but important part of the veteran general Cominius, a good and generous leader, and in the humorous old patrician Menenius, who can, in his own way, talk to and reason with the people.)

Again, in *Julius Caesar* the conspirators are determined to have Brutus of their number because he is beloved of the people. As Casca says:

> *Oh, he sits high in all the people's hearts,*
> *And that which would appear offence in us,*

> *His countenance, like richest alchemy,*
> *Will change to virtue and to worthiness.*

And so, after the murder of Caesar, Brutus does indeed establish his authority over the people, so much so that one of them, mistaking the whole purpose of the murder, cries out excitedly 'Let him be Caesar!' And it is only because Mark Antony commands an even greater popularity and a more effectively emotional brand of oratory that he wins the fickle multitude back to his side.

I have strayed a long way from *Measure for Measure* and that flattering reference to King James, praising him for being a superior being who would not court popularity with the people by 'staging himself' to their eyes in public appearances. If Shakespeare respected this attitude, he clearly did not, in ordinary terms of human affairs, think it a wise one. And it is ironic that in this play, *Measure for Measure*, where the good Duke is depicted stealing away privately and eschewing contact with the vulgar, he is really, it turns out, only doing it to deceive everyone. For he comes creeping back in disguise for the very purpose of moving unknown among his people and seeing how they are governed and what their opinion is of their laws and their rulers. Well, I mustn't make too much of that, because it is after all simply a part of the story that Shakespeare was using and may not have very much significance.

Now to turn from Shakespeare's treatment of the ruler in his relation to the people, to the people themselves. It is sometimes said that Shakespeare shows a general contempt, if not dislike, of the common people; in this, of course, we must beware of assuming that Shakespeare's opinions were the same as those that he put into the mouths of his characters. But such lines as Coriolanus' withering contempt of popular political opinions:

> *Hang 'em! They say!*
> *They'll sit by the fire and presume to know*
> *What's done i' the Capitol . . .*
> *Who thrives and who declines.*

This is not necessarily Shakespeare's own view of popular opinion.

Admittedly he puts this kind of thing very often into the mouths of his characters, despising the quick, emotional changes of the giddy-pated multitude. Casca, in *Julius Caesar*, describes with withering contempt the 'hooting of the rabblement' when Caesar refused the crown:

> If the tag-rag people did not clap him and hiss him, according as he pleased and displeased them, as they use to do the players in the theatre, I am no true man. . . . He said, if he had done or said anything amiss, he desired their worships to think it was his infirmity. Three or four wenches where I stood cried, 'Alas, good soul!' and forgave him with all their hearts. But there's no heed to be taken of them. If Caesar had stabbed their mothers, they would have done no less.

But this is Casca speaking, a character for whose opinions and conduct we need feel no great respect. Yet it is certainly true that Shakespeare in his treatment of the people in a crowd is rarely, if ever, favourable. The crowd is at best fickle – as in *Julius Caesar*, hailing Brutus with enthusiasm and half an hour later cheering Mark Antony while Brutus and Cassius, in flight, ride 'like madmen through the gates of Rome' – at worst murderous – as in the killing of Cinna the poet in *Julius Caesar*; or in the horrible hanging and beheading of their victims by the ferocious mob in Jack Cade's rebellion in *Henry VI*. These crowd scenes depicting the English populace in full revolt echo the mad, dangerous voice of a hungry out-of-hand multitude which, at moments of economic distress in the sixteenth century, was a deeply feared threat to Shakespeare's own world; and the voice of the dispossessed of Shakespeare's time, with their fear and hatred of enclosures that took away the common land, and their suspicion of lawyers and educated men, rings out in the words of the rebel leader Jack Cade: 'All the realm shall be in common,' he promises, 'in Cheapside shall my palfrey go to grass. . . . There shall be no money: all shall eat and drink on my score.' 'Let's kill all the lawyers, the first thing we do,' shouts one of his followers. They hang the town clerk of Chatham because he admits he can read and write; and when the captured Lord Say quotes a Latin tag in speaking to them, the rebel Cade cries: 'Away with him! he speaks Latin. . . . Take him away and behead him.'

These cries for the return of the common land, this animosity against lawyers and anger at any who dares to speak a language or use phrases not understood by the ordinary people, all these demands of Jack Cade's mob, would be heard again in the Civil War against King Charles after Shakespeare's death; this time not as mere brutish outcries, but respectably argued and developed and set down in pamphlets.

But if Shakespeare depicts the common people with no redeeming graces when we see them as a mob, he can and does show the individual man of the people with sympathy and admiration. Thus, in *King Lear*, in the horrifying scene of Gloucester's blinding by the unspeakable Cornwall and his wife Regan, it is one of the servants who protests at the action and is killed trying to prevent it, and the rest of the servants, after Cornwall and Regan have gone, do what they can to assist the blinded Gloucester. The soldiers, whose conversations on the night before Agincourt we listen to in *Henry V*, are intelligent men with ideas of their own; and the native generosity, good nature, and loyalty of simple people is depicted in such characters as the old shepherd in *The Winter's Tale*, Adam in *As You Like It*, the groom who visits King Richard II at Pomfret Castle, and others. In *Love's Labour's Lost*, it is the ordinary man, Costard, whose unfailing good sense, good humour, and plain speaking are used as a foil to the attitudinizing of the King and his bright young noblemen. No one would pretend that Shakespeare idealizes or makes a hero of the Common Man, a thing completely outside the conceptions of his epoch or the taste of his audiences, but his treatment of such characters, though it is best known in the uproarious comedy of *A Midsummer Night's Dream*, is by no means always comic but can be serious and sympathetic. And one cannot conceive of Shakespeare taking the view that fine actions and feelings are the prerogative of the nobly born, as, for instance, the French poet Pierre Corneille argued with all solemnity; in one of his later plays, *Heraclite*, the historic incident which he has dramatized turns on the self-sacrifice of a servant, a nurse, who saves the life of the Emperor's child in a palace revolution. Such an action, Corneille explains, cannot in a seemly heroic drama be performed by someone so low in the social scale; he changes the nurse into a lady of noble birth. It is inconceivable that Shakespeare should have done such a thing. He was too great a realist for that. If his mobs are silly and brutal, it is because the crowd – as a crowd – is both these things. But the individual man, whatever his social status, is treated with the respect he merits.

It should have appeared when King James ascended the throne of England in peace, and when he speedily made peace abroad and ended the war with Spain, that an age of settled tranquillity was at hand. The king's favourite motto was 'Blessed are the peace-makers', and his intention was to secure peace abroad by a discreet balance of alliances and to maintain order at home by the power and authority of the Crown. It was an admirable ideal, but the King failed to reckon with the complex forces at work in his new country. The inadequate revenues of the Crown, the consequent coercive power that Parliament had over the monarchy: this was one problem. The spread of Calvinism – Puritanism in its Calvinist form, that is – among his subjects, and the consequent resistance to royal power where it was felt to be at variance with the word of God: this was another problem. The failure to solve either of these problems, and worse, the positive exacerbation of both of them by the policies of James and of his son Charles, led in the end to civil war. The situation was never easy, but the incapacity of either of these kings to understand or to react to public opinion was un-doubtedly an element in hastening on the crisis of civil war.

Shakespeare died in 1616 and wrote his last play some years before that; he did not therefore live to see the situation reach the most critical stage. Yet a man so sensitive to human values and relationships must have felt already some uneasiness. He knew that King James shunned public appearances and did not care to show himself to the people, for he had commented on this with superficial approbation, or at least in terms of compliment, in *Measure for Measure*. But, as a practical observer of human affairs, we know from many other indications that Shakespeare both fully understood and valued the practice of a ruler who responds more freely to the people and has the art of pleasing them – an art not gained by keeping at a distance, an art brilliantly practised, and with no loss of dignity, by the wise and wary old Queen. It was a foreign observer, a Venetian envoy, who noticed in the reign of King James that the English, who when he first ascended the throne had been such worshippers of royalty that they would go any distance to see their sovereign pass by, did not a few years later show any particular interest in his rather infrequent public appearances. After the adulation which had been showered on the king at his first arrival, the prestige and popularity of the Crown fell gradually, and then with increasing rapidity, into a decline.

It would be an idle exercise to seek for any barometer of King James's popularity in the strength of the monarchy in the middle and later plays of Shakespeare. In his full maturity he is dealing with matters more eternal than the passing politics of England – with the storms and problems of the human soul – but when politics are a part of his theme, the clear beliefs which guided him in his earlier history plays seem to have given place to a more clouded and obscure attitude. The early history plays – the sequence which tells the story of Richard's deposition, the troubled reign of Henry IV, the victories of Henry V, the long wars under Henry VI, culminating in the murderous reign and death of Richard III – these are dominated by the idea of the king's sacred right. Richard II was a bad king, but he was the legal one. Henry IV is a usurper, and his issue (in spite of the glorious Henry V) are accursed with wars and troubles, until calm is restored by the return of the crown to its true place once again. This theme of legitimacy can even be traced out in the play of *King John*, where Shakespeare accepts the murdered child Arthur, John's nephew, as the rightful King, in touching lines:

> *The inheritance of this poor child,*
> *His little kingdom of a forcéd grave.*
> *That blood which ow'd the breadth of all this isle,*
> *Three foot of it doth hold.*

And again, when they carry away the little boy's dead body:

> *How easy dost thou take all England up!*
> *From forth this morsel of dead royalty,*
> *The life, the right, the truth of all this realm*
> *Is fled to heaven.*

Order in the state depends on the sacred authority of the Crown, passed down in due right of succession; deviation spells disaster, divided loyalties, disorder, and civil war.

In his earlier years, Shakespeare seems to accept this idea with consistency. But already, in *Hamlet*, a play which presents, among so many other facets, a complex study in politics, there are puzzling things. It contains, for instance, one of Shakespeare's most firmly phrased and most assured statements about the sanctity of kingship:

> *There's such divinity doth hedge a king*
> *That treason can but peep to what it would,*
> *Acts little of his will.*

But who is it who thus boldly claims to be protected by his Divine Right? It is Claudius, King of Denmark, a usurper, a murderer, and an adulterer. And Claudius *knows* that he is all these things; and the audience also knows it. The words are not out of character in the context; he is a bold man, bluffing out a difficult situation, quelling the armed and furious Laertes. But at a period when the sanctity of the monarch was a serious doctrine, and one to which Shakespeare himself apparently subscribed, to put it into the mouth of a king so unsanctified as Claudius gives it an ironic edge.

In the Roman plays, though he is more concerned with character than politics, Shakespeare explores the reasons for the breakdown of a society with a cooler realism than he does in the English history plays and with perhaps some glances at contemporary political theory of the popular rather than the monarchical kind, part classical, part forged on the anvil of the French religious wars.

> *My soul aches* [says Coriolanus]
> *To know, when two authorities are up,*
> *Neither supreme, how soon confusion*
> *May enter 'twixt the gap of both and take*
> *The one by the other.*

The danger of two nearly equal factions had been seen in the French religious wars; it would come soon in England in the deadlock between the power of the King and that of Parliament. In the same play the plebeian party claims that the city – Rome – *is* the people; that is, the State *is* the people, and the magistrates rule only by their consent – a doctrine already common in France in the civil wars, which would become a dominating theory in the English Civil War.

When we come to *Julius Caesar* and *Antony and Cleopatra*, if one thinks of the intensity of Shakespeare's earlier insistence on the blessings of peace and order, one is surprised to find that the character who should represent that element in the state of Rome, namely, Octavius Augustus, is treated with so little sympathy and respect by Shakespeare. He is introduced to us first in the scene in which Antony, Lepidus, and he are settling who shall be proscribed. His first words suggest a repellent character:

> *Your brother too must die; consent you, Lepidus?*

And although in *Antony and Cleopatra* he is given the opportunity to speak, rather drily, of the peace and order which he hopes the Roman world may in the end enjoy, the sympathies of the spectator are not at any moment enlisted towards this desirable end but are wholly drawn towards those two fascinating irresponsibles, Cleopatra and Mark Antony.

What does this mean? Well, probably nothing except that the mature Shakespeare found the exploration of character, with its mixture of weakness, courage, selfishness, self-sacrifice, love, folly, and calculation, more interesting by far than the politics of the Roman empire.

Whatever the faults of King James's government as King of Great Britain, his court was a generous patron of the theatre, and Shakespeare enjoyed fame, prosperity, and continuous court patronage, his plays being put on for every festival occasion. At the wedding of the King's daughter, the beautiful Princess Elizabeth, to a German prince, the Elector Palatine, Shakespeare's *The Tempest* was only one out of several of his plays which graced the festivities – though the most suitable, with its tale of love and magic and a princely betrothal. The masque shown by Prospero to Miranda and her Ferdinand, with its promise of peace and fruitfulness, was perhaps written in for the occasion. It was only partly successful as prophecy – theirs was indeed a happy and fruitful marriage – thirteen children – but Princess Elizabeth and her husband by inept policy triggered off the Thirty Years War in Germany, lost all their lands, and spent most of their lives in poverty-stricken exile.

At the time of the wedding rejoicings, Prince Charles, the future Charles I, was twelve years old. He grew up to be an enthusiastic patron of the arts and the theatre, and at his court – Shakespeare being nine years dead when he came to the throne – Shakespeare's plays were often given, indiscriminately mixed with lesser works by a new generation of dramatists – Carlell, Shirley, Davenant – as well as the securely established Ben Jonson and John Fletcher. The King's taste was for the poetic, the lyrical, the baroque. It is recorded that a performance of *Cymbeline* was greatly enjoyed by him.

The cautious suspicion of the populace felt by King James hardened in his son Charles into something like real dislike. 'He hates the people,' the observant Venetian agent reported in his dispatches. Worse, like some kings whom Shakespeare had depicted, he had no respect for their opinions and no sense of his mounting danger. And so it would happen that under his rule the English would no longer be 'singing the merry songs of peace to all their neighbours', but on the green slope of Edgehill in Shakespeare's country, a few miles only from the church where his bones lay and where 'a neat bust of that famous poet Mr William Shakespeare' was already a tourist attraction, his countrymen would stand arrayed in battle opposite each other, and in the afternoon sunlight of an October day in 1642 would 'cry "Havoc!" and let slip the dogs of war'.

1964

Good Company

'One who is very much delighted with being in good company,' wrote William Blake under a portrait of himself; and by 'good company' he did not mean merely good conversationalists. He used the expression in the wider sense from which our carelessness has narrowed it, the sense in which I once heard it aptly used to describe the novels of Scott – 'he is an author who always keeps good company'.

There is no doubt that we have failed lamentably of late years, both in literature and in life, to appreciate the value of good company. We have kept bad company for preference; I do not mean the company of the tough and the simple, which may be as good as any, but the company of the weak and the null. The high and the great qualities, or at least the expression of them, have been at a discount. There is something stoical and dramatic at first, something spuriously convincing in the reduction of all expressed feelings to a limited number of monosyllables, and coarse ones at that. But the adulation of the inarticulate leads in the end to the extinction of thought and feeling. If the supreme moments in life, whether of delight or anguish, are to be summed up in a grunt, it soon becomes impossible to distinguish the supreme moment from any other, or the moron from the genius.

This has been said before. The literary critics are all saying it, and the neo-romantic movement is already obediently at hand. But the suppression of thought and feeling has been more than a phase of literary fashion. In his *Critical Thoughts for Critical Days* Mr F. L. Lucas regrets the times when men were nourished on Plutarch. This is a significant regret, for Plutarch stands for a whole theory of moral education. To be nourished on Plutarch was to be nourished on great deeds greatly told, on the grandeur of the past, not on its trivialities. For a long time now, historians have ceased to regard this moral strengthening as an important part of their office. It is interesting to know how people lived in the past, what they ate and how they paid for it; everyone should know what the conditions of the working classes were in the early nineteenth century, and the economic causes of the Hundred Years War are not to be neglected. Yet be the mind never so full of facts, the education of the heart is incomplete if no time has been left for Sir Philip Sidney at Zutphen. Until towards the end of the eighteenth century, history was chiefly regarded as the moralist's book of examples. Without wishing to relegate a highly developed science to that place again, one may wonder whether it fulfils so innocent or even so useful a purpose to-day.

More insidious and more distressing than the propagandist perversion of history – an old and inevitable evil – is the grey meanness which has enveloped the whole study. One purpose of historians is surely to provide us with that good company which is there for the seeking. 'Lives of great men all remind us . . .' but they do nothing of the kind to-day, for we no longer read them, or at least not in that spirit. The good biographer is rare among us, the heroic biographer unknown. It was and is right to examine the sociological background and the economic structure of past society; but it is wrong in the process to lose sight of the great man and the great moment. We have more to learn to-day from the spectacle of a great man at a great moment than from any number of monographs on ancient wage-levels. For we have lost the art of living greatly, or assumed that it is no longer necessary to try.

The reasons for this flight from the heroic are evident; but they do not justify it. The social structure of Europe until very recently gave both the means of doing and of recording great deeds predominantly to one class. Those brightly illustrated children's histories which used to be in every nursery had a dozen valiant princes and heroic ladies for one Saint Joan. In our class-conscious age this unintended emphasis on the prince or the aristocrat became embarrassing; but it is futile to turn away from great minds and great actions because irrelevant factors have given them a snob value. More recently we have been afraid lest the adulation of individuals should lead to the heresy of the *Führerprinzip* and have sought to merge greatness with the undistinguished mass. But democracy should lead to a higher, not a lower, estimate of the individual, and what better standard of values have we by which to judge merit than the study of great men?

For the company of the great is good company as Shakespeare understood it, as Plutarch understood it. The past remains the source from which example and precept can still be drawn. Here, in spite of the debunkers and those who will spoil any good story by pointing out that it is poorly authenticated, here is our example and our hope. Men have been vile, stupid and self-seeking; but they have also been noble, compassionate and enduring. History has been lost too long in the desert of sociology and economics; it has been poured into the filthy conduit of racial theory or solidified in the rigid economic mould. It has lost sight of the individual and in so doing has forfeited its moral influence and more generous purpose. It should be the historian's business not to belittle but to illuminate the greatness of man's spirit.

1942

The Sense of the Past[*]

decorative divider

Ralph Penderel, the hero of that tantalizingly unfinished fragment by Henry James, *The Sense of the Past*, had written – it was his only literary achievement – an unpretending work called *An Essay in Aid of the Reading of History*. From all we ever hear of this work it sounds a not very original consideration of the magic of old places and old things, redeemed by the extraordinary intensity with which its author experienced a relatively commonplace romantic emotion. 'There are particular places', Ralph Penderel is supposed to have written, 'where things have happened, places enclosed and ordered and subject to the continuity of life mostly, that seem to put us into communication, and the spell is sometimes made to work by the imposition of hands, if it be patient enough, on an old object or an old surface.' There is nothing very remarkable in the sentiment, but we are asked to believe that Ralph Penderel's attachment to the past, or rather to surviving objects of the past, was a faith strong enough to work a miracle, and transfer him back a century in time.

Even in fiction such miracles are to be distrusted, although the surviving pages of *The Sense of the Past* suggest that Henry James would have explored the impossible situation with a rare subtlety. But I have pirated his title because it indicates the nature of a problem, part historical, part literary, which has increasingly concerned students of the past. Is there anything to be said for the cultivation of the sense of the past, for the attempt to make the imaginative leap from our own epoch to an earlier one? Is it helpful to serious historical inquiry to encourage some play of the imagination; is it a dangerous folly or an essential exercise? The frontier between scholarship and creative literature is a disputed one, over

[*] The Leslie Stephen Lecture at Cambridge, 1957.

416

which there has been much verbal combat. In this particular problem, that of historical imagination, literature has made significant contributions to scholarship and scholarship to literature.

We learn from the preface of the first edition to Henry James's posthumous fragment *The Sense of the Past* that he turned to this historical ghost story partly to take his mind off the troubles of the contemporary world during the First World War. His hero, too, found in the contemplation of the past a relief from the difficulties of the present. The desire for withdrawal, admitted or not, is often a powerful motive in driving the student, whether he be an amateur or a professional, towards the study of history. This element of escape implies also a certain lack of realism, which easily becomes a desire to idealize or at least to romanticize the past. The serious student of history, if he has, or is aware of, this weakness, has to be constantly on guard against it. On the other hand, without this romantic impetus, without this desire to remove from one age into another, to imagine and to share in the thoughts and feelings of a time remote from the present, historical inquiry would lack an essential element. Historical knowledge is in debt to the romantic writers, not so much for what they themselves did (though some of them made considerable advances in the study of the past), as for the deeper and wider scope that they gave to historical inquiry.

The summoning up of emotion like that of Henry James's hero, over some particular object or some particular place, hallowed by some great or supposedly great event, was not of course peculiar to the romantic or post-romantic epoch. Cicero spoke of 'the power of admonition that is in places'. Montaigne pondered on this way of feeling, in the sixteenth century: 'Is it nature, or by some error of fantasy, that the seeing of places that we know to have been frequented or inhabited by men whose memory is esteemed or mentioned in stories doth in some sort move and stir us up as much or more than hearing their noble deeds?'

Even the unsentimental Gibbon who was not, as he himself said, 'very susceptible of enthusiasm', was moved in this way by his first visit to Rome. 'After a sleepless night, I trod with a lofty step the ruins of the Forum. Each memorable spot where Romulus stood, or Tully spoke, or Caesar fell, was at once present to my eye, and several days of intoxication were lost or enjoyed before I could descend to a cool or minute investigation.' But that 'cool or minute investigation' was the proper occupation of an inhabitant of the Age of Reason, and Gibbon took care to let the intoxication evaporate before he began on the serious business of inquiry. To judge by this passage, he was also doubtful if these days of intoxication, which he admits he enjoyed, were not, by a more severe judgment, to be accounted 'lost'.

Dr Johnson, on the other hand, did not hesitate to ascribe some value to these intoxicating emotions. 'Far from me and from my friends be such frigid philosophy as may conduct us indifferent and unmoved over any ground which has been dignified by wisdom, bravery or virtue. That man is little to be envied whose patriotism would not gain force upon the plain of Marathon or whose piety would not grow warmer among the ruins of Iona.' This is already very close indeed to the frankly romantic fervour of John Keats:

> There is a charm in footing slow across the silent plain
> Where patriot battle has been fought, where glory had the gain;
> This is a pleasure in the heath where Druids old have been
> Where mantles grey have rustled by and swept the nettled green . . .

Clearly the feelings experienced, or manufactured, by Johnson, by Keats, and by many others, owed much less to knowledge of the past than they did to modern emotions; they were using historic sites not to strengthen their vision of the past for its own intrinsic interest, but simply to heighten their contemporary sensations of patriotism or piety. This is a very common and often enough, in literature, an effective use of history. It is clearly seen in Wordsworth's sonnet inspired by seeing the site of the victory of Dundee's Highlanders at Killiecrankie in 1689. The title underlines the point: 'In the pass of Killiecrankie, an invasion being expected, October 1803.' Dorothy Wordsworth, in her account of the Highland tour undertaken in that year, records that she and her brother, walking above the River Garry in the pass of Killiecrankie, spoke of the impending invasion; the thought of one deed of arms had instantly and naturally suggested the threat under which they were living. A story in Scott's Border Minstrelsy seems to have touched off the poem itself. A veteran Highland soldier at the battle of Sheriffmuir, maddened by the vacillations of the Jacobite commander, said 'Oh for one hour of Dundee.' Wordsworth in 1803 echoes the wish:

> Oh, for a single hour of that Dundee
> Who on that day the word of onset gave!
> Like conquest would the men of England see;
> And her foes find a like inglorious grave.

The feeling behind the Killiecrankie sonnet is one of contemporary hope and anxiety, merely heightened by reference to a past which is itself very imperfectly realized. Such lines as

> And Garry thundering down her mountain road
> Was stopped and could not breathe beneath the load
> Of the dead bodies

do not convey the impression that the poet saw what actually happened at Killiecrankie in any but theatrical terms. He makes the river human, but forgets that the men were.

This use of the past merely to heighten a modern effect is permissible in certain contexts, or at least to writers of commanding stature. But it was a common romantic vice to encourage a purely theatrical view of the past, as though history were an opera house inhabited by puppets striking noble attitudes preferably in picturesque settings, and quite removed from the ordinary embarrassments and distresses of mortal life. The facile muse of Mrs Hemans ran riot in this fashion when she turned her attention to the persecution of the Vaudois among Alpine scenery of great grandeur:

> Go, if thou lovest the soil to tread
> Where man hath nobly striven,
> And life, like incense, hath been shed,
> An offering unto Heaven.
>
> Far o'er the snows and round the pines,
> Hath swept a noble flood;

> *The nurture of the peasants' vines*
> *Hath been the martyrs' blood . . .*

and so on for any number of verses.

She had only to consider any factual account of religious, or any other, persecution to know that human life is not shed like incense. She had only to look into Milton's sonnet 'On the Late Massacre in Piedmont' and ponder nine words of it – 'whose bones lie scattered on the Alpine mountains cold' – and shudder at that, before tinkling on about men and women whose lives and deaths she had made not the slightest effort either to understand or imagine. Mrs Hemans's verses belong very much to her own time, but her type of sentimental historical fantasy is the worst legacy of the romantics and is still with us in other forms today. As a way of thinking about the past, it is devoid of any real curiosity about it, and springs merely from the desire to stimulate a flattering emotion or a vicarious thrill. It is the outlook of those ghoulishly concerned only with disaster, for whom no castle is complete without dungeons and *oubliette*, no ancient house without its priest's hole and secret panel, and who greedily lap up whatever nonsense has been invented about the alleged bloodstains on the floor.

But place has a real as well as a spurious charm and the more serious student of history does often find fascination in visiting the site of an event, quite apart from the value as evidence which it may also possess. The charm exercised by objects can be equally powerful. There is a fascination in the continued physical existence of chairs, tables, spoons, goblets, trenchers – things that were used and handled, not necessarily by the rare and famous whose names have survived, but simply by some of the millions whose names are as dead and forgotten as they are themselves.

The massive editing of documents over the last century, and the increasing use of such modern aids to research as photostat and microfilm, have relieved the historian of the continual necessity of manuscript research, though there will always remain certain things about which the manuscript and the manuscript only can enlighten us. But it is not necessity alone which draws the student of history constantly back to manuscript documents. There is a peculiar pleasure in the mere contact of the hand with the paper. I can speak with assurance only for that epoch to which most of my manuscript researches have been confined, the seventeenth century. Nothing seems to bridge the gap of the years so much as the unfolding and reading of ancient letters; sometimes minute particles of sand which had long adhered in some thick down stroke where the ink had been wet, detach themselves after three hundred years to blow away and join with yesterday's dust. This feeling for objects not merely as evidence but *for themselves* is not logically defensible; the moment we think about it we see that they do not really bring the past any nearer simply because they have existed, in one form or another, over a period of ten, twenty or a hundred generations. Landscape alters continuously. Gibbon when he trod with lofty step the ruins of the Forum was treading for the most part twenty or thirty feet higher than the footsteps of antiquity, though he did not use 'lofty' in that sense. Allowing for erosion, preservation and repair, very few surfaces of ancient things are in fact wholly ancient, and neither the ink nor the paper of that distracted complaint of the indiscipline of the Royalist cavalry, which I was reading last week, look the same to me as they did to Colonel John Boys, the governor of Donnington Castle, who wrote it, or to Prince Rupert who received it, in the spring of 1644.

It is not always the place itself but some element in it which, fused with our living knowledge, may suddenly vitalize the past. Some years ago in Switzerland I came almost by accident on the birthplace of Zwingli in the Toggenburg. The wooden peasant's house had been a good deal smartened up and restored. It had also been carefully furnished – in the praiseworthy and instructive modern manner – with such objects as would give the visitor an idea of a typical farmhouse interior at the latter end of the fifteenth century. But the house and all in it were vivid for me because I had lived for some months in childhood in a relatively modern farmhouse on the farther side of Switzerland, which was built on exactly the same plan. This is interesting evidence no doubt of the continuity of tradition in the building of Swiss farmhouses. But its immediate importance for me was that it brought a whole section of the past into my line of vision, almost into my personal experience: because I knew what it was like to live in such a house; knew the snug comfort of the wooden walls with the shutters closed at night, and the genial warmth from the oven, and – making considerable allowances for the differences between life in the last quarter of the fifteenth century and life in the first quarter of the twentieth – there remained at least a certain overlapping experience between Ulrich Zwingli and me.

Marc Bloch has said in those valuable and fragmentary reflections on *The Historian's Craft*, which he wrote during his years in the Resistance, and which were published posthumously after his capture and death, that the historian can only, in the last analysis, reconstruct the past by borrowing from, and applying, his own daily experience of life. Jacob Burckhardt was expressing the same idea in a rather different form when he described the purpose of his lectures to his students in Basle: he wished, he said, 'to make every member of my audience feel and know that everyone may and must take independent possession of what appeals to him personally'. 'Take independent possession' is the key phrase; for ultimately the understanding of the past, in so far as it is achieved at all, has to be independently achieved, by a sustained effort of the imagination working on a personal accumulation of knowledge and experience.

It was just this imaginative effort which the Romantics forced upon – or bequeathed to – historical scholarship. The foremost figure in this development was Sir Walter Scott. Leslie Stephen put the matter briefly and effectively when he spoke of the great step made by Scott when he observed that our ancestors were once 'as really alive as we are now'. The fashion for Sir Walter Scott's novels, not in the British Isles alone but over all western Europe, probably did more than any other single influence to awaken the minds of educated people to the vitality of the past. This is attested by the strongest possible witness, all the more telling because he is not altogether a favourable one. Leopold von Ranke has recorded, in an autobiographical fragment, the effect which the works of Scott had on him as a young man.

> The romantic historical works of Sir Walter Scott, which were well known in all languages and to all nations [he writes], played a principal part in awakening my sympathy for the actions and passions of

past ages. On me too they exercised their spell and I read his works more than once with the most lively interest. But I was also offended by them. Among other things it distressed me that in *Quentin Durward* he treated Charles the Bold and Louis XI in a manner quite contrary to historical evidence . . . Comparison convinced me that historical statements are more beautiful and in any case more interesting than romantic fiction. I turned away altogether from the latter and resolved that in my own works I would neither invent nor poeticize anything but would confine myself strictly to the facts.

There are two parts of this confession of Ranke, and the last half – the criticism of *Quentin Durward* – is very often quoted without reference to what precedes it. First Ranke admits and indeed emphasizes that Scott had made history a living interest to thousands of readers, and had therefore brought into being for the historian a larger and a more sympathetic audience than ever before. Only then does he go on to express his distress at the shortcomings of *Quentin Durward* as a work of history, and so to dedicate himself to the establishment of fact pure and unadorned. In the introduction to his first major work he reiterated this dedication in the form in which it is best known, and declared that it is the historian's task only to show what actually happened ('Er will bloss zeigen wie es eigentlich gewesen'). The ideal was not one that could be realized, but if Sir Walter Scott can claim the credit not only for awakening a new public but also for starting Ranke on his career of fruitful and massive achievement, our debt to him becomes greater than ever. Those who are sensitive for the honour of Scott as a student of history may also reflect that if the young Ranke had confined his attention to *Old Mortality*, *Rob Roy*, *Heart of Midlothian* and those novels in which Scott is historically and geographically at home with his subject, he would not have found him playing half so many novelist's tricks with his material.

But though the scholar may protest at the inaccuracy of the novelist or the dramatist, the imaginative writer undoubtedly brings to history a more concentrated creative power than the pure scholar usually possesses, and for that reason, however much his actual presentation may leave to be desired, he can more easily capture the interest of the beginner. This is a psychological fact that scholars have from time to time recognized: Marc Bloch wryly admitted that 'readers of Alexandre Dumas may be potential historians'.

How far the novelist, the dramatist or the poet may take liberties with historical material is a question which has often been debated, and it is a little surprising that Ranke, in his youthful innocence, expected Sir Walter Scott to treat the facts with scrupulous respect, for neither Schiller nor Goethe had done so in their dramas. Lessing had positively stated that the poet is master of history ('der Dichter ist Herr uber die Geschichte'), and had scolded Wieland for too slavishly following the facts in his play about Lady Jane Grey. Lady Jane's husband was weak, her father-in-law was ambitious and unpleasant; it would have made a better drama, Lessing argued, if Wieland had made proper use of his poetic licence to give greater nobility to these two characters.

A generation later Schiller, who as a professor and writer of history often showed a penetrating insight into the material available to him, stated the case for the use or abuse of historical material very interestingly in his criticism of Goethe's *Egmont*. The poet, he argued, can know, or not know – that is, he can use or disregard – the facts as best suits his treatment, but he ought not to leave out or misrepresent anything that is an integral part of the historical theme which he has selected. Goethe, in *Egmont*, has given his hero a sweet and loving mistress Claralchen; in order to do this he has eliminated Egmont's wife and nine (or perhaps eleven) children. Now Schiller argues that the tragedy of Egmont was the tragedy of a rooted and established man, tied by domestic, financial and family bonds to remain in the Netherlands and await the fatal coming of Alva, and that to take away his family is to alter the nature of his predicament, and consequently the nature of the conflict and calculations which delivered him into the hands of Alva when he might have sought safety – as the Prince of Orange did – in flight. Goethe's tragedy is consequently a very beautiful and touching tragedy about a simple, noble and trusting man, but it is not about the historic Egmont at all. This is sound and well argued, and is all the more impressive because in his *History of the Revolt of the Netherlands* Schiller's portrait of Egmont is a full and careful piece of historical characterization. What Schiller said in his criticism of Goethe is very much what Ranke was later to say of Scott – that the simple historical facts are more interesting and more revealing of human problems than any inventions can be. Yet when Schiller came to write his play on Joan of Arc, none of these wise considerations prevented him from making her die in the hour of victory on the battlefield, tenderly supported on either hand by Charles VII and the Duke of Burgundy – a disregard of facts that destroys the true poignant climax of Saint Joan's life; compared with such tampering Goethe's liquidation of the entire Egmont family is trivial.

Much can be said against the romantic approach to history. It tended too easily to the theatrical and the fanciful; also it came into being at an epoch when the conviction that human life was a constant, forward progress towards an attainable perfection was very strong. The romantic attitude to the past was therefore heavily tainted with the belief that the past existed chiefly to lead up to, and make way for, the glorious present and still more glorious future. Tennyson's hero of 'Locksley Hall' – 'heir of all the ages in the foremost files of time' – is only echoing Schiller's inaugural lecture at Jena: 'Ours are all the treasures which industry and genius, reason and experience have gathered in during the long ages of the world.' This inspiring frame of mind easily degenerated into the smugness which treated the past chiefly as something which could be compared to its disadvantage with the present, so as to demonstrate gratifying human progress. This was a commonplace of the nineteenth and even of the early twentieth century. We no longer believe in witchcraft. We no longer burn people alive for their religious beliefs. We have abolished public executions and installed bathrooms almost everywhere. How much more tolerant, how much cleaner, how much better we are than our forebears!

From this it is an easy step to regarding as worthy of study only such institutions and only such persons as can be shown to have some clear connection with the present, and of seeing or imagining in them only such elements as can be made to fit into the splendid story of progress towards the political or social ideal as we happen to see it. The tribal chieftain fighting the Romans, or the feudal baron defying his overlord became the conscious vindicators of nationalism or of representative government. More recently the leaders of peasant revolts have come to be hailed as the apostles of popular rights and modern democracy. The dialogue in Shaw's *Saint Joan* where the Earl of Warwick and the Bishop of Beauvais discuss the disturbing emergence of forces which they diagnose as liberalism and nationalism can be taken as an apt and ironical comment on the remarkably modern ideas and moods which even some writers of great learning have managed to detect in the past. From these misapprehensions the descent is quick towards the deliberate use of history to sustain whatever view of politics or morality suits the propagandist or the party in power.

In spite of all these drawbacks, possibly even because of them, the romantic approach to history made the understanding of the past possible in ways never attempted before. The romantics recognized the comprehensive nature of history as a study. 'In dem Gebiet der Geschichte liegt die ganze moralische Welt,' said Schiller in the same inaugural lecture at Jena; for him, the entire moral world was contained in history. There was no province of human endeavour outside the scope of history. To this general conception the romantics added the conviction that history can only be studied by entering sympathetically into the thought and feeling of the past.

This is an entirely subjective approach. The moment the student of history came into the inheritance of the romantic writers and took cognizance of the fact that his ancestors had been as much alive as he was himself, he could use his own living experience to imagine and project himself into their state of being. Nothing else would serve. The dangers of this technique are apparent, but so also are its merits. The alternative, the pre-romantic view, the approach of which Edward Gibbon is the most accomplished exponent, has its own brilliant clarity but the historian remains always at a distance from the events described, and gives the impression sometimes almost of inhumanity. To Gibbon, history really is 'little more than the register of the crimes, follies, and misfortunes of mankind'. 'Register' is a significant word. He can describe very vividly, but he constantly utters asides, or halts by the way for general reflection and comment, and by so doing he keeps the historic moment, and the men involved in it, at a safe distance both from himself and from the reader. The thunderbolts are being hurled far below the eminence on which Gibbon sits. Look for instance at his account of the murder of the Emperor Pertinax by the Praetorian Guard and the subsequent auction of the imperial title in the year AD 193. Gibbon describes the event with considerable drama – the 'two or three hundred of the most desperate soldiers' marching at noon through Rome 'with arms in their hands and fury in their looks, towards the Imperial Palace', then their confrontation by the grave and undaunted Emperor and his death. At this Gibbon concludes the chapter; he begins the next with an account of the origin and character of the Praetorian Guard – 'Such formidable servants are always necessary, but often fatal, to the throne of despotism' – and after this interlude which has broken the tension and removed us to a comfortable distance, he returns to the appalling scene from which he withdrew at the end of the previous chapter:

> Amidst the wild disorder Sulpicianus the emperor's father-in-law, and governor of the city, who had been sent to the camp on the first alarm of mutiny, was endeavouring to calm the fury of the multitude, when he was silenced by the clamorous return of the murderer, bearing on a lance the head of Pertinax. Though history has accustomed us to observe every principle and every passion yielding to the imperious dictates of ambition, it is scarcely credible that, in these moments of horror, Sulpicianus should have aspired to ascend a throne polluted with the recent blood of so near a relation, and so excellent a prince. He had already begun to use the only effectual argument, and to treat for the imperial dignity; but the more prudent of the Praetorians, apprehensive that in this private contract they should not obtain a just price for so valuable a commodity, ran out upon the ramparts and, with a loud voice, proclaimed that the Roman world was to be disposed of to the best bidder by public auction.

Again Gibbon breaks into the middle of the shocking event with a general reflection on the power of ambition over the human mind; and possibly because he removes himself, with a not unnatural distaste, from the predicament of Sulpicianus surrounded by the mutinous Praetorian Guard bent on slaughter, it does not occur to him that in this particular case Sulpicianus is more likely to have been actuated by downright fear than by ambition. Surely

Gibbon, had he been surrounded by this gang of murderers, would have admitted that fear was a powerful motive for anything that he then did. In what way, except by offering them money and at the same time trying to establish some authority over them, was the unfortunate Sulpicianus to get out of a very awkward place? Gibbon cannot and does not imagine himself in the predicament of Sulpicianus and an obvious element in the situation therefore escapes him. Gibbon's method enables him to describe and explore the surface of events with incomparable brilliance, but it rarely leads to any penetration below the surface. He does not, for instance, ask the question which must immediately occur to any modern reader of his account of the reign and fall of Pertinax – how came it that Pertinax who, according to Gibbon was both able, virtuous and beloved of the people, played his cards so badly that he came to grief after a reign of only eighty-six days?

In the post-romantic age such brilliant mapping of the surface of human events gives place to bold and by no means always successful attempts to penetrate the inner meaning, and human motives behind them. I have just made such an attempt myself, for I know nothing whatever about the character of Sulpicianus and may be wrong in suggesting that he would have been actuated on this occasion by the fear which would certainly have actuated me in his position – and which I believe would have actuated Edward Gibbon – but in the absence of more particular and definite evidence it seems a reasonable assumption that he was thinking at least a little of the immediate danger in which he stood.

Leaving aside the question of the interpretation of character (the most complicated, interesting and insoluble problem), the insistence of the romantics on the reality of past happenings, their strenuous demand that events should be thought out with the fullest sympathy, led as a natural result to a continual enlarging of historic inquiry. For though some confused imagination with fantasy and were content to imagine *in vacuo*, weaving ideas and images about the past from no knowledge at all, those seriously interested in the past fixed their imaginative ideas on anything and everything that they could find out about it. Hence, first the more or less sentimental attachment to places and things. Hence – it is triumphantly present in Scott – the desire to know about the physical surroundings, the leisure occupations, the way of living in all ranks of society, the food and drink, the ways of thought of our ancestors; and so ultimately to the widening of historical inquiry, beyond the political, the legal and the military, to embrace the social, the economic and all those branches of research and learning which are an integral part of historical study today.

But the act of imagination was often made with a glib and deceptive facility. The inquirer tended to over-emphasize all characteristics of thought and feeling that resembled his own, and even to see resemblances that were not there. Only gradually did students come to recognize the necessity for continual adjustments, for eliminating from our perspective of the past certain ways of thought which seem natural and essential to us but which did not always seem so.

Historians bred in the idea of national loyalty as almost a natural law found it extremely difficult to grasp the meaning of the different loyalties, no less strong, which have controlled and disciplined the political lives of men in the past. The meaning and sanctity of oaths is subject to infinite variations, and very few words like 'treason', 'fidelity', 'betrayal', mean exactly the same in contexts separated by long stretches of time. Meanwhile school text-books still to a great extent impose the idea that national history is the primary sort of history and thus create an unnatural division of the subject.

Our whole attitude to history, the framework within which we think of the past, the premises from which we explore and re-discover it, spring from habits of thought which are not themselves permanent. Thus, we think of ourselves as occupying a specific place in time; and of the individual life as interwoven with a continuous fabric of lives on this planet, past and future, stretching back and stretching forward. For us Man stands – or we ourselves stand – *historically* between Past and Future. This habit of thought which developed gradually in the Renaissance and Reformation has now become unconscious and instinctive with us. Whatever depth of religious faith we may also possess, we habitually think and calculate in these material terms, in a sequence of cause and effect over the years; we make deductions from the past and apply them to the future, in our own lives and in contemporary politics. In fact we think *historically*, and a very considerable effort is necessary if we are to adjust our way of thinking to a quite different outlook.

We only have to go a few centuries back in the history of Europe, to the Middle Ages, to find men framing their thought and action on entirely different assumptions. For them the individual life was set not in time, but in eternity; ideas and actions were to be thought of not in terms of time past and time future, but in terms of eternity in Heaven or Hell. This attitude persisted for many years alongside the way of thought which we have adopted and, in the sixteenth and seventeenth century either, and both, were possible. This different outlook makes religious persecution seem, if not less deplorable, at least more comprehensible.

The historian who fails to make allowance for these deep changes in ways of human thought is unlikely to develop an illuminating sense of the past. Without the capacity for entering into the fervour of our ancestors' beliefs we shall never gain any real understanding of the Reformation. Ranke said that to write justly of that earthquake epoch the historian must forget that he is a Catholic or a Protestant, but his advice is not altogether wise because a better account of the Reformation is more likely to come from the writer who is fanatical in some belief, than from one incapable of any. Our forefathers have been more traduced by those who interpret the Reformation purely as an economic, or purely as a political, conflict than by the violent partisans of either side.

A more subtle and continuous obstacle to the development of a sense of the past is that, simply by his position in time, the modern student knows too much. When he contemplates a past situation he is aware in some measure of what succeeded it and of how it was resolved. When he examines the motives and actions of an individual he knows already what their results will be. None of this knowledge formed a part of the situation at the time. Yet it is nearly impossible to expel it from the mind and to study a problem of the past as though the outcome was still unknown. I long in vain for the innocence I had when, as a child, I went to see John Drinkwater's play *Abraham Lincoln* without any previous instruction. (Its historical accuracy is not here relevant; what changes he made were mostly in the interests of dramatic simplification.)

Since I knew that right ought to triumph, I guessed at an early stage that this admirable ugly man in the funny top hat would be certain to win the war and liberate the slaves, but nothing had prepared me for the appearance of John Wilkes Booth, and for me at least the dummy pistol shot in a London theatre in the 1920s came as a shock almost as horrifying as that experienced by spectators at Ford's Theatre in Washington on 15 April 1865.

In vain have I longed to recapture that blessed ignorance – to be able for instance to consider the policy of William the Silent in the difficult year after he withdrew from Antwerp in July 1583, without the nagging knowledge that Balthasar Gerard is steadily drawing nearer, and that on 10 July 1584 he will put an end to the Prince of Orange's life and throw all his policies out of gear. In its perfect state – if such could be reached – the sense of the past should carry with it a capacity for eliminating the consciousness of the future, so that we could examine and consider the quality of an epoch *for itself alone*, without any attention to what came after it.

There is here an antagonism between two ways of looking at history, both interesting, both legitimate, but devoted to quite different ends. It is a valuable study, for instance, to trace the growth of the party system in English parliamentary government. We can distinguish and map its origins in the earlier half of the seventeenth century and note the increasing tension between crown officials, courtiers and court nominees on the one hand, and those who were outside the Court Circle. In the present state of our knowledge the growth of two parties, Court and Country, Tory and Whig, can be more or less clearly traced and demonstrated. But such a demonstration is relevant to the present rather than to the past. It is interesting because of what has happened *since* in English parliamentary life, but too much emphasis on it inevitably colours, and falsely colours, our attitude to what was actually happening in Parliament at the time, what men thought was happening, and what elements in the situation they themselves recognized and valued.

In the autumn of 1641, when the war between King Charles I and Parliament was rapidly approaching, and the House of Commons was very bitterly divided between the supporters of John

Pym and his opponents, Dr William Chillingworth was sent to
the Tower for having incautiously referred, in a private conversation, to the existence of two sides in the House of Commons. This
was denounced as a highly dangerous and subversive statement
because the House of Commons was, they most strenuously believed, a single and united body; one contemporary writer did not
scruple to compare it to 'the seamless robe of Christ'. Of course,
every sensible Parliament man in the autumn of 1641 could see
quite plainly that there *were* two sides in the House; but not one
of them had the additional advantage of knowing that this was the
beginning of the famous two-party system, a useful political invention of which their descendants would justly boast. On the
contrary they thought it disastrous; they saw it as contrary to all
that they believed about the function of Parliament, and they
pretended that it had not happened. Pym's followers explained
the fatal split in the House by assuming that *they* were the true
House of Commons and the only party of the Commonweal, and
that the King's supporters were a 'malignant faction'. The King's
supporters, with equal sincerity, assumed that they were the true
and undivided House of Commons and the others a 'juggling
junto', deliberately sowing division in the councils of the nation
and manoeuvring for personal power.

It is easier to understand the ultimate development of parliamentary government in England by tracing the party system to
its origins; but we shall understand the Civil War and the Long
Parliament better if we realize, not merely objectively, as a quaint
oddity, but with full intellectual sympathy, how repugnant this
idea of a divided Parliament was to the men of the time.

In a somewhat different sense from that which Schiller had in
mind when he said that the poet was at liberty to know or not to
know historical facts as it suited him, the historian, who really
wants to understand a situation as it was, must also know, and not
know; he must accumulate one kind of knowledge, everything
immediate to a particular situation, and reject another kind –
everything which subsequently sprang from that situation, or
came after it. He must divest his mind as far as he can – and it will
not be very far – of the wisdom, the philosophy, the prejudice,
the ways of thought and social behaviour that belong to his own
age; in their place he must try to learn and – temporarily at least –

to make his mind accept, the ideas of a quite different epoch. It goes without saying that this cannot be done without a formidable accumulation of evidence for the mind to work on.

The romantic attitude to history – this projection of sympathy into a past age – led to certain follies and excesses, and to a sentimental facility in summoning up ready-made emotions about places and things associated with the past. It led on the one hand to a picturesque idealization and poeticization of history, but it also led to a much more human and vivid appreciation of the past fate and actions of men. It encouraged in the serious inquirer a more accurate and a much fuller conception of the past. It led him to make a sustained effort fully to understand, or in Burckhardt's phrase 'to possess', the past. He tried – and still tries – to take hold of it through knowledge, and through imagination working on knowledge, so that the sense of the past is in the end no vague and hollow dream, but something based on wide and minute comprehension of assembled facts.

In the illuminating notes which Henry James left on that projected and unfinished novel, *The Sense of the Past*, he describes the increasingly painful predicament in which his hero was to have found himself during his intrusion into a previous century. It was one thing, Henry James wrote, 'to live in the Past with the whole spirit, the whole candour of confidence and confidence of candour, that he would then naturally have had – and a totally different thing to find himself living in it without those helps to possibility, those determinations of relation, those preponderant right instincts and saving divinations'.

Poor lost young man! But the historian need not (even in the gardens of Versailles) either fear or hope for one of those kinks or knots in time, dear to writers, that will project him suddenly into an earlier epoch. He will remain fixed and rooted in his own time with nothing but evidence, imagination and his own experience to minister to the 'sense of the past'. He may have now and again, an occasional flash of those 'right instincts and saving divinations', but he can never hope to acquire, however long and laborious the study, that 'confidence of candour and candour of confidence' that our ancestors had in their own age; and that we have only in ours.

1957

'Good King Charles's Golden Days'*

In England this year on 29 May falls the three hundredth anniversary of the Restoration of King Charles II. There was a time when 29 May was annually commemorated in England as Oak-Apple Day, in allusion to the oak tree in which King Charles II hid himself from Cromwell's troopers after his escape from the battlefield of Worcester. Although this date has long since ceased to be generally celebrated, there are still some institutions, with special reason to be grateful to King Charles II – Chelsea Hospital, for instance, which was founded by him for old soldiers – who remember and keep the anniversary of his happy Restoration. But, celebrations apart, King Charles II has always held a specially favourable place in the popular memory of the English.

In the long view of English history, the most significant thing about the Restoration of 1660 is its permanence. After the uneasy experiment in other kinds of government, the monarchy came back to stay. Changes of personnel and changes of dynasty were later to occur, and profound changes in the constitutional emphasis on the Crown; but the monarchy itself has remained from that day to this.

I cannot in an hour do justice to one of the liveliest, and certainly one of the most popular, characters in English history, the King himself. Still less can I do justice to the whole epoch loosely spoken of as the Restoration, and rather too flatteringly called in the old song 'Good King Charles's Golden Days'. They were not golden for everyone and certainly not 'golden' in politics, though they were wonderfully rich in intellectual endeavour, in achievement and in some of the arts. But I hope you will bear with a

* Lecture given at the Folger Shakespeare Library Washington, USA, 1960.

necessarily brief, personal, and perhaps capricious selection of some elements in an epoch as full of contrasts and problems as any in the history of the English-speaking peoples.

King Charles II entered London on 29 May 1660, eleven years and four months after the execution of his father, eight and a half years after he himself had fled in disguise from the Sussex coast with a price on his head. The whole nation seemed to have gone mad with joy. Dover and Canterbury, which twenty years before on the eve of the Civil War had witnessed violent Puritan demonstrations, now blazed with enthusiasm for the returned King. The roads and lanes of Kent were thronged with excited subjects come to see their new sovereign:

> *And loyal Kent renews her arts again*
> *Fencing her ways with moving groves of men.* . . .

The rather daring metaphor came from a very young poet, John Wilmot, Earl of Rochester, at this time an innocent twelve-year-old; he had no doubt been urged on by a zealous tutor to display his precocious talent in an ode to his returning sovereign, nicely calculated to remind him that he was the orphan son of that rather intermittently gallant Cavalier, Harry Wilmot, who had accompanied Charles on his desperate escape after the final defeat of the Royalist forces at the Battle of Worcester.

A hundred maidens all in white received the King with garlands and strewed flowers before him at Deptford, and all along the way the country gentlewomen came out to salute him and, not knowing the court fashion of kissing hands, very simply lifted up their faces to be kissed. In the streets of London the people were drinking the King's health on their knees, which Samuel Pepys thought a little exaggerated. But there was, in some hearts at least, a sense of awe and amazement, an uplifted, almost a rapt gratitude to Providence in the midst of all these noisy rejoicings. Did the King himself feel it? It seems improbable; a young man of thirty with a vigorous constitution, he had 'as little mixture of the seraphic part as ever man had'. All that he wrote to his favourite sister on the occasion was that his 'head was prodigiously dazed by the acclamations of the people and by quantities of business'. Charles II never much cared for quantities of business.

When on the evening of that glorious day the small group of venerable bishops, the survivors of the Anglican underground, assembled in King Henry VII's Chapel in Westminster Abbey to celebrate their Te Deum, they did so without the presence of the King. He was too tired to come. That was his official excuse, but there may also have been policy in it. The vexed question of the nation's religion was still unsettled and he did not want to show his hand too soon.

On his triumphal entry the King had passed through the Strand, that vital thoroughfare from the City of London to the royal palace and Parliament House at Westminster. It was in the Strand, on the eve of the Civil War, that his unfortunate father had been surrounded by throngs of Londoners clamouring for privilege of Parliament in such terms and with such faces and gestures that for the only time in his life that wrong-headed but intrepid King showed signs of personal fear. But the Strand on this May afternoon eighteen years later echoed only to the vibrating plaudits of a people gone mad with joy at the King's return. It was there that John Evelyn, a devoted if rather cautious Royalist, gave thanks with a full heart:

> I stood in the Strand and beheld it and blessed God: and all without one drop of blood . . . for such a Restoration was never seen in the mention of any history, ancient or modern . . . nor so joyful a day and so bright ever seen in this nation.

So Evelyn wrote on the day of King Charles's return. Twenty-five years later, when the King, exhausted by debauch in his fifty-fifth year, succumbed to a stroke, John Evelyn looked back in somewhat different terms on the reign which he had hailed with religious thankfulness:

> God was incensed to make his reign very troublesome and un-prosperous by wars, plagues, fires, loss of reputation by a universal neglect of the public for the love of a voluptuous and sensual life, which a vicious court had brought into credit. I think of it with sorrow and pity when I consider of how good and debonair a nature that unhappy prince was: what opportunities he had to make himself the most renown'd King that ever swayed the British sceptre. . . .

Evelyn was looking on the dark side. There had been redeeming features, of which, as an ardent member of the Royal Society, he must have been conscious, but he felt above all the decay of morality and religion at the very heart of government. In that particular emphasis he showed himself a Cavalier of the old school for whom firmness in religion was the very heart of civil government.

Evelyn's attitude to the King himself is one more of sorrow than of anger, and the same view is reflected in other statements about the King, most fully in that famous estimate of him composed by George Savile, Marquis of Halifax, the minister of his later years, who has left in his *Character of King Charles II* a classic portrait of an intelligent man gradually undermined by indolence and good nature. 'This prince', he wrote, 'might more properly be said to have gifts than virtues, as affability, easiness of living, inclinations to give and to forgive . . .'

These are admirable and useful qualities in a ruler but they are not enough. There must be, in the direction of public affairs – and the burden of direction at this epoch still fell on the King – a sustained energy, a constant, not merely an intermittent, watchfulness, and a clear sense of purpose. But Charles, as Halifax observed, if he could find a strong minister to do the job for him, 'chose rather to be eclipsed than to be troubled', and in many matters 'the power of nature was too strong for the dignity of his calling, which generally yielded as often as there was a contest'.

Too much had been expected of the King at first. His vigorous manner and fine active presence seemed to belie the stories of him as an indolent voluptuary which had been industriously spread by his enemies during the Cromwellian regime.

> *His manly posture and his graceful mien*
> *Vigor and youth in all his motions seen;*
> *His shape so comely and his limbs so strong,*
> *Confirm our hopes we shall obey him long*

wrote the court poet Edmund Waller, conveniently forgetting the streams of praise that he had poured out on Oliver Cromwell a year or two back.

Samuel Pepys, who observed the King on board the ship which carried him home from exile, was evidently both surprised and delighted to see him 'here and there, up and down, very active and stirring'. He entertained the company with a lively account of his hairbreadth escapes from the Cromwellians on the flight after his defeat at the Battle of Worcester; it was a good story and he told it well, but in the course of the next five and twenty years he was to tell it rather too often.

Samuel Pepys was singularly well placed for watching the unfolding of affairs: his work at the Navy Office put him in a particularly advantageous place to notice the interaction between the character of the Court, where decisions were taken, and the service which the King got from the different strata of officials, contractors, and those involved in the administration of the Navy. Irresponsibility and casualness at the centre could not but spread downwards, and although the King was genuinely interested, and knowledgeable, about the ships, and the Duke of York was in time to prove an able administrator, there were almost limitless opportunities for corruption and private profit. 'Good God, to see what a man might do, were I but a knave,' Pepys wrote, of a contract to supply three thousand pounds' worth of masts for ships. 'The whole business from beginning to end being done by me out of the office, and signed to by them upon the reading of it to them, without the least care of consultation either of quality, price, number of need of them [i.e., masts] only in general that it was good to have a store.'

This kind of thing was not new in spirit. It could be paralleled from the equally casual (though less immoral) court of Charles I. There was indeed a real effort made in the time of Charles II by successive Treasurers to put public finance on a sounder basis – if only to strengthen the power of the Crown – and this was hampered as much by ignorance of the principles of sound finance as by carelessness and corruption. All the same, the feckless behaviour of the Court was the most noticeable feature of the situation and was seized on by popular opinion as the cause for the incessant drain on the royal finances and the evils ensuing from it.

The conduct of the Court began to trouble Pepys little more than a year after the Restoration. 'The lewdness and beggary of the court, which I am afeared will bring all to ruin again,' he wrote on 16 August 1661, and a month later, 'I do not see that the King takes any care to bring in any money but thinks of new designs to lay out money'. The King's dislike of hard work, his 'idle courses', his dallying with Lady Castlemaine – whom Pepys thought so beautiful that he could forgive her anything – make recurrent appearances in his *Diary*, noted not with disloyalty or censoriousness but with a kind of loyal disappointment and anxiety.

It must be borne in mind that the Court was not merely a decorative addition to society, but was in effect the centre both of the government and of the civil service. There were of course many decent and sober officials at the court of Charles II striving to do their jobs efficiently, but the luxurious and improvident habits of those most closely associated with the King crossed the lines of good management at all points with bribery, jobbery, and corruption.

The reign of King Charles II (in spite of certain valiant but I think misguided attempts to whitewash it) must rank, politically speaking, as one of the least edifying in British annals. Yet, to be fair, the fault lay as much in the political atmosphere of the time, what we have come to call the 'climate of opinion', as with individuals. The return of the King had taken place without blood, and John Evelyn, giving thanks in the Strand, was not the only one who felt infinite and justified gratitude for this great mercy. But there was an evil, or rather a weakness, inherent in this intense and nationwide feeling of relief. The experience of the Civil War years, the disorders, proscriptions, persecutions and the insecurity of life and property inseparable from civil war and its aftermath; the disturbance of ancient institutions; the infringement of property rights; the threatened overturning of the entire social hierarchy by the egalitarian ideas of some of the sects and the political action of the Levellers – these things even more than deaths in battle and on the scaffold had created a morbid fear lest the troubles should return. It was still possible to appeal to this fear as late as 1681, when it caused the downfall of Shaftesbury and the Whigs. Dryden put it into words – words which came very much from the heart – in *Absalom and Achitophel*:

What prudent man a settled throne would shake?
For whatsoe'er their sufferings were before
That change they covet makes them suffer more . . .
All other errors but disturb a state
But innovation is the blow of fate . . .
The tampering world is subject to this curse
To physic their disease into a worse.

Fear of civil disturbance is apparently equated by Dryden, as by many others of his generation, with fear of anything new and any motion for reform. Fear of this kind is never a very inspiring political sentiment. Men who are guided by the desire to avoid something rather than to create something rarely achieve anything notable, and this is the dominant mood in the opening years of the reign, and recurrent throughout.

Possibly this mood explains the contrast between the negative character of the political history of the reign and the creative and affirmative spirit which is visible in almost all other spheres: art, literature, the sciences, and economic life. But in politics, fear and caution were interlinked, as they so often are, with extreme vindictiveness towards those persons and those ideas which are thought dangerous.

The King, in words nobly drafted for him by the Chancellor, Clarendon, had said in the Declaration issued from Breda on the eve of his recall that he desired to see 'all notes of discord, separation and difference of parties . . . utterly abolished among all our subjects, whom we invite and conjure to a perfect union among themselves under our protection . . .'. So in December of the same year, and again in the words of Clarendon, he spoke of the Act of Indemnity as 'the principal cornerstone which supports this excellent building'. As far as indemnity for past offences was concerned, the number of those executed at the Restoration for crimes against the King and his father was relatively few. In the words of Keith Feiling: 'Fourteen lives paid for two civil wars.' In this at least the King's natural leaning to mercy prevailed. But as for destroying all notes of discord and separation, this was prevented by the action of King Charles's first and longest Parliament, the so-called Cavalier Parliament, which was resolved to stop all danger of rebellion and civil war in future by persecuting those whom they believed responsible.

The survivors of the Civil Wars still living in 1660, who were naturally very many, and the younger generation who had grown up in those disturbed times, not having had the advantage of studying modern theories on the causes of the war, associated it less with the financial circumstances of the gentry than with the dangerous political doctrines enshrined in Puritan religious beliefs. The war, as they saw it, had been caused by the desire to elevate the ecclesiastical above the royal authority in the Calvinist fashion. 'The nature of Presbyterian government', as King Charles I had said, 'is to steal or force the Crown from the King's head.' His Cavalier Anglican subjects wholeheartedly agreed with him. Equally dangerous in their view were the numerous sects who set up the inner light and the individual conscience as the sole arbiters of right and wrong. Halifax summed up the common belief of the Anglican gentry in these years in the phrase that it was 'impossible for a Dissenter not to be a rebel'.

In this sense fear created an active – indeed an actively vicious – policy of religious persecution, which went against the judgment and the inclination of the King. In other ways the Cavalier Parliament was content to leave the constitutional situation in, or rather to restore it to, the very condition it had been in at the out-break of the Civil War: that is, with a fatal division in the powers of the State. One vital power, that to grant money, was in the hands of Parliament. The other vital power, that to use force, was in the hands of the Crown.

To understand the peculiar weakness of the Restoration settle-ment from the point of view of Parliament it is necessary to look back for a moment at the situation in 1642 on the eve of the Civil War. At that time Parliament, under the leadership of John Pym, had established its right to control taxation, and it had gravely weakened the King by abolishing the prerogative courts, the principal instruments by which he enforced his will. But there remained the King's power over the armed forces of the kingdom, and so long as this was in his hands there was something more than a possibility that he would be able to use it to regain control of the situation and reverse, or make of no account, the legislation to which he had been compelled to give his consent. This was exactly what King Charles I had planned to do, so that the question which inevitably precipitated Civil War in 1642 was just precisely this one, the question of authority over the armed forces. Pym claimed it for Parliament because he did not believe that any of the legislation passed under compulsion by the King was safe so long as the King was in a position to raise an army. Charles I in answer absolutely refused to give up the 'power of the sword' which 'God hath put into our hands'.

Again, at the time of his defeat in 1646, King Charles I had been willing to suggest a temporary, but only a temporary, relinquishment of this right. In one of his more tragic letters to Queen Henrietta Maria he argued that a temporary concession would only prune the tree of sovereignty, it would not cut it down: 'As for monarchy I will positively say that the root is left entire, and with God's blessing infallibly to spring up again as fair as ever . . . for all is but loppings, no rooting up, and being to return as entirely to the Crown as if I had entered London at a breach.'

King Charles II coming back in 1660 did not, in his father's phrase, 'enter London at a breach', did not storm and conquer the city at the head of an army and impose his will on Parliament by force of arms – as his father had tried to do, and had nearly succeeded in doing. Yet Charles II in all essential points won the Civil War which his father had lost. The right of the King to control the armed forces, the right for which the Parliament of 1640 had gone to war, was given away with a gesture that would seem slavish, were it not so apparently careless, by the Parliament of 1661. 'The sole and supreme power, government, command and disposition of the militia and of all forces by sea and land and places of strength is . . . and ever was the undoubted right of His Majesty,' they asserted, and the King, speaking on the same subject, said with truth that 'the questioning of this right was the fountain from which all our bitter waters flowed'. Simply to prevent the bitter waters from flowing again – that was the only guiding idea of the Cavalier Parliament in its earlier years.

Thus, rather than risk trouble, they left the coercive power, entire and unquestioned, to the King; which meant of course that he might one day use it to establish his absolutism. James II tried to do so, and it was occasionally also, in his later years, in the mind of Charles II.

The Cavalier Parliament checked in turn the various liberties and privileges that could be shown to have endangered the peace of England in 1642. Since pamphlets had undoubtedly done their part in the disturbances and – in the words of the poet George Wither

> Added fuel to the direful flame
> Of civil discord and domestic blows
> By the incentives of malicious prose

they naturally legislated to control the 'incentives of malicious prose' and brought in the Licensing Act to control publications. (The critics of the government were to circumvent this by publishing pamphlets with false imprints and by circulating verses and lampoons in manuscript, but it was dangerous work.) Another measure taken to prevent a repetition of the disturbances which had led to the Civil War was the Act against Tumultuous Petitioning. It could be shown that the presentation of petitions to Parliaments in the 1640s had been the cause of inspired rioting; in future therefore no more than ten people at a time were to present petitions. I have already commented on the ferocious legislation against Puritans of all kinds, or Dissenters as they now came to be called. This legislation, which not only drove them from the Church but prevented them from exercising their own religion, even in private, or from holding any offices in the country or the corporations, was designed to render them politically harmless. In this again the Cavalier Parliament was bearing out the ideas not only of King Charles I but of King James I, ideas against which their predecessors in the early Parliaments of the century had fought with great vigour.

King Charles I had regarded control of the pulpit and control of the sword as the two essential practical supports of Divine Right. King Charles II, over the martyred blood of his father, got them both, almost without asking. It was the complete abandonment, and in the religious question the reversal, of all that earlier

Parliaments had struggled for. No wonder that Andrew Marvell, a steadfast and disillusioned Parliamentarian of the old school, said that no King since the Conquest had been so absolutely powerful at home as King Charles II.

Some of the legislation of the Civil War epoch was however retained. The right of Parliament to control taxation had been settled before the outbreak of the Civil War and remained untouched, so that Charles II was to be financially in the power of his Parliaments, as much or even more than his predecessors. This had not been the first intention of the Cavalier Parliament; they had meant to grant the King an income sufficient to his needs, but did not do so owing to a serious miscalculation on the yields of the taxes assigned to him. But although the importance of this financial control of Parliament over the King has been very much insisted on by historians, there were naturally ways by which the King could evade it; Charles II found an effective one in taking money from the King of France. In the constitutional struggle, the money power, which has been so much emphasized of recent years, is really in the last resort less significant than the power of the sword.

King Charles II well understood the realities of royal power, though he talked much less about Divine Right than his father or his grandfather, and his court was certainly not a fit setting for a King who claimed to represent God on earth. Something more is needed to account for the moral laxity of this court than simply the reaction from the too great austerity of the Cromwellian period. Neither is it altogether fair to attribute the behaviour of the King and the smart set to the insidious effect of the exile which some of them had spent in France. The English have always been far too ready to attribute any laxity of morals – with total injustice – to the bad example of their neighbours the French. Only a minority of the young people at the court of King Charles II had in fact spent much time in France, and in many ways the character of the court remained obstinately English in tone, in its lack of formality, its horseplay, even in its more pastoral moments. There is a delightful account by Pepys of the King and Queen seen riding together on a July day in 1663, the Queen looking 'mighty pretty' in a 'white laced waistcoat and a crimson short petticoat and her hair dressed *à la négligence*'. The King was holding her hand, but in spite of this idyllic touch, his mistress, Lady Castlemaine, was also of the party, in a yellow plume, looking very cross. This was not on account of the Queen, but because her new rival, Frances Stewart, was also present, 'with her hat cocked and a red plume, with her sweet eye, little Roman nose, and excellent taille'. Later on the ladies all got off their hoses and Pepys saw them giggling and whispering together and trying on each other's hats like a party of schoolgirls.

The rather hoydenish coquetry of many of the court ladies, as recorded by Pepys, Grammont and others, and the tricks, masquerades, and practical jokes of Rochester, all seem to be in the familiar tough Anglo-Saxon style. The prevalence of French sartorial fashions and the increasing use of French words and phrases do not indicate any deep saturation with French culture.

English or French, the steep decline in moral standards was an inescapable fact. It can be traced in the comments of Samuel Pepys from month to month. Though he fell himself, he always retained his respect for the stronger conventions of his youth; in the early days of the Restoration he will write a pious 'God forgive me' even for such harmless slips as tuning his lute or reading French romances on a Sunday; but later these parentheses become more rare. The King had opened the reign with a proclamation against vicious or debauched persons frequenting the Court. But this presumably remained a dead letter, because he set an immediate example by taking Barbara Palmer for his mistress and rewarding the complaisant husband with the Earldom of Castlemaine. The scandal which soon followed, that of the Duke of York's secret marriage to Anne Hyde and his efforts to repudiate her, added an element of the sordid to the scene.

The younger set had grown up in peculiar conditions. Some of them had been, like the King himself, in exile, leading the aimless, demoralized existence of people who cannot fix themselves permanently because they live in constant expectation of being called home. Living uncertainly, short of money, psychologically unsettled by hope deferred but never lost, very few of them had the concentration of purpose or lively enough interests to spend their time well – like Prince Rupert, who studied engraving and helped to evolve the art of mezzotint, or Sir Robert Moray, who gave himself up to those mathematical and astronomical studies which were later to make him a moving spirit in the Royal Society.

Others of the younger generation had grown up in England, where the court of Cromwell, though not as ridiculous as the Cavaliers later liked to pretend it had been, could neither be an accepted social centre nor a model of fashion to them. They went their own way, an aimless and in many ways a selfish society, with the selfishness that comes of political oppression. The struggle to evade the pressure of persecution, to crawl out from under the fines and the taxation, to wangle a way round the laws and restraints which bound them – all this created a corrupt habit of mind, an irresponsibility towards the commonweal which could not be immediately shaken off with the return of the King and the alteration in their position.

Alexander Brome, whose witty, unpretentious verses had been popular among the Cavaliers since the beginning of the Civil War, often reveals in the sour little songs of his Commonwealth period the prevalent, disillusioned anti-idealist attitude which was common to Royalists in these years and was the background against which the younger generation had grown up:

> *Each wise man first best loves himself,*
> *Lives close, thinks and obeys;*
> *Makes not his soul a slave to's pelf*
> *Nor idly squanders it away*
> *To cram their maws that taxes lay*
> *On what he does or says:*
> *For those grand cords that man to man do twist*
> *Now are not honesty and love*
> *But self and interest.*

This was the Cavalier mood of the Commonwealth; and it bred, inevitably, the corruption and self-interest which distinguished so many of the next generation. This is, I think, the real source of the moral collapse which marks court society in the reign of Charles II, and not French influence or foreign fashions.

The King and many of his friends who were now in their late

twenties and early thirties – an age at which their fathers would long since have settled down to their responsibilities – felt that they had time to make up in the pursuit of pleasure. They set themselves at once to do so; the effect of this, to use a modern phrase, was that the age group who were sowing their wild oats in the 1660s was much larger than usual. Many of the King's war-disturbed generation never settled down at all, and their behaviour sometimes infected even those a little older than themselves. It was with dismay that Samuel Pepys saw his patron and employer, the Earl of Sandwich, begin to slide downhill. At the Restoration, Sandwich was thirty-five years old. As a youth of eighteen he had been an ardent soldier in the Puritan-Parliamentary cause; he had fought at Marston Moor and at Naseby and had been very close to Cromwell. If he was always at heart neither better nor worse than an *homme moyen sensuel*, he had kept a grip on himself in the Puritan era. But a few months after the Restoration he was recounting court scandals to Pepys in a tone of voice that made Pepys record: 'I perceive my Lord is grown a man very indifferent in all matters of religion and so makes nothing of these things.' A couple of years later when Sandwich had wandered a great deal further down the primrose path, Pepys sighs his regret: 'Though I do not wonder at it being a man amorous enough and now begins to allow himself the liberty that he says everybody else at court takes.'

The account of the court left by Anthony Hamilton, writing in the character and from the recollections of his brother-in-law, the Comte de Grammont, exposes on every page a total suspension of all moral restraint. These so-called *Mémoires de . . . Grammont* were published in 1713 and are said to have become at once *'la bréviaire de la jeune noblesse'* in the almost equally debauched period of the French Regency. Here perhaps we have an example of the English corrupting the French? Hamilton's account covers only the opening years of the reign, but the excesses continued until its close. The Queen, who had been distressed by the insolence of Barbara Castlemaine in the first year of her marriage, was seen by Sir John Reresby on the verge of tears at the insolence of Louise de Quérouaille in the last year of her husband's reign.

But this aspect of court vices has had more than its fair share of attention, both at the time and since. Much more really serious was the decline in honesty and competence that went with it. 'How loose the court is,' wrote Pepys in November 1663, 'nobody looking after business but every man his lust and gain.' Of course there were exceptions: honest officials, hard-working servants of the Crown like Pepys himself, and virtuous young ladies. There was Margaret Blagge, John Evelyn's pious and saintly spiritual friend, besides others of more ordinary and less ostentatious virtue.

The King and his courtiers had serious and intelligent interests alongside the frivolity. The King to the end of his life was intermittently capable of energy and courage. His interest in the Navy, his rather more intermittent interest in trade and the natural sciences, were never wholly overlaid by the indolence and debauchery which steadily grew on him. He could show himself in a crisis, like that of the Exclusion Bill, to have acute political judgement and a very cool head. But when everything has been said in his favour, it is still true that the atmosphere of the Court was not one to which a thoughtful father, like Sir John Reresby, wished to expose his son, even though coming to Court was the best if not the only way to get on in the world.

Yet there did come out of this Court – and it is its principal claim to respect – a great deal of intelligent patronage. This is the age of Henry Purcell in music and of Christopher Wren in architecture. It might be added that it is the age of Milton in poetry, but the age of Charles II can really take no credit for that accident of survival and genius. The poet who truly represented their best, and at times their worst, was Dryden. But some merit for encouraging the Royal Society does undoubtedly belong to the King and his court. The observant French traveller, Sorbière, visiting England in the early sixties, had been at once struck by the intellectual and scientific interests, not of all the Court, but of some of them, and especially of the King. He explained it by reference to the previous years of the Commonwealth:

Persons of quality having no court to make, applied themselves to their studies; some turning their heads to chemistry, others to mechanism, mathematics or natural philosophy; the King himself has been so far from being neglectful of these things, that he has attained to so much knowledge as has made me astonished when I had audience of His Majesty. . . . The English nobility are all learned and polite. . . .

'*All* learned and polite' is an optimistic estimate; Sorbière was evidently lucky in the people he met. But, although his view appears to contradict my own estimate of the effect of the Cromwellian period on 'persons of quality', I think he is probably right in attributing the growth of serious tastes to these years of unsettled government. The contradiction is not as complete as it sounds, for allowance has to be made for different temperaments. In a majority the uneasy years of political oppression created cynicism and irresponsibility, more especially in personal and political morals, but – as modern experience in political oppression has also shown – there is usually a minority who seek relief and release from an oppressive situation in the free atmosphere of knowledge, especially in the pursuit of such branches of knowledge as have no bearing on politics. In the seventeenth century, science had indeed very little bearing on politics.

Sorbière in another descriptive passage does seem to suggest that there was a distinction at Court between those who really understood and were interested in the new sciences and those who were not. He describes with great approval Sir Robert Moray 'making machines in St James's Park and adjusting telescopes. All this we have seen him do with great application and undoubtedly to the confusion of most of the courtiers, who never mind the stars and think it a dishonour to concern themselves with anything but inventing new fashions.'

The Royal Society is one of the real and lasting glories of the reign of Charles II. If the political story is almost wholly depressing, in the intellectual sphere the gains and achievements were outstanding. Yet both what was good and what was bad in the reign of Charles II may be seen to grow from the peculiar conditions of the years which preceded it. It can hardly be argued that the movement towards scientific investigation has any obvious connection with the rule of the Puritans – though men of Puritan sympathies were among its greatest exponents – but in fact speculation in the natural sciences had been increasing over all western Europe in the previous seventy years. A number of societies had been founded which were, like the Royal Society, devoted to the pursuit of this kind of knowledge. These came into being in Rome, Florence, Paris and several cities of Germany. But it was under the very shadow of the Civil Wars, and rather as a protest against them, that in 1646 those gatherings of thinkers and scientists began to take place in England from which the Royal Society grew. John Wallis, the mathematician, described their first meetings in these terms: 'We barred all discourse of divinity, of state affairs, and of news, other than what concerned our business of philosophy.' Thomas Sprat in his *History of the Royal Society* wrote: 'Their first purpose was no more than only the satisfaction of breathing a freer air, and of conversing in quiet with one another, without being engaged in the passions and madness of that dismal age.' At the time of the earliest meetings, the young Robert Boyle, then only nineteen and much flattered to be asked to be present, described his colleagues as 'men of . . . capacious and searching spirits . . . that endeavour to put narrow-mindedness out of countenance' – a very remarkable endeavour in a moment of fanatic political and religious warfare.

The remarkable group of men with whom it all started – Wallis, Wilkins, Ward, Boyle, and a little later the young and brilliant Christopher Wren – joined with the returning exiles like Robert Moray to form the Royal Society under the King's patronage soon after the Restoration. The King, his brother the Duke of York, and his cousin Prince Rupert were all strong supporters of it, and a very large number of the nobility, without necessarily understanding very much about it, enrolled themselves as supporting members.

Intellectually, the reign of King Charles II was marked by an eager and adventurous spirit, a passion towards the establishment of truth which is in startling contrast to the confused and negative atmosphere of the political world. But the Royal Society and scientific speculation generally had enemies as well as friends. Samuel Butler, who had attacked the Puritans with savage wit in *Hudibras*, also turned his coarse and derisive humour against the Royal Society, and Swift was later to ridicule its fellows as the scientists of Laputa. No doubt in their early years they did conduct some laughable experiments, and there was a good deal of confusion as to whether their purpose was to speculate on mathematics, physics and astronomy or to devote themselves to immediately useful tasks like the improvement of shipbuilding. Charles II himself sometimes missed the point, since he 'mightily laughed', says Pepys, to think that the members of the Royal Society were devoting themselves largely to experiments in the weighing of air, experiments which were in fact to lead to vital discoveries. Presumably he would have approved of Sir William Petty's attempt to build an unsinkable ship with a double keel, or even of the account given by Sir Richard Bulkeley of an unupsettable coach. This latter, a sort of early tank, would have been more useful on the dangerously uneven seventeenth-century roads were it not, as Evelyn put it, for some 'inconveniences yet to be remedied, that it would not contain above one person, that it was ready to take fire every ten miles, and made so prodigious a noise as was almost intolerable'.

The double keel and the unupsettable coach have passed into the limbo of lost and failed inventions; the weighing of air started a train of developments of which we have not yet seen the end.

One other thing should be said about the Royal Society. It was not insular. It had associations with the equivalent societies abroad and with individual men of science, some of whom were elected as corresponding members. The Royal Society was an important link in the international interchange of ideas which, in a time when political and religious divisions were still strong, drew together Englishmen and Dutchmen, Frenchmen and Scandinavians and Italians, in the common pursuit of truth.

One other outstanding figure of King Charles's reign must be mentioned. This was Thomas Sydenham, the great doctor, who would never be a member of the Royal Society though he knew and respected many of its members. But he had a deep distrust for systems, and even for discussion. He believed in observation and practice as the best guides for a doctor. The observations that he made during the long years that he practised at Westminster formed the basis of certain views on the seasonal character of fevers which are still interesting. But his real importance lay in the emphasis that he put on clinical as against theoretical medicine; his influence, further developed by the great Dutch physician Boerhaave at Leiden, was to be the beginning of the modern study of medicine.

Perhaps it will not be out of place here to say a word about the rise and fall of the so-called 'Chymical Physicians' during this epoch. The College of Physicians, by this time over a century old, was not quite so hidebound as its opposite number in Paris, so mercilessly lampooned by Molière in *Le Malade imaginaire*. But it was conservative. For many years it had been unwilling to accept the discovery of the circulation of the blood by one of its greatest members, William Harvey. None the less, the College was probably right when in the reign of Charles II it frowned on so-called 'Chymical' medicine. Chemical remedies had been growing in popularity since the days of Paracelsus, and in the time of Charles II the reckless use of antimony did some good and much harm. Many of the so-called 'Chymical' physicians were little better than quacks, but they were at least right in believing that doctors could make more use of these remedies than they did, and they pressed King Charles II to give them a charter separate from that of the College of Physicians. Their argument was a heroic one. It was the year of Plague, 1665. A great number of the orthodox practitioners had fled from London. The 'Chymical' physicians, led by Thomas O'Dowd and George Starkey, boldly declared that they would stay and would overcome the plague with their remedies. They stayed, but the plague overcame them. O'Dowd and Starkey both died of it, and with their deaths the movement disintegrated. Quacks and charlatans they may have been, but they had the courage to die for their convictions.

John Evelyn in his sad backward look over the reign of King Charles II spoke of plagues and fires and the general unprosperousness of the times. Yet in the economic as well as in the intellectual sphere the period was, in spite of some temporary and severe setbacks, one of expansion and of vision. That sensible optimist Sir William Petty, the inventor of statistics, which he called 'Political Arithmetic', had no patience with people who complained without ceasing (as people will) of the badness of the times. Writing in 1677, he argued: 'The buildings of London grow great and glorious.... The number of coaches and splendour of equipages exceeds former times, the public theatres are very magnificent.... That some are poorer than others ever was and ever will be.'

When he wrote that the buildings of London were 'great and glorious' Sir William Petty must have had before his eyes some of the incomparable buildings of Sir Christopher Wren which were springing up after the devastation of the Great Fire in 1666. Though Wren was not able to replan London in accordance with his splendid vision for it, he dignified and decorated the capital with his noble and beautiful churches, some of the loveliest buildings in England, with their delicate, solid, poetically imaginative towers soaring up from the dark and crowded streets. Alas, many perished in the bombing of 1940.

Commerce is too large a subject to treat of briefly, but it was in this reign that the idea of London as the commercial capital of the world became something more than a poet's vision or a businessman's dream. It was carried a long step forward towards reality. Dryden was echoing a hope already widely held when in his *Annus Mirabilis* he foretold the future of London, rising from the ashes of the great fire:

> *Now like a maiden queen she will behold*
> *From her high turrets hourly suitors come;*
> *The East with incense and the West with gold*
> *Will stand like suppliants to receive her doom.*
>
> *The silver Thames, her own domestic flood,*
> *Shall bear her vessels like a sweeping train,*
> *And often wind (as of his mistress proud)*
> *With longing eyes to see her face again.*

To anyone acquainted with the capricious behaviour of the River Thames, and its numerous loops and bends about and through London, the idea of the river as a devoted lover perpetually turning round to get another look at his lady has great piquancy. But Dryden was not merely turning fluent verses in praise of the great city. He was describing something that was beginning to happen in fact and in truth.

Outside politics, the reign of King Charles II was a time of intellectual promise. It was the time of the Plague and the Fire, the Dutch wars, the persecution of dissent, the hysterical horrors of the Popish Plot. But it was also the age of Wren and Purcell and Dryden, an age which honoured the transdendent genius of Milton though it cannot be held responsible for inspiring it; it was the age of Sydenham and Boyle and Newton and as such surely a very great age indeed.

Does this explain the enigma on which I touched at the beginning, the extraordinary popularity of King Charles II in the memory of the English people? Such an explanation would attribute too much discrimination and judgement to those blind instincts which create, in every country, a number of popular national figures who cannot precisely be called national heroes. It is assuredly not because he encouraged the Royal Society that King Charles II appears with such frequency as the benevolent genius of English inns. His saturnine features occur more often as the pictorial accompaniment of the sign 'The King's Head' than do those of any other monarch. If we add to these the number of inns in England called 'The Black Boy' and probably dating from the Cromwellian time when Cavalier innkeepers used this phrase to indicate the swarthy-skinned King in exile, he must lead by a long way in this kind of popularity.

Again, it might be argued that King Charles II owes his popularity to his sustained interest in the Navy, which would seem to provide a very solid reason for approval of him by a seafaring people. But I fear it is neither Charles the amateur scientist nor Charles the seaman who is the subject of affectionate popular legend. It is undoubtedly Charles in his idle moments: Charles and his plebeian cockney mistress, Nell Gwynn; Charles the racing man, the keen patron of a sport which is still transcendently popular.

He had from first to last an unfailing gift for pleasing and drawing near to the people. This has sometimes been attributed to his experiences on the weeks after his flight from Worcester when, disguised as a servant, he turned the spit (very inefficiently) in a kitchen, and had other experiences which do not often come the way of royalty. But accounts of him as a child suggest that his ready and easy sympathies were innate, or at least appeared very young. Sir John Reresby has left a famous account of him in his last years enjoying himself at Newmarket, which is still the centre of English horse racing and where his name still greets the visitor at every turn:

> The King was so great a lover of the diversions which that place did afford that he let himself down from Majesty to the very degree of a country gentleman. He mixed himself amongst the crowd, allowed every man to speak to him that pleased; went a-hawking in the mornings, to cock matches in the afternoons (if there were no horse races) and to plays in the evenings, acted in a barn, and by very ordinary Bartlemew Fair comedians.

The serious evils and the great achievements of his reign are still matter for the argument and investigation of historians. But the amiable, approachable, far from perfect man won a place in the hearts of his subjects which has endeared him among their descendants for twelve generations. Charles II never became, as John Evelyn sadly wrote, 'the most renown'd King that ever swayed the British sceptre' – but he became the most popular.

1960

History and Imagination

I n two senses it may be said that history embraces the whole of literature: first, because the creation of all literature occurs within the limits of history, and secondly, because all literature arises directly or indirectly out of history, for all literature arises out of human experience and all human experience is potential history. The writer may treat his material in any number of different ways. He may express himself in romance or fantasy, in poetry, drama or satire. He may adapt and organize material copied from the world before him; he may soar into realms of speculation. Yet at some point every work of creative literature is attached, however slightly, to experience. At some point it must make contact with what we think of as reality – the observed world about us. A work of literature, were this not so, would be inconceivable. No human mind is capable of ideas which have not at their source some kind of human experience. History, rightly understood, includes the whole of human experience. Therefore, it may be argued that all literature is in this wide sense historical.

But our education and the idioms that we use, emphasize certain elements of experience as though they alone were historical. A statesman is described as having 'made history' as though this were a special function of a statesman; or a nation is said to be 'making history' when it becomes involved in some particularly violent or remarkable circumstances. But every human being is making history all the time. We live in history as we live in air and we cannot escape it.

History, in the narrower and generally accepted popular sense, has supplied subjects for a very great part of the drama, the poetry and the fiction of the world. Writers have taken up and simplified or embroidered some actual situation, some story whose principal characters were at least already outlined for them. Sometimes they have imbued such individual happenings with something of universal value. This use of historical material goes back a long time before the arrival of the self-conscious and sophisticated creative writer. It is one of the earliest and most natural tendencies of man to try to distil out of harsh facts a more poetic and universal meaning, to give them at once a quality of simplicity and permanence.

In the process of turning history into the simpler and profounder stuff of poetry it was sometimes found necessary, and therefore permissible, to adapt and alter the material. From this fusion of a little that was historic with much that was poetic sprang many of the great epics, the *Iliad* or the *Chanson de Roland*, the *romanceros* of Spain, the ballads of Scotland and much of the folk literature of the world. Until recently more sophisticated writers retained something of this natural freedom in adapting the facts of recorded, or remembered, history to their needs. In this age when we are by way of making a god of accuracy – and accuracy is not necessarily at all the same thing as truth – it is worth pausing for a moment to look at the effect of this, not on historians but on creative writers who are attracted towards history.

The extent to which a writer dares to modify the facts about which he decides to write depends on the conventions of his time. Schiller was perfectly at liberty to arrange a meeting between Mary Queen of Scots and Queen Elizabeth – a meeting which, if we are to be accurate in our history, never took place. But the liberties allowed to a modern dramatist or a modern novelist by a modern audience are not nearly so great because there is now considerable confusion in the public mind as to the purpose of the historical drama or novel – or for that matter the historical film. It tends to expect from them instruction in history as well as, or possibly even more than, aesthetic pleasure or mere entertainment. The modern writer therefore who wants to convey something more valuable than a little elementary historical instruction, and yet wants to use material taken from history, is compelled more or less strictly, to keep within the limits laid down by record.

It is instructive to notice how often in modern times a creative writer who is using historical material has to employ some different approach or some ingenious device when he wishes to emphasize the more profound message that he is seeking to convey. He has by this means to evade the possibility of purely pedantic criticism on the part of the public. Shaw in *St Joan* transferred the whole of his last act to a dream, and in dreams all laws of realism can be suspended. Again T. S. Eliot in *Murder in the Cathedral* uses throughout a vocabulary and a technique which remove the drama from the solid earth of the twelfth century and lodge it essentially in the human soul which knows no chronology.

It was possible for Shakespeare, for Goethe, for Corneille, for Schiller, even for Victor Hugo, to use historical names as empty vials into which they could pour their own conceptions and so illuminate the passions, the weaknesses or the virtues of man. Shakespeare's Macbeth is not an exact portrait of a certain eleventh-century King of Scotland but is a profound and illuminating study of a living and comprehensible man, weak, not without nobility, gradually corrupted by ambition. As such it has a value far superior to a more accurate portrait of the historic Macbeth. Schiller's *Don Carlos* is very definitely not an exact portrait of the eldest son of Philip II. But it is a most wonderfully moving and compassionate study of a young irresolute man, torn between conflicts which are too great for him. These and others like them, are great studies of human character. To ask whether they are true accounts of the people whose names they carry is irrelevant. The poetic truth is too effective to be challenged by mere historic truth.

It is a delicate and rather a dangerous thing for a historian to appear to attach only an inferior value to accuracy of statement about historical events and there are contexts in which the suggestion that poetic truth could be superior to historic truth might be dangerous. But these examples are not intended to prove that the creative writer has the right at all times and places to tamper with history. The rights and liberties which he is free to exercise in dealing with historical material vary with the conventions of his age, and liberties which are acceptable and fruitful at one time are no longer acceptable and therefore can no longer be fruitful at another. Yet whatever the present situation, it has been from very ancient times a natural and a healthy habit of mankind to poeticize and to simplify the most striking events of history: to modify individual historic truth into simple permanent forms. The creative artist may within the conventions of his epoch as legitimately use historical material in the same way.

As for the historian himself, if he has any ambition beyond that of amassing a mere catalogue of unrelated and therefore unintelligible statements, he must approach his material as any other creative artist does – with the sense that it contains some essential and permanent truths which it may be his skill or good fortune to release. It is with the character of those truths and with certain difficulties in approaching them that I am chiefly concerned.

The poet, the dramatist, the novelist are free to exercise their imagination as widely as they choose. But the historian may not be allowed so long a tether. He must fulfil his function as a creative artist only within very rigid limits. He cannot invent what went on in the mind of St Thomas of Canterbury. The poet can. He cannot suppress inconvenient minor characters and invent others who more significantly underline the significance of his theme. The novelist can. The dramatist can. The historian, as Sir Philip Sidney has said, 'is captive to the truth of a foolish world'. Not only is he captive to the truth of a foolish world, but he is captive to a truth he can never fully discover, and yet he is forbidden by his conscience and his training from inventing it.

He gains his knowledge through evidence which, at the very best, is incomplete; which is always contradictory; which raises as many questions as it solves; which breaks off tormentingly just where he needs it most, or, yet more tormentingly, becomes ambiguous and dark. He can never establish the truth. He can only grope towards it; he gropes, moreover, with an intellect which, being furnished in the twentieth century, finds it extremely difficult to understand any other, which is over-confident, apt to leap to wrong conclusions, unaware of its own shortcomings or, if aware, then unable to make allowances for them. The greatest scholar can never reach more than some kind of partial and personal version of truth as it once was. All the efforts of historical scholarship are ultimately reduced to a mere matter of human opinion. In the preface to his *Civilization of the Renaissance in Italy* Jacob Burckhardt has somewhat discouragingly said:

In the wide ocean upon which we venture, the possible ways and directions are many and the same studies which have served for this work might easily in other hands not only receive a wholly different treatment but lead also to essentially different conclusions.

The painful predicament of the historian has never been better expressed. But it is important to remember that in Burckhardt's mind this defeatist view was closely linked with another implicit assumption: that neither the uncertainty nor the personal nature of his own judgments exonerates the historian from applying the utmost of his critical faculties and scholarly abilities to establishing the truth, or the fact, according to his own lights. To do anything less is intellectual treason.

Surmounting the difficulties of discovering the truth about the historic facts, as far as in him lies, is a matter for the technical skill and conscience of each individual historian. It must be assumed of him, as of other writers, that he will have the self-respect to live up to what he considers the highest standards of his own profession. Historians certainly do commit deliberate dishonesties and, far more often, *bona fide* mistakes; there are as many blindnesses, perjuries, tergiversations, errors of judgment, blemishes of character, foibles, frailties, prejudices and short-comings among historians as among any average group of mortals – or as among any average group of other writers for that matter.

None the less there are among historians a few who have from time to time cast as much light on the predicament of man as the free creative writers. There have been a few with as much insight into the human situation (within the limits allowed them), as much vision and compassion as the greatest writers outside the special bondage of history. But there is a terrible paradox inherent in the historian's profession which has done damage both to historians as writers and to society at large. The historian ought to be the humblest of men; he is faced a dozen times a day with the evidence of his own ignorance; he is perpetually confronted with his own humiliating inability to interpret his material correctly; he is, in a sense that no other writer is, in bondage to that material. Yet it is just precisely the historian among writers who is often the most arrogant. It is just precisely the historian who will often claim that he is not merely the master of his material but, by being the master and interpreter of the past, also the master of the future. It is just precisely among historians that the most conceited assumptions of knowledge, the most assured prophecies of the future, the most *ex cathedra* judgments of right and wrong will be found. On closer examination these judgments, these prophecies, these constructions of vast philosophies explaining the past, present and future of man will all prove to be rooted in the temporary political prejudice or philosophical beliefs of a particular historian or of a particular age or society. There have been among such philosophies and among such interpretations of history on a large scale a few whose inherent nobility gave them a value of their own, not as history but as moral teaching. Great names from St Augustine onwards shine out to redeem the noble error.

But it is an error. It is the great pitfall of history. The historian who forgets to be humble, who forgets the essentially inconclusive nature of his evidence and his own fallibility, who furthermore confuses the temporary opinions of a party or a nation or a religion with absolute standards of right and wrong, can unfortunately be very persuasive. He can take the petty developments of a few generations or a few centuries for some immutable law of progress; or imagine that the ephemeral rivalries of nations are in some way eternal and inevitable; or indulge half a dozen other aberrations. He may lead whole societies with him into error and make them act upon it.

The historian, when he feels this powerful temptation, could take a lesson from the geologist. The Alps, for example, so majestically immutable as they seem, are to the geologist upstarts. They are a mere matter of thirty million years old. These youthful mountains, which came so late to their present shape and grandeur, show up the entire duration of recorded history for the wretched scantling of time that it is. From this little fragment, this few thousand years – about which we can never know more than the hundred-thousandth part and that uncertainly – historians have tried to construct systems and cycles of a scientific immutability. This is the minute kingdom over which, from time to time, a historian lords it as though he were the arbiter of the universe.

In pursuing such speculations, the historian is surely wrong – sometimes nobly wrong, sometimes foolishly so. The importance of history is not that of a science or a system; it is as a record of human beings, a source from which human experience can be studied. The purpose of this study is not to make general rules either political, economic or moral, but to get to the heart of the human problem. After several thousand years of experience in human society it is still the problem that we do not understand.

It can be justly argued that the historian's function is neither more nor less than that of any other creative writer. All literature arises from human experience and therefore all literature arises in the ultimate resort from historical material. The discipline and technique to which the historian submits his material is different from that of the imaginative writer. But the nature of his material is the same and the historian, in so far as he stands or wishes to stand within the bounds of literature at all, has the same task as that of the creative artist. He is not to judge and prophesy and create systems, but within the limits allowed to him, to illuminate the human soul.

1955

Return to Paris: Winter 1945

I

The uncouth bulk of Danton gesturing against the dusk and the pungent smell of roast chestnuts from a neighbouring barrow gave for a moment the illusion that nothing had changed. True the arrival, the struggle with luggage among tired crowds in the Métro, had been unlike any previous arrival in Paris, unlike and therefore unevocative, bringing no sudden pain of nostalgia and recognition, like the so often repeated, so familiar panorama of streets slipping past from the taxi window. This time the moment of recognition had been postponed through the sheer physical trouble of arriving and only now as I set down the luggage outside the Odéon station and rested aching arms in the half-darkness, the full flood of recognition came.

The eye travels – at home and delighted – over the high outline of the houses dwindling away down the Boulevard St Germain, the yellow pools of street lamps in the dusk, the familiar clefts which the brain seeks to identify, Rue de la Seine, Rue de l'Ecole de Médecine . . . ; delighted with the hurrying crowds, the fire-lit group round the chestnut-seller, the shawled newswomen yelling rhythmically . . . The ear detects the first evident change, for that 'Paris-Soir', that 'Ami du Peuple' which were so much a part of the oral pattern of a Paris evening have gone. They are calling strange names with as yet no associations. The ear misses in another second the clang of the trams, the whistle of the police, the discordant stridency of Paris traffic. Only a few cars devour at terrifying speed the slithering distance of the street.

It was, doubtless, sentimental, but I had not wanted for the first hours at least to see anyone I knew or had known; I had come first to see Paris, and cities are to a great extent what a personal memory has made of them. So that it was after all a purely sentimental, even an egoist approach, a desire to awaken recollections, to renew sensations half-remembered, a desire to find out as much what had become of that ingenuous and dogmatic student who so many years before had experienced in these streets the simultaneous discovery of Cartesianism and first love as to find out what had become of Paris.

Turning away from Danton I missed a familiar frock-coated figure on the neighbouring plinth. The plinth was still there, plastered with political notices, but its occupant had gone. He was not, I was to learn within the next twenty-four hours, the only one. Chiappe with his telegraph at the foot of Raspail, the two old doctors in the Avenue de l'Observatoire, Shakespeare in the Boulevard Haussman, Etienne Dolet (here even the bronze plaques which surrounded his pedestal are chiselled away) all had gone to feed Germany's hunger for metal; only a few have been spared – Henri Quatre, Joan of Arc, La Fayette brandishing his outsize sword. Not perhaps a very serious artistic loss but forgotten worthies are a part of the natural accumulation of a great city and their departure leaves a scar. Besides we shall surely never again live through a period so prone to statues as the last century and this peculiar form of urban embellishment has already a period charm it is sad to lose.

The cold and sunlight of the next morning imposed an air of immobility on the scene. The criss-crossed perspectives of the bare Luxembourg trees were deserted; the tracery of frosted branches, the stone princesses vigilant over the gravel paths, and the fountains garlanded with ice were like the drop scene for a ballet. Even the ranks of frozen cabbages where once had been flower beds and stretches of lawn gave no sense of reality. This scenic Paris unfolded itself in the sharp light unaltered, beautiful, and yet – for me at least on that day, by some trick of the intense cold – washed clean of contents, a vessel of which the life seemed for the moment stilled, waiting for the new impulse which would set all going again. An illusion of course. How could it truly be so in a city of immense, continuous, vigorous life? Yet there is undoubtedly – as I came to notice later when I talked with friends – a sense of expectancy, of transition. The Fourth Republic is still to make. The new period of Paris and of France has not yet begun.

For all the enthusiasm and excitement which renewed contact with French culture has provoked here in England, the frozen fountains have hardly yet begun to thaw.

Along the Seine the bouquinistes were not yet at their places but the sight of their green boxes clamped to the embankment wall was reassuring. The central doorway of Notre-Dame was black-draped for the inevitable funeral. Inside it seemed loftier, darker, grimmer than I remembered. There was a chill almost of Puritanism in the air. In the south transept a gaunt cross of wood, towering, narrow, to the height of the clerestory windows and sombrely draped with the tricolour, commanded attention. This cross, I read, was shortly to go to Buchenwald to mark the resting-place of the French dead.

Moving further, towards the holy murmur and the gentle glow which was coming from the Lady Chapel, I realized with a sudden shock what it was that gave so gaunt an air to the great church – that same coldness that I had noticed and again failed to identify in a brief visit to Saint Germain des Prés in the darkness of the previous evening. There are no candles to be had in Paris. In a straightforward sense, and without double meaning, the lights had been put out.

It is something – indeed it is much – that among the ruins of Europe Paris has survived almost intact. There are scars but not irreparable ones from the days of that glorious August which added another astounding chapter to the fierce record of the city. It is commemorated more tragically in the innumerable simple stone tablets which at one strategic street corner after another record the names of those killed in the fight for the liberation. Some had pots or vases of flowers beneath them, dead in the wintry wind, almost all had tricolour favours, frayed and discoloured, fixed to the stone. 'Ces pauvres petits du F.F.I. . . . ,' a woman sighed; it was indeed the word. 'Agé de 20 ans . . . agé de 18 ans . . . agé de 21 ans . . .' in monotonous succession, 'morts pour la France'. Not in vain . . .? I wondered, considering the immense drabness of the European scene, and this strangely unfamiliar city, this recognizable structure of which the life had so deeply altered. But remember their ages once again; these young men had not died for the Paris or the France which I knew. They had died, and that is the secret, for a new France. Many were too young to have died for anything else.

II

It is an easy mistake, and one often made by the English observer, to take the trappings of France for the heart of France, and to think that the effervescence and vitality which used to be the most immediately striking characteristic of the French scene was also the most essential. There is an underlying hardness, a disciplined and determined strength at the heart of the French character. A certain Puritanism is a persistent and emphatic theme in their history, and an important part of their contribution to the civilization of western Europe. We forget too often that a ferment as fundamental and as widespread as that of the Revolution came two centuries earlier out of France in the name of John Calvin. But quite apart from the importance of the Huguenot tradition – it played and still plays a part comparable to the Nonconformist tradition here – in French history itself, the harsh fighting strength of Protestantism in western Europe was the creation of a Frenchman. Moreover, there is a highly Puritan strain which recurs time and again in French Catholic thought, from the founders of Cluny and Cîteaux to the Trappists.

Discipline and austerity can be an expression as eloquent and natural to the French as the colour, the *faste*, the subtlety and the vitality, which are more obviously connected with the French tradition. It is to those depths of the national character that the France of today seems to have returned, to a fundamental seriousness of purpose; impossible to avoid the idea that the four years' ordeal has effected an immense purification.

Faced by a Paris grown grey and hard it is difficult at first to find the new bearings. The long tumultuous history of France – yet a history which has been notably consistent in the reiterant rhythm of its inconsistencies – provides explanations which we should not neglect in analysing the elements of a country which years of separation and a measure of experience wholly different from our own have made unfamiliar.

466

> *L'obscurité couvre le monde,*
> *Mais l'Idée illumine et luit;*
> *De sa clarté blanche elle inonde*
> *Les sombres azurs de la nuit. . . .*

Thus Victor Hugo from his place of exile. *L'Ideé* is perhaps the most important force in the history of France; but there have been too many of them. The French mind, riotously fertile in theory, and the French brain, vigorously active in practice, have clothed too many ideas with the flesh of practical politics for the tranquillity of their own country. Not here the blinkered forward stumble of the English down what has been on the whole a single political track. France has demonstrated to Europe, Empire and Commune, Absolute Monarchy and Revolution. The fruitfulness in theory and the experiments in practice leave behind them a trail of antagonisms: inevitable penalty of having too many ideas and too much skill and passion in carrying them out.

Yet ultimately the idea of France itself overshadows all the others. Conceptions of nationality have, unhappily, no decisive outline. *La France*, to each man or woman who died for her, meant something different – the landscape of home, a symbolic figure, a political concept in action, a vision, a recollection or a hope. Those who told us what they felt before they died tell us little – and much. 'Je suis mort pour une image plus belle que celles que je voyais depuis la défaite . . .' 'Je meurs pour mon pays et pour mon Dieu . . .' 'Je ne meurs ni pour une faction, ni pour un homme. Je meurs pour Elle, pour mon idée à moi de la servir . . .' Deeply moving these last letters, perhaps most of all in that final inarticulacy. The idea is still an idea uncorrupted by practice, unconfined by definition. Over what gulfs of misunderstanding, what differences of heritage and outlook this one luminous idea cast a cloak of heroic sameness; over the Left and the Right, the Monarchist and the Communist, the disreputable and the respectable.

If never before in the history of France has so great a disaster come upon the nation, not for centuries has come so great an opportunity. But the faith in France which originated and upheld the Resistance becomes inevitably confused in the practice of quotidian politics, and the contradictory elements which made up the Resistance had split into their component parts before the first winter of liberation.

III

The austerity and self-discipline, which are profound elements in the French tradition, should not be underestimated; but neither must it be forgotten that the major problem of France, during a vigorous and fruitful history, has been the excess of ideas. From the combination of these two qualities – mental discipline and mental fertility – comes the greatness of the French contribution to civilization as well as most of the evils of French history. Thus the combination at a single moment of extreme fertility of ideas with a renewed discipline may be in the highest degree fortunate – or disastrous. So much depends on the nature of the ideas which are in the ascendant and the form which the new austerity takes.

What is disturbing in France today is the dominance, especially among the young, of the belief that creative activity in the arts must be relevant to the political conflict of the time. I cannot believe that among a people so profoundly sane and civilized as the French this deforming Germanic doctrine will long prevail. Its influence there, and to a considerable extent here also, is the inevitable legacy of the struggle against Germany. In order to overthrow the enemy it has been necessary – as it always is – to fight him with his own weapons and to assimilate in part the very ideas against which the struggle was being waged.

It would, of course, be flying in the face of history to suggest that the subjection of all activity to political standards is an idea foreign to the French. It was, after all, in France that the theory of the all-controlling State was first most effectively put into practice and it is in the French dictionary that the word *étatisme* makes its first appearance. The fruitfulness of French theories has this result – that few if any political concepts are wholly foreign to her. The return, therefore, of ideas which since they left French soil have passed through German, or for that matter Russian, transformations is doubly dangerous. They link themselves too

468

easily to elements which already exist in the multitudinous French tradition.

All the more to be regretted therefore, at a time when the discipline of the State is everywhere increasing, is the prevalence in France of the belief that creative art should be 'engaged'. For the independence of the artist is one of the great safeguards of the freedom of the human spirit.

More immediately serious for the political future of France – since the artist in the long run can be trusted to emancipate himself – is the close and conscious disciplining of parties. *La vie parlementaire est bien malade*, a French statesman regretfully told me; it needed no very perceptive eye to see the truth of this. The fight for life, from which France has barely emerged, imposed a war discipline on the new forces in French politics and impregnated the younger generation with an attitude to politics which is not only profoundly serious – an excellent thing – but carries in its discipline and rigour the marks of its fighting origin.

To say that France today faces once more the problem of deciding the place of the individual in the State, is to say only that France is facing the eternal problem of politics, the problem which confronts us all. For eighteen months, since before the liberation until almost the end of 1945, Jean Anouilh's adaptation of *Antigone* was to be seen at the little *Atelier*. No play based on that original could be devoid of greatness and the moment could hardly have been more apt. The play, which was passed by the German censor, handles the theme of the individual in revolt against authority with so delicate a balance that the sympathetic treatment of Antigone gave secret pleasure before the liberation and the sympathetic treatment of Creon has caused some annoyance since.

M. Anouilh's version, played in modern dress, brings language and allusions up to date and here and there comes near the danger of sentimentalizing the details; but the acid sharpness of the great original is preserved. Antigone remains unreasonable, obstinate and a nuisance, the small rock on which the State splits. Even the reiterated reference to her as *la petite Antigone* makes her more, rather than less, exasperating. *Sans la petite Antigone nous aurions tous vécus bien tranquilles* . . . the chorus, suave in dress suit, concludes the tragedy and we are left to think the rest out for ourselves.

It is not good, and fortunately it is not possible, that we should all live *bien tranquilles*. When the State manages so to constitute itself as to liquidate all its Antigones, not after but *before* they can assert their intolerable and intolerant independence, there will be a great desolation of the human spirit. Against the German menace it was, in the last resort, *la petite Antigone* who revolted. It was not, of course, *la petite Antigone* who won, because discipline and organization are necessary in order to overthrow discipline and organization. But it will be a sad day for France and for the world if the society which was reborn in the collapse of Germany has no room for its Antigones.

1946

The English Civil War in Perspective*

I am truly sensible of the honour you have done me in asking me to give this, the first lecture of a new foundation. The name chosen for these lectures is beautiful and just a little awe-inspiring. Sophia, the Greek for wisdom – this indicates the goal at which your lecturer should aim. Knowledge is one thing; we can mostly scramble into a little knowledge by assiduous reading, but the application of knowledge to life – that calls for wisdom. I had this in mind when I chose this subject which may seem on the surface to show only the uncertainties and contradictions that can arise through mere knowledge of facts, or through an over-confidence in their interpretation, but I hope in the end to make out a case for the deeper wisdom which comes through striving after the unattainable truth, and approaching at least more nearly to it.

Historians sometimes find their colleagues in other disciplines, and yet more often members of the general public, asking 'Why all this disagreement about interpretation? Why not simply give the facts?' but facts are by no means always clear and even if they were, a mere catalogue of facts is meaningless without some kind of arrangement or selection. This implies, on the part of the historian, discrimination and a point of view.

It is no wonder then that history is re-written from generation to generation and that some very unkind things have been said about historians for changing their opinions. 'Although God cannot alter the past, historians can,' wrote Samuel Butler. In the eighteenth century Bolingbroke declared that history 'has been purposely and systematically falsified through the ages'. True, I

* The Sophia Lecture, University of Newcastle-upon-Tyne, 1978.

fear, but in fairness it should be emphasized that the purposeful and systematic falsification of history is generally the work of politicians and publicists rather than historians.

Leaving aside the heinous offence of deliberate falsification, different interpretations of the past, however mistaken we may think them, have something to tell us. This is especially true of events which were themselves controversial and have had consequences which are still with us today. The civil wars of Charles I come into this category. The issue involved is still relevant. The cause of the dispute was an essential problem of government: the relationship of the Crown to the people or, in general terms, of the government to the governed.

The causes and consequences, the merits and demerits of the combatants, the validity or otherwise of their ideas have been argued over for three centuries, first by contemporaries, Royalists and Parliamentarians, Presbyterians, Independents and Levellers, and later by Whigs and Tories, Roman Catholics, Freethinkers, High Anglicans, Radicals and in the present century Fabians and Marxists as well as conflicting schools of social and economic historians.

As early as 1700 we find a learned French Huguenot, Rapin de Thoyras, lamenting the political prejudices which bedevil all the writings of the English on this most interesting episode in their history. 'Was there among the English some good neuter historian,' he wrote, 'it would be he that should be taken for guide, but I know not of any.' So he wrote a history himself; it has considerable merit but cannot be described as 'neuter'. He was resolutely on the side of Parliament and laid down the basis of what later came to be called the Whig Theory. (Always suspect an historian who says he is unprejudiced. It usually means that he does not know his own weaknesses.)

To jump a century and a quarter, Isaac D'Israeli – who had no inherited prejudices about the English Civil War since his family reached London only in the eighteenth century from Spain by way of Venice – wagged a reproachful forefinger at the passions of his adopted countrymen. In his idiosyncratic but original and perceptive *Commentaries on the Life and Reign of Charles I* published in 1828, he described English histories as 'the polemics of politics . . . the Monarchist and the Commonwealth man have bequeathed their mutual recriminations and their reciprocal calumnies'.

In the 1870s that great medievalist Bishop Stubbs looked towards the troubled territory of Stuart history from his own authoritative position in the Middle Ages, and adjured historians to overcome 'the prejudices nursed by ten generations' and to cultivate understanding for both points of view.

As these quotations show, the Civil War was seen from the seventeenth to the end of the nineteenth century in predominantly political terms: Royalists against Parliamentarians – Cavaliers against Roundheads in popular usage – underpinned by the religious division between Anglicans and Dissenters. The central question *then* was: which side was right, or even more simply, which side are you on?

In the twentieth century this attitude is archaic, if not quite obsolete. Interest in social and economic history has been steadily increasing for nearly a century, and is in itself the expression of a new social awareness; it has widened the scope of historical research, opened up new fields of inquiry, revealed massive and detailed evidence of a kind not previously taken into account and thereby created a new outlook. It is now no longer a question of politics and religion above all, but of politics and religion as the manifestation of deeper social and economic tensions. The problem is to discover and assess these underlying factors and to deduce from an ever mounting quantity of evidence what were the conflicting pressures which caused an apparently peaceful England to erupt into civil war. 'Crisis' became the fashionable word, not without justification. The seventeenth-century revolution has thus been removed from the sphere of past politics and planted down squarely in the midst of the social concerns and arguments of our own time.

Do historians agree any better? Of course not: the scope for disagreement is larger than ever, but through argument based on increasing evidence we do none the less approach a fuller view of the past and a knowledge which, by the richness of its detail, must approach nearer to the truth than the old Whig-versus-Tory argument ever did.

Before examining this changing perspective in greater detail, I would like again to emphasize that the central issue of this much disputed civil war, that of the relative rights of the State and the individual, is still critical and relevant today.

To recapitulate briefly, and with as little prejudice as possible, the source of all the trouble: the seventeenth-century crisis which exploded into civil war arose from a collision between two clearly formulated ideas of government. The King never put his case better than in his last hour on earth, on the scaffold outside his banqueting house in Whitehall. Here he stated with absolute sincerity the nature of his duty to the people:

> Truly I desire their liberty and freedom as much as anybody what-soever, but I must tell you their liberty and freedom consists in having of government those laws by which their life and goods may be most their own. It is not for having a share in government: that is nothing pertaining to them. A subject and a Sovereign are clear different things.

As an elaboration of that, here is a statement made by Charles's great minister, Strafford, not on the scaffold, but in his days of power:

> Princes are to be indulgent nursing fathers to their people. Their modest liberties, their sober rights ought to be precious in their eyes ... Subjects on the other side, ought with solicitous eyes ... to watch over the prerogatives of the Crown. The authority of the King is the keystone which closeth up the arch of order and government which contains each part in due relation to the whole, and which, once shaken ... falls together in a confused heap of foundation and battlement.

For an answer to these fine sentiments I turn to that blunt Republican Edmund Ludlow, who fought for Parliament in the Civil War, served on the court which tried the King and signed his death warrant. His statement was made in his memoirs, written years later in exile in Switzerland.

> The question in dispute between the King's party and us was ... whether the King should govern as a God by his will, and the nation

be governed by force like beasts, or whether the people should be
governed by laws made by themselves and lie under a government
derived from their own consent.

These opposing statements present the constitutional issue in
its simplest form, but the same words mean different things in
different centuries. Though Ludlow spoke of parliamentary
government as though it was government by consent of the people,
he assumed that the people, by and large, were quite content to
be represented by members in whose election the great majority
of them had no voice whatever. The Civil War itself would bring
forth a vociferous party, the Levellers, who demanded a wider
franchise and a House of Commons that was in some degree in
touch with ordinary people.

To outline briefly the sequence of events: Charles, finding
Parliament impossible to control in the early years of his reign,
decided to do without it, and managed to do so for eleven years
(1629–40), but the Crown revenues were inadequate to the needs
of government without parliamentary subsidies. He had therefore
to resort to other methods, such as the imposition of fines for
infringement of obsolete laws, the increase of customs dues and,
finally, the extension to the inland counties of Ship Money, a levy
for the support of the navy which had hitherto been confined to
coastal counties. This could be interpreted as imposing a new tax
without parliamentary consent. The King's critics seized the
occasion to resist payment, in the belief that the King would
prosecute and by so doing open a way for a legal debate on the
rights of the Crown, since debate in Parliament had been stopped.
John Hampden was duly prosecuted as a test case and the judges,
on whose support the King had relied, totally weakened the royal
position by failing to agree.

Meanwhile, during his personal rule, Charles had encouraged
his energetic Archbishop, William Laud, to enforce orderly and
uniform ritual in the Church of England. Puritan opposition was
checked, though never quite stifled, by the silencing of many
preachers and by prosecutions in the Courts of Star Chamber and
High Commission. By the later 1630s a very considerable undercurrent of opposition was gathering strength in England, but the

extension of the King's religious policy to Scotland was the direct cause of the crisis. Here an active Presbyterian majority, which included a strong group of the nobility, rose in revolt. In the war which followed, the King's English subjects – for the first time since the Union of the Crowns – joined in open sympathy with the Scots, who won an easy victory. (In parenthesis, although the Scots started the sequence of events which led to the King's downfall, their own eventful and very complex Civil War embodied different problems from those of the English conflict and has inspired its own series of differing interpretations which do not concern us here.)

Bankrupted by defeat, Charles was compelled to call Parliament in November 1640. This famous Long Parliament was led in its opening years by John Pym, one of the most remarkable parliamentary leaders in the history of England. Under his skilful management Parliament compelled the King to abandon his religious policy, to send Laud to the Tower and his chief minister Strafford to the block, to abolish the prerogative courts through which, above all, he had enforced his will, and to commit himself to calling Parliament at least every three years. Charles surrendered one key position after another in the defence of his royal power. The crux came in the autumn of 1641 when a rebellion in Ireland made it necessary to raise an English army to protect – or more truly to rescue – the English settlers. Parliament now made the unprecedented demand to control all higher appointments in the armed forces. On this crucial point the King refused to yield.

John Pym and his party in the House of Commons were convinced that if Charles had an army at his disposal he would use it against them rather than against the Irish insurgents. On the evidence, they were probably right. The King was equally convinced that if he ceded the control of the army to Parliament it would make an end of the authority of the Crown. He was right, too.

He had already been involved in some ill-concealed plots for a military *coup* in the previous year, and he made his final mistake when, in January 1642, he attempted unsuccessfully to arrest Pym and five of his supporters, by coming to the House of Commons himself at the head of his personal guards. This action consolidated parliamentary support behind Pym and provoked demonstrations in the City of London which forced Charles to flee from his capital.

Thereafter King and Parliament each set about raising forces, ostensibly for the relief of Ireland but, in the event, to fight each other. Sporadic clashes occurred in the late summer of 1642 and in August Charles formally raised his standard at Nottingham.

Defeated after a four year war, Charles personally surrendered to the Scots by whom he thought he might be offered acceptable terms, but they required his full recognition of Presbyterianism, which he refused. So they handed him over to Parliament in return for the arrears of pay owed to their troops. The King, well aware of the growing dissension between the English Parliament and their own victorious but unpaid army, played for time. He was not ill-pleased when he was kidnapped by the Army and was quite willing to discuss terms with them rather than with Parliament, but he misunderstood the character of this army. The New Model Army, Cromwell's Army, as it is often and not quite accurately called, was something new in the experience of the west: an army with a political will and political opinions and ideals of its own.

Army chaplains, many of them Independent sectarians, had imbued the men with a strong sense of equality, an active belief in their rights as citizens, as Christians and as men. In the slack months after the end of the war, the soldiers had had time to read or listen to the pamphlets of John Lilburne, the immensely persuasive and popular leader of the Levellers. His following – both civil and military – had become an important political movement. It had its own weekly news-sheet, rather misleadingly called *The Moderate*, which was a good and intelligent news-sheet, as well as a party organ. Under these influences the soldiers learnt to formulate their own opinions. A vocal minority, officers and men, were strong for the Leveller programme of franchise reform, of opportunity and justice for the ordinary citizen against vested interests, and indifferent or hostile to any sort of peace with the King.

The King continued to play for time, attempted to escape, was re-captured in the Isle of Wight and there entered into a secret agreement with the Presbyterian Scots to join with the English Royalists and renew hostilities. The result was the second Civil War of 1648. The Army, outraged at his duplicity, passed a resolution to bring him to trial when they had won the war – which of course they did. The majority in the House of Commons who still favoured a negotiated peace were forcibly excluded by the Army. This cowed and much reduced House of Commons, in the name of 'the people of England', appointed a court to try the King, and the Army carried out the execution. The Levellers, who had demanded a free election and a new Parliament *before* the King's trial, were outflanked by this speedy action. The hard-core Levellers in the Army mutinied, but most of the soldiers rallied to the defence of the new Republic, or Commonwealth, of England. The mutiny was crushed, the Leveller movement disintegrated and, because it had not succeeded, was forgotten for more than two centuries.

There followed the failure of the existing Parliament to make a satisfactory settlement, Cromwell's forcible dissolution, the brief ineffective Barebones Parliament and the establishment of Cromwell as Protector – with considerable success abroad and less at home. And so to the inevitable Restoration of Charles II in 1660.

What was gained by the Civil War? All Cromwellian legislation and all legislation passed by the Long Parliament subsequent to the breach with the King was declared void. But the early legislation of the Long Parliament, to which Charles had unwillingly been compelled to assent, remained on the statute book. This limited the powers of the Crown and formed the basis of the Revolution settlement of 1688. To this degree the Civil War succeeded in safe-guarding parliamentary rule.

Histories and accounts of the Civil War began to appear before the war was over and memoirs by major and minor participants in the conflict were not slow to come. More important was the compilation of documents made by John Rushworth, a clerk in the House of Commons and secretary to Fairfax, with its strong Parliamentary slant. Thomas Nalson, an Anglican clergyman who set out to give a more balanced – by which he meant a more Royalist – view, never completed his projected collection, but his volume on the King's trial is valuable. It was not until the eighteenth century that the passage of time seemed to offer an opportunity for more dispassionate treatment, and these later works are the subject of this lecture, but it would be unseemly to pass over in silence the greatest of all contemporary works on the Civil War – Clarendon's *History of the Rebellion and Civil Wars in England* published in 1702, twenty-eight years after the author's death. It is a classic of English literature as well as a major contemporary source and I cannot here discuss its outstanding value. I would like only to emphasize one rather personal way in which Clarendon contributed to the image of what, for lack of a better term, may be called the 'good' Royalist.

As Edward Hyde, Clarendon entered Parliament in 1640 as an opponent of the King's government on constitutional grounds. He remained in opposition for the first session. But when John Pym began to claim for Parliament, as of right, things which had never been claimed before, Clarendon as a lawyer, a legalist and a devout Anglican moved over to the King's side, in company with his friend Lord Falkland. His famous account of Falkland presents an impressive image of the honourable moderate Cavalier who could not go the whole way with the extremists of either party. Tolerant, generous, highly cultivated, Falkland had kept open house at Great Tew during the years of peace for a varied and gifted circle of friends who met to talk of politics, philosophy, theology and the intellectual interests of their time. Falkland, like Hyde, was disillusioned and repelled by the extremism of John Pym and by what he and other Royalists regarded as the craft and cunning of his parliamentary management. Hyde and Falkland accepted office under the King at the same time and were soon almost equally shocked by the extremists in the King's party and the deviousness of some of his policies. Falkland, despairing of peace, rode to his death in battle and thereby inspired a lengthy and moving passage in Clarendon's history which did much to create an ideal image of the aristocratic intellectual Cavalier.

This ideal figure clearly influenced David Hume in his interpretation of the Civil War. David Hume, one of the greatest and most sympathetic figures in the intellectual history of the eighteenth century, published his *History of England* in 1754. Hume's education in the narrow Presbyterianism then prevalent in Scotland left him with a hatred of intolerant, restrictive views in religion and those of the Puritans in particular. He accepted Clarendon's picture of the high-minded Royalist, applied his own rational temperament to his researches and produced an account of the seventeenth-century conflict which eclipsed the dry compilations of earlier historians, especially those on the Parliamentary side. The opinions of King Charles's Puritan critics were, according to Hume:

> polluted with mysterious jargon and full of the lowest and most vulgar hypocrisy . . . the grievances which tended chiefly to inflame Parliament and the nation . . . were the surplice, the liturgy, the breach of the Sabbath, embroidered copes, lawn sleeves . . . on account of *these* were the popular leaders content to throw the Government into such violent convulsions, and to the disgrace of that age and this Island, it must be acknowledged that the disorders of Scotland entirely and those of England mostly proceeded from so mean and contemptible an origin . . . the fanatical spirit let loose, confounded all regard to ease, safety and interest and dissolved every moral and spiritual obligation.

Hume regarded as worthy of nothing but contempt the very aspect of the struggle, the intense religious convictions of the combatants, and especially of the Puritans, which in the following century by way of Carlyle's elucidation of Cromwell and later of Gardiner's sober comprehensive volumes became one of its greatest glories.

The eighteenth-century Whigs, rightly conscious that there was much more to the Puritan-Parliamentary cause than mere bigotry, were outraged, but as Professor Trevor-Roper has put it, 'Whig pens squeaked in vain against the sophisticated and elegant writing of Hume'. His work remained the most popular history of England well into the nineteenth century.

The Whig pen which squeaked loudest and perhaps not altogether in vain was that of a woman historian, Catherine Macaulay (born Sawbridge, she was not a blood relation of the more famous Macaulay). Her work on the Stuart epoch came nine years after that of Hume. Her fluent words vibrate with indignation at the ingratitude of those who 'enjoy privileges unpossessed by other nations but have lost a just sense of the merit of the men by whose virtues these privileges were obtained; men that, with the hazard and even the loss of their lives, attacked the formidable pretensions of the Stuart family and set up the banners of liberty against a tyranny which had been established for a series of more than 150 years; and this by the exertion of faculties which, if compared with the barren produce of modern times, appear more than human . . . Party prejudice' – Mrs Macaulay evidently regarded herself as free from this vice – 'has painted the memoirs of past time in so false a light, that it is with difficulty we can trace features which, if justly described, would exalt the worthies of this country beyond the fame of any set of men which the annals of other nations can at any one period produce.' She was certainly not afraid of superlatives nor of praising her own countrymen. Thus she tells us that at the elections for the Long Parliament, 'Patriots were returned whose number, virtues and abilities were greater than had ever been convened together in any age or country'. Incidentally she plays down Puritanism and religion throughout.

It is unfair to judge her book by its purple passages, which are declarations of faith rather than historical statements. She could be acute and sensible in her use of evidence and she read widely in the pamphlet literature of the period. She even did some manuscript research and Isaac D'Israeli asserted that she had made away with a piece of inconvenient evidence – a charge which seems to have been unjust, but she certainly displayed some of the worst symptoms of loose thinking by her habit of personalizing abstract and undefined forces. Thus she could write that, in 1640, 'the spirit of the English constitution burst its bounds and like a mighty torrent demanded a free Parliament'. Later on, 'the genius of the nation' rose to exalted heights – got thoroughly above itself in fact – and ranged itself on the side of 'its Parent Liberty'.

Yet she was impressive enough to achieve a great reputation abroad. She corresponded with and visited George Washington to whom she offered unsolicited criticism of the American Constitution. Her work was admired by Mirabeau and appeared as a shining ideal before the eyes of Madame Roland whose ambition at one time was to write a book which would make her 'la Macaulay de mon pays'.

The French Revolution was in almost all respects different from the slow-motion English Revolution of the seventeenth century although their orators from time to time made references to the

English experience and Louis XVI studied the trial of Charles I before he himself suffered the same ordeal.

But following generations in France still felt an interest in the more purposeful and less destructive march of English history. Guizot in 1826 hailed the English Revolution – by which he meant the whole seventeenth-century movement – as epoch-making in European and world history. He saw it as a revolution which had succeeded not once, but twice, because its authors created the constitutional monarchy of England and their descendants founded the republic of the United States. 'These great events', he wrote, 'are no longer hidden in darkness but are now fully illuminated by the sanction of time.'

Fully illuminated? Is history ever fully illuminated? Leaving out many other more complicated aspects, it is at least true that the Founding Fathers of the United States did cite such republican thinkers as Harry Vane the younger and certainly acted on John Hampden's principle of no taxation without representation.

Guizot singled out for admiration in English government the two-party system, traceable to the Long Parliament, a system which had proved itself as a method of peaceful argument between opposing views. He also believed that the memory of the Civil War had left in England a fear of internal conflict which ensured the bloodlessness of the Glorious Revolution of 1688 when, as he put it, 'the cause of the people triumphed by the hands of the aristocracy'. Thereafter, in his view, the different classes of the English people understood how to live together. There was no thought yet in his mind of the possible effects of industrial change on this commendable harmony.

While Guizot was writing, the young Thomas Babington Macaulay was already in his reviews and essays sketching in with splendid brush strokes the opinions and ideas which make his *History of England* the classic and most influential statement of what came to be called the Whig Theory of English history. Here is a quotation from his essay on Milton written in 1827:

He lived at one of the most memorable eras in the history of mankind at the very crisis of the great conflict between liberty and despotism, reason and prejudice. That great battle was fought for no single generation, for no single land. The destinies of the human race were staked on the same cast with the freedom of the English people. Then were first proclaimed those mighty principles which have since worked their way into the depths of the American forests, which have aroused Greece from the slavery and degradation of 2000 years, and which, from one end of Europe to the other, have kindled an unquenchable fire in the hearts of the oppressed and loosed the knees of the oppressors with an unwonted fear.

Twelve years later in his *History of England*, he hailed the meeting of the Long Parliament in 1640 as 'that renowned Parliament which in spite of many errors and disasters, is justly entitled to the reverence and the gratitude of all who, in any part of the world, enjoy the blessings of constitutional government'.

Macaulay's unfinished *History of England* – all the more for being unfinished – consolidated this proud theory of English parliamentary liberty and two-party government as the great legacy of the seventeenth-century conflict. Well, it was of course the legacy of that conflict, but was it as its admirers believed, the best solution to all problems of government in all countries at all times? This was a conviction which gained momentum as British power and prestige increased throughout the nineteenth century.

Macaulay's emphasis was essentially political and the religious aspects of the Civil War, so discredited by Hume, were not fully restored to their significance until the middle years of the nineteenth century. In 1845 Thomas Carlyle, a Scotsman of a different mind altogether from David Hume, brought his rugged, irregular, forceful, exasperating genius to the study of Oliver Cromwell. At one stroke, in his edition of Cromwell's letters, he restored the significance of Cromwell's religion and of the Puritan element in the English Revolution so long obscured and misunderstood. In his introduction he bewailed the deplorable decadence of his own time and of England and expressed a hope 'that England may yet attain some practicable belief and understanding of its history during the seventeenth century'. He demanded above all a history of English Puritanism – 'the last of all our heroisms'. Carlyle saw the Puritan as hero and made the idea convincing through his interpretation of Cromwell.

Carlyle was not always careful, was not always a good judge of evidence, could be deceived by forgeries, but his insight was true and our view of Cromwell has never been the same since. The religious element in the Civil War was extraneous to the Whig theory but, until it was illuminated, understanding of the Civil War was wholly inadequate. What Carlyle began was completed with calm understanding and deep knowledge by Samuel Rawson Gardiner.

In the last quarter of the nineteenth century Gardiner wrote what is still probably the most informative general history of this epoch. He proclaimed his belief in dispassionate history. In this he followed the teaching of the great German historian Leopold von Ranke who, earlier in the century, had established the supremacy of German influence in the writing of serious history and whose belief in the unprejudiced representation of the facts was then widely accepted as a possible goal. On closer analysis, it appears that Ranke and his disciples thought that to respect opinions with which they did not agree was to be unprejudiced. This is not so. Gardiner, who sincerely believed himself to be free of prejudice, was a humane and generous man who carefully emphasized the sincerity and personal virtues of many Royalists, but he assumed that they were wrong. His great work is firmly in the Whig parliamentary tradition, given an extra dimension by his elevation of Puritanism, in its nobler manifestations, into a Whig virtue and a dominant cause of the revolution which overwhelmed the misguided King.

The same generosity of mind and certainty of opinion is to be found in the early writings of G. M. Trevelyan on the Stuarts, though he adds an imaginative concern for the fate of ordinary people which is very much his own.

But a great change of approach was coming, slowly at first, then, from the turn of the century, with increasing speed. The publication of Eduard Bernstein's *Socialism and Democracy in the Great English Revolution* is a key point. This book appeared in Germany in 1895 and was not translated into English until 1922. Bernstein, a dedicated follower of Karl Marx, worked very thoroughly on the pamphlets in the British Museum (as Gardiner and others had of course also done). But he was searching *especially* for forerunners of socialism and democracy, and in the Leveller pamphlets he

found what he was seeking. He assumed, incorrectly but under-
standably, that when Lilburne and his supporters championed
the right of all free men to elect their representatives in Parliament,
they were advocating manhood suffrage. This error was less important, in the long run, than his achievement in bringing back to
light the buried elements of social unrest in the English seventeenth
century and the interests and demands of original political thinkers
coming from a stratum of society that had not been articulate
before.

The late G. P. Gooch, in his own vein of fair-minded liberalism,
picked up the trail in his *English Democratic Ideas in the Seventeenth
Century* published in 1898, several times reprinted and still valuable today. Older attitudes were now steadily undermined by a
new kind of research. In the decades between the two World Wars,
social and economic inquiry, on the Stuart epoch in general and
the Civil War in particular, became the dominant trend. At the
same time, studies of the mechanism of politics and administration
gradually replaced the old bi-partisan approach. Significant in the
parliamentary context was the search for parliamentary diaries
pioneered in the United States by Wallace Notestein and culminating at the present time in the scholarly series issuing from Yale
under the direction of J. H. Hexter. (Hexter himself began his
distinguished career in 1941 with the publication of *The Reign of
King Pym*, a brilliant analysis of Pym's methods of parliamentary
management.)

On the English side of the Atlantic in the 1950s a storm raged
for the best part of a decade on the financial position of the combatants. Was the Puritan interest essentially that of a rising capitalist class, according to Max Weber's suggestion, popularized in
England by the persuasive pen of R. H. Tawney? Or was the
opposite true, and the opposition to the King essentially that of
the have-nots, the smaller gentry, who resented Court favour and
Court influences of the wealthier gentry and greater landowners,
as demonstrated in the brilliant controversial thesis of Professor
Trevor-Roper? Now that the dust has settled it looks as though
there is an element of truth in both arguments, and we certainly
know a great deal more about the gentry as a result.

All this while Lilburne and the once-neglected Levellers exercised an irresistible attraction over the younger generation of historians. Strangely enough it was not until 1962 that C. B. Macpherson in *The Political Theory of Possessive Individualism* showed that the Levellers had never advocated manhood suffrage. Bernstein and others had been misled by the term 'free men' which in seventeenth-century usage excluded servants and wage-earners. Even so, the Leveller programme would have greatly extended the franchise. The disillusioning discovery that the Levellers championed not the proletariat but the small employer possibly accounts for a noticeable diversion of interest to the Diggers, that remarkable splinter group who called themselves the True Levellers, and whose ill-fated experiment in the communal ownership of land was brutally crushed.

The foregoing is not an analysis but merely a sketch of past perspectives and some more recent developments in Civil War interpretation and research. Each generation sees most clearly in the past those elements which are nearest to its own problems. The revolutionary changes and threatening dangers of our time have stimulated much deeper, wider, more penetrating and more detailed inquiry than ever before. The greater availability of documents has of course helped, together with the spread of higher education and the consequent proliferation of academic theses. But evidence in general and documents in particular turn up because they are looked for, and because historians are pursuing new lines of inquiry and asking new questions.

Historians of the Civil War today are interested in nothing less than the life and structure of a whole society. Widely different lines of research contribute to this. There are demographic studies which reconstruct the population of a limited region; there are studies of significant institutions, such as schools and universities; there are studies of individual cities, their interests and commerce; there are admirable works on county administration and county politics. Much research has been done on sectarian churches, their opinions and their effect on political thought, a line of inquiry which was thrown open by the incomparable *Liberty and Reformation in the Puritan Revolution* of Professor William Haller. The possibilities are endless and research adds to our knowledge almost every day. There are also essential works of synthesis and interpretation, aiming at a convincing overall view of seventeenth-century England and its central crisis. These works are useful, lest we lose sight of the wood in counting the trees. But a general view, in today's climate of opinion, is rarely a generally accepted one.

Can no generally accepted view then emerge from so much new knowledge? The more evidence, the greater accumulation of facts the greater room for disagreement? At the present moment the Marxist interpretation has the advantage of being the most coherent. But is that an advantage? The stuff of history is by no means coherent. No agreed consensus has yet emerged, nor ever will. But then no agreed consensus emerges in our own times about the causes of our contemporary troubles. What does emerge for the seventeenth century is a much clearer, more vivid, more immediate apprehension of what life was like for our ancestors three hundred years ago. When the arguments die down, is not this greater understanding of our fellow beings, then or now, the purpose of history as it is life?

1978

The Historian and the World

The historian has much to answer for. History – that is, written history – has made and unmade states, given courage to the oppressed and undermined the oppressor, has justified aggression and overridden law. A French historian, in the cruel light of 1870, exclaimed with unwilling admiration that the Germans used their history as a means towards unity and a weapon of war; but the story of his own country as written by his compatriots had taught the French people, he lamented, 'surtout de haïr les uns les autres'. Past glories have inspired whole nations to rise again, as witness the Risorgimento, as witness Poland and Bohemia. Past heroism breeds future heroism, past cowardice the cowardice of the future. Within the limits of the modern nation, history tends to repeat itself by a process of almost deliberate imitation. We know what to expect of ourselves and, by expecting, do it.

But what is this force? What is written history? Froude sonorously hailed it as 'a voice forever sounding across the centuries the laws of right and wrong', and thereby summed up a general if an unconscious belief. Written history is, in fact, nothing of the kind; it is the fragmentary record of the often inexplicable actions of innumerable bewildered human beings, set down and interpreted according to their own limitations by other human beings, equally bewildered. The tribunal of history judges about as fairly as an average bench of magistrates; which is exactly what it is. But only a minority of people are able to recognize this fact, and, of that minority, only a minority will act upon it. The rest of us will go through life with a silt of moral and political prejudice washing about in the brain which has been derived directly and indirectly, by way of text-book and propaganda, school and home and theatre and market-place, from historical writings. For, somewhere about the eighteenth century, history tacitly replaced religion as the school of public morals. 'Standard works' instead of volumes of sermons appeared in every gentleman's library. History was promoted from being entertainment to being the most frequent form of serious reading. Nothing has yet taken its place.

Whatever the faults of the priests and preachers and theologians who were indirectly responsible for the deplorable state of things in medieval and Renaissance Europe, they knew what their function was, even if they failed to perform it. Moreover, they enjoyed full public recognition. Their successors, the historians, enjoy no such recognition and the best men among them have often been unaware of their influence, or afraid to use it.

There are two kinds of writer concerned with history: the scholars and the popularizers. The scholars spend their time excavating small fragments of the past which, once disinterred and the dust blown off, they present, like Shelley's nosegay – O! to whom? To the second kind of writer, the popularizer; and a popularizer may be anyone from an upright and learned man to Dr Goebbels: but usually he is Dr Goebbels. It is not for the scholars, burrowing with their noses deep in the past and their eyes dimmed to the pale light of the archives, to notice who is making use of the material they industriously scratch up. Nor is it for them to give any guidance as to how it is to be used. They are no more concerned with the ultimate outcome of their studies than is the research-scientist with the use of poison gas in warfare. The final results arise not from the nature of the material but from the depravity of human beings; and historical research of the truly scholastic kind is not connected with human beings at all. It is a pure study, like higher mathematics.

Very different is the position of the popularizers. They have to use, digest, and re-deliver the material in a form palatable to the public; their business is essentially with human beings, both the living and the dead. Some of them have no conscious idea beyond that of writing a readable book; others have a very definite idea of teaching a political or moral lesson through their book. In both these groups there are good men and learned men; in both these groups there are charlatans. But as far as the world is conderned

only the learning and the goodness, only the vices and the charla-
tanism of the second group have borne fruit. For the work of those
who have no message beyond the mere reconstruction of the past
is sterile.

It used to be said that history should be written without prejudice: that the historian must not step aside to draw a moral. The
first cannot be done; the second should not. Historians should
always draw morals. If the accurate, judicious and highly trained
fail to do so, the unscrupulous and unqualified will do it for them,
and the deluded public will listen gaping to false but more emphatic prophets. It is futile for the upright man to say, 'I have set
down nothing in malice, I have made no unsound deductions, I
have neither omitted nor strained a record', unless he can add –
'And I have written a book far more persuasive than anything of
Rosenberg's and as many people have read it'. The historian who
neglects the education of his public is as much responsible for the
villainous stuff to which they go instead, as Gallio was for the dis-
graceful exhibition which took place in his court of justice. A
nation does not create the historians it deserves; the historians are
far more likely to create the nation.

Over the last century more and more people have become
literate; more and more people have become (or until recently
had become) vocal members of their community or state. The
position of the writer became correspondingly more influential
and more responsible. This was not the moment for him to go off
into abstruse mumblings about art for art's sake. The artist at all
times has a duty towards society; let him outrage it, by all means,
for its own good, but – with rare exceptions – he must not retire
from it into the private circle of his own artistic integrity. Of all
writers this is truest of the historians who have, willy nilly, been
pushed by sociological and spiritual forces outside their control
into the position of chief exponents of political morality.

It is a part which all but a few historians have been lamentably
unable to play. There have been exceptions: Mommsen, unfortunately, because his message, conveyed through a learned history
of Rome, was the worship of force; Macaulay, fortunately, because his message, conveyed through a less learned history of
England, was the worship of liberal institutions and free will.

'Four hundred editions', thundered Carlyle, incensed at the levity of its style, 'could not lend it any permanent value.' He failed to see that four hundred editions in themselves may well constitute a permanent value; his attack was based on the groundless faith that there is an absolute standard outside the praise and agreement of the public. For the historian there is not.

Macaulay may have been inaccurate and biased; but he preached a good cause eloquently. There has been a fashion for sneering at his errors, but his ghost has the laugh of us for we are all the heirs of his stalwart prejudices. If we believe ourselves to be a great democratic nation, if we believe in a broadening tradition of liberty, we believe it to a great extent because Macaulay wrote history in a manner which conquered generations of readers and filtered through text-books and the schools to become part of the common conviction of a whole people.

But the greater number of historical writers failed entirely to understand what was expected of them. They turned their faces away from their audience and towards their subject, turned deliberately from the present to the past. They began to consider with misguided conscientiousness their duty to the dead. This was nonsense, for no one has a duty to the dead except in relation to the living. The misinterpretation of a dead man causes him no discomfort though it may radically affect the lessons which posterity learns from his career. The Nazis were concerned not with the ghost of Frederick the Great but with the minds of the Hitler Jugend, when they made the traducing of German national figures a punishable offence. By 'traducing' they meant disturbing the layer of accepted prejudice in the minds of the people.

Misinterpretation of past ages is more or less inevitable, and, although a respect for truth is an essential quality for the good historian, his understanding will always be limited by individual peculiarities. That is why it is important, if his style is persuasive and his learning impressive, that he should also be a good man. The dead can look after themselves; the living cannot.

The historian's first duty is not to his subject, but to his audience – not that he should tamper with truth as he sees it, but he should write nothing without considering the weakness, prejudice and ignorance with which he is surrounded and in which he shares;

and considering too the prophetic and didactic part which has been forced upon him. It is as important for the historian today to be a good, and if possible a great, man as it was for the high dignitaries of the medieval Church. It is all too easy, armed with this romantic, this most appealing of weapons, to play unfairly on the wishful thoughts of the ingenuous. 'We see those splendid barbarians,' wrote Houston Stewart Chamberlain in an outburst of imaginative word painting, 'glowing with youth, free, making their entry into history endowed with all those qualities which fit them for the very highest place.' In this flattering mirror of their ancestors, thousands of swarthy and mouse-coloured nonentities, tightly buttoned into frock-coats, at once recognized themselves. Alas, with what results . . . Chamberlain was no scholar and his barbarians were the figment of his imagination; but fine scholarship will not save the historian from perpetrating such crimes. Mommsen and Treitschke were great scholars, but when they came to interpret their material they believed that might was right, and all their knowledge served but to poison the minds of their compatriots.

Gabriel Hanotaux, the veteran French historian, spoke as a young man of 'la courbe magnifique de l'histoire *agie*, s'insérant dans l'histoire écrite'. But this, too, is a reversal of what happens, for there is no process by which the cross-hatched complexity of acted history can be reproduced faithfully in the written word. Yet the word effectively written will reproduce itself with uncanny truth in the acts of the future.

What is the solution? There is none that can be called satisfactory, for bad men will continue to be popular writers and may even, in the technical sense, be 'good' historians. The high-minded and the morally responsible will never have the monopoly of the historian's profession or of the public ear; but they should at least recognize what is expected of them and sustain on equal terms their fight for a hearing.

1942

History and Hope*

It is a hundred and forty years since George Birkbeck founded the London Mechanics' Institution from which this college has grown. It can be said with certainty that it has, during that century and a half, not merely fulfilled the practical purpose but transcended the hopes with which it was founded. It has exercised an ever-increasing and widening influence for enlightenment, has consolidated and extended its educational scope and successfully met the needs and demands of a rapidly changing world. In Birkbeck's day there was among liberal thinkers an inspiring faith that men – that human society – assisted by the wonderful inventions of their time and by the growing wealth which flowed from expanding industries, would continue to follow the path of progress which seemed to stretch out before them. We, to-day, have misgivings about the progress, let alone the perfectibility, of man. But in some spheres at least the hopes of our nineteenth-century forefathers have been realized and even surpassed.

The pleasure which I felt on being asked to come here to speak to-day was a little damped by the uneasy thought that I must have something of sufficient importance and relevance to say. Expressions of admiration and goodwill, respect for the past, the sincerest expectations of the future – these things are not enough. My predecessors in this place have set a very high standard. Some constructive comment on the times will be expected of me. Now historians lately have come under some criticism for spending too much of their time not only in the past, but in some small corner of the past. Contemporary historians are of course exempt from this criticism, since they deal with material that is still very much alive and their interpretations of it have obvious repercussions on

* The Foundation Oration at Birkbeck College, 1963.

the formation of political opinions and judgments. But historians who work in those regions of the past which have no immediate or obvious relationship to the present have become, of late years, rather cautious about making those claims to superior powers of judgment and understanding which the study of history was at one time thought to bestow on its practitioners and its readers. Professional historians to-day are inclined for the most part to emphasize the value of historical studies as an academic discipline, a training for the mind, rather than as a means of acquiring deeper experience and understanding of human society and politics.

The seventeenth century, in which I spend so much of my time, is divided from us by the great gulf of the Industrial Revolution. During that century, the Scientific Revolution, and the fundamental changes of thought that came with it, were still in process of happening. The great sequence of discoveries and inventions had begun but had not by any means run its full course or exercised its most striking effects on the minds of educated men. Birkbeck College is the offspring of both these changes – the one a change in the material conditions of life and in the whole structure of society; the other a change in accepted ways of thinking. What, as a practising historian, what as a student of the seventeenth century, can I say which is relevant to the purpose of our meeting to-day?

Changes, however profound, however revolutionary, still leave many things unchanged, and one of the fascinations of history is to trace the interlocking patterns of new ideas and old traditions, the co-existence of new and old. Superficial observers have been heard to say that history repeats itself and there is nothing new under the sun; cautious historians are more inclined to suggest that history never exactly repeats itself and that similarities may be more apparent than real. Englishmen of the seventeenth century lived in a world entirely different from ours but some of their ideas are as valid now as they ever were. Shakespeare, who stands upon the verge between the medieval and the modern world, speaks to a larger public today than ever before. But literature, because it is a matter of the human heart which does not greatly change, is in a different category from political or social thinking. And genius is after all outside time.

But it is remarkable to find the traces, in much earlier periods, of ideas which were to become fruitful only generations, or even centuries, later. The English seventeenth century is full of such tracer ideas. Politically and constitutionally, of course, it was the century in which the balance of power within England shifted from Crown to Parliament, a crisis important in itself, though possibly more important because of the interpretations which were later made of it; the conception of parliamentary government, liberty and representation sprang not so much from events themselves as from what was thought and written about them in retrospect. It was also the century which saw the development of the two-party system, that significant English invention in government. This was not welcomed with enthusiasm at the time. In fact, about 1641, an unfortunate man who happened to fall into political discussion in a public place, and to refer to the fact that there were now two parties at loggerheads with each other in Parliament, was packed off to prison for a breach of parliamentary privilege. In theory Parliament was held to be the united representative body of the nation, so how could it possibly speak with two voices unless the nation itself were some kind of monster – a conception, to use the idiom of their day, 'not to be thought about in good English'.

The emergence of left-wing political doctrines during the intellectual and political ferment of our English Civil Wars has received a great deal of attention since the development and consolidation of modern democratic ideas in the late nineteenth and early twentieth century. The experiment in collective farming by the Digger group as well as the more widespread political demands of the Levellers have by now attracted more attention in modern times than they did in their own. To my mind one of the most interesting of the many ideas put forward in that epoch of fruitful disorder, was the demand for a great extension of university education. It was suggested that money realized by the sale of Church lands should be devoted to higher education and, now that the Puritans had got rid of the bishops, that episcopal palaces should be converted into colleges. Earlier in the century attempts had already been made to organize colleges, something on the model suggested by Francis Bacon, for the study of the natural sciences.

But I am falling into a trap of my own making. I am being drawn away into the seventeenth century and if I am not careful I shall make myself an example of the historian's exclusive preoccupation with the past. Interesting and admirable as these early aspirations are, they are more curious than relevant to our present situation. What I want to talk about is not the *intrinsic* interest of history, for that is obvious enough, but the part that the study of history has still to play in the living world.

There used to be no great argument about this. The educational value of history was more or less of a truism from classical times onwards. It is constantly cited as the form of knowledge which does most to open the mind and enlarge the judgment. Machiavelli demonstrated that it could be used as a handbook to political action. Oliver Cromwell advised his son Richard that history, together with mathematics and cosmography, would fit him for public service – though it turned out that neither history, mathematics nor cosmography fitted poor Richard Cromwell to be the Lord Protector of England.

The wisdom and special gifts of historians themselves might sometimes be questioned. Dr Johnson has one of his most crushing sayings on my profession: 'Great abilities are not requisite for an historian; for in historical composition all the greatest powers of the human mind are quiescent. He has facts ready to his hand, so there is no exercise of invention. Imagination is not required in any high degree; only about as much as is used in the lower kinds of poetry. Some penetration, accuracy and colouring will fit a man for the task, if he can give the application which is necessary.'

But even if the historian was only an industrious hack the value of what he placed before the public was assured. Against Dr Johnson's harsh words there are the comforting reflections of David Hume. Hume was, to be sure, an historian himself and therefore possibly prejudiced in favour of the profession, but in arguing the value of history as a study he implies not only the very considerable wisdom of historians but also their habitual *penchant* towards virtue. For him history is a key to judgment and understanding not only in human affairs but in other branches of knowledge. 'A great part of what we commonly call erudition and value so highly', he wrote, 'is nothing but an acquaintance with historical facts . . . History is not only a valuable part of knowledge but opens the door to many other parts and affords material to most of the sciences . . . There is also an advantage in that experience which is acquired by history, above what is learnt by the practice of the world, that it brings us acquainted with human affairs, without diminishing in the least from the most delicate sentiments of virtue . . . I think it is a remark worthy of the attention of the speculative that historians have been, almost without exception, the true friends of virtue, and have always represented it in its proper colours . . .'

He would hardly be able to say that to-day. Quite apart from the questionable adventures of historians – or at least writers of history – in the spheres of ideological and political propaganda, the study of psychology has made it often very uncertain what the true colours of virtue are, since human motives are rarely if ever quite what they appear to be.

But Hume's main proposition is that, by the study of history, we can extend almost limitlessly the bounds of human experience. 'If we consider the shortness of life and our limited knowledge even of what passes in our own time, we must be sensible that we should be for ever children in understanding were it not for this invention which extends our experiences to all past ages and to the most distant nations. A man acquainted with history may in some respect be said to have lived from the beginning of the world.'

David Hume was writing long before the intensification of research and the proliferation of historical studies had made it virtually impossible for any human being to 'live from the beginning of the world' through the simple method of studying world history. The most we can hope to get hold of to-day is a mere framework or outline of so immense a subject. Historical study, historical science in effect, has like every other branch of human knowledge expanded in a way scarcely imaginable to the lucid and masterly minds of the eighteenth century. The vast accumulation of knowledge about the past, the opening of archives, the discovery of documents, the extensive and ever more scientific excavation of survivals from the remotest times – all these things have put the real knowledge, the experience of world history, as Hume conceived of it, quite outside the range of any single mind. Though this is of course no reason why we should not at least acquire some idea of the general structure of human history on this planet; for if the bare outline, the bare framework, cannot give us the kind of understanding which Hume had in mind when he spoke of the extension of life by history, or that Raleigh had in mind when he wrote his *History of the World*, it can and does give us a perspective against which to measure our own lives and times. And that is already something.

There are still a few valiant spirits who venture into the writing of world history with the intention of providing this perspective, of keeping us in mind of the longer view of time which we are apt to forget under the pressure of our hurried lives. But the majority of historians have sought rather to concentrate on establishing the truth – or reducing the margin of error, the more cautious phrase generally in vogue – on small and relatively controllable sections of the past. As the material for historical studies has grown, the techniques of research have become more complicated, the problems we seek to solve more intricate and often also more controversial, and the standards of achievement much more exacting. The old idea of history as a record of politics, of dynasties and of wars has given way to the conception of history as the study of institutions, of societies, in short of that whole complex of elements, human, geographical and economic, which lie below the obvious political surface. History today is not only past politics, but also the sociology, the economics, the culture of the past. It touches thus on many other branches of knowledge. While this has made history a very much broader study than it once was, it has also compelled a much greater specialization. The extension of the subject has caused individual practitioners and students to concentrate on much smaller sections of the whole.

This development is not peculiar to history. It is one of the major problems of our time both in education and in professional life. The total amount that human beings have come to know is now so gigantic that no individual, however gifted and energetic, can expect to 'be brought acquainted', in Hume's phrase, with more than a fragment of the whole. Think only of the books on the shelves of the British Museum not a quarter of a mile away from here; imagination can hardly grasp the depth and scope of knowledge set down in them.

The old-time ideal of an educated person as someone who was sufficiently informed to talk intelligently and argue reasonably on a great number of different subjects both in the arts and to a lesser degree in the sciences has vanished. When I was young one still not infrequently heard the ideal expressed in the well-known formula – that an educated man should know something about everything and everything about something. It was an exaggeration of the possibilities, of course, but it bore some relation to what had once been a very sensible ideal view. The mass and the detail of our knowledge in almost every sphere, in the arts and in the sciences, have simply made such an ideal impossible.

In all branches of human activity to-day division of effort, specialization and concentration are essential if we are to achieve the kind of mastery over knowledge which can lead to further advances. And so we get in many spheres teams of specialists working together to produce results which the individual can no longer compass alone.

Yet we feel uneasily that the best use of knowledge, its wisest application to our human problems, requires the kind of general understanding, the reflective wisdom, for which fewer and fewer people now have either the time or the intellectual training. And it is a matter of ancient proverbial wisdom that knowledge without wisdom is a dangerous thing.

Sir Charles Snow, in a much discussed lecture, gave us the phrase 'the two cultures' which has become part of the modern vocabulary of intellectual argument. But this problem, presented by the sheer bulk and weight and detail of modern knowledge, affects *both* the cultures alike. It is not only *one* great divide over which people find it hard to communicate with each other; the divisions multiply. With the final collapse of the Renaissance ideal of the man of all-round knowledge, interested in everything, we begin to inhabit a world of specialists, and of specialists whose language becomes unintelligible not only to the intelligent amateur but even to each other and even in the same field. Naturally, I exaggerate. Most of us in this room can still understand each other perfectly well on most subjects of general interest and importance. But how often, if we are honest, do we find ourselves out of our depth if we seek expert knowledge from a colleague or friend in a subject which is outside our own expertise even if it is well within our sphere of interest? I once overheard at a large gathering of historians – not in this country – a fellow guest angrily breaking free from an animated discussion over the cocktails with 'I don't know *what* they are talking about. I'm a medievalist.' What *they* were talking about – I was on the edge of the group – was the Namierite controversy about George III, but carried to an extreme limit of sophistication and detail that defeated even listeners well acquainted with the subject. Meanwhile a grey-bearded gentleman intercepted the fugitive with the urgent question, 'What *kind* of a medievalist?' This was all light-hearted enough, but we do need to keep in mind that the price we pay for progress in knowledge is this intense specialization, and that it is a penalty, not an advantage. General knowledge may have to be slight or even amateurish knowledge, but it is none the less useful, and we discourage it at our peril.

In my opening sentence I deliberately, if rashly, used the word 'progress'. This is a word which has been sadly devalued in our time, so that it provokes in many people a derisive smile, in others, perhaps, a kinder feeling of nostalgia for the more confident age in which human history was thought to be the history of progress, and in a few of us still a tenuous hope. Those who founded this college knew that there was much wrong with the world in which they lived, but some of them looked forward to the solution of these problems as something which the ingenuity and goodwill of man could and would accomplish. Material progress was visible all about them; the increasing efficiency and productivity of industry, the consequent accumulation of wealth and the wise spending of it on education and on other constructive purposes would in the end create a materially comfortable and spiritually satisfactory world. It would not come immediately. There would be setbacks. But it must come.

Not many people to-day still feel that same confidence in the inevitable progress of men. Two world wars, the blind frenzies of race hatred and political violence which we have lived through, and the staggering increase in man's capacity to destroy himself have been deeply disillusioning experiences. And yet it is too soon, in the long perspective of history, to assume that the confidence once felt in the inevitable progress of the human race was wholly misplaced. Since, when I was asked what subject I would talk about tonight, I tentatively suggested the phrase 'History and Hope' it is evident that I am myself an optimist. Indeed the first philosopher who inspired my youthful admiration was Leibniz, with his comforting belief that all is for the best in the best of all possible worlds. When I was advised to read Voltaire's *Candide* as a corrective to these opinions, I was not amused. On the contrary I was outraged to find the character of Leibniz parodied in the person of the ridiculous Pangloss, and his ideas made to look absurd by inflicting on him and his pupil, the ingenuous Candide, a series of misfortunes wantonly invented by the author for that purpose. Well I am not so simple an optimist as I once was, nor, I hope, am I quite so earnest and humourless. At any rate I have learnt to appreciate at its true value one of the great comic masterpieces of world literature.

Anyone who has lived as an adult through the last thirty years, with their alternation of achievements and disasters, anyone for that matter with some knowledge of human history must be aware that human gain is always in some degree paid for by human loss. Every reform either starts new problems or throws into relief problems not previously recognized. The millennium which is hoped and worked for is never reached, and may indeed change character as one approaches it. But that is no reason for falling into the opposite extreme of asserting, often with a king of lugubrious pleasure, that no progress is possible at all, that things are worse than they are, or worse than they have ever been. Still more unreasonable is the comparison of our own time, to its disparagement, with some imaginary vision of the past in which, it is argued, men did not suffer from the same uncertainties, especially spiritual uncertainties, that we suffer from to-day. This particular misuse and misinterpretation of history is not infrequent; it is rarely indulged in by historians, more often by artists and poets and men of letters. And it is of course easy enough, by emphasizing those elements in the past that appeal to us, and leaving out almost everything else, to make some very enticing fantasies about the good old days.

In place of the dark satanic mills – not incidentally that mills are so dark and satanic since the advent of electrification, but Blake's great phrase has become a journalist's cliché – in place of dark satanic mills and industrial cities, we are told that England was once a place of pastoral peace, of quiet villages and gracious manor houses all apparently occupied by kindly patriarchal characters like Squire Allworthy or Sir Roger de Coverley. Those who idealize the pre-industrial past tell us nothing about diseased cattle, failed harvests, inadequate sewage disposal, epidemic disease, wandering beggars, inadequate social order and the hundred petty or major tyrannies of local gentry who did not conform to the two amiable patterns cited above. England a hundred years before the Industrial Revolution was probably a worse place than a hundred years after it, certainly a much worse place than it is to-day.

Another favourite idealized picture is that of the Middle Ages – precise period not exactly specified. At that time, it is suggested, all Christendom was united in a single faith, craftsmen took creative pride and pleasure in their work, everyone understood and accepted his position in the hierarchy of a society bound together by mutual obligations and loyalties. Nothing is said of the superstition and intolerance which seamed society, of the day-to-day brutality and squalor in which the great majority of the populace lived and died.

Of course there are at all times some compensations for being alive; witness the fact that most people at most times have wanted to stay alive. It would have been fun to have gone on a Canterbury pilgrimage in the company of Chaucer, or to have seen the first night of *Hamlet* . . . but these are only small parts of the picture, and all in all – twenty-four hours out of the twenty-four – the compensations for being alive in this country in the twentieth century are probably greater than at any previous time that we know of.

The understanding study of history, as the history of society, as the history of all the people, not merely of the dominating groups, can I think do something to prevent such foolish and sometimes dangerous illusions about the past.

Yet we do not need to idealize the past in order to see that the present, the twentieth century, has by no means lived up to the hopes which were once entertained by it. In 1825, on the occasion of the opening of the new lecture theatre, George Birkbeck spoke as follows:

> The treasures of knowledge being thus liberally disseminated through the world, countless multitudes will quickly become reflecting and intelligent; and a new era in the history of our species will appear, distinguished by the love of peace, the love of order, the love of knowledge and the love of virtue. Freedom, prosperity and happiness will be the great universal rewards of this amelioration, and travelling on, from perfection to perfection, man will at length, however remote the period, justify the declaration that he is 'half dust, half deity'.

Birkbeck's latest biographer has called this a 'naïve but noble profession of faith'. Certainly it is a prophecy that cannot but arouse in us mixed feelings, and it may be that the smile with which we are perhaps inclined to greet it conceals our sense of guilt at having – a century and a half later – failed to make the prophecy come true. For the treasures of knowledge have been very liberally disseminated, if not quite throughout the world. If the spread of education has not yet opened a new era in the history of our species, perhaps we are to blame? It is easy to smile at a faith in progress which seems to us ingenuous as well as noble, and to pass it off with a shrug and a comment on the vanity of human wishes. But when so much has happened – and the flourishing state of this college is but one of the many witnesses to it – may not more also happen? We might do well to imitate the confident idealism as well as the practical energy of our nineteenth-century forerunners.

In the sphere of education at least progress has been – and is increasingly – rapid. We see new schools springing up, and a development of opportunities at the university level unparalleled in any previous epoch. We see all around us the signs of a new appetite and taste for intellectual things – our shops are bright with the display of attractive paperback volumes containing all the best of modern and ancient thought, knowledge and literature. Our art galleries and our concert halls are gratifyingly full. Shakespeare plays to full houses at Stratford-on-Avon for eight months of the year and the doors of the National Theatre are besieged by a public which can't have too much of *Uncle Vanya*.

The present popularity of pleasures such as these is evidently one result of better, wider, more persuasive education. For knowledge, said a Baptist preacher, a contemporary of Birkbeck, 'expands the mind, exalts the faculties, refines the taste of pleasure and opens innumerable sources of intellectual enjoyment'. The words occur in a sermon by the Reverend Robert Hall *On the Advantages of Knowledge to the Lower Classes*. And they were approvingly quoted by Birkbeck in his inaugural address. There are indeed many signs in our increasingly classless society that education is working in precisely this way.

George Birkbeck and his associates hoped and predicted that 'countless multitudes will quickly become reflecting and intelligent'. Let us make no mistake about it. Countless multitudes have done so, have become more thoughtful, more perceptive, equipped to understand more, to enjoy with greater discrimination, to reason with greater judgment, and to live life more fully than ever before.

Unfortunately there are also countless multitudes who either through their misfortune or their fault, have failed to become reflecting and intelligent, and whose literacy enables them the more easily and swiftly to fall victims to exploitation by propaganda.

So that the 'great universal rewards of education' – freedom, prosperity, love of peace, love of order, love of virtue – are still very imperfectly and partially achieved. And even where they have in some measure been brought nearer, the whole of our civilization lies under a threat of extinction more potent than anything conceived of by our great-grandparents, and certainly not allowed for in the visions of the future that appeared to those who founded the parent institution of this college, only eight years after the Battle of Waterloo.

Eight years after Waterloo – that takes us a long way back, to just before the dawn of the Railway Age. The world has done some 'spinning down the ringing grooves of change' since then. It was still by and large the world of the sailing ship and horse traction in 1823, not the much more compact world of the steam ship and locomotive. Distance, the slowness of movement and communication, was a factor in world affairs just as the immense speed of communication and swiftness of movement is a factor today. This does and should bring the peoples of the world very much closer together, as we have felt sometimes at moments of national or international excitement when the television screens made us participants in events half the world away; or more solemnly and sadly in these last days when we wholeheartedly shared in the grief and loss of the American people.

But looked at in terms of progress only, the changes for the better and the positive achievements have been such as to change the conditions of human life, among the more fortunate peoples, beyond all recognition. The prevention and treatment of illness, the control of the ravaging epidemic diseases under the shadow of which our Victorian ancestors still lived, the steady improvement of public health, the expansion of social services – all these things have made the expectation of life both longer and happier. All these things represent sustained efforts of human intelligence and goodwill. All these things undoubtedly represent progress.

We are too much inclined to take the advances for granted and to count only the evident failures of our time – unsolved problems of national and race hatred, the uncertainty of moral values which is typical of a period of rapid change, the divisions of interest and ideology which threaten the peace of the world, and the ever-present anxiety that man, proud man, having mastered nature, will use his powers only in some final orgy of self-destruction.

These things loom very large. And since I have several times stressed the differences between the Modern Age, the mechanized age, and the far longer stretch of man's history that preceded it, it may seem odd to end with a general reflection on history. But the basic equipment of mankind, our minds and hearts, the enigmatic ultimate essence of our being, changes less rapidly than the inventions we make or the societies we create. It has been a common thing throughout the ages for men to make more of the dangers and disasters that threatened them than of their advantages. In quoting George Birkbeck's hopes about the virtues of education I did not quote alongside them the many quotations, some of which will be known to all of you, from newspapers or from eminent statesmen of the day predicting every kind of social breakdown, immorality and disorder as a result of the rash extension of education throughout all classes. The prophets of gloom, all told, were far more wrong than the optimistic reformers.

We would be unwise – indeed I think it would be blindly foolish – to view the conditions of 1963 with any complacency. But because our very considerable advances have been accompanied by setbacks and are threatened by both new and old dangers, this is no reason to abandon, I will not say the *faith*, but I will say the *hope* in progress. The 'great universal rewards of more education', and let us hope more wisdom, are still a long way off. But let us go on believing that one day they will be attained. History may not be correctly interpreted as essentially the story of man's progress; but it does sometimes record the progress of men and women towards better things, and some of the human record over the last century and a half has been in that direction.

1963

T. C. Smout

A History of the Scottish People 1560–1830

'By far the most stimulating, the most instructive and the most readable account of Scotch history that I have read . . . this splendid work carries us from Knox to Neilson, from the hot gospel of Calvin to the hot-blast smelting process – and incidentally seeks to explain the change. For always, in following this lucid narrative, we see an original mind at work, questioning and explaining as well as illustrating.

The illustrations, incidentally, are original and delightful too. The whole book has delighted me. I cannot praise it too highly.' Hugh Trevor-Roper, *Sunday Times*

'This is a fine history of Scotland. It combines rich and deep scholarship with an elegant and lucid style . . . No one who professes an interest in Scotland can afford to miss reading it.' *Times Literary Supplement*

'This remarkable book leaves the reviewer with little to say except that all Scots, and even Englishmen who are interested in Britain's development, should read it. It is admirably proportioned, based on vast reading, and brings all the main topics together.' *Economist*

FONTANA PRESS

EARLY VICTORIAN BRITAIN, 1832–51

J. F. C. Harrison

For people in all walks of life, the period between the passing of the Great Reform Bill and the Great Exhibition was one of turbulence and change, where massive events such as the new Poor Law, the coming of railways, Chartism, the repeal of the Corn Laws and the Great Irish Famine were set against a background of political manouevring and violent economic fluctuations. Professor Harrison offers a thorough and entertaining survey of this crucial phase of British history.

'I read . . . with uninterrupted delight, entranced that English historians could combine so dazzlingly scholarship and art.'
A. J. P. Taylor, *Observer*

Also by J. F. C. Harrison

The Common People: a History from
the Norman Conquest to the Present

Rose Elliot

The Bean Book

Beans are an invaluable part of our diet, for not only do they provide an inexpensive source of protein, but they are rich in iron, phosphorus and B vitamins. Throughout history the bean has sustained generations, and here Rose Elliot's flair and inventiveness bring us a host of delicious recipes using more varieties of beans than you ever imagined existed.

Rose Elliot is Britain's top writer on vegetarian cookery and in this classic collection of original recipes the humble bean is utterly transformed. There are spicy dals from India; crisp, tasty rissoles; delectable pâtés and bean salads, shiny with dressing and fragrant with herbs. Delicate bean dishes from France, robust ones from Italy, others from the Middle East, with more than a hint of olive oil, lemon and garlic, full of earthy charm.

Vegetarian or non-vegetarian, nobody can resist Rose Elliot's imaginative and colourful dishes, a sheer delight to the palate and the eye.

A Fontana Original

Rose Elliot

Not Just a Load of Old Lentils

Rose Elliot has long been one of Britain's top vegetarian cookery writers. Apart from being healthy, vegetarian food is delicious, tasty and colourful and Rose Elliot's many books are packed full with hundreds of creative and original recipes which appeal to everyone, vegetarians and non-vegetarians alike.

Not Just a Load of Old Lentils is a classic in the world of vegetarian cookery and has been a best-seller since it was first published. With more than 400 recipes covering everything from soups and starters through to desserts, cakes and biscuits it offers mouth-watering ideas for every taste and occasion.

For already devoted vegetarians Rose Elliot provides fresh inspiration, and the vitality and enthusiasm of her writing will send many a meat-eater rumaging through the vegetable racks.

'*Not Just a Load of Old Lentils* makes an impact from the first'
– *Health for All*

A Fontana Original

ƒp
Fontana Press

Fontana Press is the imprint under which Fontana paperbacks of special interest to students are published. Below is a selection of titles.

- ☐ A Century of the Scottish People, 1830–1950 *T. C. Smout* £6.95
- ☐ The Sociology of School and Education *Ivan Reid* £4.95
- ☐ Renaissance Essays *Hugh Trevor-Roper* £5.95
- ☐ Law's Empire *Ronald Dworkin* £6.95
- ☐ The Structures of Everyday Life *Fernand Braudel* £9.95
- ☐ The Wheels of Commerce *Fernand Braudel* £9.95
- ☐ The Perspective of the World *Fernand Braudel* £9.95
- ☐ France 1789–1815: Revolution and Counterrevolution *D. M. G. Sutherland* £5.95
- ☐ Crown and Nobility, 1272–1461 *Anthony Tuck* £4.95
- ☐ Racial Conflict in Contemporary Society *John Stone* £3.50
- ☐ Foucault *J. G. Merquior* £3.50

You can buy Fontana Press books at your local bookshop or newsagent. Or you can order them from Fontana Paperbacks, Cash Sales Department, Box 29, Douglas, Isle of Man. Please send a cheque, postal or money order (not currency) worth the purchase price plus 22p per book (maximum postal charge is £3.00 for orders within the UK).

NAME (Block letters) _____

ADDRESS _____

_____

_____